VALUE CHANGE
IN CHINESE SOCIETY

VALUE CHANGE IN CHINESE SOCIETY

edited by

Richard W. Wilson
Amy Auerbacher Wilson
Sidney L. Greenblatt

PRAEGER SPECIAL STUDIES • PRAEGER SCIENTIFIC

Library of Congress Cataloging in Publication Data
Main entry under title:

Value change in Chinese society.

   Includes bibliographical references and index.
   1. China--Social conditions--1945-1976--Addresses,
essays, lectures. 2. Taiwan--Social conditions--
Addresses, essays, lectures. 3. Social values--
Addresses, essays, lectures. 4. Social change--
Addresses, essays, lectures. 5. Popular culture--
Addresses, essays, lectures. I. Wilson, Richard
W., 1933-   II. Wilson, Amy Auerbacher, 1934-
III. Greenblatt, Sidney L
HN737.V34   309.1'51'043   77-83479
ISBN 0-03-023046-2

PRAEGER PUBLISHERS
PRAEGER SPECIAL STUDIES
383 Madison Avenue, New York, N.Y. 10017, U.S.A.

Published in the United States of America in 1979
by Praeger Publishers,
A Division of Holt, Rinehart and Winston, CBS, Inc.

9   038   987654321

Printed in the United States of America

PREFACE

This book contains the work of scholars who presented papers on the subject of value change in Chinese society at a conference held at Princeton University on November 18, 19, and 20, 1977. The value-change conference was the second in a series with an overall objective of applying selected social science paradigms to Chinese data. Materials on China are still not widely utilized by those in the social science disciplines and, conversely, the explicit use of current social science techniques for analyzing Chinese data is still not widespread. This book, therefore, represents an effort at furthering a convergence of the disciplines and the China field in such a way as to benefit both China scholars and discipline-oriented social scientists.

The goal of this volume is to set forth ideas concerning the problem of value change in modern Chinese society. The term society, as used here, refers to several contemporary political units whose citizens are overwhelmingly Chinese in origin. The majority of the essays, therefore, deal with the People's Republic of China, but others, where appropriate, analyze data gathered in Taiwan or Hong Kong. Clearly one volume cannot cover all aspects of a subject as broad as value change. Rather, the present efforts have been aimed at presenting a series of studies, closely related by a common theme, that can elucidate the general question of value change and that can also show the worth of this approach as an aid to understanding the modern Chinese.

The scholars who contributed to this volume represent a variety of disciplines and each, therefore, addresses the question of value change from a unique perspective. In setting the framework for the conference where these papers were initially discussed, an explicit decision was made not to ask the conferees to structure their work in terms of a specific series of questions or around a set of interlocking hypotheses. Although the subject of value change has a venerable history in the social sciences and has, in one way or another, also influenced a great deal of work on modern China, hypotheses in the general field of value change are still in the process of evolving; various theories are still hotly debated, and there is no consensus even on definitional matters. For these reasons it was believed that too rigid a framework would lend only a pseudo-scientific aspect to the conference proceedings and might inhibit anticipated creative and exploratory aspects. These caveats notwithstanding, there were set forth for those invited to the conference some definitions of value change derived from social science literature, and the authors were asked to explore the implications of value change in terms of work that they knew best, attempting to draw them out in a flow of correspondence that preceded the conference. Moreover, the conference itself was organized in such a way as to maximize thoughtful and critical involvement by all concerned. The subject of value change in and of itself was thoroughly discussed and an effort was made to debate the utility of this approach. As a consequence the papers reflect, in their discussion of Chinese materials, problems and issues from the general field of value change itself.

In this volume the papers are presented in a manner that, it is hoped, will clearly reveal for readers the goals and flavor of the conference at which they were initially presented. A general introduction that raises definitional and theoretical issues precedes the papers which utilize Chinese materials. Following the introduction, several studies discuss, in broad terms, the question of defining values in a Chinese setting. Papers on more specific topics then follow, dealing with value change in terms of social stereotyping, socialization, ecology, sexual differentiation, and subgroup orientations. The hope is, of course, that these works will stimulate others to further research on other topics that are relevant to a value-change approach.

Two papers have been added by scholars who were not present at the conference. The contributions presented at the conference largely addressed the question of value change in modern China, but the participants agreed unanimously that a study that specifically focused on traditional values would be an essential ingredient in this volume. For this reason Tu Wei-ming was approached, who kindly assented to the request for use of his previously published paper. The editors also felt that no book on the subject of value change should ignore the subject of childhood socialization. Fortunately a study was done in this area by Carolyn L. and Richard Baum, who also graciously granted permission to include their work.

An attempt has been made throughout the volume to use the *pinyin* system of romanization. However, in the case of Professor Tu's article, many references are to historical figures who are best known in their Wade-Giles transliteration. For this reason, no attempt was made to change the Wade-Giles system of romanization used in Professor Tu's paper. Well-known place names in all the papers have also been left in the form most commonly understood by Western readers.

The tasks of the editors have been of several types. Initially general parameters were formulated for a conference dealing with value change in Chinese society. A number of scholars who, it was felt, might have an interest in pursuing this topic from the vantage point of their own scholarly perspectives were then approached. During the conference organization phase close liaison with the authors was maintained, informing them on progress toward the stated goals. All three of the editors helped in the general selection of conference topics, the preparation of guidelines, the selection of participants, the organization of the conference, and the subsequent editing of the proceedings.

The editors wish to give special thanks to the East Asian Department of Princeton University for providing partial funding for the conference. A debt is due to Marion J. Levy, Jr., chairman of the East Asian Department at Princeton

University, who encouraged and supported this project. For help in organizing the conference the editors extend their gratitude to Janice Gibson of the Princeton University East Asian Department and to Catherine Tranfo of the Rutgers University International Center, who also provided invaluable assistance in the preparation of the manuscript.

CONTENTS

LIST OF TABLES AND FIGURES

VALUE CHANGE
IN CHINESE SOCIETY

METANOIA: AN INTRODUCTION

Richard W. Wilson

The process of value change, of conversion, or of a fundamental change of mind or character has been and remains a central question in the social sciences. In the twentieth century, analyses of the attitudes and values that people hold have sharpened in terms of definition and measurement; yet there still remains an elusive quality to the study of values and value change. While one speaks superficially of the beliefs and feelings that individuals and groups hold, knowledge of how to measure these qualities—how they relate to each other, how they are acquired and how they change, and what the relationship of such changes are to antecedent and subsequent social conditions—is in some respects as difficult to pin down as the ability to understand and predict the weather. Justine Aronfreed has put it succinctly: "We know very little about the acquisition processes through which ... cognitive competence ... develops. And we know even less about how this competence interlocks with social experience to product internalized structures of value."[1]

Although historically there has been great disarray in the study of values and a discouraging failure by scholars to work with a set of concepts linked so as to yield a unified body of cumulative knowledge,[2] the field is not entirely without a growing coherence. In fact, the study of values and value change still holds the promise of being a useful and parsimonious way of understanding the motivations and behavior of individuals and groups. It is, after all, relatively clear that without shared values, emotionally satisfying interpersonal relations and individual self-regard and sense of purpose would be greatly hampered.[3] Without some set of mutually held principles there would be no way to identify with others; meaningful individual and social life would be impossible.

It is from commonsense feelings such as these, often loosely articulated, that modern social scientists have begun systematically to examine values and value change. The process of developing a coherent conception of values has led to the formulation of a number of questions. What are the properties of values that can serve as the basis for a definition? What is not a value? How are values acquired? In what order and with what salience? Why do certain values tend to be manifested in recurrent situations? What is the difference, if any, between individual-level values and those that are shared by the members of a group? What is the process of value change and what is the effect of change on social life? And is value change a process that is syncretic in nature?

THE PROPERTIES OF VALUES

There is no single accepted definition for the concept "value" in the social sciences. Values have been variously defined as "affectively toned fixations,"[4] as prescriptive or proscriptive beliefs or as "abstract ideals, positive or negative, not tied to any specific attitude object or situation, representing a person's beliefs about ideal modes of conduct and ideal terminal goals."[5] Values have been referred to as preferences that are felt to be justified; they are codes or standards that persist through time and that contain an undertone of the desirable, not just the desired.[6] In perhaps one of the best known definitions a value is defined as "a conception, explicit or implicit, distinctive of an individual or characteristic of a group, of the desirable which influences the selection from available modes, means and ends of action."[7] If values refer to the desirable, then clearly they have an implicit dual nature, with a positive conception linked inseparably to a negative or undesirable perception that is its reverse image. In another definition values are thought of as "standards which determine the type of action by which . . . one will give vent to one's needs."[8] Here values are thought of as guides for the fulfillment of basic wants.

Donald Campbell, who prefers to use the term "attitude" rather than "value," feels that there is already a common but implicit agreement on an operational definition of attitude. A social attitude, he says, is marked by "consistency in response to social objects."[9] It is "a syndrome of response consistency with regard to social objects," a definition that he notes has the advantage of conveying a common meaning and the disadvantage of being appropriate to a large number of social science concepts.[10] As there is a plethora of terms for standards or codes that are learned or acquired (Campbell himself notes 78 of them), he feels the entire genus should be represented by the phrase, "acquired behavioral dispositions."[11] These predispositions to respond in certain ways are presumed to broadly represent "motive attributes, preferences for certain types of goals, or predilections for certain types of outcome."[12]

Values, however, are more than mere predilections. They are particular types of cognitions that are organized in a consistent pattern, have an evaluative quality, refer to desirable end-states, and imply choice and action.[13] Values may be differentiated from each other in terms of what they prescribe—such as honesty or cooperativeness—or in terms of particular characteristics of their cognitive, affective, and conative components—such as intensity (strength of feeling), salience (prominence), flexibility, degree of interconnectedness, complexity, overtness, and consciousness.

As standards, values provide criteria by which goals are chosen, indicating that something ought to be preferred. They deal with modes of conduct (instrumental values) and end-states of existence (terminal values) in which they serve as guides, helping individuals size up significant aspects of the environment by giving these aspects meaning. They also help an individual to get along with others by serving as standards for one's concept of oneself. In addition, values have an ego-defensive function in that they serve to recast unacceptable feelings and actions into acceptable forms.[14] Above all, values have emotional content in the sense that ideal goals are not presented in an affectively neutral manner but are to be striven for as highly desirable. In helping a person to test reality, defend his ego, and adjust to others, values maintain and enhance a basic sense of self-esteem and self-regard.[15] The designation of certain goals as desirable and the enhancement and maintenance of self-esteem are, in fact, the two critical inter-related functions that values serve in helping to organize individual behavior.

In attempting to determine what is valued, either observed behavior or verbalizations concerning behavior are usually examined first. From observations of individuals, consistent behavior patterns in given situations can often be noted. Where a consistency can be established, it is then possible to infer a degree of liking, of commitment, for certain kinds of behavior.[16] At the group level this motivating aspect of values is necessarily an abstraction studied by ascertaining socially sanctioned ends and socially approved modes and means for securing these ends.

There may, of course, be deviant values and values may be in conflict. It is, therefore, essential in the study of values to be clear as to whether analysis is at the most general cultural level, at a level determined by age, occupation, sex, SES, and so forth, at a lower social level such as family, school, and so on, or at the individual level.[17] Studying values at different levels may provide one measure for understanding the dynamics between individual-level and system-level behavior and especially for understanding deviance and conformity in given cultural settings.

VALUES AND ATTITUDES

Although the concept of value occupies a critical position in analyses of human behavior, it by no means stands alone, but is surrounded by other concepts for attitude, need, norm, and belief. Of these perhaps the concept most persistently linked to values is the one for attitude. As might be expected from the discussion on values, there is as yet in the literature no uniformity concerning what constitutes an attitude or, in fact, even what the precise analytic difference is between attitude and value. Occasionally the two concepts are used interchangeably, although most serious studies differentiate them. They are, in fact, similar in the sense that both are part of a blueprint of desired outcomes that function as criteria against which the inputs from the senses are checked and that guide behavior.[18] An attitude, however, is a more special case of the genre in that it is more specific in focus. If terminal values refer to absolute goals, to end-states that are valued for their own sake, and if instrumental values refer to ideal modes of behavior, then attitudes differ in the sense that they are not as broad in scope. Rather, an attitude is an acquired preference to respond to or to evaluate some quite specific event in a favorable or unfavorable manner.

An attitude contains beliefs (but not all beliefs are attitudes) and a feeling and action component as well. While there may be an imperfect correlation betwen an attitude and either a verbal statement or behavior, the most common view is that attitudes have both dynamic and directive qualities and that they therefore function as mental habits which, when aroused, act to dispose a person to perform a particular set of actions.[19] In this vein, Milton Rokeach defines an attitude as "a relatively enduring organization of beliefs around an object or situation predisposing one to respond in some preferential manner."[20]

One analytical distinction between values and attitudes is that values have a more central position in the individual's personality structure; they function as standards. Attitudes are not standards. Values, which are components of attitudes, are standards, but an attitude itself is merely an organization of several beliefs focusing upon some specific object or situation. Values guide attitudes in the sense that they impel action "across specific objects and situations and beyond immediate goals to more ultimate goals,"[21] whereas attitudes are focused on a specific object. Although an attitude, like a value, has cognitive, affective, and behavioral qualities, it is not a basic element in the personality, but rather a frame of reference that provides a basis for induction and deduction and the organization of knowledge.[22] An attitude is not a single predisposition to respond but is, rather, an agenda for action, which when activated will lead to a response, although not necessarily always in the same manner or to the same degree. It is, therefore, a set of interrelated predispositions that are organized around an object (which may be concrete, as a group, or abstract, as an issue) or around a situation, which provide an agenda for how to behave.[23]

Either singly or in clusters, attitudes function in a number of important ways. At the most general level they can be thought of as translating general desired ends into more specific guides to action. In so performing, attitudes simplify the task of evaluating new information and they dispose an individual toward certain lines of action that are instrumental to achieving one's goals. In short, it can be said that "An attitude toward some state of affairs is defined as a composite of the valence (positive or negative) of all the values or goals to which that state of affairs is perceived to have positive or negative instrumentality."[24]

Some Other Conceptual Dimensions

Some researchers believe that statements about an object or about actions do not literally reveal attitudes but are, rather, indicants of attitudes. In this view beliefs and intentions can be analyzed independently; the problem, then, is to isolate the dynamic and directive qualities of attitudes (and values) and examine how they interrelate with these other dimensions.[25] For instance, beliefs are part of values and attitudes but in themselves have only a true and false, incorrect and correct dimension, whereas values and attitudes also have a dimension of good or bad.[26] Opinions, which are close to beliefs, are presumed to be more directly observable than attitudes or values and also to lack a dynamic behavioral predisposing quality. Interest, which is a term sometimes used in social analysis, is conceptually narrow in focus since only some values are self-interested in nature. Needs, which some scholars link with values in the sense that values presumably both originate from needs and create, inhibit, or block still others, are differentiated on the basis that values contain a cognitive dimension that reflects societal demands as well as innate individual wants.[27] Only humans, therefore, have values, whereas both men and other living creatures may have needs.

A persistent source of confusion in the study of values and value change seems to be the tendency to use the terms value and attitude at both the individual and the group level. The result has been to blur the dynamic interrelationship between preferences at the individual level and prescriptions at the social level that are external to the individual. For this reason the choice has been made here to define group-level evaluative structures as norms and ideology. It is important to remember that there is a feedback relationship involved between the two levels in which social level prescriptions may be internalized and become individual-level preferences and where individual-level preferences, widely shared, can be abstractly noted as social-level prescriptions. There is, however, no necessarily direct correspondence between the preferences of any single individual and the prescriptions that may be noted at the social level.

Norms, which most directly reflect societal demands, refer to appropriate forms of behavior within specific situations and have a consensual quality in terms of some reference group. They become especially important in social analysis when they embody the objectives of elite groups so that they reflect social control demands. Ideology, like norms, also has a consensual quality in terms of some reference group. Unlike norms, however, ideology is a framework of desired ends (terminal) and of appropriate means to these ends (instrumental) that goes beyond specific situations and refers to the ultimate goals of the group. It is a belief system that may be partly codified in a doctrine (such as Marxism) but goes further as a representation of the conscious and unconscious attributes of the world view of a people. It is an abstraction found by ascertaining socially sanctioned ends and socially approved ways of obtaining these ends.

Values, Attitudes, and Behavior

What is the relationship between values and attitudes and behavior itself? The problem is complex, for there is no reason to suppose that behavior will uniformly correspond to attitudes on any given issue or in any given situation.[28] Concerning values, Neil Smelser says that in most situations values are too general to be useful as guides for behavior, with the result that people actually conform to norms, which are more specific, by behavior that is acted out in terms of roles and is affected by situational factors.[29]

Generally, a person behaves routinely in terms of a very few roles and because of this has a relatively well-defined sense of self. Moreover, in most situations one's sense of self is relatively habitual; behavior is motivated toward relatively well-articulated goals and has a kind of unconscious quality readily understood both by oneself and by others. Prior learning and experience predispose the individual toward certain particular ends among alternate possibilities. It is, therefore, usually not difficult, following an act, to pair actions with reasonably well-articulated attitudes. However, granted that one never has an absolute sense of self in any situation, where this sense becomes overly problematic, the meaning of what one does may become obscure, and considerable confusion may arise as to which values and attitudes actually apply.[30] To further complicate matters, behavior toward objects occurs within situational contexts, and this behavior is therefore related to two types of attitudes—one relevant to the object and one relevant to the situation.[31] Since it is possible to have a favorable attitude toward the object but a negative one toward the situation (or vice versa), similar behavior by two different individuals may be related to a different qualitative mix of attitudes.

The potential complexity in research in determining which values and attitudes actually apply in a given situation has led to the attempt to take into account a factor that might be called self-esteem. Succinctly, as one's self evaluates one's behavior against internalized standards, self-esteem will vary according to one's ability to approximate the requirements of the standard. The anxiety (from shame, guilt, and the like) that one feels when one falls short of one's ideals is deemed to be the actual motive force for particular kinds of behavior rather than the standard itself.

If two people are observed engaging in different behavior within the same situation and toward the same object, or the same person in the same context showing two kinds of behavior at two different points of time, one may ask why. One possible response is that the individual, in a particular context, had a feeling of esteem (or disesteem) regarding his behavior and, if asked, he might go on to explain the reason for this. Underlying values will be revealed by these rationalizations when behavior (which is measurable in some degree) is accorded some feeling state (which can be typed—love, hate, and so on) at some level of intensity (which, at least in theory, is also measurable). Presumably the more intense the feelings of esteem, the more positively salient will be the value dimension that is noted, and the less the degree of esteem, the more negatively salient will be the value dimension that has been expressed. As the intensity of feeling, positive or negative, declines less salient values are encountered. When one asks for reasons for behavior one is asking for motives, or attempted justifications, which it is hoped will indicate in what way the observed behavior is valued, with what intensity it is valued, and whether the goals of the behavior are direct or whether they are merely means to a further end.[32]

Observed behavior is always only a rough guide to underlying attitudes and values. For instance, caution should always be taken not to automatically equate conformity to norms with internalized standards. One should also be wary of uncritically equating a statement about what is desirable or undesirable with the salience of a value, for while a statement may be a manifestation of salience, it may also be only a memorized response designed to win group approbation and avoid sanctions for deviance. In cases such as these one may obtain evidence concerning the intensity and salience of norms, but only genuinely and freely elicited strong emotional responses, usually best observed in choice situations and often evoking feelings of guilt or shame concerning one's self-esteem, can give clues as to the actual nature of the internalized standards that a person holds.[33]

VALUE CHANGE

In early childhood learning, norms relating to honesty, cooperation, filiality, gentleness, and so on are often given separate stress. But as these norms are internalized as values they do not continue to be differentiated from each other but rather, over time, gradually begin to form into a hierarchically organized value system that is highly resistant to change. This system has been defined as "a learned organization of rules for making choices and for resolving conflicts—between two or more modes of behavior or between two or more end-states of existence."[34] While it is not yet known precisely why among alternate possible preferences some become valued, there is a presumption that the rightness for individuals of certain preferences structured in a distinctive system originates from having learned the norms and ideology of the social system of which they are members, and that these prescriptions serve as overarching ideals for individual behavior. Of course, the ranking of values will differ among the individuals of any society, as will the ranking of normative and ideological prescriptions among cultures. Within societies, individuals can be analyzed according to whether their value systems are conformist or deviant in terms of the system of prescriptions found in the society's norms and ideology.[35] A similar analysis can be made between the system of norms and ideological prescriptions of subgroups and the system pattern at the societal level. In the analysis of societies the degrees of variation among the value systems of individuals and among the normative systems of subgroups will often be one crucial comparative distinction among the societies themselves.

Values may be differentiated in terms of their function and relative position within a given value system. For instance, in terms of function, values are characterized as either instrumental or terminal with a concomitant presumption that on a central-peripheral dimension of salience the terminal system (although not necessarily all of its constituent values) is most central. Although the instrumental and terminal value categories are related, they can be thought of as representing two different value systems, each with its own rank order. According to Rokeach, for all individuals regardless of culture there are approximately 60-70 instrumental values and only about 18 terminal values.[36] Whether Rokeach is definitively correct in this enumeration or not, probably the total number of values is, in fact, quite small.

In terms of position, the more a particular value relates to a self-conception of existence, identity, or esteem, the more likely it is to be central within its own system. This will be particularly the case where clusters of such values are widely shared, and are thus reinforced by social consensus, and where such values are closely connected with other less salient value clusters. Central values, it is presumed, will be the most difficult to shift within a value system and, when shifted, will result in the greatest repercussions for the value system as a whole. There is a commonly held assumption among those who study values that individuals will strive to maintain consistency among the cognitive, affective, and behavioral components within one value, between two or more related values, and among all the values in a value system. Changes in values that are peripheral within the system will raise the least repercussions in terms of maintaining the consistency of the value system as a whole. There is good evidence that where adherence to central values is strong there will be great resistance to alterations in the prevailing value system, but when central values have been dislodged from their position of primacy there will be relatively greater repercussions for the overall system.[37]

Values help the individual in a number of ways: to be socially adjusted in the sense of maximizing the possibilities for obtaining rewards and minimizing punishments; to be ego-defensive in terms of preventing certain impulses from surfacing and in terms of selectively screening knowledge of threatening external forces; to be expressive in the sense of establishing one's identity; and to categorize knowledge in terms of providing a frame of reference for understanding one's environment.[38] A value generally serves to maintain these functions in some generally stable distribution. A value may become inadequate, however, in terms of fulfilling one or more of these functions. When this happens the inadequacy is likely to be related to new situational contexts, more specifically to such factors as a changed environment, need deprivation or the creation of new needs, new and more meaningful information about problems, a shifting pattern of rewards and punishments, threats to self-esteem, and/or feelings of dissatisfaction or inefficacy.[39]

Values tend to cluster within a value system. Their position on a central-peripheral dimension is noted by a preference for behaving in terms of one cluster of values rather than another. On the basis of the information that is incoming to the individual, certain values are activated and the utility of the values as guides for behavior are monitored on the basis of feedback, where the viability of the values in terms of fulfilling their functions is compared to the requirements of the continuously incoming information.[40] Chief among the factors that determine viability are the "contingencies of reinforcement" surrounding the behavior that has been manifested—that is, rewards versus punishments for particular actions and the degree of frustration that concomitantly results.[41] When a substitution or revision of a cluster of controlling values occurs, four stages in this process can be discerned: a new goal is implicitly or explicitly established; information relevant to this decision is analyzed; a form of behavior that will achieve the goal is selected; and a "signal" is given to begin the process of carrying out the new behavior.[42]

Dissonance and Attitude and Value Change

In the sense that values exist as learned justifications for particular actions, distress (or dissonance) can be expected when an individual is forced to comply overtly with an unfamiliar norm or is required by novel situational conditions to engage in unfamiliar behavior. In terms of attitudes and values there appear to be three principal ways in which a state of dissonance occurs: inducing a person to engage in behavior that is inconsistent with attitudes and values; exposing a person to new information from a credible source that is inconsistent with current information in the attitude-value system; and exposing a person to inconsistencies within his current attitude-value system.[43] When new behavior occurs following dissonance, it will not for some time occur spontaneously, but will rather be a response of overt compliance to unfamiliar requirements.

Although dissonance theories are disputed, they do shed light on paradoxical feedback effects of behavior on attitudes and values. Dissonance theory states that distress will occur when two cognitive elements are contrary to each other and the amount of dissonance will be a function of the importance of the elements in the dissonant relationship. There is also an implicit assumption that there is a tendency to bring cognition into consonance with reality.[44] Reduction of stress can occur by changing one or more of the dissonant elements, by adding new elements that are consonant with existing cognitions, or by decreasing the importance of the dissonant elements.

The functions of values—social adjustment, ego-defense, identity expression, and knowledge categorization—can also be thought of as serving an even more fundamental function of maintaining and enhancing one's total conception of oneself. In situations where one feels one is immoral or incompetent there is likely to be distress. Since values serve as guides for evaluating oneself as well as others, distress that involves values is also likely to encompass one's concept of oneself.[45] These conceptions are the innermost core of an individual's total belief system. They relate to personal qualities and abilities and to the various social positions (sex, generation, occupation, and so on) that one occupies in society. Unlike some values and many attitudes these self-conceptions are activated in almost all situations.[46] Since individuals generally seek to maintain a degree of emotional balance, a change at the core of the personality system is likely to arouse the greatest dissonance and also lead to changes in functionally related terminal values, instrumental values, and functionally related attitudes and behavior. Real fundamental change in individuals comes from changes in self-conceptions and in the terminal values that are related to these conceptions, and results from dissatisfaction with one's concept of oneself or with associated values.

It should not be assumed, when attitudes and values are in conflict, that the attitude, being less central, will always be the one to change. It may be, of course, that in most circumstances people are more likely to find their attitudes uncongenial with their values than to find that their values are inappropriate. Nevertheless, it is basically the contradiction between the value and one's self-conception or between the attitude and one's self-conception that determines whether the attitude or the value will change. The crucial question is where in the total attitude-value system is there an inconsistency with one's self-conception.[47] The principle is as follows: "Contradictions are resolved so that self-conceptions will, at the least, be maintained and, if at all possible, enhanced."[48]

Despite the fact that it cannot be stated that change at the individual level, when it takes place, must first occur either for attitudes or for values, it is known that many attitude changes are typically short-lived (since underlying values are still intact). When values underlying a changed attitude remain intact there is no reason to expect behavioral change, since behavior will still be oriented toward consistency with underlying values. When there is a shift in the hierarchical position of a value within a value system, however, permanent changes in attitudes can be expected and, ultimately, changes in behavior as well.

Attitudes may, in fact, shift or change slightly with few repercussions up to the point where genuine inconsistency with anchoring values seems imminent. At that point resistance to dissonant feelings will make further change in attitudes very difficult. Minor changes, caused by such things as disagreement among peers, being in a suggestive situation, or receiving a persuasive message, will have no real repercussions for the value system unless reinforced by other factors such as radical situational change or intensive group discussion or indoctrination.[49]

When change in attitudes does take place it can be toward an object, toward a situation, or toward both. Behavior is a function of both an attitude toward an object and one toward a situation in which a number of terminal and instrumental values may be associated with each attitude. It is expected that the greatest propensity for change will exist when two or more terminal values that apply in any given context are persistently inconsistent. Such inconsistency is the product of changes in attitudes toward either objects or situations that call into question the relationships of terminal values within the value system.

People can acquire new values and related behavioral dispositions through trial and error, through personal observation and understanding of a situation, by perception of another's responses, by observation of the outcome of another's actions, by verbal instruction, or by a combination or sequence of such learning experiences.[50] Regardless of the type of experience, the process of attitude and value change first involves paying attention to information that contains novel content, then comprehension of the content of the information and grasping the implications for oneself, and finally retention (or internalization) of the information's requirements, followed by action. During this process the rate of change will tend to be negatively accelerated over time and the amount of change will be an increasing function of the discrepancy between the initial value position of the person and the value expressed in the content of the information.[51] In the communication process whereby information is transmitted one can identify a number of salient features including the attributes of the source, the content and structure of the message, the way in which the information was transmitted, the nature and character of the recipient, and the ultimate destination of the message.[52]

One crucial factor that will determine whether a recipient will tune in to a message and eventually retain it is whether the recipient's self-esteem is enhanced through some form of identification with the originator of the information. Perceived competence and similarity, perceived empathy, and judgments concerning the communicator's ability to administer sanctions are all important factors in feelings and judgments about the credibility of the source.[53]

Individual- and Societal-Level Change

Within any society the value systems of individual members are never formed into exactly the same pattern. However, at least one definition of a group states that its member individuals will generally have shared value orientations. Such sharing fosters group solidarity by providing common meaning for recurrent situations, readily understood criteria for minimizing intragroup conflict, labels for deviance, and common justifications for sanctions against the errant. Shared values help individuals to identify with other group members; emotional responses of guilt or moral righteousness concerning deviance or conformity presumably have their origins in the sanctions and rewards that have emanated from one's reference group and that are sanctified in the group's norms and ideology.[54] There is a presumption that individuals, by and large, will attempt to reduce dissonance by configuring their values to conform to the prescriptions contained in the norms and ideology of the social system within which they live. In traditional societies such conformity was no doubt largely ubiquitous, but this condition poorly characterizes the modern world where the disjunctive reordering of priorities within the value systems of individuals and within the norms and ideologies of subgroups and societies has become the order of the day for the majority of mankind. The anguished feelings that many people feel as a result of this aspect of modernization are well known.

Societies throughout the world are currently modernizing in a process that is by no means unidirectional and is also markedly uneven, both within and among societies. Such change need not be traumatic but often is, as different preferences become salient within the value systems of individuals and as different prescriptions become prominent within the norms and ideologies of subgroups. Historically, young people and intellectuals often appear as *loci* for the impetus to such change, perhaps because both groups (although they are not mutually exclusive) have not made a final commitment to beliefs and values that will constrain future behavior. In the case of young people the reason for this appears to be age-related, since youth occupies an ambiguous position in the social structure, and in the case of intellectuals the reason appears to be occupational, since some intellectuals, by the very nature of their profession, may become critics of established ways.

Individuals may reorder priorities within their own value systems as a response to idiosyncratic internal needs and, to the extent that the new configuration is noticeably variant from social norms, they may be labeled as deviant or eccentric. Or individuals may reorder priorities only among those clusters of values that are relatively peripheral on the central-peripheral dimension. Since such values are largely derived and are characterized by less constraint in terms of the impact that a reordering will have on the overall value system (as compared with central values where even very tiny shifts may have large repercussions), such a reordering may mark a person as "different" from others. Should the reordering occur relatively uniformly for a group of individuals, it may become the basis for a new definition of a social strata or a particular subgroup. Or, if basic value orientations are not "tightly tied to known and understood empirical states of affairs" there may be leeway for a reinterpretation by some individuals of these orientations which may serve "as an important basis for the legitimation of new departures."[55] Depending on situational context and perspective, such "reinterpreters" may be seen as villains, fools, heretics, traitors, and rebels, as revolutionary fighters, heroes, and martyrs, or as heroic captains of change. From the standpoint of the person who is the reinterpreter, the process may be highly energizing and self-fulfilling or it may be psychically excruciatingly painful, involving loss of identification with others, ambivalence, and feelings of persecution accompanied by anger. For some individuals a process of alienation, of withdrawal of support and identity from the established social order, which at first is only passive and felt with regard to isolated parts of society, may become more active and be generalized to the whole social system.[56]

Alterations in normal and expected patterns of life may lead to a number of different types of responses, ranging on a continuum from slightly inappropriate with regard to established norms to violent and revolutionary. When alterations occur one begins to look at the actual type of behavior that is subsequently manifested as well as at possible external influences. In trying to ascertain what antecedent influences might help explain particular kinds of behavior, some scholarly reports indicate that certain feelings and thoughts—including, among others, normlessness, a socialization experience that does not give one a firm sense of place and identity in the social system, a feeling of inefficacy, and a desire to explain society's ills and locate the causes—may all be partial explanations for a search by individuals for a new system of personal values and a new normative and ideological order.[57]

In a situation of fleeting novelty, prevailing individual value systems may be distorted only slightly, if at all. However, where repetitively unfamiliar situational contexts occur and where certain values within an established value system are repeatedly and grossly inadequate as guides for behavior and as anchors for individual sense of self, of identity within a previously explained and understood framework, there is a fertile environment for the formation of a new system of values.[58] The emergence of new individual value systems marks the attempt by some, often the young, to respond to the strain they are experiencing. In turn the response by agencies of social control, which are often staffed and led by older generations, to the holders of new value systems will vary in terms of the capabilities of these agencies, of their assessment of the consequences that may result from lack of conformity among value systems and norms and ideology, and of their feelings of threat about these consequences.

When people begin to be alienated from the established social order in which they live, their withdrawal is likely to be only partial at first and their behavior reformist in nature. Should reforms fail, however, there is likely to be intensification of personal feelings of threat and inefficacy. The behavior that is then manifested, which may or may not affect the political system, is likely to be intensified if deviant subgroups reinforce and stimulate the desire to withdraw from the current order. Such groups may also foster a desire by the individual to reinvest identity with these groups, for they provide and promise a way for feelings of threat and inefficacy to be reduced. Subgroups that are themselves alienated serve as powerful reinforcers for the behavior of otherwise isolated individuals (moderated always by individual factors of social background and personality), in some cases providing merely a new focus for different but still purposefully conformist activity, while in other cases serving as the triggering device for retreatism, reformism or, more rarely, revolutionary behavior.[59]

Although value change may begin among selected individuals and remain a relatively isolated social phenomenon there are times when change may come to embrace an entire subgroup. Whether the behavior that results aims at changing only facets of the established social system or whether there is a call for a sweeping reorganization of the entire society will be largely dependent on the type and extent of the original situational disruption, on the ultimate goals of those who seek change, and on whether they perceive themselves as having the capability and resources to reconstitute the social system. If the aggrieved group does not possess the means to reconstitute the social system, is prevented from expressing hostility that will punish some individual or some group that is considered responsible, and cannot change the normative order or influence those who have the power to do so, then the feelings of inefficacy that result may well lead to withdrawal of support for the system and the beginning of efforts to change the prevailing ideology of society.[60] At this point what may well occur is a "collective attempt to restore, protect, modify, or create values in the name of a generalized belief."[61] Since hostility is almost always one component of the feelings of inefficacy that precede a social movement, there may well be a potential for violence. Certainly moral outrage will be manifested toward some objects or situations and will be expressed in a manner that is consonant with the dominant belief orientations of the social system. Thus, for instance, where the dominant belief orientation is religious in nature, those who are presumed to be guilty of usurious loans may be labeled as sinful, but where the dominant belief orientation is Marxist in nature, these same individuals will be labeled as bourgeois.[62]

Efforts at change may initially originate in only one institution or in a limited number of institutions within a society. If such an institution is a major one (family, educational system, religious organization, and the like), change in it will soon impinge upon other institutions to the extent that their functions are perceived to be linked. Change may begin, for instance, with reorganization of the military, but if there is also a perceived need 'for new military knowledge, changes in the educational system may soon be initiated. Eventually, as the ideology changes, even the family, among other institutions, may experience a transformation. It is most likely that the political system will also be involved, especially where the government is a major legitimator and a guarantor of the traditional ideology. Since the great mass of people, especially in peasant societies, may not share the same patterns of belief as do relevant elites, or even be aware of their membership in a broader common culture, they may not initially be involved in the process of change. However, as soon as institutions that include them as members (such as the village or the family) become caught up in the process of change, they too will become involved. Finally, if a movement takes control of the government and establishes its own normative and ideological prescriptions as a blueprint for the rest of society, the transformation process may become one that is deliberately directed by agencies of social control. In such cases, now increasingly common, value and behavioral change for members of societies does not appear as an undirected process but is, rather, consciously induced and led by social control authorities.

Fundamental, long-term, and highly persevering social change will not occur unless there has also been a change in the ideology of society. But new emergent ideological prescriptions generally develop at the same time that certain older prescriptions are diminishing in importance, so that considerable confusion is apt to persist for some time concerning the overall nature of the predominant normative and ideological structure. Change among subgroups will not be uniform in speed nor necessarily follow a predetermined course, with the consequence that lack of congruence among subgroups may extend over a considerable period. At the societal level prolonged negotiation and conflict among subgroups espousing various systems of norms and ideology will frequently ensue.

Whatever the nature of social change, either reformist and gradual or rapid and revolutionary, it is not to be expected that a society's ideology will be totally reorganized. Rather, the ideology that evolves will be syncretic in nature with some prescriptions from the old system remaining in an unchanged position within the new emergent system.[63] Individual and subgroup behavior, even when superficially similar to that of the past, will overall be in conformity to a new system of normative and ideological prescriptions that will contain, however, older prescriptions that have survived.

CONCLUSION

The current state of research in the area of values is clearly in a transition phase. It is still difficult to correlate, in an invariant way, an expressed attitude or value with a particular mode of behavior or to explain why two people who share an attitude or value behave differently in the same situation. At root remains the question of how attitudes and values relate to particular forms of behavior and, more especially, how particular subsets of values—both terminal and instrumental—become operative under some circumstances but not under others. As a consequence a situation remains in which measures of values and measures of behavior are linked by probabilistic statements and statistical inference. The measures, in effect, are still crude and related only by assumptions. The assumptions themselves, however plausible and even ingenious, still await definitive tests for confirmation or disconfirmation.

Value change appears to occur when conventional ideas and modes of behavior are perceived as inappropriate for a new problem and when people begin to feel distress about this condition. The process of change, however, does not require that every value in the prevailing system be eliminated or transposed. Rather there will be syncretism where new values join with existing values to form a new and distinctive overall pattern. Those who espouse a new value system may, at least initially, be called deviants or revolutionaries, but during the later stages of change they may be thought of as innovators or heroes. In psychological terms these individuals have risen above fears of inconsistency and dissonance and have embraced complexity and a liking for the unexpected.[64] As the values which they espouse adequately solve new problems, others come to perceive the utility of the new pattern and slowly change their own orientations.

In previous sections a number of factors have been set forth that are, it is hoped, useful for analysis of value change and its implications within any given specific context. The most important of these factors include the following: description of the context, level of analysis (individual or group), the relevant prescriptions within the established ideology and their ordering on a central-peripheral scale, the values held by those individuals who are involved in the context that has been described and the ordering of these values on a central-peripheral scale, and the capability and determination of agents of social control.

Although the link between values and behavior is still unclear, observed behavior as noted in a description of a situational context is a crucial variable that throws light on the ability adequately to set forth the values that are operative within that context. Where the ranking of individual values is inconsistent with the ranking of prescriptions in the established normative structure or ideology, there will exist a variable condition of social tension whether it is directly observable in behavior or not. Knowledge of this condition allows the observer, with varying degrees of precision depending upon the nature of the data, to assess the intensity of tension in terms of a verbal index of severe, moderate, slight, nil, and the like.

To the extent that there is incongruity between individual values and normative and ideological prescriptions, one may expect a manifestation of the resulting tension to be revealed in one form or another. For instance, where the incongruity exists only for isolated individuals, the manifestation may take the form of varying degrees of stigmatization and/or degrees of control of individual deviance. Where such incongruity links numbers of individuals and where social control methods are permissive, changes in practices within certain social institutions may become sufficiently noticeable and also sufficiently widespread to indicate a qualitative change in the ideology of the whole society. Where social control is restrictive, however, the manifestation of tension may well be violent and involve large-scale revolutionary activity on the part of some subgroups. Or, of course, social control agents may rigidly structure educational form and content or may initiate indoctrination campaigns, often with a concomitant stress on the primacy of solidarity and conformity. In any case, knowing the values that are elicited in a situation, who holds them and with what intensity, the congruence of individual values with prescriptions in the established ideology, and the power and flexibility of social control agents and agencies, can provide a powerful if still inexact tool for social analysis.

NOTES

1. Justin Aronfreed, "Moral Development from the Standpoint of a General Psychological Theory," in *Moral Development and Behavior: Theory, Research and Social Issues*, ed. Thomas Lickona (New York: Holt, Rinehart and Winston, 1976), pp. 54–69.

2. M. Brewster Smith, *Social Psychology and Human Values* (Chicago: Aldine, 1969), pp. 97–98.

3. Clyde Kluckhohn, "Values and Value-Orientations in the Theory of Action," in *Toward a General Theory of Action*, ed. Talcott Parsons and Edward A. Shils (Cambridge, Mass.: Harvard University Press, 1951), p. 400.

4. Muzafter Sherif, *The Psychology of Social Norms* (New York: Octagon Books, 1973), p. 117 (first published by Harper and Brothers, 1936).

5. Milton Rokeach, *The Nature of Human Values* (New York: Free Press, 1973), p. 7; and Milton Rokeach, *Beliefs, Attitudes and Values: A Theory of Organization and Change* (London: Jossey-Bass, 1968), p. 124.

6. Kluckhohn, *Values and Value-Orientations*, pp. 391–95.

7. Ibid., p. 395.

8. Everett Hagen, *On the Theory of Social Change: How Economic Growth Begins* (Homewood, Ill.: Dorsey Press, 1962), p. 113.

9. Donald T. Campbell, "Social Attitudes and Other Acquired Behavioral Dispositions," in *Psychology: A Study of a Science*, Study II. Empirical Substructures and Relations with Other Sciences. Vol. 6. *Investigations of Man as Socius: Their Place in Psychology and the Social Sciences*, ed. Sigmund Koch (New York: McGraw-Hill, 1963), p. 96.

10. Ibid., pp. 96–97.

11. Ibid., pp. 97, 100–1.

12. Ibid., p. 148.

13. Vern L. Bengtson and Mary Christine Lovejoy, "Values, Personality and Social Structure: An Intergenerational Analysis," in *Linking Social Structure and Personality*, ed. Glen H. Elder, Jr. (Beverly Hills: Sage Publications, 1973), p. 105.

14. Rokeach, *Human Values*, pp. 15–16.

15. Ibid., pp. 14–15.

16. C. Wright Mills, "Situated Actions and Vocabularies of Motives," in *Social Psychology Through Symbolic Interaction*, ed. Gregory P. Stone and Harvey A. Farberman (Waltham, Mass.: Xerox College Publishing, 1970), pp. 476–77.

17. Bengtson and Lovejoy, *Values, Personality and Social Structure*, p. 107.

18. Campbell, "Social Attitudes," pp. 143–44.

19. William J. McGuire, "The Nature of Attitudes and Attitude Change," in *The Handbook of Social Psychology*, 2nd ed., vol. 3, ed. Gardner Lindzey and Eliot Aronson (Reading, Mass.: Addison-Wesley, 1954 and 1969), pp. 147–48; and Frederick J. Fleron, Jr. and Rita May Kelly, "Personality, Behavior and Communist Ideology," *Soviet Studies* 21, no. 3 (1970): 308.

20. Rokeach, *Beliefs*, p. 112.

21. Rokeach, *Human Values*, p. 18.

22. Rokeach, *Beliefs*, p. 131.

23. Ibid., pp. 118–20, 135.

24. McGuire, "Nature of Attitudes," p. 151.

25. Martin Fishbein, "The Relationships between Beliefs, Attitudes and Behavior," in *Cognitive Consistency: Motivational Antecedents and Behavioral Consequents*, ed. Shel Feldman (New York and London: Academic Press, 1969), pp. 203–4.

26. Kluckhohn, *Values and Value-Orientations*, p. 432.

27. Ibid., p. 428; Hagen, *Theory of Social Change*, pp. 104–11; Rokeach, *Human Values*, p. 20.

28. M. Brewster Smith, "A Map for the Analysis of Personality and Politics," in *A Source Book for the Study of Personality and Politics*, ed. Fred I. Greenstein and Michael Lerner (Chicago: Markham, 1971), pp. 38–39.

29. Neil J. Smelser, *Theory of Collective Behavior* (New York: Free Press, 1962), pp. 29–32.

30. Nelson N. Foote, "Identification as the Basis for a Theory of Motivation," in *Social Psychology Through Symbolic Interaction*, ed. Gregory F. Stone and Harvey A. Farberman (Waltham, Mass.: Xerox College Publishing, 1970), pp. 482–86.

31. Rokeach, *Beliefs*, p. 126.

32. Andrew C. Theophanous, "In Defense of Self-Determination: A Critique of B. F. Skinner," *Behaviorism* 3, no. 1 (1975): 103.

33. Kluckhohn, *Values and Value-Orientations*, pp. 403–7.

34. Rokeach, *Beliefs*, p. 161.

35. Kluckhohn, *Values and Value-Orientations*, p. 415.

36. Rokeach, *Human Values*, p. 11.

37. Thomas M. Ostrom and Timothy C. Brook, "Cognitive Bonding to Central Values and Resistance to a Communication Advocating Change in Policy Orientation," *Journal of Experimental Research in Personality* 4, no. 1 (1969): 42; Rokeach, *Beliefs*, p. 55.

38. Daniel Katz, "The Functional Approach to the Study of Attitudes," in *A Source Book for the Study of Personality and Politics*, ed. Fred I. Greenstein and Michael Lerner (Chicago: Markham, 1971), pp. 202-7.

39. Ibid., p. 218.

40. James G. Miller, "The Nature of Living Systems," *Behavioral Science* 21, no. 5 (1976): 311-13.

41. B. F. Skinner, *Beyond Freedom and Dignity* (New York: Knopf, 1971), pp. 115-17.

42. Miller, "Nature of Living Systems," p. 315.

43. Rokeach, *Beliefs*, p. 167.

44. Smith, "Map," p. 91.

45. Rokeach, *Human Values*, pp. 216, 225, 228.

46. Ibid., pp. 215-16.

47. Ibid., pp. 217, 229.

48. Ibid., p. 230.

49. McGuire, "Nature of Attitudes," pp. 169, 175-76.

50. Campbell, op. cit., pp. 107-10.

51. McGuire, "Nature of Attitudes," pp. 223, 243.

52. Ibid., pp. 172-73.

53. Ibid., pp. 187, 191-92, 194.

54. William A. Scott, *Values and Organizations: A Study of Fraternities and Sororities* (Chicago: Rand McNally, 1965), pp. 56-59.

55. Marion J. Levy, Jr., *Modernization and the Structure of Societies: A Setting for International Affairs* (Princeton, N.J.: Princeton University Press, 1966), p. 352.

56. David C. Schwartz, *Political Alienation and Political Behavior* (Chicago: Aldine, 1973), pp. 96-97.

57. Ibid., pp. 12, 16, 17, 95, 154; Smelser, *Theory*, pp. 290-92.

58. Miller, "Nature of Living Systems," p. 302.

59. Schwartz, *Political Alienation*, pp. 28, 42-43, 94, 156-57, 160.

60. Smelser, "Nature of Living Systems," pp. 272-73, 325.

61. Ibid., p. 313.

62. Ibid., pp. 313, 319, 320.

63. Levy, *Modernization*, p. 55.

64. William J. McGuire, "The Current Status of Cognitive Consistency Theories," in *Cognitive Consistency: Motivational Antecedents and Behavioral Consequents*, ed. Shel Feldman (New York and London: Academic Press, 1969), p. 37.

PART 1

CHINESE VALUE ORIENTATIONS

The initial study in this section discusses the relationship between traditional and modern Chinese values. It is followed by a study written from the perspective of contemporary psychology; it deals with the nature of value orientations in modern Chinese society and linguistic factors that constrain the range of these orientations. The next study, written by a sociologist, discusses questions of social stereotyping with special emphasis on how value orientations may be imputed to others. The last two studies focus on socialization, with an analysis of processes whereby new value orientations may be acquired by both children and adults.

1

CONFUCIANISM: SYMBOL AND SUBSTANCE IN RECENT TIMES

Tu Wei-ming

In this essay, I shall discuss the symbol and substance of Confucianism in the light of the Cultural Revolution and the ensuing events. Although I am fully aware that issues of power and policy on the economic, political, and social levels may have exerted a greater transforming influence on the brute facts of life in present-day China, I will in this study address myself mainly to the ideological question.

As an apparent digression, which it is actually not, I shall begin by an examination of Levenson's renowed thesis on *redness versus expertise*, or *value-priority*, in his works on the fate of Confucianism, and suggest that this "Levensonian" interpretation needs to be broadened and modified if it is to account for the ideological struggle in the Cultural Revolution. The Confucian element will be introduced in a discussion of the Maoist approach to vital problems in China in order to show that Confucian ideas have dominated much of the intellectual discussions in contemporary China notwithstanding the making of a new "state cult" of Maoism. The essay concludes with a series of reflections on the relevance of Confucian symbolism in identifying substantive issues in China's quest for a new value system.

This article originally appeared in *Asian Thought & Society: An International Review* (April 1976): 42–66. The author wishes to note that the article had been presented to the 4th Annual Sino-American Conference on the People's Republic of China in Airlie House, Virginia (December 12-16, 1974), prior to its publication, without change, in *ATS*.

THE LEVENSONIAN THESIS

In an article entitled "Marxism and the Middle Kingdom," published in the September 1966 issue of *Diplomat*, Joseph R. Levenson makes the following observation:

> Ch'ien-lung, proclaiming that the imperial virtue was acknowledged everywhere, could write complacently to George III, "We are in need of nothing. . . ." Mao, however, knows how desperate the needs are—the intervening century and a half had ruined any complacency and the Confucian pretension to virtue that explained it—and his prescription to banish the needs is *science* (very far from Confucian values), most especially including a 'science of society.' The *red* of *red vs. expert* is not an eternally Chinese demand, whether Confucian or Communist, that officials profess to a world view transcending technical skill and specialization. It implies something else, that the modern world is incompatible with the Confucian, not congruent with it—so incompatible that science and technology are in the ascendant everywhere, and Marxism has to own them or lose its own ascendancy.[1]

Although this observation seems incongruent with the "spirit" of the Great Proletarian Cultural Revolution, it does point to a central *Problematik* in contemporary China: how to adapt herself to the modernizing world without losing her own cultural identity.

Reviewed from this perspective, the *red vs. expert* controversy has been interpreted as a conflict between an emotional need to be attached to that which defines what the uniqueness of China is and an intellectual choice to develop a highly sophisticated technology. Of course the conflict between identity and adaptation is not new. Indeed it smacks of the conciliatory attempt of Chang Chih-tung (1837-1909) in his "substance-function" (*t'i-yung*) formula. And Levenson's pioneering work itself suggests that the conflict was apparent in the mind of Liang Ch'i-ch'ao (1873-1929).[2] Without stretching the point, the anti-traditionalism of the *New Century* (*Hsin shih-chi*) and the advocacy of democracy and science in the *New Youth* (*Hsin ch'ing-nien*) can also be understood as a by-product of an inevitable confrontation between the so-called *redness vs. expertise*. The triumph of scientism in modern China may thus be described as a clear indication that the amateur ideal of the red will eventually be supplanted by the "technic skill and specialization" of the expert. The true test for Marxism as well as for Confucianism is its ability or inability to *own* science and technology.

Actually, it has been widely argued that the Cultural Revolution represents no more than a desperate attempt to rescue the dying fervor of the red. According to this view, the young Maoist radicals fear that the revolutionary spirit has been seriously eroded by party functionaries, factory managers, and academic teachers, and that the take-over generation as a whole has become bourgeois in mentality and revisionist in attitude. Therefore they contend that unless a major transformation in the political culture takes place, China will face the danger of following the capitalist road at the expense of socialism. The tasks of the Cultural Revolution, as adopted by the Central Committee of the Chinese Party, were:

> First, to struggle against and overthrow those persons in authority who were taking the capitalist road; second, to criticize and repudi- ate the reactionary bourgeois "academic authorities" and the ideol- ogy of the bourgeoisie and all other exploiting classes; and third, to transform education, literature, and art and all other parts of the superstructure that did not harmonize well with the socialist eco- nomic base.[3]

This program may very well be seen as hoisting a red flag against bureauc- ratization in the party, systematization in the economy, and professionalization in the university. It can be seen as a declaration of war against the emergent tendencies of what Max Weber calls "rationalization" in political, economic, and educational institutions. If Levenson is right in holding that the *red* is not an eternally Chinese demand that officials profess a world view transcending tech- nical skill and specialization and that the ascendancy of science and technology is irresistible, then the Cultural Revolution, too, will be doomed to failure, and the *redness* will also in the end become "a shade, living only in the minds of many, treasured in the mind for its own sake after the society which has pro- duced it has begun to dissolve away."[4]

Levenson's thesis can be further developed against the background of modern Chinese history which he perceives in "The Province, the Nation, and the World: the Problem of Chinese Identity" as

> a history of movement from the politics of Confucian faction (deriving at times from provincial fellow-feeling, but in a world com- manded, overall, by a common Confucian fellowship) to the politics of a new world, an international politics conceived in terms of class.[5]

Implicit in this description is his strong belief that science and technology as manifested in the universalizing process of industrialization will give rise to "the diversity of many vocational types that come with specialization." This is neither a Confucian nor a Maoist value. And since "specialization makes new elites, of professionals, not amateurs on the Confucian model," he concludes, the fields of expertise will eventually provide "particular identities."[6] Redness, we may add, will be neutralized as Confucian amateurism and gradually relegated to a second- ary role.

If we take this line of argument seriously, how can we account for the "fantastic drenching in ideology that China began to take" during the Cultural

Revolution, directed not only against the experts but against the past as well? Levenson explains the obvious dilemma in terms of a sense of danger, "the danger of a war that could not be left to experts, because they would not choose it and could not win it with their expertise alone." With a touch of irony, Levenson continues:

> And it was this danger that gave the Cultural Revolution its dual targets, the two cultures, western and traditional. The concurrent attack on the latter confirms danger as the source of attack on the former, on the cosmopolitan spirit which the experts represented. For the tendency to "museumify" the past, instead of rooting it out, belonged to the age of self-assurance. It had not been there in the early days of struggle, when the communists had the passion of engagement: and it vanished now in an embattled age of possible destruction. The god of history was a hidden god again. Relativistic historicism, coolly accounting for one-time foes by giving them their niches, went out of fashion. The dead were no longer monuments, but ghosts and monsters to be slain again.[7]

BEYOND *REDNESS VERSUS EXPERTISE*

However, provocative as it is, the Levensonian interpretation is flawed in both conceptual sophistication and historical accuracy. Only five years after the untimely death of the brilliant scholar, we have witnessed too many fundamental problems in post-industrial societies to feel comfortable in giving unqualified support to the assertion that "science and technology are in the ascendant everywhere." The awareness that the life-supporting resources are finite, that the available energy for mass consumption is exhaustible, that the ecosystem in the world is disintegrating, and that the human environment is rapidly deteriorating, at least suggests that modernization, in the sense of industrialization, is no longer to be conceived as a process of quantitative growth. The newly emergent global consciousness recognizes basic limits not only in economic growth but in scientific and technological developments themselves. The United Nations Stockholm Conference on the Human Environment in 1972 and the politicization of natural resources engineered by the Organization of Petroleum Exporting Countries recently further testify to the vulnerability of highly industrialized countries. One wonders whether with this hindsight Levenson would still have insisted that "expertise" rather than "redness" was the wave of the future?

Historically the case against the Levensonian interpretation is even more compelling. The available literature on the Cultural Revolution seems to indicate that the *red vs. expert* controversy has not been a central concern. No serious attempt has been made to demean expertise at all. Only a few professionals in science and engineering have experienced public humiliation. Mao Tse-tung is alleged to have given special instructions to protect science and engineering professors from Red Guard assaults. Indeed, technical expertise is fully accepted as a positive value. The slogan "first red, then expert" is not intended to discourage specialized knowledge; it simply demands that such knowledge be applied in the total ideological, political, and economic context. After all *scientific* materialism is taken seriously as a guiding principle for action. And the ability to solve concrete problems with particular skills acquired through actual experience is highly prized. If an expert is under attack, and in the case of Ch'ien Wei-ch'ang, usually it is not his expertise but his limited vision in its application that matters.

The plight of the high-level cadres and the professors in the humanities is an entirely different story. They are the real "rootless cosmopolitans,"[8] in Levenson's characterization. For the experts are neither rootless nor cosmopolitan. To be sure, they are not as ideologically secure as the peasants or the workers, but they have found a permanent niche in the total scheme of "building socialism." Although they cannot yet claim the universality of science and, as Levenson observes, "see their association with professional colleagues on the other side of national and ideological walls," they are rooted and localized in China's established institutes of science and technology. The cadres and the professors, especially those in literature, history, and philosophy, are the modern counterparts of traditional China's "bureaucrat-literati" or "scholar-officials." They are the targets of attack because, from the scientistic point of view, they are the expendables (rootless) and yet, with the power of the pen, they have exercised enormous influence throughout China (cosmopolitan).

The case of Wu Han is well-known. His political power as deputy mayor of Peking, combined with his historical knowledge and literary expressiveness, gave tremendous weight to the *Dismissal of Hai Jui* (January 1961). The play was not only a satire but also an act of defiance against Mao's handling of the *rightists*, especially P'eng Te-huai, Mao's first defense minister, in 1959. Ostensibly Wu seemed to be pleading for the rehabilitation of P'eng Te-huai, but underlying the theatrical plot was a serious attempt to advocate a new cultural mode. Of course Wu Han was not alone. He was joined by Liao Mo-sha, head of the United Front Department of the Peking Municipal Party Committee, and Teng T'o, former chief editor of the *People's Daily*. The three of them, beginning in October 1961, under the joint pseudonym of Wu Nan-hsing, collaborated in writing a series of morality tales for the Municipal Party Committee's journal *Front Line (Ch'ien-hsien)*. Under the heading "Personal Notes from a Three-Family Village" *(San-chia ts'un cha-chi)*, these tales comment on education, the arts, morals, and current events. As a whole, they represent a masterful use of historical allegories.[9] Again, the political message was subtle but clear: a fundamental transformation of the revolutionary way of life was in order.

What was this new cultural mode or way of life that Wu Han, Liao Mo-sha, Teng T'o, and others advocated? At first glance, it appears to be absolutely innocuous. One wonders why some of their seemingly modest protests have been labeled as extremely poisonous. A brief analysis of Teng T'o's short essays, published under the general heading of *Evening Chats at Yenshan (Yen-shan teh-hua)* in the *Peking Evening News* from March 1961 onwards, may provide part of the answer. The "chats" were originally designed to serve the workers, peasants, and soldiers. Teng explains in his preface to the first anthology of his essays; however, since the majority of the readership consists of cadres, teachers, students, scientists, technicians, and practitioners in the arts, the "chats" at the present juncture cannot fulfill the needs of the masses. After all, Teng continues, the demands of the cadres and other above-mentioned comrades are different from those of the masses. He acknowledges the duty of high-level cadres in the party, the government, and the army to represent the interests of the people, but given the present situation, he intends to satisfy those who have already achieved a considerable level of cultural sophistication.

Teng T'o's "chats," numbering more than one hundred and fifty articles, are all written in elegantly composed vernacular or *pai-hua*. Stylistically they are reminiscent of the "short, superfine-quality essays" (*hsiao-p'in wen*) of late Ming (1368–1644). And the essays are so rich in historical allusions that they can be fully appreciated only by those who are highly cultivated in their literary tastes. Teng does talk about mundane things such as the earliest recorded political march of the workers in Peking and the alleged pessimism in Taipei. But the bulk of his literary effort is devoted to subjects which are historically informative and aesthetically appealing. He talks about the art of calligraphy, paintings, the difficulty of understanding the classics, the necessity of correct identification of archaeological sites, and a host of other subjects. A salient feature of his comments on a wide range of topics from natural phenomena to current events is his consistent inclusion of primary sources from historical texts, especially those of the Ming dynasty.

Indeed, Teng's "chats" are laden with direct quotations from the Four Books, the Five Classics, the writings of the pre-Ch'in philosophers, the dynastic histories, the works of the Sung thinkers, and a variety of "miscellaneous notes" (*pi-chi*) by Ming scholars. His essays on Confucius's most beloved disciple Yen Hui (521–490 B.C.),[10] the Han general Wu Han (d. 44),[11] the hero and statesman of the *Romance of the Three Kingdoms* Chang Fei (d. 221) and Chu-ko Liang (181–234),[12] the T'ang poet Chia Tao (779–843),[13] the Tung-lin scholar Ku Hsien-ch'eng (1550–1612),[14] the Ming statesman-scientist Hsü Kuang-ch'i (1562–1633),[15] and a relatively unknown Ming official Li San-Ts'ai[16] further indicate his preoccupation with traditional personalities.

Actually if we delete those perfunctory references to Marx, Lenin, and Mao, which are made often inconspicuously as dispensable trappings, Teng's "chats" are fitting companions to Peking opera, top-grade Lung-ching tea, and other exhibits of the *haute culture* in old Peking. Teng's delightful comments on poinsettia,[17] snow-flakes,[18] eagles,[19] bees,[20] dogs,[21] and a long-lost game called "*t'an-ch'i*"[22] may even create the illusion that the "cultural essence" of Peking has remained intact after twelve years of revolutionary education. More important perhaps is the complex of fundamental values permeating Teng's published works: it includes a respect for things past, a concern for exquisite taste, and a caution against any form of extremism. One easily detects in it a kind of self-indulgence, verging on the snobbishness of a traditional "literatus" (*wen-jen*).

Apparently the genteel world of Yenshan (even the name itself evokes memories of old Peking) was extremely contagious. It would not be far-fetched to suggest that in the pre-Cultural Revolution days, the ethos of "intellectuals" in the capital of the People's Republic was very much a reflection of the cultural values advocated in Teng T'o's *Evening Chats at Yenshan*. From the outside, it seems that these cultural values are not necessarily incompatible with "building socialism." But if they in fact became the central concerns of the power elite, supplanting revolutionary ideas, notably the idea of "struggle," it was a real cause for alarm, especially for those who could not bear witnessing the demise of the "spirit of Yenan." The indignation of Mao and his radical comrades at this "unwholesome" development is quite understandable.

On the ideological front, the "revolutionary situation" must have been equally distressing to the Maoists. Among the forty-two issues of *Philosophical Research (Che-hsüeh yen-chiu)*, published between 1959 and 1965, only one takes note of the philosophical expressions of the masses. And it was the winter and the very last issue of the 1965 series. Before then, it probably did not even occur to the editors of the prestigious journal that philosophical inquiries could have been conducted by people other than the professional philosophers. Understandably the scholars who had gained their reputations long before the founding of the People's Republic continued to dominate the intellectual scene. To mention just a few obvious examples, an article on the principle of objective verification by the logician, Chin Yüeh-lin, attracted considerable attention;[23] the aesthetician, Chu Kuang-ch'ien, aroused great interest by publishing a couple of technical comments on the art of aesthetic appreciation;[24] and the Buddhologist, T'ang Yung-t'ung, made a rare appearance by contributing a highly refined piece on textual criticism, while his student, Jen Chi-yü, was very active in other scholarly debates.[25] The only visible new presence was the defender of genuine Marxism and Leninism, Kuan Feng. But even Kuan devoted much of his time to historical analyses of Lao Tzu and Chuang Tzu.

Several controversies surfaced in the six-year period. Fung Yu-lan made quite a few lengthy self-criticisms, repeatedly denounced his early thoughts on Neo-Confucianism, and declared that he had been seriously wrong in advocating "abstract inheritance" as a guide for appropriating brilliant ideas in the past. But in the summer 1965 issue, he again raised the problem of transmitting the Chinese philosophical heritage. He proposed that (1) the linguistic expressions of the ancients be properly used (as in Mao's modern poems written in the style of Sung *tz'u*), (2) a conscious attempt be made to link up with philosophical issues in the past (as in Mao's *Practice* and *Contradiction*), (3) stories in ancient philosophical texts be adopted for allegorical purposes (as in Mao's ingenious handling of the parable of "The Foolish Old Man Who Moved Mountains" from the *Lieh Tzu*), and (4) experiences of the past be made to serve as lessons for the present (as in Mao's creative application of ancient military tactics).[26]

The prominence of "tradition" is evident in almost every issue. With notable exceptions, such as a study on the nineteenth century Indian philosopher, Swami Vivekananda, in the winter 1962 issue,[27] the majority of the articles dealt with philosophical interpretations of Chinese history. Although methodologically Kuan Feng, Lin Yü-shih, and others insisted that "the arena of the history of philosophy is the battlefield of the struggle between materialism and idealism,"[28] more contributors seemed to question the wisdom of imposing Western categories on the study of Chinese philosophy. Some strongly urged that research emphases be placed upon China's unique contributions to world philosophy, especially in areas of education, ethics, and spiritual life. Liu Chieh even declared that the Confucian idea of "humanity" (*jen*) is the primary symbol in philosophy and advocated a new appreciation of the Confucian ideal of the "unity of man and Heaven."[29]

The national Conference on Confucius (November 6-12, 1962), held in the capital of Shantung, near the birthplace of the sage, was therefore not an isolated phenomenon. Attended by one hundred and sixty philosophers and historians representing sixteen provinces and cities, the conference of "scholarly discussion" (*hsüeh-shu t'ao-lun hui*) examined several position papers and heard comments made by distinguished scholars among whom were Fung Yu-lan, Yang Jung-kuo, Chao Chi-pin, Lü Chen-yü, and Kuan Feng.[30] According to a report in *Philosophical Research*, Kao Tsan-fei's essay on "The Core of Confucian Thought—Humanity (*jen*)" attracted much attention. Kao maintained that the "total thought content" of the Confucian idea of *humanity* must be differentiated from its concrete "forms of expression." Thus, the validity of the inner logic in the Confucian formulation of the concept of *humanity* cannot be negated solely on the ground of its historical manifestations. Yang Jung-kuo, on the other hand, maintained that since "class analysis" is essential to any metaphysical construct, Confucius's thought must be examined against the background of the actual economic and social conditions of his times as well as his own class origin and attitude. Kuan Feng and Lin Yü-shih further contended that Kao had significantly departed from the guiding principle of Marxism. However, Lü Chen-yü argued that the best way to study a great personality is to see him in the light of critical scholarship. Imposing alien categories on him will not advance the spirit of science in Marxism.[31]

Contrary to Levenson's interpretation, the rehabilitation of the Confucian point of view did not reflect any intention of the Party to "museumify" the Confucian heritage as an archaeological relic. Rather, it was symptomatic of a massive effort at reshaping the official ideology or, as it were, redefining the whole notion of "redness."

Whether or not Liu Shoa-ch'i was instrumental in making these scholarly exchanges possible, the ethos as manifested in them has been labeled as Liu's "rightist" tendency. The implication is not that since Liu and his cohorts have adopted the "capitalist road" at the expense of "building socialism" they have put much more emphasis on "expertise" than on "redness." It seems that the real issue lies in the "superstructure" itself: at this particular juncture of the People's Republic, what should be the correct ideological line? Should bureaucratization in the Party be encouraged? Should academic elitism be justified? Should the normalization of higher education be continued? Should centralized economic decisions be maintained? Underlying these considerations is of course a host of questions concerning "value priority." What kind of cadres are to be trained? What does it mean to be an "intellectual" in a socialist country? What is education for? And what strategy of economic development is to be implemented? The "rightists" would certainly opt for a gradual, normal, institutional, and elitist approach to these problems. The operating principles would be harmony rather than struggle, calculation rather than spontaneity, and leadership rather than mass participation. This would presuppose that a high level of integration in society, even if it has been achieved by conciliatory and compromising measures, is tolerable and even desirable.

If we follow this line of thinking, "contradiction," a central kernel in Mao Tse-tung's thought, would have to be relegated to the background. Whether or not he was actually instigated by Liu, the philosopher Yang Hsien-chen did urge just that. In 1964, Yang published his theory of "combine two into one" (*ho-erh wei-i*) as an obvious critique of Mao's *On Contradiction.* [32] While Mao asserts that "everything divides into two" and "the law of contradiction in things, that is, the law of the unity of opposites, is the basic law of materialist dialectics," [33] Yang claims that Lenin's thesis on the identity of contradiction means one should seek for "common points," "common things," and "common needs." [34] He further advocated the idea of the inseparability of opposite aspects and suggests that learning dialectics means "learning how to link the two opposing ideologies." To him, "synthesis" represents a more advanced development than mere "analysis." Thus, he calls for "conciliation of contradictions" and even "class collaboration." [35]

Yang's philosophical assault on Maoism found a sympathetic echo in Fung Yu-lan's articles published in the same period. On the surface, Fung's assumption that "universal forms" transcend class distinctions has little in common with Yang's notion of "combine two into one." However, like Yang, Fung's intention is to establish a common ground on which people of different class origins can begin to share certain "basic" values. Inherent in Fung's monographic studies then is a critique of Mao's theory of "class nature," and by extension his strategy of "class struggle." [36] This demand for reconciliation is in perfect accord with Wu Han's message in the *Dismissal of Hai Jui*, and, we may add, it is also quite compatible in spirit with Teng T'o's *Chats at Yenshan.*

MAOISM IN PERSPECTIVE

From Mao's perspective, the whole situation must have appeared to be extremely provocative. The record of his informal talks in this period of time clearly shows that he was deeply distressed by what was happening. He remarked ruefully that class struggle had been discontinued for a whole decade[37] and that education on socialism had become a shambles.[38] He complained that the so-called intellectuals were in fact stupid and ignorant.[39] He felt that the *People's Daily* was not worth reading[40] and he probably refused to take seriously the intellectual debates in *Philosophical Research* for years. His distaste for scholasticism had become more intensified and his distrust for professional philosophers had become more pronounced. He contended against the facts that among the great Chinese philosophers and literati, such as Wang Ch'ung (27–91), Fan Chen (ca. 450–ca. 515), Fu Hsuan (217–278), Liu Tsung-yuan (773–819), Wang Ch'uan-shan (Fu-chih, 1619–1692), Li Chih (1527–1602), Tai Tung-yuan (Chen, 1723–1777), and Wei Yuan (1798–1856), none "specialized" in philosophy. This was also the case in the Marxian tradition. Even Hegel and Kant, he continued, were not merely specialists.[41] With a touch of sarcasm, he said that conducting counterrevolutionary activities under disguise of writing fictions was a great invention.[42] Perhaps only half seriously, he even suggested that Peking opera singers, poets, literary writers, and dramatists be chased out of the city.[43] Using the example of Russian revisionism, Mao warned that the high-salary bracket appeared first among the writers and artists in the Soviet Union.[44]

In the May 1963 address delivered at the Hang-chou Meeting, Mao instructed that five "essential points" (*yao-tien*) be implemented by the Party to ensure a higher level of efficiency among the cadres in carrying out their socialist responsibilities: (1) practicing class struggle, (2) strengthening education on socialism, (3) depending upon poor peasants for actual experiences, (4) continuing the movement of "four purifications" (*ssu-ch'ing*) in economics, politics, organization, and thought, and (5) participating in collective productive labors. On June 16, 1964, Mao revealed his concerns in cultivating the "successor generation" (*chieh-pan jen*). Again, he instructed that five factors be taken into consideration: (1) adequate education in Marxism and Leninism, (2) identification with the masses, (3) ability to unite the majority, (4) democratic attitude, (5) self-criticism.[45] Undoubtedly Mao was deeply concerned about the fate of his most cherished principles, notably "social practice," "class struggle," "mass line," and "continuous revolution." Therefore, what he actually proposed was no less than a restructuring of the existing "value priority." It did not take him long to realize that the completion of the task required more than issuing directives.[46]

Historically the Cultural Revolution began with the publication of Yao Wen-yuan's devastating criticism of Wu Han's *Dismissal of Hai Jui* in the Shanghai paper *Wen-hui pao* on November 10, 1965. Recently available information confirms the suspicion that Mao was personally responsible for the publication of the article.[47] Thus, in a sense, Mao was instrumental in creating the climate of opinion in which the Cultural Revolution became possible. Whether Mao actually supervised the formation of the Red Guards, his sanction and encouragement of the students' demonstrations clearly show that he was very much in favor of the movement. The stabilizing effect of the Army during the period also indicates that Mao, through the apparent, if not real, cooperation of Lin Piao and other military leaders, was really in command. And the fact that the supreme rule of Mao Tse-tung Thought has become fully established only since the downfall of Liu Shoa-ch'i in 1966 further points to the interpretation that Mao not only initiated the "revolution" but actually led it to its logical conclusion. However, Mao's active role in the Cultural Revolution does not at all suggest that he personally "manufactured" the whole thing. Nor does it imply that he was in perfect control at each stage as the Cultural Revolution unfolded.

In an address delivered at the enlarged meeting of the Standing Committee of the Politburo on March 17, 1966, Mao remarked that the antisocialist influence of Wu Han, Liao Mo-sha, and Teng T'o was so pervasive that "cultural revolutions" were urgently needed in literature, history, philosophy, law, and economics.[48] Similarly, on April 28, 1966, Mao, in his criticism of P'eng Chen, who was listed as one of the six most influential members of the Party in September 1966, described the situation in Peking as so tightly controlled by the "rightists" that "even a needle could not stick into it, nor could a drop of water leak into it."[49] Mao's feeling of powerlessness in exerting an immediate impact on Peking is evidenced by his painful decision to initiate the Cultural Revolution from Shanghai. A recorded conversation of Mao on February 3, 1967, reveals that he originally intended to have a critique of Wu Han published in Peking, but no one there could be entrusted with the task. Therefore, he had to go to Shanghai and discuss the matter with Yao Wen-yuan. And Mao mentioned in passing that the Shanghai base had been established by Chiang Ch'ing. After Yao had completed the article, as a precautionary measure, Chiang insisted that it not be shown either to Chou En-lai or to K'ang Sheng for fear that Liu Shao-ch'i, Teng Hsiao-p'ing, or Lu Ting-i might gain access to it and intervene in its publication. Mao complained that even after it had been printed and widely circulated throughout the country, Peking still refused to cooperate.[50] However, it should be noted that a remarkable change of emphasis in *Philosophical Research* did take place in winter 1965 when a special issue on the philosophical essays of the workers, peasants, and soldiers was published on December 21, 1965. Mao happily stated that he had read three of them with great interest and encouraged others to do the same.[51]

The three 1966 issues of *Philosophical Research*, which were among the last to have been published before the journal was abruptly discontinued, contain exclusively articles denouncing Wu Han and intellectual elitism in the first and the third, and one hundred concrete examples of the principle of "identity of contradictions" in the second. On May 25, 1966, seven members of the Department of Philosophy at Peita launched an attack against the university's chancellor, Lu P'ing. Their poster of criticism, displayed on the walls of the university and commonly known as the *tatzupao* (large-character news), was the first sign of "student" rebellion against an established educational authority during the Cultural Revolution. Mao's personal decision to have the content of the *tatzupao* broadcast over the national radio system on June 1st gave a great impetus to impending student demonstrations in Peita, Tsinghua, Nanking, and other famous universities. The "initiators" of the Cultural Revolution, as the seven signers of the *tatzupao* were to be called by the press, opened the floodgate of protest with, as it were, a few strokes of the brush.[52] The story of the subsequent events is now widely known, although interpretations on Mao's "counter-current" activities continue to be proliferating. Admittedly the intellectual confrontation thus outlined might have been a surface manifestation of what many China experts believe to be a much more substantive issue, namely an intense power struggle in the highest echelon of the Chinese communist leadership. However, the "power struggle" thesis is inadequate, not because it is "wrong" but because, as advanced in current literature, it is too restrictive even to account for the actual exercise of power in the Cultural Revolution.

Needless to say, power has been a central concern. The downfall of Liu Shao-ch'i, later the death of Lin Piao, and the displacement of an overwhelming majority of leaders in virtually all segments of the "establishment" can very well be interpreted as a change in the mode of exercising power unprecedented in the history of the PRC. The Cultural Revolution, in this particular connection, has been a "snatching power" (*tuo-ch'üan*) movement. And it does seem plausible that Mao, with the support of the Shanghai "radicals," reemerged from the Second Line to the First Line and in the process managed to destroy the power bases of his rivals: Liu's Party, Lin's Army, and, with a stretch of the imagination, probably also Chou's Government. This interpretation is, however, oversimplified. Given the complexity of events of the last decade in the PRC, it is deceptively naive to subsume the whole "political" process under the rubric of power struggle, assuming the existence of a conscious design to restructure the leadership so that those who were "power holders" (*tang-ch'üan*) would be drastically replaced by those who were originally powerless. Of course the slogan that *tsao-fan yu-li* (there is reason to rebel or rebellion is justified) during the heyday of the Cultural Revolution could be easily understood as a militant attempt to transfer power from one group to the other. But are we to accept the speculation that Mao was able to mobilize the Red Guards and, with the support of the People's Liberation Army, successfully destroyed the Party; then through an ingenious manipulation of the Government managed to paralyze the leadership of the Army, and that now his radical supporters are busily trying to discredit the Government as well? Even if phenomenologically one can perceive such a pattern, as an explanation it gives no more than an impressionistic account. For it fails to take into consideration the underlying issue of value priority, without which the Cultural Revolution could not have happened in the first place.

It is generally recognized that Mao's real strength in mobilizing a nation-wide revolution did not come from the power centers of what constituted the web of day-to-day political control but from the authority of ideology. Paradoxically Mao's ability to exert a profound influence in shaping the direction of national sentiments in the last ten years is, in a significant way, attributable to his choice of remaining relatively detached from directly exercising power through the party apparatus. Had Mao been closely associated with the educational policies of the party, for example, he would not have had the leverage to deal effectively with the student revolts in the summer of 1968.[53] Indeed, without any irony at all, Mao could very well subscribe to Lord Acton's observation that power tends to corrupt and absolute power corrupts absolutely. The struggle of the Cultural Revolution, in this connection, can even be characterized as an attempt to search for an uncorruptible power base—"dictatorship of the proletariat." Whether or not this is labeled revolutionary romanticism, the Maoist strategy was to define power in so broad and comprehensive a context that it could never be legitimately "localized" to become the weapon of a special interest group. And a monolithic order, achieved through a routinized handling of public problems, was thought to have been a direct threat to social revolution precisely because it seemed that inherent in its power relationships was a tendency toward particularism. It was not power alone but power based on ideology that gave Mao the authority to challenge the everyday management of national affairs.

The ideology behind the Cultural Revolution, commonly known as Maoism, stresses among other things (1) social practice (*she-hui shih-chien*), (2) class struggle (*chieh-chi tou-cheng*), (3) mass line (*ch'ün-chung lu-hsien*), and (4) continuous revolution (*chi-hsü ko-ming*). Without describing in detail each of the principles, it may be helpful to discuss in brief some of their ideological implications.

Social practice superficially resembles the notion of *engagement* in modern existentialism, but since its philosophical basis is not individualism but collectivism, it points to an entirely different area of concern. The individual choice to confront the unknown as an authenticating act for one's real existence is diametrically opposed to the idea of "eradicating self-centeredness" (*ch'ü-ssu*) as a precondition for genuine practice. In Maoism, a person is perceived as an integral part of a collectivity; his real worth, as it were, can be fully manifested only by a process of objectification through which selfishness is overcome and unity with the "great self" (*ta-wo*) achieved. The idea that one's inner truth can be discovered by probing the ground of spiritual subjectivity is completely alien to this mode of thinking. Practice in Maoism must be empirically verifiable and socially recognizable. It is intended to subordinate the needs of the part to the needs of the whole. It aims at a total solution, rather than an individual response to a partial situation.

As a form of social practice, *class struggle* aims to ensure that egalitarian measures be universally implemented. The purpose of "struggle, criticize, and reform," to use a current expression, is to achieve a higher level of justice in society by destroying apparent orderliness. This is premised on the judgment that latent contradictions among people, brought about by an unequal distribution of economic commodities, social privilege, and political power, can be resolved only through struggle. Conciliatory arrangements are frequently pretexts for perpetuating injustice. The leveling of inequalities by heightening conflicts between "classes" is thus an indicator of the societal commitment to revolutionary change. Since contradictions, in a practical sense, cannot cease to exist, the struggle has to be renewed continually.

The *mass line* is to see to it that cadres, intellectuals, and other leaders do not forsake the revolutionary spirit of struggle. And the idea of "unity with the masses" is intended to foster an exemplary morality of self-sacrifice. The task of socialist education therefore involves the establishment of centers for training revolutionaries with a profound sense of mission. The prominence of totalism is particularly pronounced in the principle of *continuous revolution*. Much emphasis is placed on the power of the people by their own will to bring about an egalitarian society. To be sure, revolution is dependent upon "a capacity for building large-scale and highly disciplined forms of human organization,[54] but the boundless creative power of the masses is believed to be more reliable as the basis for socialist transformation. Mao is absolutely serious in asserting that "the people, and the people alone, are the motive force in the making of world history."[55]

However, contrary to widely held belief, *social practice* as a form of praxis is not necessarily anti-intellectual. Mao fully recognizes the significance of intellectual activities in building socialism;[56] he also acknowledges that the intellectuals themselves have a key role to play in social revolution. To him, it is vitally important that the cadres be thoroughly trained in the "theory" of Marxism-Leninism. for unless they are adequately equipped with an ideological tool, they cannot very well fully realize the creative potential of the masses.[57] Mao once stated that "truths, all truths, in the beginning, are always held in the hands of a few, and are always suppressed by the majority." And to illustrate his point he cited the examples of Copernicus, Galileo, and others.[58] His "counter-current" thesis is therefore predicated on the assertion that the real vision of how to apply Marxist and Leninist ideas to a concrete situation is sometimes the property of a small minority in society. But only through an experiential involvement in studying and working with peasants, workers, and soldiers can the insight of this creative minority become socially practicable.

Similarly, *class struggle* and *mass line* are not necessarily anti-rational. It is true that faith in the people as a source of inexhaustible energy and a belief in the intrinsic value of identifying with the lower classes are unquestioned "background assumptions" of Maoism. But the actual process of achieving social goals, far from being an emotional solution to China's "authority crisis," is often pragmatic and programmatic. The emphasis on study and research further suggests a commitment to empiricism, not as a philosophical doctrine but as a practical necessity. *Continuous revolution*, accordingly, is not so much against structure itself as against any form of essentialism. Mao believes that the dynamic process, rather than the achieved equilibrium, is a more effective way to release creative energy from below. It is better, Mao seems to contend, for the present to be chaotic than for the future to become stagnant.[59]

Obviously the Maoist line is in basic conflict with, for lack of a better term, the Confucian line advocated by Wu Han, Teng T'o, and other intellectuals in Peking. So far as the Cultural Revolution is a struggle on the ideological plane, the confrontation of the two lines can very well characterize what the major points of contention have been in the cultural arena over the last ten years. With the upsurge of anti-Confucian campaigns after the Lin Piao incident in 1971, it seems that the attack on the Confucian tradition may have been a logical extension of the Cultural Revolution. If we leave genetic reasons aside, critiques of Confucianism may appear to be inevitable consequences of shaping up the cult of Maoism. This interpretation of course presupposes that Maoism is absolutely incompatible with Confucianism and that Mao himself has a very strong aversion to Confucian culture.

Despite the apparent total negation of Confucianism, however, in the light of the available information, Mao himself is ambivalent towards the Confucian heritage. It is true that Mao has repeatedly attacked intellectual elitism, academic scholasticism, and bookish knowledge devoid of an experiential basis. Yet this does not entail that he is consistently critical of Confucianism itself. He may think more highly of revolutionaries, inventors, poets, and folk heroes than of Confucian scholars, but there is no evidence of any systematic effort at eradicating the Confucian influence in his thought.

Suggestively, Mao has time and again acknowledged that six years of Confucian education in his youth have had a profound influence in shaping his world view. He is familiar with the Four Books and the Five Classics. For example, he can still recite long passages from the *Book of Poetry*.[60] And he has expressed the wish to go through all of the twenty-four dynastic histories.[61] He has also noted that his knowledge about warfare did not come from the *Sun Tzu*, as many people suspected, but from books much closer to the Confucian tradition, such as *Tso-chuan* (*The Tso Commentary to the Spring and Autumn Annals*), *Tzu-chih t'ung-chien* (*General Mirror for the Aid of Government*), and *San-kuo yen-i* (*Romance of the Three Kingdoms*).[62] Even in his philosophical writings, despite their apparent Marxist-Leninist stance, perennial issues in Confucianism are often taken into serious consideration. On the Chinese New Year of 1964 (February 13), Mao, in an informal conversation with Chang Shih-chao, Huang Yen-p'ei, and others, made a few references to the Confucian "six arts" (ceremonies, music, archery, carriage-driving, writing, and mathematics). He expressed regret that the "main stream" (*chu-liu*) of Confucianism had been lost and urged his followers not to throw away the Confucian heritage.[63]

A further evidence of this seemingly open-minded attitude toward the Confucian tradition is found in the January 1972 issue of *K'ao-ku* (*Archaeology*), the first scholarly journal to resume publication after the Cultural Revolution. The editorial reiterates the necessity of continuing the struggle of the two ideological lines. It also stresses the importance of applying Mao's policy of "making the past serve the present" to archaeological studies.[64] But the first article by Kuo Mo-jo, president of the Academy of Science and for decades a close personal friend of Mao, is on a hand-written scroll of the Confucian *Analects* dated 710 with poems and miscellaneous notes added toward the end.[65] The scroll was discovered in 1969 at T'ulufan in Hsinkiang province. The copier, P'u T'ien-shou, was identified as a twelve-year-old student of a frontier community school. Kuo claims that P'u's calligraphic skill and ability in poetic expression amply testify that his familiarity with the basic literary education in T'ang China was very high. Kuo proudly concludes that if a twelve-year-old schoolboy at an ordinary community school in the remote region of Hsinkiang was able to demonstrate such a level of competence in Confucian education more than a thousand years ago, the claim of the Russian sinologists that Chinese culture has never spread beyond Szechwan and Kansu is obviously false.[66] It should be noted in passing that this "Confucian" scroll was included in "The Exhibition of Archaeological Finds of the People's Republic of China" in Paris, London, and Toronto. It was replaced by a "land contract" only after the anti-Confucian campaign had been launched.

CONFUCIAN SYMBOLISM IN HISTORICAL CONTEXT

It may not be far-fetched to suggest that the actual organization of massive campaigns against Confucius launched after Lin Piao's death was a surprising development even to some members of Mao's inner circle. The politics of anti-Confucianism, which is inseparable from the eradication of Lin's ideological influence in the Party, is beyond the scope of the present study. Suffice it to say that the "power" issue is directly involved, but many journalistic accounts about an implicit attack on Chou En-lai are yet to be substantiated. Some guesswork, such as the attempt to prove that the target was indeed Premier Chou by suggesting the phonological approximation of Chung-ni (Confucius's style name) and *tsung-li* (the modern term for premier) is highly speculative. However, it should be noted that the recent upsurge of anti-Confucian sentiments, despite its uncertain political consequences, is not at all a new phenomenon in modern Chinese intellectual history.

In fact, underlying these uncertainties and occasional absurdities is a consistent theme not only in the political thought of the People's Republic but in the whole intellectual development since the fall of the imperial system in the early twentieth century: cultural iconoclasm. In other words, a strong commitment to see China reconstitute herself as an integrated political system independent of Western influence has been closely linked with an equally strong commitment to see her cultural values supplanted by new ideas imported from the West. The belief that the quest for political self-determination necessarily involves a willingness to cast away traditions which account for much of China's cultural heritage has been widely shared by modern Chinese intellectuals of different political persuasions. As a result, Confucianism, the most influential value-system in China since its revival in the eleventh century, has become the principal object of iconoclastic assaults.

Actually, ever since the May Fourth Movement in 1919, Confucian symbolism has been attacked from without and corrupted from within. Indeed, systematic campaigns against "Confucius and Sons" (*Kung-chia tien*) in the twentieth century are traceable to the publication of the *New Century* in 1907 and surely to the commencement of the New Culture Movement in 1916. As a matter of fact, the effectiveness of the *New Youth* as a weapon against Confucianism significantly outweighed its ability to promulgate *Te hsien-sheng* (Mr. Democracy) and *Sai hsien-sheng* (Mr. Science). A brief survey of the well-known anti-Confucian heroes should substantiate the claim that the only consensus of virtually all articulate Chinese intellectuals at the turn of the century was that the roots of the Confucian tradition must be eradicated before China could be "modernized." The socialist Ch'en Tu-hsiu (1879–1942), the writer Lu Hsün (1881–1936), the Kuomintang leader Wu Chih-hui (1864–1953), the classicist Chang Ping-lin (1868–1936), and the anarchist Liu Shih-p'ei (1884–1919) had little in common, except their anti-Confucian sentiments.

Undoubtedly these influential minds made the odds overwhelming against the possibility that Confucian ideas would reemerge as meaningful and creative symbols in Chinese intellectual circles. But ironically it was the ostensibly staunch supporters of Confucianism who really committed the devastating blow. The elaborate scheme of Yuan Shih-k'ai to make Confucianism a "national religion" as a way of legitimizing his imperial ambitions probably did more to discredit Confucian symbols than all the anti-Confucian articles of the *New Youth* put together. The haphazard efforts of the warlords, notably Sun Ch'uan-feng and Chang Tsung-ch'ang, to "promote" Confucian studies as a way of enhancing their prestige discouraged sensitive youth from having any association with Confucian symbols. The politicization of Confucianism in the Republican era further strengthened the belief that, as a political ideology, Confucian values had always supported the despotic system in imperial China.

Damaged by external attacks and internal corruptions, Confucian symbolism seemed to have become ossified long before the founding of the People's Republic. This enabled Levenson to observe the modern fate of Confucian China as follows:

> The sageliness of Confucius may still be felt in China (or felt again), like Socrates' Europe. But Confucian civilization would be as "historical" as Greek, and modern Chinese culture as cosmopolitan as any, like the western culture that reaches now, in paper-back catholicity, to "The Wisdom of Confucius." In a true world history, when all achievements are in the museum without walls, everyone's past would be like everyone else's; which implies that quite unConfucian thing, the loss of the sense of tradition.[67]

Yet recent events in the West as well as in China impel us to take issue with this observation.

For one thing, it is inconceivable that an anti-Socratic campaign, if one could ever be launched in modern Europe, could have an impact beyond the academic ivory tower. Cultural iconoclasm, and the recent anti-Confucian campaign is in a sense a variation on the same theme, may itself be a subtle manifestation of the latent power of the Confucian tradition in contemporary China. Admittedly this is most intriguing. One possible interpretation is that the Confucian civilization has been so deeply rooted and widespread in Chinese society that its influence is still pervasive, despite more than half a century of concerted efforts to extirpate it. To be sure, many Confucian symbols have been so thoroughly ridiculed and discredited that they probably can never be re-established as meaningful guides for social action, but the "substance" of Confucian power, so to speak, as manifested in "new" values which are structurally identifiable as of Confucian origins, is an entirely different matter. Of course this claim can only be substantiated by a sophisticated analysis of what may be called the modern transformation of Confucian symbolism. Suffice it now that there are definite signs to show why this line of inquiry may be fruitful.

One example readily comes to mind. Systematic efforts to eradicate Confucian influence, in the case of many modern Chinese intellectuals, were frequently accompanied by "unconscious" identifications with Confucian values. Hu Shih's militant refutation of Confucian passivity, for instance, did not at all prevent himself from becoming a "mild, kind, courteous, restrained, and magnanimous"[68] gentleman. Liu Shih-p'ei's fascination with Wang Yang-ming (1472–1529) forced him to conclude that the greatest Confucian thinker of the Ming dynasty was in essence "anti-Confucian." Wu Yü's ruthless denunciation of Confucian institutions did not divert his attention from the importance of moral rejuvenation in China. Chang Ping-lin's involvement in revolutionary activities went parallel with his commitment to "ancient text" (*ku-wen*) scholarship. And it is probably more than an irony that the champion of anti-Confucianism, Ch'en Tu-hsiu himself, is now labeled a "Confucianist" at heart. On the other hand, those who tried to use Confucian symbols for political gains did not fare very well either. Lu Hsün's devastating caricatures of the so-called "reactionaries" have made them no more than a group of laughingstocks. It is common knowledge that most attempts at the formulation of a mere Confucian political ideology have met with failure.

Thus, the Confucian symbols could not be destroyed simply by intellectual critiques; nor could they be easily manipulated for political expediency. The phenomena seem to suggest that underlying the apparent trend of cultural iconoclasm was a strong sense of confidence—no matter how much destruction there is, the identity of Chineseness will remain powerful. This partly explains why decades of iconoclastic attacks on traditional authorities have not yet brought about a fundamental transformation of Confucian symbolism. It is quite plausible that beneath the sound and fury of current campaigns against Confucius lurks an urgent need to demonstrate the uniqueness of the Chinese ideological line.

It is certainly false to identify Confucianism with the uniqueness of Chinese culture. This not only commits the fallacy of boundary confusion but also lacks any intellectual sophistication. But since Confucianism has significantly contributed to the formation of basic Chinese cultural traits, it would be ill-advised to advance an interpretation of the salient features of modern Chinese political culture, for instance, without an adequate knowledge of some of the basic Confucian values. Unfortunately the problem is much more complicated than that. To begin with, since the Confucian tradition does not constitute one massive whole, exhibiting solid uniformity, it cannot very well be reduced to a few core ideas such as ancestral worship, filial piety, the "three bonds" (*san-kang*), and the "five constancies" (*wu-ch'ang*). Moreover, as one of the oldest and the longest humanistic traditions in the world, Confucianism involves a highly complex process of integration, enveloping many divergent currents in religion, philosophy, arts, economics, politics, and education over a very long period of time. The spiritual orientation of pre-Ch'in Confucianism was significantly different from the institutionalized Confucian value-system of the Han; the appropriation of Confucian ideas in the T'ang central bureaucracy did not at all resemble the Confucian concerns as reflected in the ethos of Sung scholar-officialdom, and the struggle of Confucian "intellectuals" against the despotic rule of the Ming court must not be confused with the plight of Confucian officials under the literary inquisition of the Ch'ing.

The diversity and richness of the Confucian heritage makes it possible to accommodate many seemingly contradictory claims. This "ecumenical" nature of Confucianism helps it to coexist with all kinds of alien forces on the one hand and in the process assimilate much of their strength on the other. Ch'ü T'ung-tsu's analysis of the Confucianization of law[69] and Kenneth Ch'en's study of the Chinese transformation of Buddhism[70] are outstanding cases in this respect. On the other hand, having adapted itself to a variety of changing social and political conditions, Confucianism has come very close to a form of eclecticism, occasionally verging on a total disintegration of its inner identity. Thus the Jesuit scholar, Matteo Ricci (1552-1610), could vehemently criticize Neo-Confucianism and find substantive compatibility between classical Confucianism and Catholicism at the same time.[71] Equally illustrative but in a different context, T'an Ssu-t'ung (1865-1898) could claim in his *Jen-hsüeh* (Philosophy of Humanity) that the notion of "humanity" (*jen*) in Confucian thought is identical to the Buddhist precept of compassion and also to the Christian doctrine of universal love.[72] Numerous other examples can be cited to show that the range of possibilities in Confucian symbolism is truly great. It should be stressed that its adaptability could also account for much of its influence on imperial institutions. The pervasiveness of Confucian symbols in Chinese culture is certainly the main reason why the unprecedented change in China since the Western impact of mid-nineteenth century has brought about many waves of anti-Confucian campaigns.

Still, one can rightly complain that generic concepts such as "Confucian China" are extremely misleading. We must not forget about other prominent traditions like Taoism and Buddhism. We should also take into account the development of Christianity since mid-nineteenth century and the visible presence of Islam in the southwestern parts of China. If we start to probe the resources of the folk culture and the syncretic tendencies of belief-systems in the lower echelon of the society, the case against the domination of Confucianism in Chinese culture seems more compelling. It is interesting to know that this was precisely how the anti-Confucian forces of the May Fourth generation shaped up their tactics: to relativize Confucianism as one of the several major traditions in China and to neutralize its influence by characterizing it as merely the ideology of the educated elite. In a sense, this continues to be the strategy of current anti-Confucian campaigns. It is probably too early to predict whether it will actually work, but, in the light of historical experiences, it is not difficult to detect some serious problems.

A prelude to the current anti-Confucian campaign was Kuo Mo-jo's article on the periodization of ancient Chinese history, published in the summer of 1972, more than a year before the campaign was formally launched. Kuo's article announces the official position that the end of slave society and the beginning of feudalism in China, after many years of debate, are now to be identified as the transition from the Spring and Autumn (722-481 B.C.) to the Warring States (403-222 B.C.).[73] Confucius (551-479 B.C.), as a product of the slave society, was therefore advocating an outmoded ideology at the time when inevitable social changes had already occurred. Consequently, it is only fitting that Confucius is characterized as extremely "reactionary." The historicist argument attempts not only to relativize and neutralize Confucian influence in traditional China but also to "localize" Confucian thought in a definite historical context. However, it leaves a crucial question unanswered: How did the ideology of the slave society continue to play a dominant role in the feudal period for two thousand years?

Yang Jung-kuo, whose emphasis on class analysis was noted in the 1962 Conference on Confucius, has emerged as a leading theoretician for the anti-Confucian movement. In his recent book on *The Sage of the Reactionary Class—Confucius*, he again focuses his attention on Confucius's class origins and class attitudes. He flatly denies that Confucian ideas of "humanity," "loyalty," "filiality," "reciprocity," "goodness" and "rectification of names" can be abstracted from their historicial specificities and claim a kind of trans-temporal validity.[74] He does concede that Confucian symbols were effectively used by feudal institutions. He explains that this is because (1) the land-owning class changed its historical character and held on to its political power, and (2) the feudal government, in its search for an ideology of control, abandoned the more progressive Legalism and adopted Confucianism for its selfish interests.[75] He then briefly outlines how Tung Chung-shu (c. 179-c. 104 B.C.), a leading philosopher of the Han dynasty, synthesized salient elements in Confucian teaching and formulated his "idealist transcendentalism," which eventually became the reactionary ideology of feudalistic rule in China.[76]

Having characterized Confucianism as the reactionary ideology of the ruling elite in the feudal period, Yang further argues that the mainstream of Chinese intellectual history can even be seen as a continuous appropriation and manipulation of Confucian symbols for the service of despotic governments. This naturally leads to the interpretative position that those who rebelled against the Confucian tradition were the real revolutionary spirits in Chinese history. So far, only a few have been identified. Aside from the historically controversial figures, Chih of Liu-hsia and Mao of Shao-cheng, the list includes Han Fei (d. 233 B.C.). Li Ssu (d. 208 B.C.), Shang Hung-yang (150–80 B.C.), Wang Ch'ung (27–7?), Liu Tsung-yuan (773–819), Wang An-shih (1021–1086), and Li Chih (1527–1602).[77] Among the modern writers, Lu Hsün alone is considered absolutely uncompromising in his anti-Confucian stance. Great "materialists," such as Chang Tsai (1020–1077) and Wang Fu-chih (1619–1692), are no longer mentioned. The long-ignored Legalism has suddenly surfaced as a progressive ideology. The First Emperor of the Ch'in dynasty, whose coercive measures at centralization have been universally denounced throughout Chinese history, has now been rediscovered as an anti-Confucian hero.[78]

Surely, far from being an intellectual exercise of a philosophical debate, the main purpose of the anti-Confucian campaign is to generate a nation-wide mass movement in order to "fix up the superstructure." By that is meant, among other things, a total weeding out of the poisonous thought of elitism in order to achieve a true "dictatorship of the proletariat." Putting theoretical niceties aside, can this be achieved simply by exposing Confucianism as the most insidious reactionary ideology in Chinese history? Perhaps the anti-Confucian campaign was only designed to liquidate Lin Piaoism. If so, the implications for the formulation of new policies on arts, literature, philosophy, history, and even archaeology would be too far-reaching to be restricted to one concrete political event. The Chinese leadership today may genuinely believe that once the Confucian "shackle" is removed, the real creativity of the masses will be naturally released, and that this will at last silence what the current literature describes as the "dark spirits" (*yu-ling*) of Confucianism.[79] Perhaps Levenson was right after all in suggesting that "the dead were no longer monuments, but ghosts and monsters to be slain again."

However, we must not forget that the "fate" of Confucianism is widely thought to have been sealed before the founding of the People's Republic. Moreover, since the majority of Chinese intellectual historians outside of China still feel that the Confucian tradition definitely ended before the Republican era, the attempts to salvage it in the '30s and '40s are generally labeled neotraditional, if not outright reactionary. Some scholars, depending on their vantage points, further argue that the debate on science and metaphysics in 1923, or the May Fourth Movement in 1919, or the abolition of the Examinations in 1905 was really the single most devastating blow to Confucian symbolism. This inevitably leads to the puzzling question why long after the death of Confucianism, the Confucian "ghosts and monsters" have to be slain again and again. If we take Yang Jung-kuo's interpretation seriously, this seemingly extraordinary phenomenon actually has been characteristic of Chinese thought for centuries: Confucian symbolism should have perished together with the slave society in the third century B.C., but its "dark spirits" have been haunting the Chinese for two thousand years. Without being unduly sarcastic, I would contend that the modern Chinese "obsession" with the dark side of Confucian symbolism is itself a reflection of the relevance of the Confucian tradition in defining substantive issues in China's emergent superstructure.

SUBSTANTIVE ISSUES OF VALUE PRIORITY

In conclusion, I would simply note how these issues are delicately entangled with what may be called "perennial problems in Confucianism." However, to stress the relevance of Confucian symbols in defining some major problem areas in contemporary China is not at all to suggest that Maoism is in a sense still Confucian in character. Actually the Maoist value orientation is so alien to the ethico-religious intention of Confucianism that there is absolutely no way that the "inner sensibilities" of the Confucian tradition can be holistically grasped simply by an analysis of the articulated ideology of Maoist China. On the other hand, it is inconceivable that one can have a sophisticated appreciation and critique of the "value priority" in China without being aware of the Confucian dimension both as an intractable reality of the past and as a viable alternative for the future.

(1) As an all-embracing humanist tradition, Confucianism seeks to find *integrated* and *holistic* solutions to sociopolitical problems. Any exposure to the *Great Learning* (*Ta-hsüeh*) or the *Evolution of Rites* (*Li-yün*)[80] should convey the impression that the Confucian approach is comprehensive in character. Unlike Taoism, Buddhism, or other historical religions, Confucianism is oriented toward the peaceful but fundamental transformation of this world. Although the Confucian choice is to harmonize with, rather than to master over, the existing conditions, a confirmed Confucian often stands in tension and conflict with the status quo. As a result, one of the central concerns in the Confucian tradition is how to be an integral part of the social collectivity without losing one's sense as an individual moral person. A Confucian is a social being but never merely an atomized entity in the crowd. The notion of continuous revolution is also intended to bring about total solutions. To be sure, it aims at a radical, not merely a gradual, transformation of the existing society. But by focusing on the human factor it has so far avoided the danger of causing irreparable damage to the human environment. It is vitally important to know how this emphasis on continuous mass mobilization, equipped with a highly advanced control mechanism, can continue to adopt an "ecologically" sound policy of social development

without ever trying to harmonize with the existing conditions. Is it possible to envision the cadre as an integral part of the totality and yet at the same time as a responsible critic of it? If not, the "counter-current" phenomenon is inconceivable.

(2) One of the core ideas in Confucianism is self-cultivation. A key passage on this matter in the Confucian *Analects* is: "To conquer yourself and return to propriety (*li*) is humanity."[81] Due to Lin Piao's alleged preocuppation with this statement, two anthologies including more than twenty essays critical of this six-character line were published in the spring of 1974.[82] Whether or not "return to propriety" means to accept unconditionally the ideology of the slave society in the Chou dynasty, "conquer yourself" as a way of learning to be human certainly resembles the whole idea of "eradicating self-centeredness" (*ch'ü-ssu*). It is true that Confucian self-cultivation, unlike self-criticism, is intended to help one to become a *chün-tzu* (a superior or profound person) rather than to become a *kan-pu* (cadre), but the primacy of moral self-discipline is assumed in both cases. Of course the total ideological context in which the cadre cultivates himself has nothing to do with Confucian emphasis on the "transformation of one's material nature" (*pien-hua ch'i-chih*).[83] Neverthelss, it is quite possible that once moral qualities are stressed, the way of identifying leaders becomes not only compatible with but also reminiscent of the pattern of social mobility in a Confucian value-system. Moreover, even if prescriptive conditions, like class origins, are established as major criteria of selection, cadres will still be evaluated in terms of personality traits and acquired attitudes. After all, the language of "redness" as an ethical as well as political category is often indistinguishable from the language of Confucian moral philosophy. It is certain that the Confucian symbols, at least in the near future, will not be appropriated the way Liu Shoa-ch'i did in his "Black Book," *On How To Be a Good Communist.*[84] But substantive issues are likely to be discussed in a similar context.

(3) The Confucian idea of human nature is thought to be in basic conflict with the doctrine of class nature. If there were absolutely no universalizable human nature, either Mencius's belief in the moral propensity of man or Hsün Tzu's belief in man's intrinsic cognitive power to know good would be considered false. For underlying the apparent contradictions between the Mencian theory of *hsing-shan* (goodness of human nature) and Hsün-tzu's theory of *hsing-o* (the evil tendencies of human nature) is a strong commitment to man's malleability, transformability, and perfectibility through self-effort.[85] This is predicated on the assumption that despite the diversity of human conditions, which certainly include various kinds of natural environments, primordial ties, and methods of socialization, there is a common potential shared by all persons called "humanity." Without this assumption, the Confucian insistence on universal education would be groundless. The doctrine of class nature, I suppose, is intended to bring about a more egalitarian society through class struggle. Accordingly the "dictatorship of the proletariat" does not necessarily aim to destroy other undesirable classes by sheer force; a better choice is perhaps to

exercise the transforming power of education so that political goals can be reached through the art of persuasion as well. Class struggle therefore entails ideological self-criticism and psychological conversion. One wonders how this can be achieved without an awareness that class nature as well as class attitude are changeable by educational processes and that these processes are not merely superimposed from outside. If such an awareness does exist, the quest for genuine mass participation will probably lead to the question whether human nature is really definable in terms of class origins alone.

(4) As of now, formal education in China is still dominated by pragmatic and scientistic methods. To be sure, in Mao's new educational directives, the old university entrance examination has been virtually abolished, the curriculum at all levels of schooling shortened, practical application of knowledge emphasized, and close cooperation between productivity and academic research established. On the surface, this "politicization" of education may seem likely to have an adverse effect on theoretical sciences. In the language of "redness versus expertise," this seems a clear indication of leaning toward redness at the expense of expertise. But, to reiterate an earlier point, the real issue is not the fact of technological expertise which, I believe, will continue to be highly regarded no matter how "red" the country becomes. The very fact that the universities in China are in essence institutes of science and technology should make the point clear. Certainly the question of developments in basic research in the theoretical sciences is more intriguing. But there is no reason to believe that critical studies in mathematics, physics, health-related sciences, and the like will be curtailed in China because of the educational reform. The phenomenon in the humanities and social sciences is an entirely different matter. This is, in a broad sense, inseparable from the complex problem of defining or redefining "redness." It seems that the "priority of values" will continue to be a crucial concern in China for years to come. Some traditional Confucian value orientations, like bias against profit-making activities and predilection for government service, will probably remain powerful. Others, such as preferring generalists to specialists, will likely be more seriously challenged.

(5) The policy that literature and art must serve the people at the present time may not be in conflict with the notion of historical continuity. Nor must the creative energy of the masses take the form of anti-traditionalism. In fact folk culture in China can exhibit a wide range of possibilities beyond the comprehension of established forms of artistic or literary expressions in the "great tradition." However, the "two-culture" concept is not fully adequate as an analytical scheme for understanding Chinese history. In fact one can learn as much about substantive Confucian issues from the *Romance of the Three Kingdoms* or the *Dream of the Red Chamber* as from the Thirteen Classics. The inability of the "culture workers" to rediscover enough popular theatrical performances that have not yet been tainted by Confucian "feudal" thought of "emperors, kings, generals, and prime ministers" is also a case in point. The

whole repertoire of the Peking opera tradition as well as many other local operatic literatures are now slated for extermination. But if Lin Piao, who is alleged to have been so "anti-intellectual" that he refused to read even newspapers and books, was in fact familiar with the basic Confucian ideas, the presence of similar ideas among educated Chinese must be considerable. After all, Mao himself in his informal conversation with Wang Hai-jung revealed that he had read the *Dream of the Red Chamber* five times and found its fourth chapter a good lesson for understanding the class situation of imperial China.[86] The subtle question then is to differentiate anti-Confucianism from anti-traditionalism. Such a differentiation may also lead to a distinction between the appropriation of traditional symbols as weapons for political control and the original meanings of those symbols. It is difficult to believe that just because Wu Han has "misused" Ming history, historical allegories will no longer play an important role in political education.

(6) One of the most serious charges against Confucianism is its elitist tendency. A frequently quoted documentary evidence of this has been Mencius's distinction between those who labor with their mental strength and those who labor with their physical strength. Since the distinction is thought to have implied the supremacy of the mental laborers, it is concluded that there has been a strong bias against working people in the Mencian tradition of Confucianism. However, historically Mencius made the remark in his debate with a physiocrat. What he intended to do there was simply to point out that it is neither possible nor desirable to have every person involved in agricultural production. He stressed the functional necessity of division of labor and argued that the scholars (or, if you wish, the intellectuals) could justify their existence and usefulness without making a direct reference to productivity. For the scholars, as the articulate members of society, must perform other equally significant duties such as government service and education.[87] Since Mencius also affirmed that the people are more important than the king and that the people have the right to rebel against tyrannical rulers,[88] he was certainly not an enemy of the people by conscious choice. The current policy to send intellectuals downward and to recruit members of the least advantaged groups to become university students might have been an utter surprise to Mencius, but the Mencian concern for the role of the intellectual in society is still a very relevant issue.

(7) The Confucian emphasis on cultural diversity is being attacked as a form of "restorationism." The idea of "restoring perished states, continuing broken lines of large families, and recruiting hermitic people for government services,"[89] which is alleged to have been another of Lin Piao's favorite quotations, is a Confucian approach to displaced people and their cherished traditions. It is diametrically opposed to the Legalist demand for conformity. The issue is partly centralization versus decentralization, but in a broader sense it is a conflict between two different ways of achieving political integration. At present, the Legalist line of uniformity seems in command. But in areas like minority relations and international cooperation, the spirit of peaceful co-existence is clearly

visible. The policy toward the Five-Black Groups (the landed, the rich, the reactionary, the rotten, and the revisionist) is likely to be uncompromising for some time. But it seems inevitable that eventually a conciliatory arrangement will be made. After all continuous revolution presupposes the continuous presence of not only diversity but also contradictions in society.

(8) Confucianism, as an ethico-religious philosophy, has put much emphasis on society as a "fiduciary community." The primacy of harmonizing human relations in Confucian political education is one of the many manifestations of the particular focus. Even the idea of ordering society in a hierarchical structure, based on merits rather than birth, is reflective of this concern for social stability. It is often thought that this Confucian model of society has been supplanted by the need to build socialism through total mass mobilization. And the harmonizing intention of Confucian social thought is believed to have been a path to stagnation, inequality, and in current parlance, revisionism. However, this is not necessarily a flat rejection of the Confucian model of "fiduciary community." It is difficult to envision that a critique of Confucianism in this connection will lead to the reorganization of society according to an adversary system of law. Given the existing "legal" practices in China, it seems unlikely that China will soon become "legalistic" in the sense that the American society is. On the contrary, the cohesiveness of the social structure will continue to depend upon the basic trust of the people, and since the appearance of control is fundamentally different from the substance of collective participation, the real challenge to the mass line is not merely the promotion of orderliness but the disciplined expression of creative dynamism. This can only be achieved when a sense of community is shared by the overwhelming majority. Psychological terms, such as "pride,'" "confidence," and "dedication" are different ways of describing the same phenomenon. The angry response to Antonioni's movie on China[90] and the strong attack on Western music[91] may also be understood in this context as attempts to form a new group self-definition. As China enters into the pluralistic world of nations, her self-image will probably undergo many metamorphoses, but it seems that the notion of "fiduciary community" will remain strong.

Undeniably, despite the fact that Confucian ideas are still relevant in identifying substantive issues in contemporary China, Confucian symbolism as a whole has been discredited and corrupted almost to a point of no return. Ironically, just as during the Cultural Revolution every faction of the Red Guards evoked the name of Mao to justify its activities, so all conceivable "enemies of the people" are now labeled as Confucian. In his "Directive to the Great Cultural Revolution in Shanghai" on February 12, 1967, Mao remarked that even if China was completely communized, there should still be a party, a center. It matters very little whether the party is called, in his words, "the Communist Party, the Social Democratic Party, the Social Democratic Labor Party, the Nationalist Party (*Kuomintang*), or the One-Thread Way (*I-kuan tao*).[92] Perhaps, after the Confucian "ghosts and monsters" are absolutely subdued, a new and comprehensive ideological structure will emerge. Call it Socialism, Humanism,

Marxism, or Maoism; for the symbol is not as important as the substance of a total and integrated value system.

NOTES

1. Reprinted in *Modern China: An Interpretive Anthology*, edited by Joseph R. Levenson (New York, 1971), pp. 231–32.

2. Levenson, *Liang Ch'i-ch'ao and the Mind of Modern China* (Cambridge, Mass., 1953). See a summary of his argument in his *Confucian China and its Modern Fate: A Trilogy* (Berkeley, 1969), general preface, ix–x.

3. See *Decision of the Central Committee of the Chinese Communist Party concerning the Great Proletarian Cultural Revolution*, adopted on August 8, 1966 (Peking: Foreign Languages Press, 1966), p. 1. This statement is taken from Chester C. Tan, *Chinese Political Thought in the Twentieth Century* (New York, 1971), p. 370.

4. Levenson, *Confucian China and its Modern Fate*, general preface, x.

5. Originally published in Albert Feuerwerker, Rhoads Murphey, and Mary C. Wright, ed., *Approaches to Modern Chinese History* (Berkeley, 1967), pp. 268–88. Reprinted in *Modern China: An Interpretive Anthology*, p. 68.

6. Ibid.

7. Levenson, "The Past and Future of Nationalism in China," *Survey*, no. 67 (April 1968), pp. 28–40. Reprinted in *Modern China: An Interpretive Anthology*, p. 15.

8. A term used by Levenson in "The Past and Future of Nationalism in China," *Modern China: An Interpretive Anthology*, p. 14.

9. For a succinct account of this development in English, see Jean Esmein, *The Chinese Cultural Revolution*, trans. from French by W. J. F. Jenner (New York, 1973), pp. 43–54.

10. Teng T'o (pseudonym, Ma Nan-ts'un), *Yenshan yeh-hua* (Peking, 1965), pp. 182–85. It should be noted that in *The Chinese Cultural Revolution*, Teng's pseudonym is misidentified as "Mao Nan-tun."

11. *Yenshan yeh-hua*, pp. 110–12.

12. Ibid., pp. 469–72 (Chang), pp. 315–18 (Chu-ko).

13. Ibid., pp. 18–20.

14. Ibid., pp. 156–58. The essay is entitled "Shih-shih kuan-hsin," taken from part of a line of Ku Hsien-ch'eng's famous couplet in front of the Tunglin Academy.

15. Ibid., pp. 339–42.

16. Ibid., pp. 530–32.

17. Ibid., pp. 277–79.

18. Ibid., pp. 280–82.

19. Ibid., pp. 473–76.

20. Ibid., pp. 359–62.

21. Ibid., pp. 477–80.

22. Ibid., pp. 113–16.

23. For Chin's article on the verification of objective facts and the first three basic laws of thought in formal logic, see *Che-hsëh yeh-chiu* (abbreviated as *CHYC*) 3 (1962), pp. 1–11. Also see Chin's article on class nature and the idea of necessity in logic inference, *CHYC*, 5 (1962), pp. 69–83.

24. For Chu's essay on Kant's aesthetics, see *CHYC*, 3 (1962), pp. 72–93; for his essay on Goethe's aesthetics, see *CHYC*, 2 (1963), pp. 62–74.

25. For T'ang's article, see "Lun Chung-kuo Fo-chiao wu 'Shih-tsung,'" *CHYC*, 3 (1963), pp. 47–54. Jen Chi-yü has apparently emerged as a leading scholar in contemporary China. See his *Han-T'ang Fo-chiao ssu-hsiang lun-chi* (Peking, 1973). It should be noted that

Mao has spoken highly of Jen's works, which are basically critical analyses of Buddhist thought in China from the perspective of dialectical materialism.

26. Fung Yu-lan, "Chung-kuo che-hsüeh i-ch'an te chi-ch'eng wen-t'i," *CHYC*, 1 (1965), pp. 63–7.

27. The article was written by Huang Hsin-ch'uan, see *CHYC*, 6 (1962), pp. 81–91.

28. This is, of course, merely restating A. A. Zhadanov's assertion in his *Speech in the Discussion of G. F. Alexandrov's History of Western European Philosophy*. See Kuan Feng and Lin Yü-shih's article on "Several Problems Concerning the Class Analysis in the Study of a History of Philosophy," in *CHYC*, 6 (1963), p. 29.

29. Liu's articles originally appeared in *Hsüeh-shu yen-chiu*. For a critique of his position as well as a summary of his argument, see Liu Yuan-yen, "P'ing Liu Chieh hsien-sheng te 'Wei-jen lun' ho 'T'ien-jen ho-i' shuo," in *CHYC*, 1 (1964), pp. 32–9.

30. For a brief report on the Conference, see *CHYC*, 1 (1936), pp. 54–7.

31. Ibid., p. 57.

32. For two rather different interpretations of the Yang Hsien-chen controversy, see Ch'en Fung, "I-fen-wei-erh te lun-chan Yü Yang Hsien-chen te shih-fei chen-hsiang,"*Tsu-kuo Yüeh-k'an* (Feb.–March, 1965) and "The Theory of 'Combine Two into One' Is a Reactionary Philosophy for Restoring Capitalism," in *Three Major Struggles on China's Philosophical Front (1949–64)*, published by Foreign Languages Press (Peking, 1973), pp. 48–66.

33. Mao Tse-tung, "On Contradiction," quoted in *Three Major Struggles*, p. 48.

34. *Three Major Struggles*, p. 54.

35. Ibid.

36. The case of Fung Yu-lan is too complicated to be adequately summarized here. For our limited purpose, his pre-Cultural Revolution intellectual struggles can be characterized as attempts to formulate a positive interpretation of Confucian values in the light of the ideological trend at the time. See *CHYC*, 6 (1963), pp. 45–53. However, Fung's most recent self-criticism, after having criticized his own interpretative positions on Confucius for several times since 1949, took the form of a radical denunciation of the Confucian tradition. See his "Tui-yü K'ung Tzu te p'i-p'an ho tui-yü wo kuo-ch'ü te tsun-K'ung ssu-hsiang te tzu-wo p'i-p'an" and "Fu-ku yü fan-fu-ku shih lien-tiao lu-hsien te tou-cheng." The two articles originally appeared in *Pei-ching ta-hsüeh hsüeh-pao*, 4 (1973). They were reprinted in *Kuang-ming jih-pao*, December 3–4, 1973.

37. The recently available material includes Mao's recorded conversations, directives, articles, and other sources. Most of them have never been published before. The anthology seems to have been compiled by dedicated Maoists during the Cultural Revolution. The preface is dated August 1968. My copy is based on the Hoover Institute version. Since the material is not yet widely circulated, it will be referred to as *Mao's Unpublished Statements* (abbreviated as *Statements*). The remark was made on March 28, 1965. See *Statements*, p. 480.

38. The remark was made on April 15, 1964. See *Statements*, p. 487.

39. See *Statements* (March 1964), pp. 476–77. It should be noted that Mao, in this connection, did not intend to be anti-intellectual; what he tried to convey was simply the necessity of social practice as the real basis for acquiring useful knowledge. In an informal conversation with his niece, Wang Hai-jung, on June 24, 1964, Mao asked Wang, a student of English at the Foreign Languages Institute, the English word for *chih-shih fen-tzu* (intellectual). When Wang failed to provide the answer, Mao himself tried to look it up in a Chinese-English dictionary. To his regret, only the English equivalent of *chih-shih* (knowledge) was found. See *Statements*, p. 503. Mao's preoccupation with the problem of the intellectual is reflected in his other conversations as well. In particular, see *Statements*, p. 469.

40. The remark was made is his conversation with Mao Yuan-ch'ing in March 1964. Although Mao dismissed the *People's Daily* as boring, he spoke highly of the *Liberation Army News* and *Chinese Youth News*. See *Statements*, p. 471 and pp. 579–80.

41. The remark was made at the Heng-chou Conference in March 1963. See *Statements*, p. 442. For his criticisms of Yang Hsien-chen, see *Statements*, pp. 557–627.

42. The remark was made in an address to the Tenth Plenum of the Central Committee on September 24, 1962. See *Statements*, p. 435.

43. The remark was made on February 13, 1964. What Mao really had in mind was to transfer them downward to the rural areas. See *Statements*, p. 462.

44. The remark was made in his talk on the Third Five-Year Plan on June 6, 1964. See *Statements*, p. 499.

45. *Statements*, pp. 443–45. For a monographic study on this, see R. Baum and F. C. Teiwes, *Ssu-ch'ing, The Socialist Education Movement of 1962–1966*, China Research Monographs 2 (Berkeley, 1968).

46. *Statements*, pp. 501–3.

47. A most comprehensive statement on this matter was made on February 3, 1967. See *Statements*, pp. 664–65. Also, see his remark on March 1, 1967 in *Statements*, pp. 673–75. However, it seems that Mao was not particularly impressed by Yao's article. He merely stated that it managed to identify the issue, but failed to tackle it. See *Statements*, p. 626.

48. See *Statements*, p. 640.

49. See *Statements*, p. 641.

50. See *Statements*, p. 664. The same expression noted on page 641 is repeated here: "Neither a drop of water nor a thin needle could enter into the Peking Municipal Party Committee."

51. See *Statements*, p. 640.

52. Jean Esmein, *The Chinese Cultural Revolution*, p. 99. Since the "seven signers" were actually instructors on the faculty, in a strict sense, they did not themselves represent the beginning of the student rebellion.

53. The fascinating confrontation between Mao and the student leaders took place on July 28, 1968. See *Statements*, pp. 687–716.

54. An expression from Lucian W. Pye, *The Spirit of Chinese Politics* (Cambridge, Mass., 1968), p. 235. It should become clear that the problem of what Pye calls the gap between the phenomenon of control and the substance of development is not a central concern in my study. See *The Spirit of Chinese Politics*, pp. 235–40.

55. Mao Tse-tung, *Selected Works*, 4 vols. (Peking, 1961), 3:257.

56. *Statements*, p. 496.

57. See his conversation with the Educational Delegation of Nepal on August 29, 1964, in *Statements*, p. 574.

58. *Statements*, p. 472.

59. For a sophisticated analysis of some of the basic intellectual issues in Maoism, see Frederic Wakeman, Jr., *History and Will: Philosophical Perspectives of Mao Tse-tung's Thought* (Berkeley, 1973), pp. 302–33.

60. *Statements*, p. 550.

61. He further remarked that the *Chiu T'ang-shu* is better than the *Hsin T'ang-shu* and the *Nan-shih* and *Pei-shih* are both better than the *Chiu T'ang-shu*. He was most dissatisfied with the *Ming-shih*. See *Statements*, p. 479.

62. It should be noted that Mao's real message was the futility of bookish knowledge. Even though he learned more about warfare from these three books than from the *Sun Tzu*, they did not help him a bit in his military campaigns. The only way to learn about warfare, he claimed, was to be involved in it. See *Statements*, p. 627.

63. *Statements*, p. 461 and p. 463.

64. *K'ao-ku*, 1 (1972), p. 2.

65. Kuo Mo-jo, "P'u T'ien-shou 'Lun-yü ch'ao-pen huo te shih-tz'u tsa-lu," *K'ao-ku*, 1 (1971), pp. 5–7. And as the editor noted, the text itself, together with annotations, was published in the following issue.

66. Ibid., p. 7.

67. Levenson, *Confucian China and Its Modern Fate*, 3:123.

68. A statement in the *Analects* describing the virtues of Confucius. It is quoted in Mao's "Report of an Investigation into the Peasant Movement in Hunan." It should be noted that Mao's description of the brute reality of revolution here is diametrically opposed to Hu Shih's liberal approach to social change. Mao argues: "A revolution is not the same as inviting people to dinner or writing an essay or painting a picture or embroidering a flower; it cannot be anything so refined, so calm and gentle, or so 'mild, kind, courteous, restrained, and magnanimous.'" See Stuart R. Schram, *The Political Thought of Mao Tse-tung* (New York, 1969), pp. 252–53.

69. See his *Law and Society in Traditional China* (Hague, 1961), pp. 267–79. The book was originally published in 1917 under the title *Chung kuo fa-lü yü Chung-kuo she-hui*.

70. See his *The Chinese Transformation of Buddhism* (Princeton, 1973), pp. 3–13.

71. See Matteo Ricci, *T'ien-chu shih-i* (preface, 1607, Wan-li edition), 1:37b–57b, especially 46b–47b. Ricci criticized both Neo-Confucianism and Buddhism by evoking the authority of classical Confucian ideas.

72. See Wing-tsit Chan, "The Philosophy of Humanity *(Jen)* in T'an Ssu-t'ung," *A Souce Book in Chinese Philosophy* (Princeton, 1973), p. 738.

73. Kuo Mo-jo, "Chung-kuo ku-tai-shih te fen-ch'i wen-t'i," in *Hung-ch'i tsa-chih*, 7 (1972), pp. 56–62. The article was reprinted in *K'ao-ku*, 5 (1972), pp. 2–4.

74. Yang Jung-kuo, *Fan-tung chieh-chi te "sheng-jen" K'ung Tzu* (Peking, 1973), pp. 26–65. It is interesting to note that 560,000 copies of the book were printed for the first edition.

75. Ibid., pp. 71–2.

76. Ibid., pp. 73–5.

77. For this see, *Chung-kuo li-tai fan-K'ung ho tsun-K'ung te tou-cheng* (Hong Kong, 1974), Ching-ch'ih, et al., ed., *Lun tsun-Ju fan-Fa* (Hong Kong, 1973), and Chao Chi-pin, *Kuan-yü K'ung Tzu chu Shao-cheng Mao wen-t'i* (Peking, 1973). It is not at all far-fetched to suggest that the list almost exhausts the "genuine" anti-Confucian heroes in Chinese history, even though the case of Wang An-shih is still ambiguous.

78. See Hung Shih-ti, *Ch'in Shih-huang* (Shanghai, 1973), pp. 55–72. It should be noted that since its first publication in May 1972, the book has been reprinted four times. And in total 1,350,000 copies have been printed.

79. See Sha-ming, *K'ung-chia-tien chi-ch'i yu-ling* (Peking, 1970), pp. 53–68.

80. See Wing-tsit Chan, *A Source Book in Chinese Philosophy*, pp. 84–94. Also, see Wm. T. de Bary, Wing-tsit Chan, and Burton Watson, comp., *Sources of Chinese Tradition*, 2 vols. (New York, 1960), 1:175–76.

81. *Analects*, 12:1.

82. See *P'i "k'o-chi fu-li" wen-chang hsüan-chi* (Hong Kong, 1974) and *Tsai p'i "k'o-chi fu-li"* (Hong Kong, 1974).

83. A very common idea in Neo-Confucian literature. It is closely associated with the Ch'eng-Chu school of Neo-Confucianism.

84. Originally entitled *Lun Kung-ch'an-tang-yuan te hsiu-yang* (On the Self-Cultivation of Communists), it is a short essay on the importance of self-cultivation in the Confucian tradition to the formation of a Communist personality. Mao is alleged to have characterized the book as absolutely unMarxian in character.

85. For an analytical discussion on this issue, see Donald J. Munro, *The Concept of Man in Early China* (Stanford, 1969), pp. 49–83. For a discussion of the contemporary implication of this issue, see Munro, "Man, State, and School," in "China's Developmental Experience," ed. Michel Oksenberg, *Proceedings of the Academy of Political Science*, 31 (March 1973), pp. 121–43.

86. For Mao's reference to the *Dream of the Red Chamber*, see *Statements*, pp. 444, 529, 556, and 567.

87. *Mencius*, 3A:4. See Wing-tsit Chan, *A Source Book of Chinese Philosophy*, pp. 69–70.

88. *Mencius*, 1B:7, 8 and 4B:32.

89. See *Lin Piao shih ti-ti tao-tao te K'ung lao-erh te hsin t'u* (Peking, 1974), pp. 86–89.

90. See *P'i-p'an An-tung-ni-ao-ni p'ai-she te fan-Hua ying-p'ien "Chung-kuo"* (Hong Kong, 1974). The anthology includes more than twenty angry denunciatory articles on Antonioni's approach and motivation.

91. See *Kuan-yü piao-t'i yin-yüeh, wu-piao-t'i yin-yüeh wen-t'i te t'ao-lun* (Hong Kong, 1974).

92. *Statements*, p. 671.

2

THE ROLE OF THE CHINESE LANGUAGE IN COUNTERFACTUAL/THEORETICAL THINKING AND EVALUATION

Alfred H. Bloom

The field of psychology has been undergoing radical changes in recent years that seem to bear important implications for understanding the sources of individual as well as culturewide value orientations. The long-accepted notion that man is a direct and exclusive product of his environment and its corollary that values are acquired directly and intact from external sources have been seriously challenged. The rise of Chomskyan grammar, experimental work in perception and memory, studies in linguistic, cognitive, and moral development appear to converge in suggesting that internal cognitive structures play a crucial role in mediating and organizing mental and behavioral interaction with the environment and, by extension, in shaping the form and content of values. From the perspective of this latter view, the study of value formation must be integrated with the study of cognitive development as a whole. Any factor that affects the way an individual cognitively structures his experience may act indirectly to impose constraints on, to influence the development of, and to guide change within the values he holds.

For example, any factor that influences an individual's general tolerance for cognitive ambiguity may translate in the value realm into an influence upon that individual's readiness to maintain situationally relative values as opposed to an absolute standard that is applicable across situations; any factor that influences an individual's facility for adopting distinct cognitive perspectives may translate into an influence on that individual's readiness to view political and social situations in multidimensional terms; any factor that influences an individual's propensity for logical argument may translate to influence the

The research reported in this chapter was supported in part by grants to the author from the National Endowment for the Humanities and from Swarthmore College.

importance that individual attaches to logical consistency in the construction and application of his own value system; any factor that influences an individual's level of moral development, if one accepts Lawrence Kohlberg's notion of a universal developmental sequence of stages of moral reasoning,[1] may translate to influence that individual's readiness to sense a personal obligation to reject unanalytic adherence to conventionally defined values in favor of constructing a value system of his own. Finally, any factor that influences an individual's capacity to work, cognitively speaking, in the abstract theoretical and hypothetical realms may translate to influence that individual's readiness to seek definitions for his values in abstract, theoretical terms, to seek support for those values in abstract, theoretical systems, and to alter his value commitments on the basis of abstract, theoretical argument.

Moreover, of the factors that are likely to influence the development of cognitive structures in one or more such ways, and thereby influence in turn the formation of value orientations, none seems both as accessible to study and, on the basis of psycholinguistic research, as potentially significant in its effects as the structure and content of the language spoken. Some would argue that cognitive representations of the world are in fact determined exclusively by the structure and content of language, which would imply that it is necessary only to analyze language to gain direct insight into the cognitive foundations of value orientations. Others react against attributing to language such a deterministic role and go so far as to assert and/or assume that the cognitive structures, through which the environment is represented and hence understood and interpreted, and the linguistic structures into which those representations are translated for the purpose of communicating them, are distinct aspects of competence, devoid of mutual influence. If this latter view is correct, linguistic analysis is not a channel through which one can venture into the cognitive and value worlds. But investigations into psycholinguistic development suggest a relationship of language to thought which, as one might intuitively expect, lies about midway between the extreme "language-as-determining" and "language-as-irrelevant" positions and which carries its own guarded implications for the analysis of the impact of language, by way of cognitive structure, on value orientations. An integration of this research views the ability to make sense of the empirical world as dependent on the prior development of cognitive miniplans or schemas.[2] Each schema provides a cognitive categorization of that world which makes it possible in turn to recognize, understand, and remember the individual phenomena experienced in terms of the categories to which they belong and to store information gained with respect to experienced instances in such a way that that information can readily be applied to future instances of the same category. During his first 18 months, a child proceeds to the construction of such schematic divisions of the world without the aid of language and hence free of its influence. For example, he will develop cognitive schemas for dividing the world into types of objects, such as furry things, moving things, and friendly things; types of actions such as crawling, rattle playing, and balloon tossing; and types of situations such as those in which someone gives something to someone else or those in which someone does something to an object.

Then around 18 months to two years, the capacity for symbolization will emerge and with it the capacity for associating linguistic labels with already constructed cognitive schemas. The child will begin to associate distinct nouns and verbs with his already constructed object and action schemas as communicative labels for the specific objects and actions that fall within their domains and to associate specific grammatical endings or word orders with his already constructed situational schemas as means for communicating whether he is talking about a situation in which both an agent and a beneficiary are involved or one in which only an agent and an object are involved. Once associated with underlying cognitive schemas, however, linguistic labels, both lexical and grammatical, will begin to act not only as devices for communicating about the instances to which they refer, but also as guides to a reorganization of his own cognitive mapping of the world. Observation of adult speech, as well as adult reactions to his own speech, will lead the child gradually to redefine the conceptual and referential boundaries of his verbal labels until they are in sufficient conformity with those of the adults of his culture to permit the child to mean and understand by his words the same categories of instances that adults do by theirs.[3] If the child has, for example, during the first years of life grouped together in his own nonlinguistic way all furry things, the arrival of the words "dog" and "squirrel" and "blanket" will lead him to reorganize his way of categorizing experience so that German shepherds, dachshunds, and Pekinese are all placed in one category, small, furry, acorn-eating animals in another, and flat, furry, inanimate objects in another. Categorization of experience independent of the influence of language will continue. Schemas will develop for recognizing unnamed faces, unnamed emotional states, and unnamed personality types, but at the same time linguistically guided categorizations will increase dramatically in both number and complexity.

While, however, acquisition and use of the words "dog," "squirrel," and "blanket" lead to a reorganization of nonlinguistic categorization of those objects, one is well aware in one sense, long before these labels are mastered, what dogs, squirrels, and blankets are and even with the cognitive reorganization induced by the labels, one's understanding of those objects, one's knowledge of their perceptual characteristics, habits, and so on, will most likely depend for a long time at least much more on first-hand experience with them than upon any linguistic information obtained about them. With respect to such schemas, in other words, language will intervene into thought processing only so far as to alter the boundaries between things that have already been experienced and have come to be understood in a nonlinguistic way.

Such seems not to be the case, however, when it comes to more abstract words such as "sister," "marriage," "bachelor," "theory," "abstraction," "epiphenomenon," and "counterfactual." It is hard to imagine understanding the notion "marriage" before the advent of the word "marriage" as a fundamental node of organization, since there is no perceptual feature or set of perceptual features that can act in that capacity—much less understanding what "theories," "epiphenomena," or "counterfactuals" are without having the labels as focuses of cognitive organization and at the same time in addition developing a whole web of supportive concepts like "explanation," "phenomenon," and "cause," under the guidance of and within the constraints imposed by their own respective verbal labels. Language seems on one level, to intervene to catalyze a cognitive reorganization of the the representation of the perceptual world, yet, on another, moving up the hierarchy of increasing abstraction, to begin to furnish the structures through which one thinks.[4] Confrontation with a new term in a new discipline, just as confrontation with a term in another language which does not translate exactly into one's own language or map directly into perceptually apprehensible instances, will act as a conceptual challenge to create a schema for understanding the parameters of the perspective on reality that that term provides. Language at this level, rather than acting as a deterministic straight jacket on cognition or a mere organizer of preexisting cognitions, becomes a creator, an inducer of new modes for organizing and hence for viewing experience.

The implication for this present pursuit is that when one considers where a given language might be expected to exert important influence on cognitive structure—an influence that is likely in turn to translate into the value sphere— there is reason to expect that such influence will be greatest in those areas of cognition where language provides rather than reorganizes cognitive structures, those areas of thought in which language has to compete least with the pull of perceptual experience.

Yet previous attempts to investigate the impact of language on cognition within a cross-cultural context have focused almost exclusively on the question of whether or not the existence within a speaker's lexicon of a name for a specific color will affect the speaker's ability to remember that color.[5] Such research has, in other words, focused on the potential effects of language in just those areas of cognition where the pull of perceptual experience, of nonlinguistically derived schemata, should be strongest and hence the effect of linguistically induced categorizations of experience least significant. Even within this area, however, where linguistic effects on cognition should be at a minimum, experimental results suggest that as one moves from colors like red and blue, which are perceptually distinct and salient because of the retina's physiological properties, to colors such as orange and brown, which do not represent physiologically imposed divisions of the color spectrum, language begins to play a more influential role in the cognitive process.[6] The existence or nonexistence within a speaker's lexicon of names for red or blue seems to have little effect on his/her ability to remember those colors.[7] By contrast, memory for orange and brown appears to be significantly facilitated by the existence of verbal labels in the speaker's lexicon for these nonphysiologically determined colors.[8]

Previous experimentation in this area has been limited not only by its emphasis on categorizations of the perceptual world; in focusing almost exclusively on the cognitive impact of specific lexical items rather than on the cognitive impact of more generalized (for example, syntactic) linguistic structures, it has in addition severely circumscribed the range of cognitive effects it could expect to uncover. As one moves up the ladder of increasing abstraction, it is highly likely that the existence of specific lexical items within a speaker's lexicon will have an effect on that speaker's cognitive organization of experience—an effect, moreover, that is likely to translate into the value realm as well. Consider how such words as "national honor," "national pride," "domino theory," "capitalist," "class struggle," and "Gang of Four" can act as elicitors of nodes of cognitive organization around which entire value clusters are built. However, the impact of the presence of such lexical items will in general confine itself to influencing the content of particular value orientations.

By contrast, the impact of more generalized linguistic structures is more likely to pervade overall development of cognitive structures and hence to influence in a much more wide-ranging and fundamental way value formation processes within an individual or even a society at large.

The specific project that forms the core of this study focuses on the lack in the Chinese language of one such generalized structure, common to English and other Indo-European languages, and on the possible impact of the lack of this structure on Chinese thinking and evaluation.

AN EMPIRICAL SEARCH FOR THE
CHINESE COUNTERFACTUAL/THEORETICAL

While working in Hong Kong a few years ago on the construction of a questionnaire designed to measure levels of abstraction in political thinking, the author repeatedly asked subjects questions of the form, "If the Hong Kong government were to pass a law requiring that all citizens make a weekly report of their activities to the police, how would you react?" and just as repeatedly received answers such as, "They won't" or "They didn't." Trying to press the subjects into a cognitive shift into the realm of the theoretically possible served only to make the subjects increasingly frustrated and as often as not led to such exclamations as, "We don't think/speak that way," "it's un-Chinese," "it's unnatural," "it's unaesthetic," "it's Western."[9] Two years later, the author was in Taiwan attempting through linguistic and experimental analysis to get a better idea of exactly what it is in this domain that the Chinese do not speak and/or do not think and, perhaps most importantly, of what kind of relationship might hold between the two.

In analyzing English grammatical structure, or that of other Indo-European languages, one quickly becomes aware that there is a distinct grammatical form to express what will be called here the "counterfactual/theoretical mood." It is the mood marked in English in the present by "were to + would," as in "If the kingdom of Swat were to conquer China, the world would be shocked," and in the past, by the past perfect + "would have," as in "If the kingdom of Swat had conquered China, the course of Asian history would have been somewhat different and the Pakistanis would never have been able to live it down." This counterfactual/theoretical mood calls for an examination of the might-have-been, the granting of temporary reality to a state of affairs one knows did not occur, in order to treat that state as a basis for examining the consequences one hypothesizes would have been engendered by it, had it in fact occurred.

In English, sentences employing the counterfactual/theoretical mood stand in contrast both to sentences one might term straightforwardly descriptive, such as "The Mongols conquered China, but did not succeed in conquering Japan," in which events that have or have not taken place are directly described; and in contrast as well to sentences one might term implicational, such as "If the Mongols invaded Swat, they conquered it," in which what has or has not happened is neither straightforwardly described nor is what has happened intentionally contradicted in order to examine the implications of the might-have-been, but rather an implicational relationship is stated, believed to hold between two events, regardless of whether or not either event has in fact occurred.

Such implicational sentences can be uttered with varying presuppositions as to how likely it is that the event described in their first clause or premise has or will in fact happen. One might presuppose that the Mongols invaded Swat and state in an almost rhetorical way, "If they invaded Swat they conquered it" as if one were about to add, "and that is all there is to it." Or one might have no notion of whether or not they in fact invaded Swat, as to the likelihood of the premise of the implication, and simply state "If they invaded, they conquered it." Or, a little more atypically, perhaps, one might think in fact that the Mongols never got that far south, but state with a disbelieving air for the purposes of at least getting the reasoning straight, "*If* they invaded it, they conquered it." But whatever the presupposition, the use of an implicational sentence as opposed to a counterfactual/theoretical one has the effect of signaling that one is intending the statement as a description of a relationship between events rather than as a summons to the listener to shift from the realm of empirical generalization to the realm of theoretical/hypothetical postulation and implication.

A grammatical analysis of Chinese, confirmed by intensive interviewing of both native unilingual speakers and English-Chinese bilinguals, yields a very different picture of that language's treatment of descriptive, implicational, and counterfactual sentences. The Chinese language expresses descriptive statements as English does, and in fact expresses implicational statements in more explicit terms than does everyday English speech. While English speakers use only context and/or intonation to indicate how likely they feel it is that the premise of an implicational statement has in fact taken place, the Chinese can make use of a much more precise linguistic device to signal that presupposition—namely, alternative forms of the word "if." For example, the use of the word "jiaru" for "if" in the sentence, "If the Mongols invaded Swat, they conquered it," will communicate the notion that the Mongols are unlikely to have invaded that kingdom and at the same time play its role in expressing the implicational relationship between invasion on the one hand and successful conquest on the other; while the use of the alternative form "ruquo" will, by contrast, not commit the speaker to any presupposition as to whether Swat was invaded. Moreover, in everyday English, one does not normally differentiate between "if-then" and "if-and-only if-then" interpretations of implicational sentences. When we utter the sentence "If China conquers Swat, it will acquire a new summer resort," whether this is the only means by which it could acquire such a resort (the if-and-only-if interpretation) or whether in fact there is a chance it might acquire one by some other means is left ambiguous. By contrast, Chinese, through the use of alternative forms of the word "then" (jiu versus cai), makes the distinction clear in normal grammatical speech. Yet despite Chinese grammatical precision in expressing both the degree of likelihood of the premise of implicational statements and the distinction between if-then and if-and-only-if-then interpretations of the relationship of the premise to its consequence there is no simple lexical, grammatical, or intonational means in Chinese to signal that a given statement is intentionally counterfactual, intended to be entertained and interpreted as an exercise in hypothetical theory construction. There is, in other words, no grammatical device for signaling directly what in English is called the counterfactual/ theoretical mood.

But certainly the fact that there is no such device does not necessarily imply that cognitively speaking speakers do not make that shift. Just because English does not have a distinct word for bank, meaning "financial institution," does not mean that that kind of bank is confused with the one that lines a river; and just because the expression "everyone loves his wife" is ambiguous between the "everyone loves John's wife" and the "everyone loves his own wife" interpretation does not mean that those interpretations are confused in thought. Is it then only that the linguistic apparatus for signaling the counterfactual/theoretical mood is missing in Chinese, or does the lack of that signaling device reflect and perhaps, in part at least, explain an important difference between the way English-speaking people and the Chinese categorize experiences, leaving aside of course the case of those Chinese who have experience in Western languages and thought?

There were many pointers to the more interesting thesis that the lack of a linguistic apparatus in Chinese for signaling the counterfactual/theoretical bears important cognitive implications. The suggestion of the idea had sprung in the first place from repeated evidence of reluctance among the Chinese to shift into the counterfactual/theoretical realm in response to questionnaire queries. When one points out the difference between the implicational and counterfactual/ theoretical to English speakers they grasp it immediately; yet the large majority of the Chinese unilingual speakers who were interviewed and worked with encountered difficulty in grasping the concept—a difficulty that often persisted over a substantial time period, despite repeated efforts at clarification. At a recent conference, while discussing these ideas, a Chinese professor who had been in the United States approximately three years suddenly interrupted the discussion to exclaim, "Wait a minute: what does 'would have' mean? It is the one aspect of English I haven't been able to grasp." A group of native Chinese, Chinese-English bilingual subjects who understood the English distinction between counterfactual/theoretical sentences and implicational sentences, were asked to attempt to construct pairs of Chinese sentences differing only in terms of that distinction. No subject could accomplish the task and each admitted, though at times reluctantly, that the notion "would have" is not only inexpressible directly in Chinese, but somehow foreign to the way Chinese think about implicational sentences. A content analysis of a leading Chinese newspaper in Taiwan over a period of three weeks led to the discovery of only one use of what one might call counterfactual/theoretical argument expressed by the circumlocution, "X is not the case, but if X then Y," and that turned out to be in a translation of a speech by Henry Kissinger. Mao tended likewise to use counterfactual/theoretical reason in this way, but he was heavily influenced by German and Russian writings; and it is interesting to note, moreover, that while Westerners find Mao's writings relatively easier to read than typical Chinese prose, for the Chinese it seems the opposite is very much the case.

There are some instances of the use of implicational sentences among Chinese, however, which at first glance at least appear to reflect counterfactual/theoretical reasoning and hence to lead to a questioning of the hypothesis that the counterfactual/theoretical mood is absent from Chinese thinking. For example, imagine a situation in which everyone has been waiting for John and as a result arrives late for a movie. Under such circumstances, one could say in Chinese, "If John came earlier we are able to arrive at the movie on time," meaning in English, "If John had come earlier we would have been able to arrive at the movie on time." The language does not signal the counterfactual/theoretical, and yet it seems as if a counterfactual/theoretical thought is being expressed. Yet, paradoxically, the ability to work with counterfactual thoughts does not generalize from such reality-oriented situations to newspaper speculating or theoretical questions about the Hong Kong government.

To suggest a resolution to this apparent paradox it may be useful to take a look at what it might mean, in terms of the model of language and thought discussed earlier in this chapter, to say that the counterfactual/theoretical mood plays a role in the cognitive life of the normal unilingual speaker of English that it does not play in the cognitive life of the normal unilingual speaker of Chinese. One might imagine that persistent exposure to and use of such forms as, "If X had happened, Y would have happened," would tend to catalyze the development with the English speaker's mind, by contrast to the Chinese speaker, of a schema that integrates the notion of an implication linking two events with the additional notion that neither of these events constitutes a factual occurrence— a schema, in other words, that permits instantaneous comprehension of the fact that a given statement is intended as describing a relationship in the realm of the might-have-been rather than in the realm of actual fact. Before developing such a counterfactual/theoretical schema one might be able to use and understand counterfactual implications in specific contexts (for example, the use of sentences like, "If Daddy were here we could go to the movies," when it is obvious that Daddy isn't here), just as it is possible to understand the notion of an adult, male, who is not married before one has developed the notion "bachelor." But development of a schema for the counterfactual/theoretical mode, just as development of a schema for "bachelor," affords one a higher cognitive perspective on what one was able to pull together only by dint of some cognitive effort at an earlier stage. Unequipped, mentally speaking, with a counterfactual/theoretical schema, one can understand counterfactual sentences only by holding both implication and context in mind and on the basis of those two pieces of information inferring that the sentence is intended to describe a nonfactual state of affairs. Once mastery of such a schema is developed, however, the "were" or "would have" can be immediately understood as signals of a theoretical mode of speech and thought, that any sentence marked by them is to be classified as one that talks of the might-have-been. Just as mastery of the schema for "bachelor" will eliminate the effort of thinking about bachelors in the three simultaneous dimensions of maleness, adulthood, and unmarriedness, mastery of the counterfactual/theoretical schema will eliminate the effort, in thinking about a counterfactual/theoretical sentence, of having to first resolve the tension between a statement about two events and a context that precludes its being about actual facts. Just as "bachelor" will take its place as a node of cognitive organization in one's memories, to which information that is not true of its composing parts taken separately can be attached, so counterfactual/theoretical will become one of the structures through which one views, interprets and gathers further information about one's experiences. Just as "bachelor" will act as a node of mental organization to which one can direct attention in thinking about and solving problems relating to individuals who fall within that category, so will the counterfactual/theoretical serve as a node of mental organization to which one can direct attention in thinking about and solving problems relating to counterfactual/theoretical sentences.

Use or understanding of situationally tied counterfactual reasoning cannot then be taken as evidence of the development of a counterfactual/theoretical schema, but the ability to stand back from a sentence and judge it as counterfactual/theoretical as distinct from implicational, the ability to venture forth outside of a situational context in a purely counterfactual/theoretical vein, and the ability to hold the theoreticality of some statement in mind in the pursuit of a more complex logical task are likely to require the higher level of abstraction that the schema provides and hence to count as evidence that a counterfactual/theoretical schema has developed in the subject's mental world.

According to this interpretation, then, the difficulty the Chinese encountered in grasping the distinction between the implicational and the counterfactual/theoretical, as well as their reluctance to venture forth, cognitively speaking, out of the constraints of a given situation into the hypothetical realm supports the central hypothesis that the lack of a counterfactual/theoretical marker in Chinese grammar does bear important cognitive consequences. To put this hypothesis to a more stringent test, however, stories were prepared of the form, "X was not the case, but if X had been the case, then Y would have been the case, Z would have been the case, and W would have been the case."*

Following each story, subjects were asked whether on the basis of the story as read they perceived W, the final consequent of the string of implications presented, as intended to indicate something that had or had not happened. Chinese versions of the stories (written in the form, "X is not true"; if X then Y, then Z, then W—the only way to convey the meaning intended in Chinese) were presented to a group of hotel workers in Taiwan, as well as to a group of students at Taiwan National University, the college of highest prestige in Taiwan. English versions were presented as a control to a group of students at Swarthmore College in the United States. It was hypothesized that if the Chinese do not have a cognitive schema available for coding and interpreting the counterfactual/theoretical mood, they would have no point of orientation to which to direct their attention in processing stories, and although possibly able to figure out that one or perhaps two of the implications were intended as counterfactual/theoreticals, would have increasing difficulty as they moved through the story and encountered more and more of the same. By contrast, equipped with counterfactual/theoretical schemas, the Western subjects, upon seeing the words "would have," would know immediately to shift into the counterfactual/theoretical mode of processing and understand without effort and in fact in almost a self-evident manner that all the implications including of course the last must be intended as counterfactual/theoreticals. The experimental question, in other words, is whether or not the Chinese will impose a counterfactual/theoretical way of thinking upon the stories, even though the linguistic device necessary to signal that mode of thinking is absent—whether or not counterfactual/theoretical thinking constitutes a salient aspect of the way the Chinese subjects categorize and work with experience. The results are rather dramatic. At Swarthmore, 25 out of the 28 or 89 percent of the students tested consistently responded that the events referred to in the last statements of the stories were false—that is, interpreted the counterfactual/theoretical as intended; and the remaining three students gave only one inconsistent response each, which on the basis of later interviewing turned out to be attributable to ambiguity with regard to the "if" versus "if-and-only-if" distinction rather than to ambiguity with regard to the

---

*Sample story: In ancient times there was a Greek philosopher named Decos who could not speak Chinese. If he had been able to speak Chinese he would have been influenced by Chinese culture, because at that time China and Greece maintained a commercial relationship. He would have isolated the best points of Greek and Chinese logic and integrated them into a new advanced form of logic which would have constituted an important contribution to the development of both Greek and Chinese philosophy.

counterfactual/theoretical distinction. By contrast, among the 54 Chinese students tested, all of whom had had some exposure to English, only 37 or 69 percent made consistently correct responses; and among the working-class subjects, who had had little exposure to English, the number of consistent responders dropped to 6 out of 36 or 17 percent. Degree of training in English was positively and significantly correlated with ability to grasp and work successfully with the counterfactual, as measured by the task. For the working-class subjects, the relationship was significant at the .01 level; for the students, at .05. It was in fact the case that many of the subjects who responded correctly wrote the words "would have" in English in the margins of the stories they were reading as if they needed some linguistic point of orientation in order to maintain a conscious involvement in the counterfactual/theoretical mood. Moreover, later interviewing of the subjects who responded incorrectly indicated that for the most part, as they proceeded from the first negated premise through the various subsequent implicational statements, they lost track of the fact that the original premise was in fact untrue (that is, counterfactual) and failed to focus on any relationship it might bear to interpreting the later implicational statements. As a result, the subsequent implications, including of course the last, were viewed as separate entities to be interpreted on their own terms. In this light, without any grammatical marking like "would have" to guide them, some subjects assumed the statements to be ones of fact, others descriptions of generalized relations between events. Failure, in other words, to use the original negated premise as a key to shifting into the counterfactual/theoretical mood had led to a misinterpretation of the story and lent support to the suspicion that not only are the words "would have" absent for the Chinese subjects, but likewise the disposition to impose the kind of reasoning they represent.

It is interesting to note, in addition, that if one looks up the word "theoretical" in an English-Chinese dictionary and then looks at the meaning of the translation equivalents given within a standard Chinese dictionary, one finds that the word theoretical is taken to mean "from the perspective of a particular theory," rather than to mean, as the term is usually used and as it is presently used, a way of rejecting in thought and speech the description of actual events in favor of postulating a set of premises about how things might be or might have been, and reasoning and drawing implications within the constraints imposed by those premises. It is understandable that the counterfactual/theoretical schema developed under the guidance of the grammatical labels "were" and "would have" would come, in time, to be labeled by a descriptive term such as "theoretical" or "hypothetical," and it stands to reason that if such a schema does not play a role in Chinese cognitive life, it does not give rise to equivalent descriptive entries in the Chinese lexicon.

REALITY-CENTERED VERSUS THEORETICAL VALUES

There is then a hypothesis, supported in part at least by some suggestive observation and experimentation, concerning the way in which the general grammatical structures of two distinct languages may intervene into the thought worlds of their native speakers to guide the development of distinct cognitive frameworks of rather significant dimensions. It is a hypothesis, moreover, about a linguistic effect on thought which is likely to translate into an important influence upon the value realm as well. It is interesting to indulge in such questions as how one would act or should have acted if, how one would act or should act if, and on the basis of those indulgences extend, as it were, one's experience to form a broader basis for constructing, differentiating, and refining a set of principles according to which one will act and evaluate. But it is a basis which, at the same time one ventures forth into the theoretical, becomes more and more detached, alienated from the constraints of the actual situations one has encountered. It is a mode of reasoning to which one could respond as Xun Zi did in commenting on a theoretical discussion of hardness and whiteness as opposed to hard and white. "There is no reason why problems of hardness and whiteness should not be investigated, but the superior man does not discuss them. He stops at the limit of profitable discourse."[10] But it is likewise a mode of reasoning that Piaget sees as necessary to the development of scientific hypothesizing, scientific theory construction, and controlled scientific experimentation,[11] and a mode of reasoning that may stand as a necessary prerequisite to the development of a facility for building and critically questioning abstract theoretical systems, whether in the scientific or philosophical or moral realm—a mode of reasoning that may stand as a necessary prerequisite to the development of a faculty for departing from the use of traditional prescriptions and models as guides to moral behavior and evaluation, in favor of the construction of abstract theoretical principles that can be applied to novel situations as they are encountered. As Marxian counterfactual/theoretical thought and language, scientific counterfactual/theoretical thought and language, and Western everyday counterfactual/ theoretical thought and language persist in exerting their influence on the Chinese world, there may be observed a process of value change in China leading for better or worse toward the theoretical system approach so characteristic of the West. Many students of comparative Western and Chinese cultures have dealt with the perceived contrast between the reality-centered values of China and the theoretical abstract values of the West.[12] F. S. Northrop in his *Meeting of East and West* contrasts, for example, the Orient's propensity for analyzing things with respect to their aesthetic component with the Occident's propensity for analyzing things with respect to their theoretic component.[13] But what he and others have not said is that the sustaining vector of this difference may lie not only in general culture tendencies, but in the language and its effects on individual psychology, and that hence any narrowing of that difference may be reflected in and, in fact, at least in part induced by concomitant changes in the structure and use of the Chinese language.

NOTES

1. Lawrence Kohlberg, "Stage and Sequence: The Cognitive-Developmental Approach to Socialization" in *Handbook of Socialization Theory and Research*, ed. David A. Goslin (Chicago: Rand McNally, 1969), pp. 347–480.

2. Jean Piaget, *Psychology of Intelligence* (Totowa, N.J.: Littlefield, Adams, 1966).

3. Herbert H. Clark and Eve V. Clark, *Psychology and Language* (New York: Harcourt Brace Jovanovich, 1977), pp. 485–514.

4. See Lev Semenovich Vygotsky, *Thought and Language* (Cambridge, Mass.: MIT Press, 1962); and Marion Blank, "Mastering the Intangible Through Language," in *Developmental Psycholinguistics and Communication Disorders*, ed. Doris Aaronson and Robert W. Rieber (*Annals of the New York Academy of Sciences*, Vol. 263), pp. 59–69.

5. See Roger Brown and Eric Lenneberg, "A Study of Language and Cognition," *Journal of Abnormal and Social Psychology* 49, no. 3 (1954): 454–62; Delee Lantz and Volney Stefflre, "Language and Cognition Revisited," *Journal of Abnormal and Social Psychology* 69, no. 5 (1964): 472–81.

6. See Eleanor Rosch, "On the Internal Structure of Perceptual and Semantic Categories," in *Cognitive Development and the Acquisition of Language*, ed. Timothy Moore (New York: Academic Press, 1973), pp. 111–14; Eric Lenneberg and J. M. Roberts, "The Denotata of Color Terms," paper read at Linguistic Society of America, Bloomington, Indiana, August 1953, cited in Brown and Lenneberg, "Study of Language"; Volney Stefflre, Victor Vales, and Linda Morley, "Language and Cognition in Yucatan: A Cross-Cultural Replication," *Journal of Personality and Social Psychology* 4, no. 1 (1966): 112–15.

7. Rosch, "Internal Structure."

8. Lenneberg and Roberts, "Denotata of Color Terms"; Stefflre, Vales, and Morley, "Language and Cognition in Yucatan."

9. Alfred H. Bloom, "Two Dimensions of Moral Reasoning: Social Principledness and Social Humanism in Cross-Cultural Perspective," *Journal of Social Psychology* 101 (1977): 29–44.

10. Xun Zi, Ch. 2, p. 49, as cited in Joseph Needham, *Science and Civilization in China*, vol. 2 (Cambridge: Cambridge University Press, 1956), p. 202.

11. Barbel Inhelder and Jean Piaget, *The Growth of Logical Thinking from Childhood to Adolescence* (New York: Basic Books, 1958).

12. See André Malraux, *The Temptation of the West* (New York: Vintage Books, 1961); F. S. C. Northrop, *The Meeting of East and West* (New York: Collier Books, 1966). See Joseph Needham, *Science and Civilization in China* (Cambridge: Cambridge University Press, 1956), vol. 2, Chs. 13 and 14 for discussion of the lack of development of a theoretical orientation to science in early China; Ch. 15, especially pages 473–75, for a discussion of the surprisingly minor impact of Buddhist theoretical systems on the development of Chinese thought; Ch. 18, especially pages 524–25, for a discussion of the lack of development of a theoretical approach to law in China; and vol. 3 (1959), Ch. 19, especially pages 91, 152–68, for a discussion of the lack of development of a theoretical geometry and of a theoretical, as opposed to an applied, approach to mathematics in general.

13. Northrop, *Meeting of East and West*, pp. 291–374.

3

INDIVIDUAL VALUES AND ATTITUDES IN CHINESE SOCIETY: AN ETHNOMETHODOLOGICAL APPROACH

Sidney L. Greenblatt

THEORETICAL PROLOGUE

The student of Chinese society, seeking guidance from the social science literature on the subject of value and attitudinal change, opens what appears to be a Pandora's Box. The literature serves up a bewildering array of definitions of what values are and how erstwhile scientific observers are to identify them. Donald Campbell, for example, lists 76 equivalents in current use.[1] In some of these definitions, values and attitudes are seen as basic human needs and drives; in others, they are seen as "dispositions," "orientations," or "propensities" anchored in needs and drives but at some distance from them. In still others, they are seen as measurable activities rather than propensities.[2]

In short, definitions of values and attitudes range all the way across the behavioral spectrum from needs and drives to activity. To make matters worse, values and attitudes are not themselves distinguished in much of the literature. Nor is it very clear how the two are related to such other concepts as "beliefs," "motives," "interests," or to use Herbert Blumer's list, "impulses, drives, appetites, antipathies, feelings, sentiments, habits, ideas, opinions, judgments, and decisions."[3]

Even those sympathetic to the effort to give meaning and operational significance to the study of values and attitudes are appalled by the state of confusion that attends the field. As Milton Rokeach puts it,

> despite the central position of attitudes in social psychology and personality, the concept has been plagued with ambiguity. As the student pores over and ponders the many definitions of attitude in the literature, he finds it difficult to grasp precisely how they are conceptually similar or different from one another. Even more important, it is difficult to assess what differences these variations in conceptual definitions make.[4]

The literature on attitude and value change raises similar problems. An enormous amount of scholarly effort has been expended to produce volumes of research findings that signify very little, since it is not changing attitudes or values themselves but opinions about them (that is, expressed attitudes) that are, in fact, the objects measured. The failure to come to grips with a theory of attitude and value change looms large in the production of such measurements.

Rokeach has done a good deal to clarify the conceptual issues surrounding the study of attitudes and values as well as to put the empirical study of value and attitude change on firmer foundations. Careful conceptual distinctions are drawn among "beliefs," "belief systems," "ideologies," "values," "value systems," "faith," "sentiments," and "attitudes." An attitude, for example, is defined as

> a relatively enduring organization of interrelated beliefs that describe, evaluate, and advocate action with respect to an object or situation, with each belief having cognitive, affective and behavioral components. Each of these beliefs is a predisposition that, when suitably activated, results in some preferential response toward the attitude object or situation or toward others who take a position with respect to the attitude object or situation, or toward the maintenance or preservation of the attitude itself. Since an attitude object must always be encountered within some situation about which we must also have an attitude, a minimum condition for social behavior is the activation of at least two interacting attitudes, one concerning the attitude object and the other concerning the situation.[5]

A value, by contrast is

> a type of belief, centrally located within one's total belief system about how one ought or ought not to behave, or about some end-state of existence worth or not worth attaining. Values are thus abstract ideals, positive or negative, not tied to any specific attitude object or situation, representing a person's belief about ideal modes of conduct and ideal terminal goals. . . .[6]

Ideal modes of conduct, "personally and socially preferable in all situations with respect to all objects" are described as instrumental values. Ideal goals, end-states of existence that are personally and socially worth achieving, are described as terminal values.[7] Rokeach argues that both instrumental and terminal values form two separate though interrelated systems, rank-ordered in terms of importance to the individual. Systems of values are, in turn, linked cognitively and functionally to attitudes toward specific objects and situations. Although values are defined as beliefs that transcend specific objects and situations, situational factors do affect value choices and behavior because of the linkage between values and attitudes. In other words, people may behave in ways that are not congruent with their values because of attitudes they hold toward themselves and others and because of the situational constraints with which they are faced.[8] It is proper, then, to speak of an individual having a "value-attitude system," a complex organization of motive forces, subject to situational constraint, that propels an individual toward action.

Were all the theoretically possible permutations among attitudes, values, and situational norms operative in actuality, research into value-attitude systems and the changes they undergo would be virtually impossible. Rokeach holds, however, that the organization of value systems, the social structure, and the individual proclivity toward consistency and the reduction of dissonance combine to shape value-attitude systems and to reduce the number of actual variations.[9]

The organization of value systems reduces the range of possibilities, Rokeach posits, because "an adult possesses thousands, perhaps tens of thousands of attitudes toward specific objects and situations but only several dozens of instrumental values and perhaps only a few handfuls of terminal values."[10] Culture and social structure operate through socialization processes and structural constraints on opportunity to reduce the number of possibilities. Finally, the predilection of individuals to maintain cognitive consistency and to reduce dissonance, especially in those choice situations where self-esteem is likely to be involved, functions also to reduce the number of possibilities.

Since the ability to research value change rests on these considerations about the structure of values, culture, social structure, and personality, it is important to raise a number of questions about them. First, just how limited is the number of instrumental and terminal values? It seems reasonable to propose that any answer to that question must depend on an appreciation of the dynamics of culture. It also seems reasonable to propose that both instrumental values and terminal values are elastic categories of belief. To the extent that a society's members subscribe to a single, coherent cultural system, one would expect a limited number of instrumental and terminal values. To the extent that a society's members subscribe to multiple cultures or syncretistic traditions or are subject to cultural diffusion or transition, one would expect expansion in the number of values and consequent complication of value-attitude systems. Several dozens of instrumental values and a handful of terminal values might well expand to several hundreds of instrumental values and several dozens of terminal values.

Second, how much of the variation in patterns of behavior is explained by the predisposing and controlling features of culture and social structure and how much by the more amorphous processes of social interaction and personality? In Rokeach's terms, attitudes are defined as predispositions to action; values as imperatives to action. That view is open to criticism, and Herbert Blumer's critique is particularly pertinent:

> The human act is not a release of an already organized tendency; it is
> a construction built up by the actor. Instead of a direct translation

the tendency into the act there is an intervening process which is responsible for the form and direction taken by the developing act. . . . this intervening process is constituted by a flow of self-interaction in which the individual indicates various things and objects to himself, defines them, judges them, selects from among them, pieces together his selections, and thereby organizes himself to act. It would be a grievous error to assume that this intervening process through which the human actor constructs his act is nothing but a tendency working itself out. Quite the contrary, this intervening process works back on the tendency, sometimes guiding it, sometimes shaping it, sometimes transforming it, sometimes blocking it, and sometimes ruthlessly eliminating it.

In a new and different situation a person has the need of carving out a new line of activity. He has to size up the situation, get cues, judge this or that, and piece together some line of activity that will enable him to fit the situation as he sees it. The situation will pose new demands and present new possibilities. By definition, these demands are not incorporated in the tendency which antedates them and which has been built up without regard to them. To presume under such conditions that a knowledge of the antecedent tendency will forecast the act that is to be built up in the new situation is presumptuous indeed.[11]

It is not that Blumer's position is irreconcilable with that of Rokeach. Rather, Blumer emphasizes individual freedom of action; Rokeach stresses structural determination.

Third, what are the situational factors that affect the drive toward cognitive consistency and reduction of dissonance? As Rokeach notes, the drive for cognitive consistency depends on the salience of particular values to the individual who is confronted with a choice between competing values. Situational factors may, however, intervene to determine salience, as the Milgram experiments on authority demonstrate.[12]

These questions, while important in any research setting, are particularly vexing when research on value change is applied to Chinese society. Direct tests of Rokeach's lists of instrumental and terminal values may be informative, but they impose a set of value relevancies on Chinese subjects that ignore China's own rich and diverse cultural legacy. Derivations from that legacy raise other problems. Researchers are faced with a choice between classical Confucianism and Neo-Confucian values, values drawn from heterodox Buddhist, Taoist, and popular traditions, imported and adopted Western values, modern socialist, capitalist, and Maoist adaptations, and the various syncretic permutations of these systems that may coexist in Chinese society, its subgroups, and even in individuals. It is not all that clear, in the Chinese case at least, that the number of instrumental and terminal values is limited to several dozen of the former and a handful of the latter.

The knowledge of how culture and social structure interact to shape values in Chinese society leads to further questions. Numerous authors have observed how authoritarian organizational practices, a collectivist orientation in socialization processes, and the absence of Western-style individualism, in both traditional and contemporary China, operate to produce a high degree of outward conformity in Chinese behavior. But reference to these features of Chinese society tells more about public expression in Chinese society than about private values. Too little is known about how Chinese people negotiate their way through the labyrinth of social rules and expectations—the microsociology of interaction in Chinese society—to evaluate the relative weight to be accorded structural determinants of behavior as opposed to social construction and social negotiation. It seems that it is safe to say only that the line drawn between the public and the private, the prescribed and the negotiable features of society, freedom and determinism, is drawn differently in Chinese society than in the West.

As for cognitive consistency and the reduction of dissonance, observers of Chinese behavior have taken note of the fact that syncretistic belief systems are accompanied by syncretistic practices. It is not uncommon for members of Chinese families in Taiwan and Hong Kong to hold different religious affiliations, Western and non-Western, or for a single individual to pass through several such affiliations without manifesting signs of conflict and dissonance that are typically associated with such behavior. Nor is it uncommon, in these same settings, for individuals and families to frequent Western-trained medical doctors, mediums, and fortune tellers for treatment of an illness without evincing signs of dissonance. One might, of course, argue that none of these behaviors implicates values that are salient to self-esteem or that all of these behaviors are rooted in an underlying and consistent commitment to Confucianism. It is, however, equally plausible, given the current grasp of Chinese behavior, that self-esteem in Chinese society and culture does not depend on cognitive consistency.

Because considerations of culture, social structure, and personality are so crucial to an understanding of value change in Chinese society, this study resists the temptation to test Rokeachean lists of instrumental and terminal values. Rather, it seeks to raise two prior questions. How do Chinese, within a given situational setting, impute the hidden dimension of human behavior to one another? What implications does the process of imputation have for an understanding of value change? Since these questions ask not what the values are that Chinese hold, but what methods Chinese people use to construct the sense that there is, indeed, a hidden dimension of human behavior, the approach is labelled ethnomethodological.[13]

The term "hidden dimension" forms a broad conceptual category that includes the many commonsense pre-social science labels ordinary people use to describe the motive forces that underlie overt acts. In various cultures and societies those labels may include "beliefs," "ideas," "thought," "motives," "springs-to-action,"* and so forth.[14] The terms "value" (*jiazhi*) and "attitude" (*taidu*) are available from the Chinese lexicon to characterize evaluative and cognitive dimensions of overt behavior, but the more appropriate term is "motive" (*dongji*), for it refers to the covert sources of overt behavior. One is interested, therefore, in the processes by which Chinese impute motives to one another and in the implications of that process for an understanding of Western social scientific concepts of "attitude-value systems" and "value change." While the terms "motive" (*dongji*) and "value and attitude" have different referents (differences in culture make it impossible to establish precise conceptual equivalents), they deal with the same range of behavioral problems.

The report that follows this introduction begins by describing the research setting, in this case fortune telling in Hong Kong, and the methods employed. It then goes on to examine three issues raised in the introduction: culture and Chinese values in the attribution of motives; social structure and social construction in the attribution of motives, and situational aspects of cognitive consistency and dissonance. The report concludes with a section entitled: Implications of Motive Attribution for an Understanding of Value Change.

FORTUNE TELLING IN HONG KONG AS A RESEARCH SETTING

The author's first visit to a Chinese fortune teller (to any fortune teller, for that matter) occurred some twelve years ago on an earlier research stint in Hong Kong. It left an enduring impression. Along with other experiences derived from intensive interviews with refugees from the People's Republic of China, the visit contributed to a hunch that Chinese methods for assigning personal and social identities, attributing motives, and typifying social roles and situations were culturally distinct from those methods commonly attributed to Westerners. At the time, both the impression and the hunch were filed away for lack of either a theoretical or methodological framework for testing the hunch or elaborating the impression. Several years were spent building a theoretical and methodological base. Then, a sabbatical leave in the spring of 1977 provided an occasion for revisiting Hong Kong. In the course of four months, between April and August 1977, a combined program of documentary study and participant observation focused on fortune telling was undertaken.

The documentary phase of the program involved the collection and analysis of both classical and contemporary, and scholarly and popular works on Chinese fortune telling, as well as handbooks, almanacs, charts, and other technical paraphernalia used in the practice of fortune telling. Analysis of these

---

*"Springs-to-action" (*ji*) or "promptings to act" describe how action is immanent in the mind's operations.

materials focused essentially on four items: the various traditions represented in the textual material, the contrast between classical and modern texts, the central values contained in the textual materials, and the logic-in-use—that is, the logic that permits a user of the textual materials to construct practical answers to the practical problems a client brings to the fortune teller.

The participant-observer phase of the program involved participation in and observation of transactions between professional fortune tellers and their clients. Of the thirteen readings obtained, four were readings with the author as client, three involved the author's five-year-old son as client, two were readings with entire families as clients, and the remainder were readings with individual friends and relatives as clients. Introductions to the fortune tellers were provided exclusively by friends and relatives with one proviso: that any fortune teller introduced be able to carry out the reading in the Mandarin dialect, the only dialect over which the author has some command.

Each reading took from one to three hours depending on the number of clients involved, the type of reading requested, and the fees charged for a reading. The fees, paid by relatives and friends when they served as clients, ranged from HK $80 (approximately U.S. $16) at the public fortune-teller stalls at Wongtaisin Temple in Kowloon, to HK $100 (approximately U.S. $20) charged by fortune tellers operating out of their private apartments on the island of Hong Kong.

All the readings were tape-recorded, and each tape was analyzed for evidence of the services professional fortune tellers performed for their clients and for indicators of the process by which a reading developed to completion. Readings thus obtained were then compared to the models derived from textual materials in order to assess the importance of face-to-face transactions in the construction of a client's biography.

In a few individual cases and in one instance involving a family there were opportunities to observe reactions to the readings for some time after they were performed. Impressions derived from these observations provide the bases for an interpretation of cognitive consistency and dissonance.

As a Chinese-speaking foreigner in a Chinese field setting, there were features of intercultural interaction that both facilitated and impeded participant observation. Time and financial limitations also forced choices concerning the type of situation in which there could be participation or observation. It is worth taking a moment to describe these conditions and their impact upon the participant-observer role.

First, in theory at least, professional Chinese fortune tellers are practitioners of the "five arts" (*wushu*):

1. Chinese astrology (*suanming or suangua*)—calculations of a client's past, present, and future—based principally upon the eight characters of one's birth (*bazi*), the symbolic relationships between the *bazi* and the five elements (*wuxing*) of earth, fire, wood, water, and metal, as well as the hexagrams of the

Yi Zhing (*Book of Changes*) and frequently astrological calculations based on named and unnamed stars.

2. Palmistry (*kanshou*)—based on "readings" of the markings on and topographical features of the hands.

3. Physiognomy (*kanxiang*)—based principally on "readings" of the markings on and topographical features of the face.

4. The medical arts (*yixue*)—acupuncture, moxibustion, and pharmacology—based on medical "readings" taken from physiognomic, palm, and astrological indicators or from the feeling of the bones (*mougutou*).

5. The therapeutic arts (*shanxue*)—including the martial arts (*wuxue*), nutritional therapies, meditation, and self-cultivation techniques, and geomancy (*fengshui*).

Only a few of the fortune tellers observed advertised an ability to practice all five arts; most focused on the first three. But, since each art can be practiced at varying levels (that is, with more or less elaborateness) and since the first three are the bases for the last two, the greater the depth and breadth of the arts a client calls for, the higher the price. While Chinese clients were expected to haggle, a foreigner was expected to pay the full rate unless a Chinese client friend haggled over the price on his or her behalf. The author's own limited budget forced some hard choices between depth, breadth, and the number of readings. He settled for thirteen less elaborate readings of the first three arts to assure incorporation of the most frequent types of readings, and modified the impact of the cost, as was noted earlier, by having several interested friends and relatives take him along as an observer for in-depth readings of their fortunes at their expense.

Second, while most readings take place on the spot (only one fortune teller calculated the *bazi* in advance of a face-to-face encounter), fortune teller-client transactions were often complicated by the involvement of third parties, and third party involvement had an impact on the participant-observer role the author had assumed. This complication requires an extended explanation.

Fortune tellers, who operate out of street-side booths, practice their art in settings that are open to all potential clients. The booths at Wongtaisin in Kowloon, for example, are enclosed within a lengthy wood-frame and tin-roofed structure that resembles a long Quonset hut. A stone aisle separates adjoining three-sided booths arranged on either side of the structure's inside walls. Multiple stone stairways, entering the structure from a road alongside that leads to a neighboring Buddhist temple, permit potential clients to survey the services within or to wait their turn if all chairs are currently occupied. This device also serves to separate potential clients from uninterested passers-by en route to or from the temple. Each booth has a desk or table and several chairs. The tables sit on a platform elevated slightly above the level of the aisle and set at a 90-degree angle to the aisle so that one end of the table abuts it. On one side of the table is a single chair for the fortune teller; two or three chairs occupy the space on the other side of the table facing the fortune teller for the clients' use. Other chairs are arranged in semicircular fashion in the aisle at the end of the table for clients who are awaiting their turn or for the extra members of a family group or peer group of clients.

The structure of the setting assures that any remark made by the fortune teller or client will be within audible range of the client "audience," but out of range for passers-by. It is quite common for a fortune teller to address some observations (usually moral maxims or general remarks) to his client audience. Intimate remarks are addressed to the client face-on, and though they are made in a lower tone of voice, they are audible to the client "audience," but typically subject to "civil inattention" unless the client audience consists of kin or close friends.[15] Civil inattention is not accorded by strangers when the client happens to be a Chinese-speaking foreigner. In this case the audience is wide-eyed and all ears and will interrupt to offer comments or await commentary from the fortune teller.

There were several strategies for dealing with the client-audience problem. One was to engage the fortune teller in direct eyeball-to-eyeball contact to minimize the impact of the audience. Another strategy was to use the author's five-year-old son as a client. Though he is part Chinese and speaks some Mandarin, he did not have sufficient command of the language to understand client-audience remarks and, hence, was not bothered by audience participation. This strategy also afforded a special advantage. Because the boy was unable to manage a systematic presentation of himself in Chinese, fortune tellers would develop only the bare bones of the model of his character and turn to me for additional cues. The models they developed were useful as training devices, and by manipulating the cues offered on the boy's behalf, the author could get a sense of the difference between the results produced by a simplified model of a reading and the outcome of a negotiated face-to-face transaction.

After several trials, however, the author began to search for other less public settings, and turned to more expensive fortune tellers who operated out of their own private apartments. To minimize his own presence as much as possible, he enlisted the aid of friends and relatives who presented themselves as clients and him as an interested observer. The problem of audience effect was not, even in this setting, altogether under control.

Clients of fortune tellers in Hong Kong are often families or groups of friends rather than individuals, and a fortune teller may come to serve a family in the same capacity as a family doctor. Family members who are not themselves the subjects of a particular reading may participate actively in the transaction by offering up or rejecting cues given by either the fortune teller or the client. Unlike the strangers awaiting their turn at Wongtaisin, family members do not accord "civil inattention" to matters of an intimate nature when it is a kinsman whose fortune is being read, and discussion of such matters may continue well beyond the transaction itself. The author was not an exception to that rule, when relatives were present. It was difficult, under such circumstances, to play the role of silent observer. On the other hand, it afforded access to family discussions that took place after the transaction with a fortune teller. In addition, the author's relatives are northerners or Mandarin-speaking Fukienese, and when they had difficulty grasping the Shanghai accents of a fortune teller (11 of the 13 fortune tellers were Shanghai men), knowing at the same time of the author's traffic in the lore of fortune telling, they would often turn to him for an explanation or translation of the fortune tellers' remarks. That too made it impossible to play the role of silent observer. Furthermore, once the fortune tellers discovered that the author spoke Mandarin and was familiar with fortune-telling practices, they would often stop to detail an item for his benefit. While that was occasionally an advantage, it interrupted the natural course of a reading and shifted attention away from the client at hand.

A third problem area concerns the character of fortune teller and client "talk." Except for a brief period of silence when fortune tellers are engaged in the calculation of the *bazi* (side-engagements of family and friends with occasional responses to fortune tellers' questions mark this interlude), transactions between fortune tellers and their clients consist of an enormous volume of talk carried on at great speed. To make matters more difficult, a good deal of fortune-teller talk contains literary, poetic, and historical allusions. Taking field notes on the spot is difficult if not impossible; if one is a client attending to the fortune teller's reading of his case, it is impossible. Reliance on memory to reconstruct talk is out of the question, given the speed at which it takes place, its volume, and its literary, poetic, and historical content. Hence all readings were tape-recorded, for this was the only sure-fire means of obtaining an accurate record of the transactions—the principal source of data for this study. The use of literary, poetic, and historical allusions is often beyond the clients' capacities, and simplified explanations for clients rebounded to the author's advantage. He also had resort to a fortune teller informant and to a research library from which he could draw support for the interpretation of certain segments of a reading.

A fourth and final problem area concerned the interpretation of nonverbal gestures in fortune teller/client transactions. Here the problem derives from the fact that there is no authoritative literature on the meaning of nonverbal gestures in Chinese culture and society. Thus the interpretation of kinesic (body language) and proxemic (body distance) cues rests largely on the Western language literature that addresses this subject matter.

The author has chosen to take up these problems in the body of the report in order to highlight the difficulties of undertaking participant observation in Chinese society and to stress the need for additional work on the dynamics of face-to-face interaction in Chinese society and culture.

CULTURE AND VALUES IN THE CHINESE
FORTUNE TELLERS' ATTRIBUTION OF MOTIVES

The Chinese fortune teller in Hong Kong draws from an extensive cultural stock of knowledge for the practice of his profession.* It is a stock of knowledge that extends back to the early history of Chinese thought and religion to include the *Book of Changes, Book of Songs, Book of Rites,* the Confucian, Taoist, and Buddhist classics, selected Neo-Taoist and popular Buddhist works of a later period, Neo-Confucian works—particularly of the Sung and Ming periods—and a technical lore that belongs to all these traditions and to popular folklore.[16] It is a complicated and highly syncretic literature.

The term "syncretism" applies especially well to this genre, since its creation appears to have centered on the periods in which "The Combination of Three Teachings in One" (*sanjiao heyi*)†—that is, the combination of the teachings of Confucianism, Taoism, and Buddhism—prevailed in the realms of Chinese philosophy and religion.[17] Many of these classical works are reprinted from late imperial editions, published in Taiwan and reissued in Hong Kong. They are readily available in selected Hong Kong bookstalls.

To the classical works must be added an enormous body of contemporary popular works related to one, several, or all of the "five arts." The popular materials take several forms. There are *wenyan* texts (written in the literary idiom) that excerpt portions of the classical works for detailed commentary.[18] There are also *baihua* versions (written in the vernacular idiom) of the classical works with excerpted portions of the classical originals, and there are innumerable *baihua* secondary sources that introduce fortune telling generally, or various of the five arts to general audiences. Many of these works are bound in flashy paperback covers akin to popular Western paperbacks on astrology and other occult topics. Some contain cartoon or pornographic drawings that bear no relationship whatsoever to the contents of the books. A few book in this vein, in both English and Chinese, compare Chinese fortune telling to Western astrology, palmistry, and physiognomy. A lesser number relate Chinese fortune telling to Western science, particularly to Einsteinian physics. Finally, there are technical aids such as almanacs, charts for the calculations of the *bazi*, calendars for converting lunar and solar time, time-zone charts, face charts for readings of physiognomy, and hand charts for the palmist.

While these contemporary popular works are available in most bookstalls, some bookstalls specialize in the sale of fortune-telling materials. Second-hand bookstalls carry editions of popular works printed in the late 1800s and again in the 1930s and 40s. Technical aids are more difficult to obtain from bookstalls; they are produced by specialized publishers who distribute to professional

---

*The term "his" is appropriate here, since all the fortune tellers in the study were male.

†Also known as the "Combined Practice of the Three Teachings" (*sanjiao jianxiu*).

fortune tellers. Most of the fortune tellers with whom the author dealt used technical manuals produced in Shanghai in the 1930s and 40s.

Both the classical and the contemporary literature on fortune telling are complicated by the fact that there are several schools of thought and practice among fortune tellers, and by the fact, mentioned earlier, that each of the arts may be practiced at different levels. Calculations derived from the date and time of birth are differently treated by the *Xing-zong, Zuping,* and *Cewei* methods. Calculations based on the permutations of the five elements differ among the *Taiyi, Dunjia,* and *Liuren* schools, and readings of the face and hands are differently handled by *fengshui, yangshou,* and *renxiang* practitioners. Presumably, at different levels in the exercise of fortune-telling skills, predictions may be made for individuals, families, nationalities, and whole societies. Some of these differences in schools of thought and levels of practice are reflected in the published literature. The *Cewei doushu* and *Zuping* schools and the *Dunjia* and *Liuren* methods are the most prominently represented in bookstall collections.

While it might be thought that Chinese fortune tellers, like their Western counterparts, rely principally on contemporary popular materials for the practice of their profession (few Western physiognomists are familiar with, say, John Lavater's classical work on physiognomy),[19] all the author's informants claim they are scholars as well as professional practitioners of their art. They also claim that fortune tellers who use the contemporary popular works for the practice of their profession are "unprofessional."

If it is indeed true that Chinese fortune tellers utilize a large part of this cultural stock of knowledge for the pursuit of their profession, then culture, as embodied in the stock of knowledge, is not an objectified form of knowledge "out there" in fortune tellers' texts and handbooks, appropriated in some unspecified unconscious or semiconscious way. It is, rather, a cultural stock of knowledge available "here and now," part of the fortune tellers' habitual "recipes" for fulfilling their conscious intent to identify and resolve clients' problems.* The appropriate term to use is, then, not "stock of knowledge" but "stock of knowledge in-trade."† The latter term stresses the intentionality of the

---

*"Habitual knowledge presents 'definitive' solutions to problems, which are organized in the flow of lived experience without one having to give them attention. That means that they can be subordinated and coordinated to a core of experience, and above all to a predominant act. I can whistle a song while I walk *and* think about a mathematical problem. I can smoke while I write, write while I look for words, etc. I can play a musical instrument without being careful about the fingering, even without 'consciously' reading the notes and concentrate 'completely' on the meaning (the thematic articulation) of the piece being played. Naturally as many examples of this can be given as one wants. They all concern combinations of skills, useful knowledge, or knowledge of recipes."[20]

†"Each step of my explication and understanding of the world is based at any given time on a stock of previous experience, my own immediate experiences as well as such experiences as are transmitted to me from my fellow-men and above all from my parents,

fortune teller's cultural consciousness and helps to distinguish the professional fortune teller's cultural consciousness from that of amateurs, most clients, and certainly foreign participant-observers attempting to reconstruct the patterns by which Chinese fortune tellers impute motives to their clients. As a neophyte, the author cannot take for granted those features of culture that the professional fortune teller can and must take for granted in order to practice his art.

For that reason, the reconstruction of the fortune teller's imputation of motives is an ideal-typical construction of how the fortune teller treats his cultural stock of knowledge. It cannot be a precise replica of the fortune teller's logical reasoning because the author is not Chinese and because he is not a professional fortune teller. However, the rendition of the imputation of motives is plausible.

No one can fail to be struck by the enormous array of signs and symbols that populate classical and contemporary fortune-telling texts. There are "named" (*youmingxing*) and "unnamed" stars (*wumingxing*), the "five elements" (*wu xing*), the "ten stems" (*shi gan*), and "twelve branches" (*shier zhi*), *yin* and *yang*, the "sixty-four stems and branches" (*liushisi ganzhi*), the signs of the Chinese zodiac, the sixty-four hexagrams of the *Book of Changes*, the "five, eight, and ten gates" (*wu, ba, shi gong*), "five, eight, and ten courts" (*wu, ba, shi tang*), the "five, eight, and ten official positions" (*wu, ba, shi guan*), and so on. Taken in and of themselves, these and other signs and symbols constitute the symbolic elements of an intricate cosmology.

Out of these signs and symbols the Chinese fortune teller constructs practical answers to practical problems. The question is, How? One might begin by noting that signs and symbols are not randomly distributed. They are elements in a cosmological system that has a definite structure. That structure is composed of several levels of symbolization from the most abstract, the level at which signs and symbols are merely presented, to the most concrete level where signs and symbols are linked to concrete indicators of behavior on the topography of the hands, the body, and the face. In between these two levels are multiple levels of symbolic elaboration and commentary that make each cluster of symbols more concrete and specific.

---

teachers and so on. All of these communicated and immediate experiences are included in a certain unity having the form of my stock of knowledge, which serves me as the reference schema for the actual step of my explication of the world."[21]

The concept "stock of knowledge in-trade" is intended to narrow the definition of stock of knowledge to a specific situation—that is, the fortune telling situation. This usage derives from the concept "logic-in-use." As Aaron Cicourel notes, "The rehearsal of elements of role-taking involve 'logic-in-use' because the actor is taking more than 'internalized norms' or stored information into account, for it is the appearance, behavior and reactions of others in a particular setting that activates normative categories."[22] Since the fortune teller's stock of knowledge is applied in a particular interactive setting, the stock of knowledge in-trade is conceived to have the same relationship to the stock of knowledge that logic-in-use has to logic.

At the most abstract levels of this structure, symbols are grouped to form dimensions of the cosmos. Stated in the most parsimonious way, the cosmos is depicted as having five irreducible dimensions: time, space, conditions, relationships, and direction.[23] Each new combination of symbols and signs forms an elaboration of these basic dimensions into more specific and concrete dimensions of human action. Time, for example, taken abstractly as cosmic time, is related to the zodiacal cycle to establish calendrical time; space is elaborated into heavenly, human, and earthly zones; conditions are elaborated into various environmental effects; relationships are elaborated into superordinacy and subordinacy; direction is elaborated into movement and rest. At the next level in the combination and recombination of signs and symbols, calendrical time devolves into biographical time-specific ages marked year by year in the stars, the permutations of elements in the calculations based on the date and time of birth and on the structural features of the face, body, and hands. Spatial zones similarly devolve into locations in the kinship structure and occupational location again marked on the face, body, and hands and in the stars. Environmental effects devolve into events such as illness, accident, marriage, divorce, birth, death, love affairs, and travel. Movement and rest devolve into decisional choices such as bold action, cautious action, retreat, withdrawal, and passivity.

Popular maxims and homilies complete the structure of the system. They comprise the composite experience of fortune tellers of the past, handed down generation after generation. Each such maxim is linked to particular topographical features of the face, hands, and body: the forty-two modular types of eyebrows, the twenty modular structures of the eyes, the mouth, the ears, and the nose; the three facial zones; facial lines, facial hair, moles, bone structure, facial shape; skin texture and coloration; the lines, squares, circles, ellipses, stars, and dots on the hands; finger joints, fingernail shape, color, and texture; the fleshy protuberances on the hands, hand shapes; the length and shape of the torso, arms, legs, hands, feet, and head; the tenor and timbre of the voice.

The maxims and homilies associated with these features combine with indicators of movement to depict demeanor (*mianmao*), or character, and the prospects for success or failure, poverty or wealth, a long or short life, many successors or none. For example, the eyebrow formation known as *guimei* (rough eyebrows that press on the eyes, shorter than the length of the eyes, where the starting point of the eyebrow is minute and the hair disperses as it sweeps upward) implies unstable character, improper behavior, lack of success in affairs, short life, and a tendency to resort to plunder to make a living. Eyebrows that "grow like wild grass," the so-called "chaotic eyebrows" (*meimao sangluan*), depict a person of unstable mind (*xin wu ding xiang*), a person who is narrow-minded, full of doubts, wanting in affinity with others, and clumsy at things (*fan ren lu, you zhou yu shi*). In connection with the "five longs" (*wuchang*) meaning long head, long face, long body, long hands, and long feet, it is said of one who has short hands but long features in other regards, "though one has *wuchang*, even if he comes from a prosperous family, he cannot avoid poverty." The poetic form is:

Wuchang zhi ren, gu mao cu,
zhi xia jie zhi quo bo lu,
You qian gu gao wu zi ru,
yi liang kan lai bu shi chu.[24]

The fortune teller's stock of knowledge in-trade is thus an elaborate, logically closed, cosmological system to which entry is secured by the practice of the three arts (astrological, palmist, and physiognomic) that are the focus of attention here. As has been pointed out, it is a highly syncretic system, for it draws upon Confucian, Taoist, and Buddhist sources, among others. Yet, insofar as it emphasizes doctrines of harmony and balance, and in its overall this-world-liness and pragmatic vision, it is quintessentially Confucian. The doctrine of harmony and balance is present throughout.

Guidebooks, for example, warn practitioners against treating any specific feature in isolation and rendering an interpretation on the basis of that feature alone. The face, for example, is depicted on a single frontal plane, divided into three horizontal segments or "zones" (*santing*). The area from the hairline to the bridge of the nose is the top zone (*shangting*) or heavenly zone (*tian*). The area from the bridge of the nose to the base of the nose is the middle zone (*shongting*) or the zone of human kind (*ren*), and the area from the base of the nose to the chin is the lower zone (*xiating*) or the earthly zone (*di*). Another imaginary line divides the face vertically into left and right hemispheres. Any particular feature found in one zone must be seen in terms of features in other related zones of the face before an interpretation can be legitimately rendered.[25] Thus, interpretations rest on prior considerations of balance and harmony.

Both the hands and face are divided into principal and subzones which mark years of age, environing events, occupational aptitude, social, familial, and sexual relationships, and demeanor. Permutations of the symbols derived from the calculation of the *bazi* are similarly subdivided. Taken together, the face, the hands, and the calculations of Chinese astrology are mutually complementary microcosms of the universe. The mechanics by which each abstract cosmological symbol is elaborated into a concrete indicator of human behavior and the obverse—that is, the techniques by which the fortune teller associates each concrete indicator with the appropriate cosmological symbols from which the indicator's meaning is derived—create what ethnomethodologists would describe as a "relevance structure": a set of recipes and typological formulas that constitute a basic model of the human actor.*

---

*"My knowledge of everyday life is structured in terms of relevances. Some of these are determined by immediate pragmatic interests of mine, others by my general situation in society. It is irrelevant to me how my wife goes about cooking my favorite goulash as long as it turns out the way I like it. It is irrelevant to me that the stock of a company is failing, if I do not own such stock; or that Catholics are modernizing their doctrine, if I am an

Just as the cosmos may be described as having five interrelated, irreducible dimensions, the model of the human actor derived from this cosmological system may also be described in terms of five interrelated, irreducible dimensions: identity—constituted by age and event indicators that depict the actor's past, present, and future; character—constituted by indicators of the actor's demeanor; conditions—constituted by indicators of important events in the actor's life cycle; relations—constituted by indicators of the actor's social, sexual, and familial relations and relations of superordinacy and subordinacy; and orientation—constituted by aspects of the actor's demeanor that mark tendencies to action or passivity. Each of these dimensions can be more specifically elaborated with respect to health, occupation, familial, sexual, and social relations, and financial, travel, and educational prospects.

This model of human action approaches an individualized biography because it reduces the number of possibilities for the construction of such a biography to five. To put it in a slightly different way, if any given individual's "real" biography consists of everything that individual has said and done in every situation in which that same individual has been involved over a lifetime of involvements, the model of human action in the fortunetelling literature reduces the infinite number of possibilities that empirical reality offers to five basic categories of biographical data that cover the most important aspects of an actor's social existence.

Individualization is more closely approximated when the dimensions of the model are fleshed out with the social types contained in the maxims and homilies in the fortune tellers' texts. At the apex of such types is the person most likely to register continuous successes in life. Persons who fill this type manifest the symbols of wood (*mu xing*) and fire (*huo xing*) in astrological calculations and in body type. They they certain topographical features: smooth, slightly glossy, light-colored skin; curved eyebrows that conform to the shape of the eyes and brow bone, and full eyebrow hair that flows in a single direction; finely shaped eyes with clear, centered, and luminous (*liang*) irises; balanced and slightly elongated nose and ears; finely shaped mouth; slightly rounded facial, hand, and body shape; high forehead and a full, slightly glossy head of hair. Their characters are upright and morally correct; they pursue all things in moderation. Their cleverness, marked in the lines clearly etched across the forehead, is a sign of wisdom. Auspicious events mark their courses through life and assure their health through old age. They have the power to attract the support and affinity of others. In their relationships with superiors and subordinates they

---

atheist; or that it is now possible to fly non-stop to Africa, if I do not want to go there. However, my relevance structures intersect with the relevance structures of others at many points, as a result of which we have 'interesting' things to say to each other. An important element of my knowledge of everyday life is the knowledge of the relevance structures of others."[26]

are loyal, and they command the loyalty of others. They are loving and filial in their familial and sexual relations, and they are destined to have many successors and to prosper in their careers. In terms of orientation, they are active and confident in their pursuit of life's opportunities.

At the nadir of such social types is the one most likely to suffer disaster in life. Fire (*huo*) and metal (*zhin*) predominate in the astrological calculations. The face is typically triangular in shape; the eyebrows are choppy and out of balance with the eyes and brow bones. The eyes manifest irregularities; irises are off-center, and if the white of the eyes shows on three sides, it is a sign of demented, homicidal, or suicidal demeanor. Ears, nose, and mouth may be misshapen and out of balance with other features of the face. The limbs are distorted. Criminal cunning is indicated. Immorality pervades such a character. Inauspicious events mark such a one's career from early childhood on. A short, disastrous life is likely. Relations with others are chaotic and disruptive. Deviant careers are a certainty. Orientation may be now active, now totally withdrawn.[27]

Centered between these polar types is one that depicts a meteoric rise and decline in fortune, and both between apex and center and between nadir and center are a host of other social types that depict mixed destinies. Thus, most of the social types that populate the literature are open-ended typifications, drawn from the same basic model of human action, but possessing interchangeable features—some favorable and some unfavorable.[28]

VALUES AND MOTIVES

The fortune tellers' stock of knowledge in-trade and the more individualized typifications that fortune-telling lore provides, are sources for both values and motives. The simplest way to categorize motives is to employ a set of concepts shared by both ethnomethodologists and phenomenologists. Drawing from the work of Alfred Schutz, motives, understood as concepts in commonsense logic, are divided into the two types: "because" motives and "in-order-to" motives.* The identification, characterological, conditional, relational, and orientational dimensions of the model of human action, derived from the stock of knowledge in-trade, provide cues to both forms of motive. Biographical events,

---

*"The term 'motive' is equivocal and covers two different sets of concepts which have to be distinguished. We may say that the motive of the murderer was to obtain the money of the victim. Here 'motive' means the state of affairs, the end, which the action has been undertaken to bring about. We shall call this kind of motive the 'in-order-to motive.' From the point of view of the actor this class of motives refers to this future. . . . Over against the class of in-order-to motives we have to distinguish another one which we suggest calling the 'because' motive. The murderer has been motivated to commit his acts because he grew up in an environment of such and such a kind, because, as psycho-analysis shows, he had in his infancy such and such experiences, etc. Thus, from the point of view of the actor, the because motive refers to his past experiences."[29]

relational and orientational dimensions of the model, are the principal sources for "because" motives—the more elaborate of the two. "Because" motives may relate to early childhood experiences (illness, accident, the death of parents or siblings, or conversely, the birth of siblings, the success of parents), opportunities taken or missed (chances to meet a benefactor, to secure a position, or to make money), social, familial, or even ancestral facilities or impediments (family resistance to or support for a choice of career or marriage partner, for example), or characterological predilections to fear, aggression, caution, or withdrawal, or some combination of these.

The drive for fame and fortune, the desire for knowledge, the desire for progeny (preferably male), longevity and good health, marriage, a happy and secure family, and sexual fulfillment are typical "in-order-to" motives. "In-order-to" motives are often linked to specific careers in a career hierarchy. The drive for fame and fortune and the desire for knowledge are most likely to be linked to careers that stand at the apex of the hierarchy—the careers of statesmen, scholars, and military strategists. Fame and fortune may also accrue to careers next on the ladder—those of professionals not already mentioned, big business men, and creative artists. Lesser motives underlie the lesser careers of the artisan, the farmer, the worker, the petty tradesman, the housewife, and the ordinary soldier. At the nadir of both motives and careers are the deviants: gamblers, swindlers, prostitutes, petty thieves, and the like.

A list of terminal and instrumental values can be culled from these typified motives, though it must be remembered that motives, as they are presented in the stock of knowledge in-trade, are not exactly equivalent to values. "In-order-to" motives must be termed "conditionally terminal" because they represent not universal end-states that transcend situational considerations, but the highest ends to which occupants of particular kinds of careers may aspire. They are, therefore, situationally embedded. So are "because" motives. Both, however, strongly suggest more transcendent values drawn principally from the Confucian tradition. Human kindness (*ren*), loyalty (*zhong*) and filiality (*xiao*) are held to accompany the successful pursuit of typical goals. The absence of moderation in oneself or one's kin or the absence of reciprocity in social and familial relationships often underlie the treatment of the sources of failure under the heading of "because" motives. Typified motives are thus either "conditionally terminal values" or they are linked to underlying instrumental values drawn from the Confucian tradition. Either way, a value-motive hierarchy is implicit in the structure of the fortune tellers' stock of knowledge in-trade.

By making available a model of human action, a set of relatively individualized social types and typified motives and values, the stock of knowledge in-trade makes it possible for the fortune teller to construct a reading of a client that has all the appearance of being uniquely and personally "true" for that client. Indeed, it might be hypothesized that both fortune teller and client, to the extent that they share culturally given typifications such as these, will perceive such a reading as uniquely and personally "true," even in the absence of a face-to-face transaction.[30]

In fact, however, most readings are incomplete without a face-to-face transaction between fortune teller and client. Likewise, an understanding of the dynamics of motive attribution is incomplete without a consideration of the way culture, social structure, and social interaction operate to shape the attribution of motives in the course of a transaction between fortune tellers and clients. For a variety of reasons, including professional ones (which will be addressed shortly), fortune tellers cannot assume that clients fully share their frame of reference. In a similar way, culture cannot be assumed to be the sole determinant of how motives and values are attributed to others. It may provide a list of values and motives, but it does not provide a description of the process by which values and motives are negotiated, modified, or transformed.

Social Structure and Social Construction in the Attribution of Motives

The most evident structural feature of transactions between professional fortune tellers and their clients is the fact that these are transactions between unequals. The fortune tellers are, after all, professionals. Like other professionals, they legitimate their claim to professional status and the fees they charge by defining clients as people who have problems that can be resolved only by the exercise of the fortune tellers' training and skills—especially client-oriented professionals.[31]

It is not always evident that clients intend to activate an unequal relationship of this kind when they call upon a fortune teller. Young people in particular often regard a visit to a fortune teller as a lark or simply something interesting to pass the time (though their subsequent interest in the transaction may belie their expressed intent). Yet, by calling upon a professional fortune teller, they activate a "calling" that sets in motion an interaction between unequals.* Fortune tellers identify and define clients' problems, not the other way around. Though the client pays the fees, it is the fortune teller who sets the pace of the transaction, determines its length, defines the skills to be employed and the depth of the reading, dominates fortune teller-client "talk," and, generally, takes the client in hand.

Fortune tellers' domination of the situation is manifested in a number of different ways. First, fortune tellers talk like professionals. It is rare to hear

---

*When a client is discovered to be competent in the knowledge and/or practice of fortune telling, it is an occasion for the redefinition of the relationship from one between a professional and a client to either one between a master and a disciple or one between two masters.

fortune tellers hem and haw. Their pronouncements are typically unhesitating and spoken in confident and authoritative tones of voice. As the taped record demonstrates, while clients frequently forget their own remarks in the course of a transaction, not to mention the remarks of the fortune teller, fortune tellers seldom forget any cue they themselves author, or fail to respond to any cue offered by a client, though a transaction may last anywhere from 20 minutes to 3 hours. This is an important facet of social construction, and it will be discussed further in the pages that follow.

Second, the relationships are unequal because fortune tellers have greater command of the stock of knowledge in-trade than clients. Again, age plays a role. Clients over 40 are more likely to have knowledge of the linguistic idiom of fortune telling, to be familiar with the cosmological system fortune tellers utilize, and to grasp the typifications, maxims, homilies, and poetic, literary, and historical allusions. People under 40 usually require translation into the vernacular and explanation. Yet, even where older clients are involved, the professional's mastery of his stock of knowledge in-trade, the speed with which he can manipulate signs, symbols, and interpretations, and his mastery of the technical facets of his art establish his dominance over the transaction.

Third, professional command of the situation is frequently manifested in the fortune tellers' use of nonverbal gestures. Although Hong Kong is an ethnically and racially mixed society and subscribes to a syncretistic culture of its own, certain aspects of traditional Chinese society and culture are still visible. Interpersonal distance between strangers is still greater than for most Americans and certainly greater than for many Europeans. Eyeball-to-eyeball contact between strangers (excluding Westerners) is still not common in most ordinary encounters; nor is body contact in situations other than those occasioned by public transport, waiting lines, and the mad dash for sales counters. The fortune teller, however, is a practitioner of the fine art of "tactual politics."[32] With a freedom and confidence akin to that of the family doctor, the fortune teller closes interpersonal distance to what is ordinarily an extremely discomforting range. He engages clients in direct eyeball-to-eyeball gaze; he grasps them firmly by the hands. He may suddenly stand and close a hand over the back of the client's head (to feel the skull structure), or he may grasp a client's chin and pull the client's head toward him for a closer examination of facial features.

Such body contact is limited to those regions of the body that are the legitimate concern of the physiognomist and palmist—the face and hands. But the fortune teller often saves his comments on the intimate aspects of a client's life history for just such moments of contact, thereby disarming his client, affirming his control of the situation and the authority of his pronouncements.

All of these facets of the fortune teller's domination of the situation stem from his role as a professional and the functions he performs for a client or client group. In the broadest sense, the fortune teller has one overarching function to perform. It is his job to develop a consistent, logically closed biographical "account" of the client's past, present, and future.[33] That overarching function can be subdivided into several subfunctions, including identification, diagnosis, prognosis, prediction, and counseling. Diagnosis and prognosis can be further subdivided into characterological and medical diagnoses and prognoses.

These several subfunctions are manifested in the structure of fortune teller/client "talk." The fortune teller's contribution to this "talk" consists of several kinds of statements, congruent with the functions he performs, that are linked to form a composite account of the client. These statements and their referents are listed below.

Identification Statements: *"Ni shi yige. . . .";* *"Ni yiqian zou yige. . . .";* *"Ni yinggai zou yige. . . ."* ("You are. . . ." "You were. . . ."; "You ought to be or ought to have been a. . . .")—statements establishing the social identity of a client.

Diagnostic Statements: (1) Characterological diagnoses—statements that typically take the form, *"Ni shi shenma yang de ren"* ("You are such-and-such a type of person"), or *"Ni daode shang shi. . . ."* ("Morally, you are. . . .")—with reference to a moral trait or characterological attribute. (2) Medical diagnoses—statements locating a medical problem in some region of the body.

Prognostic Statements: statements that typically take the logical form, *"Yinwei ni shi shenma yang de ren, souyi ni jianglai hui. . . ."* ("Because you are such-and-such a type of person, in the future you will. . . ."), or *"Yinwei ni yu dzemma yige wenti, souyi ni jianglai hui. . . ."* ("Because you have such-and-such a problem, in the future you will. . . .")—whether the statements refer to characterological or medical prognoses.

Predictive Statements: These statements can be distinguished from prognostic statements insofar as the former are not demonstrably rooted in the identifications or diagnoses already made. Such statements may be highly specific or very general. *"Mingnian sanyue wuhao ni hui kaidao; bu yaojin."* ("On March 5th, next year, you will undergo surgery; it's nothing important."); or *"Ni jiang lai hui zhuan qian."* ("In the future, you will make money.").

Statements of Counsel: These statements are rooted in identifications and diagnoses already made. *"Ni zheige ren tai zhin jiang; ni yao dou xiuxi."* ("You're too uptight; you must relax more.")

Elaborative Statements: These statements are situationally specific elaborations on statements already made. They play a role in the transaction similar to the role played by the conditional, relational, and orientational dimensions of the model of the human actor in the fortune teller's stock of knowledge in-trade. *"Yinwei ni xiaonian de shihou shou hai, souyi ni gen tongshi de guanxi bu da hao."* ("Because you were harmed as a child, your relations with colleagues are not very good.") Elaborative statements recur throughout fortune teller/client transactions and can be tagged as primary, secondary, tertiary, and so on, elaborations of a single identification, diagnostic, prognostic, predictive, or counseling statement.

Explanatory Statements: These are statements explaining technical lore or the stock of knowledge in-trade being applied by the fortune teller. Explanatory statements typically establish the salience of abstract signs and symbols to the client's particular case. As such, they may function like elaborative statements in the building of an account of the client's biography.

These seven types of statements form the core of the fortune teller's account of the client. There are, however, other kinds of statements that are peripheral to the core of the account but essential to the relationship between the fortune teller and his client. They include statements legitimating the fortune teller's role—*"Wo sishi dou nian suangua; Dun Jia suanfa shi zui kekao de."* ("I have been an astrologer for 40 years; the *Dun Jia* method is the most reliable."); statements legitimating the relationship between the fortune teller and client— *"Ni kan, Wo duiyu ni de wenti shenma dou zhidao."* ("You see, I know everything about your problems."); and cue-searching statements—*"Ni zui jin you meiyu gen furen chaojia?"* ("Have you argued with your spouse lately?").

The structure of the fortune teller's contribution to fortune teller/client "talk" illustrates how the fortune teller's role both dominates and is built into the very nature of the transaction. It also demonstrates that the process of account building mirrors the mechanisms that create a "relevance structure" from the abstractions contained in the fortune teller's stock of knowledge in-trade.

There are, however, significant differences between the stock of knowledge in-trade and the account building that occurs in the course of a fortune teller/ client transaction. While the fortune teller dominates the situation, the client is seldom merely a passive target for the practice of a fortune teller's skills. There are several reasons for this.

First, the fortune teller has a vested interest in the client's active participation in the transactions. The more the fortune teller is able to generate the client's interest in a reading, the greater the likelihood that a one-time client will return for more, and the fortune teller, as a professional practitioner of his role, has a vested interest in the cultivation of a long-term client population. The more the client shares in the process of building his or her own account, the greater the likelihood that the client will view the fortune teller as engaged in a legitimate role—one that effectively addresses the client's problems.

Second, the client is a principal source for the cues a fortune teller uses to flesh out the model he derives from the stock of knowledge in-trade. To borrow from Erving Goffman, cues may be given or "given off" by the client; that is, the client is a source of both conscious and deliberate messages about himself or herself and unconscious, unintended messages.* Dress, body posture, items in

---

*"The expressiveness of the individual (and therefore his capacity to give impressions) appears to involve two radically different kinds of sign activity: the expression that he *gives*

"identity tags," locution, may "give off" cues about the client's social status.[35] Body posture, the shape of limbs, skin discolorations, hair texture, and even mouth odor may provide useful cues for medical diagnoses without the client being aware that such cues are being "given off." To messages and cues "given off" the client may add, verbally, messages about his or her own occupational and social status, medical history, relationships with kin and colleagues, and other information pertinent to the building of an account. Indeed, the first step in the calculation of the *bazi* depends on information about date and time of birth supplied by the client.

Verbal and nonverbal cues serve not only to provide information useful for the building of an account; they also serve to indicate the client's acceptance or rejection of, or ambiguity about statements made by the fortune teller. A quizzical expression on the client's face may engender a search for additional cues, a more thorough explanation, an elaboration of an earlier statement, or a recalculation of the *bazi*, physiognomic, or palmic indicators on the part of the fortune teller, though recalculation seems to occur only when nonverbal and verbal signals of rejection are combined. In short, it takes a very persistent client to break through the fortune teller's domination of the situation.

The role of the client is evident in the structure of fortune teller/client "talk." The client's contributions are typically responses to the statements of the fortune teller, though some clients may begin the transaction by asserting social identity at the outset and/or presenting themselves as persons with problems to be resolved. The pertinent client statements are listed below:

Identification Statements: *"Wo shi shenma shenma ren."* ("I am so and so; I am such and such a person.") Such statements may establish social and/or occupational status.

Problem Statements: *"Wo xia ge yue xiang qu MeiGuo youxing; bu xiaode yinggai bu yinggai qu."* ("I am thinking of taking a trip to the U.S. next month; I don't know whether or not I should go.").

Statements Accepting or Rejecting the Fortune Teller's Identifications, Diagnoses, Prognoses, Predictions, and Counsel: *"Bu co, ni dzemma zhidao?"* ("Not bad; how did you know that?"); *"Bu dui!" "Wo cunglai meiyu gen furen chaojia!"* ("You're wrong! I've never had an argument with my spouse!").

Just as there are statements that are peripheral to the core of the fortune teller's account of the client, so too there are statements that are peripheral to

---

and the expression that he *gives off*. The first involves verbal symbols or their substitutes which he uses admittedly and solely to convey the information that he and the others are known to attach to these symbols. This is communication in the traditional and narrow sense. The second involves a wide range of action that others can treat as symptomatic of the actor, the expectation being that the action was performed for reasons other than the information conveyed in this way."[34]

the client's self-accounting. Like peripheral statements in the case of the fortune teller, these statements bear on the relationship between the fortune teller and the client. They include statements offering or denying legitimacy to the fortune teller's role—*"Zhen shi mo ming qi miao; Ni hao xiang dui wo shenma dou zhidao!"* ("It's really unbelievable; you seem to know everything there is to know about me."), or *"Hushuo!" "Zhen meiyu shenma chuxi!"* ("Sheer nonsense! It's useless!"); statements offering or withdrawing legitimacy from the fortune teller/client relationship—*"Duo xieh, Ni zhen bang wo mang."* ("Many thanks, you have really been a help to me."). (Negative statements are the same as those noted above.); and explanation search statements—*"Ni shuo wo you san ge 'mu' zi, you shenma yisi?"* ("You say I have three characters for wood; what does that mean?").

Obviously, while statements clients make offering or withdrawing legitimacy from the fortune teller's role or the relationship between fortune teller and client are peripheral to the account, they are central to the outcome of the transaction.

Clients' identifications, problems, and acceptances or rejections are cues for the framing of statements made by their fortune tellers. They are thus occasions for modifications in an account. Such modifications may be registered in any one or all of the statements made by fortune tellers. *"Ni shuo ni zou shangyi; ni yinggai zou guan."* ("You say you are in business, but you ought to be an official.") *"Ni shuo ni cunglai meiyou gen furen chaojia, keshi wo kan ni de meimao sangluan; bu hui jiang co."* ("You say you have never argued with your spouse, but your eyebrows are of the 'chaotic' type; I can't be wrong.") When clients are persistent in their rejection of fortune tellers' statements, the conflict is typically channeled into a reexamination of the stock of knowledge in-trade. The *bazi* may be recalculated and responsibility shifted back to the client because clients are seldom confident of the time of birth. Such a device relieves the fortune teller of the burden of error and permits a recasting of the account. In the face of similar persistent disclaimers, a physiognomist and palmist may take a second, more detailed look at zones of the face and hands to uncover new indicators that permit a recasting of the account.

Ambiguity in the stock of knowledge in-trade, caused by the difference between the model of human action the stock of knowledge provides and actors as they actually present themselves to their fortune tellers, serves to make accounts negotiable. This is the principal difference between the stock of knowledge in-trade, abstracted from situational considerations and considerations of social structure, and the stock of knowledge in-trade as it is worked out in the course of social interaction. The negotiability of accounts also explains why a reading in the absence of a face-to-face encounter is never the same as a reading with the client present, and to turn a phrase, "accounted for."

The Negotiation of Motives and Values

Through the application of culturally given social types, ranked occupational stereotypes and the attribution of typified motives and values to the client's case, the fortune teller attempts to persuade the client not only of the usefulness of his skills and services, but also of the accuracy of his moral judgment. His accounting of the client is thus a moral accounting, and moral judgment is implied in each of the functions a fortune teller performs: identification, diagnosis, prognosis, prediction, and counseling. The negotiation of an account is distinct from the negotiation of roles,[36] for it is not the relationship of a professional practitioner of some particular skill to a client that is the subject of negotiation, but the moral career of the client as the fortune teller seeks to depict it.[37]

That clients recognize the moral dimension of the fortune teller's imputation of motive is partly demonstrated by the character of client responses. In one extreme case, a client who sought a fortune teller's prediction of a winning horse at the Happy Valley Race Track responded, in English, to a very negative imputation of motive on the part of the fortune teller with a moral counterimputation of his own. "I told you he's full of shit. The only thing he's interested in is a fast buck!"

In another instance, a fortune teller told a middle-aged male client that his facial features indicated that the client had frequent arguments with his wife. From the context of the account, it was clear that this item was an elaboration of an earlier statement that the client was driven by a desire for position that led him to be "insincere" in his relationships with colleagues and kin. The client protested vehemently that he never argued with his wife; that their relationship was very harmonious, and by implication, that the fortune teller had erred both in his imputation of motive and his judgment that the client placed position above harmonious relationships. Both parties thus acknowledged the link between motives and values, and in this instance, the fortune teller, after a prolonged and unsuccessful effort to impose his judgment on the client, recast the account by reexamining the client's facial signs. The new version stressed the danger of excessive concern with position and counseled cultivation of the client's newly revealed potential for sensitivity to others. It might be said, then, that the client was negotiating to revise the fortune teller's account of him by altering the hierarchy of values imputed to him. The fortune teller's compromise left the account intact but acknowledged the client's claim to a modified hierarchy of values. In these and other instances, the imputation of motives suggests that a negotiable value-attitude system is being formulated.

SITUATIONAL ASPECTS OF COGNITIVE CONSISTENCY AND DISSONANCE

Within the confines of the transaction between fortune teller and client, cognitive consistency and dissonance take on meaning as aspects of the situation.

For the fortune teller, cognitive consistency is a characteristic of the account of the client he constructs, and dissonance derives from the client's response to the account, particularly a response that rejects the legitimacy of the fortune teller's work. Given the fortune teller's domination of the situation and the advantage proffered by his familiarity with the stock of knowledge in-trade, maintaining consistency in the construction of an account is relatively easy. In those rare instances where clients reject the legitimacy of an account and its author, fortune tellers may resort to a variety of strategies. They may take a dogmatic and unyielding stance, reiterating the authority of their sources, asserting their personal authority; they may ignore the rejection or pass it off as "mere talk" (*"Bu yao ting ta de hua; ta zong shi zemmayange jiang."*["Don't listen to him; that's the way he always talks."]), or they may withdraw into silence.

Though the author was witness to a number of transactions where fortune tellers were forced to modify their accounts by clients, no instance was witnessed in which a modification of this sort involved the acceptance of values foreign to the fortune teller's stock of knowledge in-trade. There is, however, some evidence that the literature of fortune telling does seek to adapt to values not derived from the stock of knowledge in-trade. This is a theme which will be discussed in the conclusion.

Cognitive consistency and dissonance as they pertain to clients are more difficult to assess. For the fortune teller, presumably, cognitive issues raised in the course of the transaction are either resolved when the transaction ends or are carried over to the next transaction with that same client. For the client, however, cognitive issues raised in the course of the transaction transcend the transaction itself.

The client walks out of the transaction as the owner of an account of himself or herself. Indeed, clients may walk out with charts or an entire book containing the record of the account. That record, as it is written or remembered, may figure in social interactions that take place beyond the confines of the fortune-telling situation. If the client is a member of a client group of friends or relatives, the account is socially shared, and its may be revived or recounted at the behest of other members of the group. Furthermore, almost every account contains predictions of events that are supposed to take place in the world beyond the fortune-telling situation at some future date. These are events that only the client or client group is in a position to monitor and interpret unless, of course, clients choose to share the monitoring and interpretation of predictions with others. An account can thus be described in terms of its social career, and the social career of an account transcends the situation in which it was originally constructed.

The implications for a treatment of cognitive consistency and cognitive dissonance, and their impact in turn on value change, are considerable. It may mean that cognitive issues raised in the course of the transaction between fortune teller and client will be forgotten by the client shortly after the transaction ends. It may also mean that the client will not be permitted to forget such issues or the value conflicts they engender because others, privy to the account, will not let such matters pass. Then again, it may mean that future events will occur that cause cognitive dissonance long after the account has been filed away as insignificant by both the client and by others familiar with its contents. Situational factors, other than those related to the original transaction may thus have an import for the process of value change.

Since it is the social career of an account and the relationship of that career to the value-attitude system of the client that are of interest here, consistency can refer to three different phenomena: the consistency between values and motives in the internal structure of the account, an issue already discussed; consistency between terminal and instrumental values in the internal structure of the client's value-attitude system; and consistency between the values and motives in the account, as they are shaped by social interaction and social construction, and the values contained in the client's own value-attitude system. For purposes of conceptual clarity, the first may be termed "logical consistency," the second, "cognitive consistency" (the sense in which the term is usually used), and the third, "cognitive congruency."[38] The question being raised then, is, Under what conditions will cognitive incongruency produce cognitive dissonance in the client? It is important to note that any attempt to answer the question here must be highly speculative, since the focus of the study is on the fortune-telling situation, not on client value-attitude systems outside that situation. No tests for dissonance were applied, but some observations undertaken in the course of the study might be useful indicators of the dimensions of the problem.

Liu Zhangsan: Cognitive Incongruency and Dissonance

Liu Zhangsan* is a young businessman recently returned to Hong Kong after spending most of his adolescence and early maturity in England and the United States. His training encompassed both a strong liberal arts background and a highly specialized career in engineering. He returned to Hong Kong to assume a managerial post in his father's firm at his father's request.

Liu Zhangsan appears to adhere to a highly syncretic system of values and attitudes. On the one hand, he espouses a commitment to principles of Western science as they apply both to the technical side of the business and to management practice. On the other hand, he cleaves to a modified version of traditional Chinese values in matters concerning family. In this area, he espouses a strong commitment to filial piety, reciprocity, and sincerity. Conflict between these two commitments has been evident. Staffing in Liu Zhangsan's branch of his father's firm has been partly determined by his father's "relationships" (*guanxi*), and Liu's commitment to scientific management practice has been frustrated by

---

*Names used here are fictitious.

considerations he regards as improper in the business realm. At the same time, his father's failure to respond to Liu Zhangsan's commitments to filial piety have frustrated Liu's pursuit of the role of eldest son. Liu himself regards the compromises he has had to make as "manageable," and the social structure of both the family and the firm have aided him in this regard. Many of his business and family activities are invisible to his father, and that allows him opportunity to make decisions for both family and firm on principles of his own choosing. Conflict is thus intermittent, though a high state of tension often prevails.

Liu Zhangsan's visit to a fortune teller was his first as a client rather than an observer. Other members of his family are frequent users of a fortune teller's services, including Liu's father. In this instance, Liu was accompanied by his mother and younger brother. As Liu made clear before the transaction began, fortune telling was strictly a mix of superstition and self-fulfilling prophecy. He was present more out of curiosity about what it was the author found of value in it than any desire to present a problem of his own for a fortune teller's resolution.

When the transaction began, Liu Zhangsan, encouraged by other members of the group, requested a reading of his *bazi* and face and hands. The entire accounting was aided immeasurably by the constant interruptions of Liu's brother and mother who provided both factual information and cues as to the accuracy of the reading. Liu himself participated actively in the calculation of the *bazi* (especially with the time-zone calculations), but remained silent through most of the process except where information was explicitly requested or explanation was required.

The fortune teller's account laid emphasis on several aspects of Liu's character. He pointed out that Liu had experienced an unhappy childhood, marked by separation from kin. With no self-identification statement from Liu, the fortune teller identified him as a statesman, pointing to his high intelligence, extremely quick mind, and high moral principledness. When Liu pointed out that he was a businessman, the fortune teller retorted that Liu was in the wrong career. His proper career was politics and not business. The fortune teller elaborated by identifying a problem. Liu Zhangsan's moral principledness was unsuitable to the contingencies of a business career. Frustration in his moral pursuits were leading him toward moral dogmatism. Liu's "human feelings" (*renqing*) were insufficiently cultivated, because he allowed himself too little time for rest from the demands of his career. The lack of rest and resultant intolerance would, he predicted, lead to severe disruptions of family relationships and threaten Liu's mental and physical health, if not counterbalanced. The fortune teller counseled Liu to cultivate moderation and tolerance and to learn to enjoy life and give rein to humor.

When the transaction ended, Liu described the outcome as moderately impressive and acknowledged that the fortune teller had skills comparable to those of a good psychoanalyst. Many features of the account, however, he found to be rather ludicrous. The fortune teller's account of his early childhood and his suitability for a statesman's career were silly "shots in the dark." He was, however, impressed by the fortune teller's treatment of his character (though he thought it exaggerated) and about one fact of Liu's family history that startled all of the group. (It is not material here.) Liu's mother and brother were, however, impressed with the accuracy of the fortune teller's overall analysis. In several conversations among members of the family (now that others were made privy to the contents of the account) Liu's tensions and intolerance, as revealed by the account, were incorporated into a continuing dialogue about Liu's relationship to his father and his frustrations with the family business. Portions of the account were thus being made supplemental to an ongoing family concern. It might also be said that the account provided additional armament for those members of the family convinced that Liu Zhangsan should extend values, heretofore limited to family relationships, into Liu's business relationship with his father and his father's colleagues. What Liu deemed a relatively successful compartmentalization of values and attitudes was thus being challenged, and the challenge suggests a potential for the experience of additional dissonance.

Mei Liwu: Cognitive Incongruency and Dissonance

Mei Liwu is a young woman in her early thirties. She has served in a number of capacities, principally as a legal secretary and administrative assistant to law firms and research organizations. She was educated abroad and has travelled widely. Her encounter with a fortune teller was not part of the project reported here, but her experience is one that many fortune teller clients claim they share, and it offers a stark outline of the problem. When the opportunity arose to talk to her at length about her experience, it was eagerly accepted.

Mei Liwu had participated in several visits to a fortune teller, both as an observer and as a client. Her visits, according to her own account, were never taken seriously. They were intended as a way of passing time, and most such encounters occurred in the company of friends. Two years ago she paid a visit to a Cantonese fortune teller, again in the company of a few select friends. According to Mei Liwu, the account was not particularly memorable in any regard but one. The fortune teller predicted that she would fall ill in a year's time. He stated that she would undergo six successive operations, and he named the dates of each of the operations and described the character of their outcome. She was not to be concerned, however, for the operations would, in the end, be successful, and she would recover her health. Mei Liwu claims that she gave little credence to the prediction, though she was bothered that it had occurred. In the following year, she did indeed fall ill, and the six operations took place exactly as predicted. Today Mei Liwu confesses to a considerable fear of fortune tellers and no desire to engage in another transaction.

Whether Mei Liwu's report is taken at face value or not is, perhaps, less important than the way it had been brought to the author's attention. She was engaged in a conversation with several friends about fortune tellers, and the author happened to be within range. In response to others' reports of their experiences, Mei Liwu pointed out that "I never remember what a fortune teller has told me." The conversation turned to other matters of interest for about 20 minutes and then returned to the subject of fortune tellers. It was then that Mei Liwu described her experience. The incident offered rather direct evidence of cognitive dissonance.

It is very likely that Mei Liwu's account, like other accounts, underwent a social career in which the fit between event and account was socially constructed. The shock produced by Mei Liwu's six operations may be less a product of a fortune teller's specific prediction than a product of the account's social career. The experience of shock was sufficient to lead Mei Liwu to express signs of dissonance and, in the course of the discussion, to question the appropriateness of a strictly empirical approach to the nature of reality.

Mei Liwu and Liu Zhangsan offer grounds for the speculation that change in individual value-attitude systems is a long-term process involving situationally specific interactions between authoritative, socially defined accounts of an individual and the individual's own value-attitude system.

IMPLICATIONS OF MOTIVE ATTRIBUTION FOR AN UNDERSTANDING OF VALUE CHANGE

The purpose throughout this paper has been to demonstrate how an ethnomethodological approach might modify the Rokeachean view of value change. By describing in some detail how motive attribution derives from the fortune teller's stock of knowledge in-trade, how motives and values are first attributed to clients in the transaction situation and then negotiated to form an account, and how account building and modification may have an impact on cognitive dissonance and the potential for value change, it is hoped that stress will be given to the role of situational considerations in the study of value change wherever it occurs. The intent has also been to point out some aspects of culture, social interaction, and social construction that are particularly Chinese. In that regard, the syncretistic character of both the stock of knowledge in-trade and of the value-attitude systems clients bring to the fortune-telling situation are among the most important Chinese features of the setting for value change.

Speculation might be allowed to run rampant for a moment to take up a few implications of the syncretistic character of Chinese culture as it is represented in this instance by the Chinese fortune-telling case. Though the young in Hong Kong no longer confer the same legitimacy upon the fortune-telling profession that older residents do, there is still an enormous number of people, both young and old, who frequent fortune tellers. One might speculate that the continued popularity of fortune telling owes much to the syncretistic character of the fortune teller's stock of knowledge in-trade. By comparison to more dogmatic and doctrinaire systems of knowledge, the culture of fortune telling is flexible and adaptable. Though the social types and typified values and motives belong to an era that is passing, they still survive when fleshed out with new contents. Marriage is not what it once was, but the typification of marital behavior in the fortune-telling literature is sufficiently flexible to accommodate changing mores.

The focus here has been on individual value change, but one might speculate a bit further on change, not in an individual's values, but in the stock of knowledge itself. As noted earlier, the author was not witness to any instance in which values foreign to the stock of knowledge in-trade were accepted by the fortune teller in the course of a transaction. But the contents of popular works on fortune telling suggest that the kinds of cases fortune tellers typically encounter in this modern day and age are finding their way into the stock of knowledge in-trade. Modern problems of marriage and divorce, the juncture between science and the pragmatic approach of the fortune teller, and modern problems of business management are often used as illustrations of the viability of the fortune-telling profession in the industrial era. Syncretistic flexibility may help to keep fortune telling vital in changing times.

There is, however, another implication. The stock of knowledge in-trade presumably embodies the experience of fortune tellers over the centuries. It reflects both conceptual elaboration on the part of more thoughtful fortune-telling practitioners and the problems clients have negotiated into past accounts. Change in the stock of knowledge in-trade might be looked upon as a continuous dialectical movement incorporating both the fortune teller's accounts and the reactions of persistent clients to those accounts. If this is true, and this is mere speculation, then the attribution of motive that takes place in any given individual instance can be linked to change in the stock of knowledge in-trade, taken as a whole. Any negotiation between fortune teller and client provides the potential grounds for a change in the values, institutionalized and objectified, in the fortune teller's stock of knowledge in-trade. Institutionalized and objectified values, the resultants of the social constructions in which fortune tellers and clients are mutually engaged, are, in turn, the grounds upon which any new attribution of motive and negotiation of account will occur. The dialectical transformation of values is a subject for further research.

NOTES

1. Donald T. Campbell, "Social Attitudes and Other Acquired Behavioral Dispositions," in *Psychology: A Study of A Science*, vol. 6, ed. Sigmund Koch (New York: McGraw-Hill, 1963), pp. 100–1.

2. George Casper Homans, *Sentiments and Activities: Essays in Social Science* (New York: Free Press of Glencoe, 1962), pp. 280–81.

3. Herbert Blumer, *Symbolic Interactionism: Perspective and Method* (Englewood Cliffs, N.J.: Prentice-Hall, 1969), p. 92.

4. Milton Rokeach, *Beliefs, Attitudes and Values: A Theory of Organization and Change* (San Francisco: Jossey-Bass, 1970), p. 110.

5. Ibid., p. 132.

6. Ibid., p. 124.

7. Ibid., p. 160.

8. Ibid., p. 161.

9. Ibid.

10. Ibid., p. 162.

11. Blumer, *Symbolic Interactionism*, pp. 94, 95, 96.

12. Stanley Milgram, *Obedience to Authority, An Experimental View* (New York: Harper & Row, 1974).

13. Harold Garfinkel, *Studies in Ethnomethodology* (Englewood Cliffs, N.J.: Prentice-Hall, 1967). Another approach that draws generative linguistics into ethnomethodology is spelled out in Aaron V. Cicourel, *Cognitive Sociology: Language and Meaning in Social Interaction* (London: Penguin Books, 1973), pp. 99–140.

14. The Neo-Confucian elaboration of this concept can be traced to the *Book of Changes* (Yi Zhing). See Donald J. Munro, "Belief Control: The Psychological and Ethical Foundations," in *Deviance and Social Control in Chinese Society*, ed. Amy Auerbacher Wilson et al. (New York: Praeger, 1977), pp. 18–19.

15. "Civil Inattention" is defined in Erving Goffman, *Behavior in Public Places: Notes on the Social Organization of Gatherings* (New York: Free Press, 1963), pp. 83–88.

16. Huang Wenliu, *Mingyun xue* (Kowloon, Hong Kong: Tianxia Publishing House, no date), p. 24.

17. See W. Theodore deBary, "Introduction," in *Self and Society in Ming Thought*, ed. W. Theodore deBary and the Conference on Ming Thought (New York: Columbia University Press, 1970), pp. 22–24.

18. An example is Chen Xizhou, *Wan Ling Shen Chi Xiangfa* (Kowloon, Hong Kong: Chan Wing Tai Book Co., no date).

19. John Caspar Lavater, *Essays on Physiognomy Designed to Promote the Love of Mankind* (London: William Tegg, 1855).

20. Alfred Schutz and Thomas Luckmann, *The Structure of the Life World* (Evanston, Ill.: Northwestern University Press, 1973), p. 108.

21. Ibid., p. 7.

22. Cicourel, *Cognitive Sociology*, p. 25.

23. These five dimensions are a derivation from Helmut Wilhelm's interpretation of the *Yi Zhing. Change: Eight Lectures on the I Ching* (Princeton, N.J.: Princeton University Press, 1960), particularly pp. 15–22.

24. Li Kangjie, *Renxiang xue gailun* (Hong Kong: Zhenru Publishing House, 1972), p. 18.

25. Ibid., p. 20.

26. Peter L. Berger and Thomas Luckmann, *The Social Construction of Reality: A Treatise in the Sociology of Knowledge* (Garden City, N.Y.: Doubleday, 1967), p. 45.

27. Li, *Renxiang xue gailun*, pp. 9–18.

28. Ibid., pp. 9–30.

29. Alfred Schutz, *On Phenomenology and Social Relations: Selected Writings* (Chicago: University of Chicago Press, 1970), pp. 126–27.

30. This hypothesis derives from a counterpart study of psychics, astrologers, tea-leaf and tarot card readers in the metropolitan New York region. One aspect of the perceived "fit" between psychics' accounts of clients and clients' self-accountings may be due to a phenomenon known as the "Barnum effect." See Douglas A. Davis, "Bias, Barnum and Base Rates: Rethinking Labeling and Attributional Effects on Diagnostic Accuracy." Paper prepared for publication, September 1977. Mimeographed.

31. See Wilbert E. Moore, *The Professions: Roles and Rules* (New York: Russell Sage Foundation, 1970), especially p. 92 and pp. 100–2.

32. Nancy M. Henley, *Body Politics: Power, Sex, and Nonverbal Communication* (Englewood Cliffs, N.J.: Prentice-Hall, 1977), especially pp. 101–6. Though Henley focuses on gender differences between "touchers" and "touchees," the dynamics of tactual politics are applicable to this situation too.

33. The classical treatment of "accounts" and the accounting process can be found in "Accounts," in Stanford M. Lyman and Marvin B. Scott, *A Sociology of the Absurd* (New York: Appleton-Century-Crofts, 1970), pp. 111–43. Lyman and Scott attend to situational rather than biographical aspects of the accounting process. For a usage more akin to the one applied here see Jack D. Douglas, ed., *Understanding Everyday Life: Toward the Reconstruction of Sociological Knowledge* (Chicago: Aldine, 1970), p. 10.

34. Erving Goffman, *The Presentation of Self in Everyday Life* (Garden City. N.Y.: Doubleday, 1959), p. 2.

35. For a description of "identity tags," see Erving Goffman, *Strategic Interaction* (Philadelphia: University of Pennsylvania Press, 1969), pp. 22–24.

36. Cicourel, *Cognitive Sociology*, pp. 11–41.

37. Erving Goffman, "The Moral Career of the Mental Patient," in *Asylums: Essays on the Social Situations of Patients and Other Inmates* (Garden City, N.Y.: Doubleday, 1961), pp. 128–69.

38. Percy H. Tannenbaum, "The Congruity Principle: Retrospective Reflections and Recent Research," in *Theories of Cognitive Consistency: A Sourcebook*, ed. Robert P. Abelson et al. (Chicago: Rand McNally, 1968), pp. 52–72.

4

CREATING THE NEW COMMUNIST CHILD: CONTINUITY AND CHANGE IN CHINESE STYLES OF EARLY CHILDHOOD SOCIALIZATION

Carolyn Lee Baum
and Richard Baum

In the course of various travels to Hong Kong, Taiwan, and the People's Republic of China, the inability to fully comprehend the nature of the affective bonds that serve to link Chinese parents and their young children has been repeatedly and profoundly perplexing. The major puzzle was the existence of what seemed to be a substantially different sense of the parent-child attachment bond—a bond regarded as critical to "healthy" child development by Western psychologists and human development theorists.

This chapter represents an attempt to explore the nature and cultural particularities of the bonding process in Chinese society—both traditional and modern—and to reflect on some of the possible behavioral ramifications of contemporary Chinese styles of early childhood socialization.

THE ATTACHMENT BOND

In a classical study of the etiology of psychopathology in young children, psychoanalyst René Spitz observed the development of human infants reared in clean—but emotionally sterile—foster-care institutions, devoid of consistent, individualized maternal nurturance. He discovered numerous signs of severe emotional distress in the institutionalized children, which he attributed to the absence of sustained maternal warmth.[1] Indeed, some of the children observed by Spitz literally withered away and ultimately died from emotional neglect—a condition known as "marasmus"—which occurred despite the provision of adequate nutrition and physical care.

Building on the work of Spitz and others, the English psychoanalyst John Bowlby constructed a pioneering theory of human attachment behavior.[2] According to Bowlby, there are critical, identifiable periods in the early development of human infants in which the infant forms a humanizing attachment bond with a "significant" nurturing figure. In the absence of such early bonding, Bowlby observed, children are likely to develop certain pathological character traits, centering on the inability to form trusting or lasting human relationships. Such traits include aggressive sexual behavior, dishonesty, distrust of others, and lack of emotional responsiveness. Deep, lasting affection is regarded as impossible for such psychopathic individuals, who lack a strong superego and tend to regard other people as objects to be manipulated for their own benefit.

The theories of Spitz and Bowlby have had widespread and profound influence upon Western child-development theory. Indeed, it has become quite common in Western psychology to equate "good mothering" with healthy child development—and, conversely, to blame the occurrence of psychopathology in young children on infantile deprivation caused by the lack of sufficient maternal nurturance.[3]

In recent years, however, criticism of the Bowlby-Spitz theories has been articulated with increasing frequency. Such criticism has been both technical and political. On the technical side, many child-development specialists now argue that since the theories of infant deprivation formulated by Spitz and Bowlby were based upon limited studies of "special" (institutionalized) foster-care children, their results cannot mechanically be extrapolated to apply to children raised in more "normal" (that is, noninstitutionalized) environments.[4] Politically, the criticism stems from the implication—spelled out by subsequent interpreters of the Bowlby-Spitz hypotheses—that "healthy" children cannot be reared in any setting other than that of the nuclear family, preferably with a mother who devotes the major portion of her time to the nurturance of her children.[5] The implication is that mothers who work outside the home or who are otherwise unavailable for full-time maternal duty may be depriving their offspring of one of the essential requisites for healthy emotional development—a symbiotic physical and psychological reciprocity with a mothering person. This latter implication has been strongly questioned by some contemporary observers on the dual grounds that it both denies, a priori, the nurturant potential of pluralistic styles of child rearing and fails to allow for cross-cultural variations in the social context of maternal nurturance.[6]

Bearing in mind both the Spitz-Bowlby hypotheses and the recent criticisms of them, one may ask whether Western theoretical interpretations of personality development, with their (often unstated) bias in favor of a strong nuclear family and a maternal-centered attachment bond, are too ethnocentric and culture-bound to be of significant utility in helping to understand the process of human attachment bonding in other, substantially different cultural and institutional milieux. Specifically, the following questions may be asked: Just how "different" is the parent-child relationship in contemporary China? Just how significant are such differences in terms of the "healthy" emotional development of Chinese children? What kinds of "bonding messages" are communicated to these children, and how are such messages transmitted? Have these messages (and/or the mechanisms of their transmission) changed appreciably from traditional times to the present? And what are the sociopsychological implications of such continuity/change?

PERSONALITY DEVELOPMENT AND THE FORMATION OF THE "I"

The authors begin this inquiry by relating a remark made several years ago by a young Chinese mother in Hong Kong. "You know," she said, "the Chinese child does not belong to the mother as in American society. The Chinese child belongs to the entire [extended] family." This almost off-handed remark is at once both exceedingly obvious and extremely profound—obvious because conventional anthropological and sociological wisdom indicate that Chinese culture has always emphasized the importance of collective bonds of human solidarity over individualized bonds, and profound because it points to a fundamental difference between Western and Chinese styles of early childhood socialization.

In all societies, regardless of cultural particularities, the infantile ego must be supported and nurtured for the human being to achieve a "normal" adjustment to its external environment. Thus, all infants need food, shelter, and affection in order to survive in a physical or human sense in any culture. But the form and boundaries in which such basic support is provided may be highly variable. Such structural variation, in turn, has a differential impact upon human personality development.

It is generally believed that the human infant is born into an undifferentiated world. No boundary is perceived between the "self" and the external environment. It is also believed that the very young infant, from the age of two months on, perceives himself to be united with his mother in an "omnipresent system—a dual unity within one common boundary."[7] This period is known as the symbiotic phase of infantile development. Mother is perceived as a separate "object" only gradually, over a period of many months. According to Margaret Mahler, the infant's tentative experimentation at separation-individuation begins at about six months of age.[8]

It is widely believed that the very young infant perceives himself to be omnipotent—"the creator of the world." Food arrives *because* he is hungry. Mother and father exist *because* he needs them. This stage of "primary narcissism" is regarded as a critical phase of development, with profound implications for both healthy and pathological personality growth.[9]

In the West it is generally held that the stage of primary narcissism lays the foundation for strong ego growth. If the child experiences overwhelming frustration of its early needs, the budding infantile sense that the "I" can achieve some mastery over its environment is diminished. At the same time, however, and in the natural course of events, a certain amount of "healthy" frustration occurs—frustration that is necessary for the growth of a strong ego. For if the world does not impose itself on the growing child, how else can he learn that he is not, in fact, omnipotent, and that—of critical importance—there are boundaries between himself and the outer world? Thus, for example, one of the prime symptoms of schizophrenia is a weakened or nonexistent ability to distinguish between one's inner fantasies and the realities of external life—that is, a blurring of the boundaries between the internal and external environments. In this connection it is interesting to note that schizophrenia is the one mental disorder that is currently acknowledged to exist in the People's Republic of China (PRC).[10]

American culture encourages a strong one-to-one attachment bond, and consequently fosters a powerful sense of the individual ego's impact on its environment. Feeding, for example, has largely moved away from being a strictly scheduled affair to one where the demands of the hungry infant are attended to when and as they are initiated by the baby. Moreover, American society imposes rather strict cultural sanctions against group care of infants. Reflecting the theories of Spitz and Bowlby, mentioned earlier, American society is biased in the direction of valuing a lengthy one-to-one dependency period wherein the symbiotic ties between mother and infant are regarded as vitally important to healthy infantile emotional growth.

A young American infant, nurtured primarily by one adult to whom it must adapt in the absence of other significant care-taking persons, typically develops a strong cathectic bond with this primary nurturing figure. Within this dyadic structural context, the infant normally begins to regard himself as an enormously important individual vis-a-vis his or her "significant other." An infant is generally fed and otherwise comforted upon its own demands within a bonding structure characterized by a powerful, undiluted relationship with primarily one adult. From the beginning of life, American society thus provides the foundation upon which a powerful sense of the significance of the individual ego can flourish.

Even in unconventional settings—such as Synanon, one of the few successful communes in the United States where children are reared collectively—mothers are required to live with their own infants for the first six months of life. Thereafter, when the infant normally is able to distinguish between its own mother and others (as well as between itself and the external environment), the infant is moved to the "children's house," where it receives more pluralistic and diffuse nurturance. Here is an example of how one American counter-culture has adapted a basically alien style of communal child rearing to what is essentially—and probably unconsciously—a culturally syntonic pattern of maternal-centered bonding. In this manner a collective institution has been infused with the American preoccupation with individualism. Synanon's infants consequently receive a basic initial foundation in an individualized relationship wherein the infant "belongs" to its mother, albeit temporarily.

PERSONALITY DEVELOPMENT AND CHINESE CULTURE

Just as Americans unconsciously express their individualistic value orientations through subtle behaviors toward their children, so too does the contemporary Chinese approach to child rearing express a fundamentally culturally syntonic style.

According to Erik Erikson, a good portion of that which is regarded as identity is unconsciously determined.[11] Identity is the synthesis of many aspects of socialization but, according to Erikson, all societies foster child-rearing values that insure that their members will become functional in the adult culture.[12] For example, the "rugged individualist"—a highly valued American archetype—would be an outcast in Chinese society. And this is as true today, under communism, as it was a hundred years ago, when individual entrepreneurial initiative was regarded as a threat to Confucian cultural orthodoxy.

Because the process of identity formation begins at birth, is gradual, subtle, and partially unconscious, much of what individuals and societies regard as "correct" child-rearing practice is highly resistant to induced change, or manipulation. Thus, Richard Wilson has noted that "while a government or party may decree or advocate changes in the ways in which people interrelate, the styles of speech that adults use with children, the daily and generally mild sanctions employed in child training, parental expectations about what constitutes good behavior, are types of attitudes and actions that are extremely resistant to radical change."[13]

The Chinese child begins life as a member of a group. He does not belong to the mother alone, but to the entire extended family. Consequently, Chinese society does not emphasize the nurturance of the ego-centered "I" as the core element of the budding personality. This early socialization pattern is reflected in adult culture by the well-known traditional Chinese emphasis on group norms and group membership—an emphasis that in many important respects continues to be paramount in contemporary China.

While contemporary Chinese propaganda may encourage loyalty to the collective or state, above loyalty to one's family (or self), the Chinese government has been remarkably tolerant of traditional child-rearing practices in many parts of rural China, interfering only minimally with the strong local (village and family) ties that were a hallmark of premodern agrarian culture.[14] And those changes that have occurred in contemporary China, such as the growth of group care for infants and children in urban areas, have integrated traditional elements of the cultural emphasis on group solidarity and the submersion of the self.

Thus, there is a continuity of values on two levels. First, government interference in the dynamics of family life in rural China has often been more rhetorical than real. And second, in those sectors where change has occurred, as in schools and urban child-care centers, both the language and the style of communication utilized continue to manifest long-standing Chinese values and modes of presentation.

Examples of stylistic continuity in value emphasis include the following:

The five Confucian kinship relations have been replaced with the "five loves" (love of country, love of leaders, love of labor, love of science, and love of public property).

There is continued emphasis on the notion that patriotic conduct and public spiritedness are rooted in love for parents and relatives. (Thus, Charles Ridley et al. observe that while strict conformity with traditional rules of obedience between family members of varying statuses is no longer official policy in the PRC, the family is still regarded as the foundation for obedience and proper behavior toward the state.)[15]

The duty of children to parents has been supplanted by the duty of children to "serve the people," to respect and love Chairman Mao (at least until his recent death), the Party, and the People's Liberation Army (PLA)—a substitution that retains the traditional style of piety while providing new objects to be loved and cherished.

Traditional deemphasis of the individual ego, or self, vis-a-vis the interests of the family or clan has been superseded by the subordination of self-interest to the collective or state. In either case, adaptation of the individual to group norms and values is paramount; and while the parents no longer theoretically "own" the child's body, the state, as a surrogate parent, does.

The Confucian notion that external standards of conduct and behavior, once internalized, can serve to eliminate conflict and generate harmony remains a firmly held cultural value in contemporary Chinese society. As Wilson notes, "although the socialization process may initially emphasize a formalistic learning and enactment of morals, it is assumed that ultimately these precepts will be internalized as an aspect of one's positive identity and that one will become completely 'sincere.' In other words, there will be harmony between the ideal of the self and the actuality of behavior and thought."[16]

Although Confucian ideology is no longer the guiding doctrine of the Chinese state, this contemporary equation of the inner person with the totality of its external behaviors is clearly traditional in origin.

INFANCY: THE FIRST STAGE

While other stylistic similarities and parallels exist, some possible ramifications of the above-mentioned continuities in cultural orientation for the personality development of the Chinese child will now be explored. First, what is the significance of the child's attachment and adjustment to family and society where group solidarity (as opposed to an intense mother/infant dyad) is emphasized as the foundation of child rearing?

Wilson, believing that there is a common value base governing parenting styles in both Taiwan and mainland China, has argued that the solidarity of the group and the submersion of the individual's identity into a larger, more important identity is perhaps the most constant and enduring theme of childhood education for both Mainlanders and Taiwanese. . . . Norms of conformity and deviance are among the most heavily sanctioned in the society. Whatever one's inner feelings, loyalty to the group—to one's family, school, friends, and above all, political loyalty to the state—is the *sine qua non* of adequate conformity. From early childhood on, expressions of disloyalty or deviance, of whatever nature, call into question one's membership status in the group and subject one to punishment, usually ostracism and shaming.[17]

In order to foster a reasonably sturdy personality as well as a capacity to submit to collective interests, the young child's psychic (emotional and libidinal) needs must be brought into balance both internally and with the demands of his external environment. In this connection, a recent study by William Parish and Martin Whyte sheds light on the balancing process. In their investigation of family life in Kwangtung, Parish and White found that young infants are generally attended to on demand for the first year of life, during which time they are nurtured freely according to their needs.[18] According to Erikson, a child's basic trust in the safety and responsiveness of his earliest environment provides the foundation for an adult personality that is on balance more trusting than mistrusting—both of itself and of the external world. Such security must be provided in infancy lest the completely vulnerable baby feel totally overwhelmed and impotent, in which case severe physical, mental, and emotional damage would occur. But since such damage is apparently no more in evidence in contemporary China than anywhere else, it must be assumed that Chinese children are given sufficient infantile support and nurturance, and that their ego-building requirements are thus basically satisfied, in the first years of life. In this regard, Parish and Whyte's observations concerning infantile nurturing are highly instructive.

However, the Chinese infant's needs are rarely met within an exclusive, one-to-one relationship. Thus, Parish and Whyte found that in rural Kwangtung

a variety of ways are found to care for young children while allowing their mothers to work in the fields. The most common is to have the paternal grandmother . . . serve as a baby sitter during the day. The mother will then nurse the infant when she comes home for meals, and at other times a hungry child may be carried out to the fields by the grandmother, to be nursed there by the mother. . . . Most of the attention comes from the womenfolk of the family: the mother, grandmother, and older sisters.[19]

In a similar vein, Ruth Sidel has observed that in the context of urban group child care, "children from a very young age receive multiple mothering—from the mother, while she is nursing, from the time the work day ends until it begins again the next day, and on her day off; from the several "aunties" in the nursing room, for they all care for the children; and quite possibly from a grand-mother who may live with the family."[20]

While many foreign observers have reported that Chinese infants generally receive tender affection in the first years of life, the care givers are frequently multiple and the child must therefore develop its sensitivities so that it can be responsive to several adults. (In this connection, it should be noted that the human infant is never a totally passive receptor, but adapts, responds to, and initiates subtle behaviors in the adults who provide for its care. Thus, babies adjust their behavior and physical responses to the feel, sound, sight, and touch of the "mothering" person or persons.)[21]

It may be hypothesized that Chinese society provides the framework in which the infant learns, from the beginning, to be sensitive to subtle signals from a small group of primary care-giving adults (as opposed to a single primary care giver). Since parent/infant bonding is not usually exclusive in Chinese society, the child's sense that it and its mother are omnipotently and symbiotically united is interrupted from the start. Parent/infant bonding is therefore diluted, and the intensity of the bond is thus proportionately lessened.

While American mothers and infants typically tend to become acutely attuned to each other, signals from children who are the recipients of multiple mothering may be less discretely discerned. Hence, the Chinese child not only must learn to adjust to multiple signals, but must also, from the outset, learn that he is not the central and exclusive focus of life to one mothering figure. Insofar as the infantile ego gradually develops from the internalization of both the satisfying and frustrating aspects of its own body as well as its external environment,[22] the Chinese infant's ego must therefore adapt to and internalize a group-oriented, group-centered world.

The fact that contemporary Chinese culture seems to encompass clear and standardized beliefs concerning the nature of children, and the proper style in which to rear them, provides a needed consistency in the multiple-style approach to child care, while at the same time subtly diminishing the Chinese child's individuality.[23] Thus, a visiting delegation of American child-development specialists, observing the interaction between a Chinese mother and her infant, noted that "she seemed to be more concerned with keeping the baby comfortable than with engaging [its] attention, a pattern we often observed in the treatment of infants in China and consistent with the view we heard expressed on several occasions by nursery school personnel that in the first year of life 'children can't do very much.'"[24]

A further example of the contemporary Chinese deemphasis of childhood individuality is contained in a remark made to the American child-development team in course of its visit to the PRC. The researchers were attempting to discuss children's innate differences in intelligence when their host stated, "It is important for us to believe that all children are the same."[25]

As mentioned earlier, all societies—often unconsciously—induce behaviors in children that are consistent with adult values and cultural norms. Similarly, all societies tend to foster beliefs about the nature of children that will support efforts to mold the desired adult personality or character traits. In China the lack of highly focused attention to the infant's particular (individual) needs and behaviors, coupled with the belief that "infants sleep a lot, . . . prefer not to play, and adults accommodate to the infant's 'basic nature,'"[26] combine to induce conforming behavior in children with little effort made to elicit or foster individualized differences through stimulation of, or interaction with, the child.

In rural China, families are generally far too busy with the business of survival to stimulate too many aspects of the infant's individuality. In city nurseries, on the other hand, infants are trained to conform to an externally imposed schedule for eating, sleeping, and eliminating. Moreover, babies in such nurseries cannot be picked up every time they cry—there are simply too many of them for such individualized attention.[27]

Fortunately (and probably not accidentally), Chinese beliefs concerning the nature of children are such that standardized adult behavior toward children is felt to be in accordance with human nature. Hence, there is a notable lack of conflict between cultural expectation and social behavior, with the result that Chinese parents do not seem to experience the same type of emotional turmoil often expressed by American parents—turmoil occasioned by the fear that they are somehow inhibiting the healthy psychological growth and development of their children. While the Chinese may be highly conformist, they are clearly able to provide a strong and unambivalent value base that is both reassuring to—and highly supportive of—their young children.

One of the major complaints frequently articulated by American parents is the feeling that they do not "know how to raise their children." American society is in a transitional state. Young parents no longer have the traditional support of and advice from senior members of the extended family; and new support systems have been extremely slow to evolve. Moreover, while Americans generally tend to value a lengthy dependency relationship between mother and child, upwards of 40 percent of the American labor force is now female.[28] Thus, while mothers are increasingly leaving the home to accept outside employment, American society has been shockingly slow to develop adequate alternative forms of child care. In this situation, cultural expectations (the "good mother") and socioeconomic needs (the "working mother") seem to be drastically out of synch on many levels, leaving many American parents anxious and bewildered. Hence, there are considerable costs being paid by the American family for its adherence to such traditional cultural values as "rugged individualism" and the inbred fear of and hostility toward community planning and group conformity. This is not to say that Chinese society incurs no human costs in its rigid emphasis on planning and conformity—only that the costs are quite different. This point will be discussed later.

THE TODDLER PERIOD

Thus far there have been briefly described some of the ways in which Chinese early child-rearing practices lay the foundation for group-oriented identity formation and a high degree of social conformity in adult behavior. Children who are well nurtured, but who are believed to need—and therefore receive—fairly standardized care as infants, are not likely to develop strong feelings that they, as individuals, can exert a major impact on their environment. From the beginning of life, Chinese society communicates the message that group or collective effort, and attachment, is both necessary and preferable to more individualized endeavor.

Although such communications commence, as has been seen, in early infancy, it is during the subsequent toddler period (ages one to three) that a new equilibrium must be achieved between the normally heightened strivings of the growing child and the increasing demands of the dominant culture.

According to Mahler, the young infant psychologically separates himself from the symbiotic attachment to his mother and begins to individuate as a distinct "self" over an extended period (roughly three years) of "hatching."[29] In her view, motility is a key development in the process of individuation:

> The importance of walking for the emotional development of the child cannot be overestimated. Walking gives the toddler an enormous increase in reality discovery and testing of the world at his own control and magic mastery. . . . We found in boys and girls alike that in the very next month following the attainment of active free locomotion, great strides were made toward asserting their individuality. This seems to be the first step toward identify formation.[30]

In a similar vein, Erikson hypothesizes that the years between one and three are those in which the child develops a strong urge for autonomy. He describes this normal developmental stage as a critical period in which the foundation is laid for the subsequent, crucial perception that individual autonomy may be attained without suffering a debilitating sense of shame and self-doubt.[31] According to this hypothesis, the toddler gains an increasing sense of autonomy when his newly acquired ability to walk and move away from his caretakers is not met with overly humiliating control or anxiety on the part of parents and family. Erikson postulates the additional notion that control over bodily functions—including both motility and elimination—provides the toddler with an added sense that his budding ego is master of his own body.

On this latter point, Richard Solomon has argued that the traditionally relaxed approach of Chinese parents toward toddler motility and bowel training conveys the message that personal control (individual autonomy) is not highly valued.[32] While this view is highly suggestive, it can be argued that the reverse is more likely true. According to Erikson, the child's rudimentary sense of personal autonomy is significantly enhanced when the adult permits him to gradually develop his own bodily controls, at his own pace.

It appears that a subtle balance is achieved in Chinese childhood socialization between the toddler's newfound freedom to move and gain gradual control over his own body (which is highly supportive of the budding ego) and the imposition of strict external discipline vis-a-vis the toddler's outward behavior (which may provoke anxiety, shame, and doubt). Thus, the Chinese child's primitive ego is permitted considerable autonomy through the relaxation of certain parental controls, while outward displays of deviant behavior are at the same time harshly and unambivalently curtailed. Accordingly, it is the hypothesis here that this delicate balancing of individual needs for bodily autonomy and societal needs for behavioral conformity may contribute to the formation of basically intact and "healthy"—but highly controlled and other-directed—adult Chinese citizens. Rather than blindly echoing the common cultural bias which holds that a "mature" adult must be an American-type autonomous and independent citizen, it can be simply pointed out that Chinese culture supports the growth of a healthy infantile ego, while at the same time ensuring that the ego has the capacity to submit to external control and discipline.

This combination of a relaxed attitude toward infantile motility and bodily functions and the subsequent imposition of strict behavioral control during the toddler period is a phenomenon that clearly dates back to pre-Communist Chinese society. Writing in 1946, Olga Lange described the Chinese approach to toddler socialization in the following terms:

> Children under two years of age are the only family members not subjected to any discipline. At the age of two, and sometimes before, the children hear the first "don'ts," as their education begins. As of old, the main aim of education is to raise obedient children, devoted to their family, working hard at school or in the house, and living peacefully with their sisters and brothers and with the neighboring children. . . . To educate their children in the spirit of obedience and virtue, Chinese parents of all classes . . . find it useful to submit them to strict discipline.[33]

As an illustration of the hypothesis concerning the continuity of values and parenting styles in pre- and postliberation China, the following passage from a contemporary study of Kwangtung villages proves highly illuminating when taken in conjunction with Lang's 1946 observations:

> The life of the toddler in our villages seems to be one of lax supervision but fairly harsh discipline. Once children are weaned and able to get around on their own they are not kept at home, but are allowed to roam and play about the village. . . . But when toddlers are disobedient or get into trouble, parents or other caretakers are strict

in a traditional sense. . . . A naughty child may be yelled at, cuffed in the ear or rear, or beaten with a bamboo rod. . . . The Chinese government's campaign . . . against corporal punishment of children may have reduced reliance on this tactic in urban areas and even in rural schools, but apparently not in homes in rural Kwangtung.[34]

It is interesting to note that the traditional emphases on group norms and group conformity seem to receive even greater stress in contemporary China's urban areas than in rural environments. Certainly, there are proportionately more nurseries and child-care facilities in China's cities; hence, relatively greater numbers of urban youngsters can be cared for in such collective institutions.

It is in the group-care setting that Chinese children receive the most orderly and preplanned indoctrination into what are considered "modern" Chinese values. Teachers are employed not only to provide proper care for the children while their parents are at work, but also to insure a proper "moral" environment as well. And since teachers are able to devote more time and thought to implementing programs that foster the "proper" kinds of attitudes and values in children than the children's own hard-working (and hence only intermittently care-taking) parents, the traditional emphasis on obedience and group conformity is consequently fostered with great clarity and purposefulness in the group setting—particularly (and paradoxically) in the more modern urban schools and child-care centers.

Joerome Kagan noted many interesting examples of how adult behavior in urban group child-care settings served effectively to communicate values of group conformity and submersion of self to Chinese infants and toddlers. The phenomenon of free toddler motoricity observed in rural settings was seen to be more strictly inhibited in urban facilities. Additionally, there seemed to be greater demands placed upon urban youngsters to adjust to group norms and expectations. Kagan thus observed that

> Caretakers do not generally encourage nursery-aged children to be freely mobile or to play alone for long periods of time. They also discourage infants one year or older from crawling, . . . walking about freely, or choosing a preferred solitary activity. . . . All activity is typically initiated by the adult teacher. . . . Infants were described to us as dependent, helpless, and relatively inactive, and they appeared to be cared for without great effort to stimulate their sensory and intellectual development. . . . There was an obvious preference by teachers for group over individual activity. . . . There was adult restraint of what is apparently considered excessive spontaneity and motoricity, and, for an American, surprisingly little discernible variability among the children.[35]

Kagan et al made another interesting observation about the youngest preschool-aged children—that they were "quiet and subdued" relative to older children. "Children under three years of age, at least in the presence of strange visitors, were quiet and affectively subdued—in some contrast to the kindergarten children who were verbal, expressive, and socially responsive. The nursery children loosened up after a while, of course, but the younger ones especially never showed the gaiety and liveliness of kindergartners."[36]

Children of the age described by Kagan are those whose motor abilities have been only recently attained. According to Mahler, children in this "practicing subphase" are subject to periods of exhilaration, when they are "impervious to knocks and falls." At other times, such children manifest "low-key" behavior, as "when they became aware that mother was absent from the room. At such times, their gestural and performance motility slowed down, their interest in their surroundings diminished, and they appeared to be preoccupied with inwardly concentrated attention."[37]

It is noteworthy, according to Mahler, that it is at about three years of age that the separation-individuation process is more or less resolved, for better or for worse. Observers of Chinese children have frequently noted that at around three years the children tend to be, on the average, quite lively. Perhaps at three a sufficient resolution of the process of separation-individuation has been achieved so that energy previously absorbed in adjusting to the various separations to which the children are subjected can be released in the form of an active interest in the external environment. In any event, the manner in which (and the degree to which) separation-individuation is achieved during the toddler years remains important throughout the lifetime of the individual. As Mahler has noted, this early period of childhood development "reverberates throughout the life cycle. It is never finished; it remains always active; new phases of the life cycle see new derivatives of the earliest processes still at work."[38]

It may thus be hypothesized that the (primarily urban) Chinese emphasis on control and restraint of motoricity, combined with the necessarily limited availability, on group-care settings, of what Mahler terms "nurturing supplies" from which the child may "refuel" during the toddler "hatching" period, may have significant implications for the Chinese adult's mode of relating to others in his/her environment; for in contemporary urban group child-care settings, those adaptive mechanisms that provide a necessary balance between instinctual gratification and instinctual denial appear to be weighted in favor of greater behavioral control. As a result, one wonders if adults reared in the contemporary urban group-care setting are likely to be less autonomous—and to manifest greater self-doubt—than adults socialized in the traditional rural settings.

It is not suggested here that it is the group setting that is, in itself, a cause for concern; for as Sidel and others have noted, Chinese infants and toddlers receive warm and loving attention from their urban group caretakers.[39] Rather, attention is simply called to the fact that the apparent lack of balance between self-gratification and external control that characterizes the contemporary urban group-oriented style of infant and toddler socialization may have certain unanticipated behavioral consequences in the future. Since the institutionalized style of group child care is relatively new in China, and since most societies are only imperfectly capable of critical self-examination with regard to such subtle factors as their mode(s) of value transmission to young children, it may be many years before Chinese authorities sense that they may have unintentionally over-emphasized one aspect of their traditional culture—external behavioral control and conformity—at the expense of another, equally important balancing ele-ment—autonomous motility and body control. Thus, one is left to ponder the psychological implications of such recent urban innovations as the imposition of "orderly," group-oriented bowel-training techniques, as described by Sidel. "Toi-let training is collective and is begun at a year or a year and a half. . . . Between twelve and eighteen months, the teachers begin toilet training the children in the nursing rooms. After breakfast, the children set on white enamel potties and all have their bowel movements together!"[40]

While there may be greater attention paid to obedience and conformity in urban than in rural Chinese environments, there are also certain continuities in methods of child training in both settings. In both, infantile needs and impulses are gratified, but external behaviors are clearly and unambivalently controlled. Thus, for example, in rural Kwangtung, fighting and stealing among children are absolutely prohibited by adults,[41] while in urban settings conflict is denied an external outlet by teachers who maintain control by initiating frequent changes in activities. In both settings, the child learns to gratify his libidinal and aggres-sive impulses within the context of an adult expectation that children must curtail overly aggressive or disharmonious behavior.

All societies, theoretically, unconsciously rear children so that instinctual gratification will be modified by social and cultural expectations. Indeed, ac-cording to Sigmund Freud, such modification (or repression) is the very essence of civilization.[42] The point is, however, that societies do this in vastly differing ways. While theorists can never be certain just why certain cultural styles evolve, the product—the adult culture—can be observed, as can the methods employed to socialize children to fulfill adult cultural expectations.

One can only speculate, for example, as to why Chinese parents have his-torically been lenient toward motility and bodily functions in very young chil-dren. Clearly, not all agrarian poverty cultures resolve the tension between grati-fication and control in the manner of the Chinese. Thus, in one study of the rural poor in Guatemala, it was found that infants and toddlers were severely restricted motorically. The children of impoverished Guatemalan peasants were rarely permitted to venture outside their huts, where their mothers remained virtually full time.[43] These poor Guatemalan women did not work in the fields as rural Chinese mothers have historically done. Hence, the fact that the Chinese mother had traditionally allowed others in her extended family to share the tasks of child rearing in order that she might work in the fields is not entirely explicable in purely economic terms.

Whatever the reason, one culture almost totally inhibits motoricity, while the other culture allows great freedom. Additionally, one culture mandates a strong mother/infant symbiotic bond, while the other shares the child with the extended family. It may not, therefore, be strict economic necessity that has fostered the traditional Chinese child-rearing style of motoric freedom combined with strict behavioral discipline.

Undoubtedly, many factors have contributed to the evolution of Chinese socialization techniques. There is a strong suspicion that, for whatever reasons particular child-rearing styles evolve (and these have not been satisfactorily explained in the existing anthropological literature), they are not simply accidental, but rather are shaped by (and in turn help shape) unconscious cultural motifs that lay the foundation for the development of certain discrete combinations of adult personality traits.

One example of the Chinese adult culture's expression of an early and unconscious approach to child training is provided by the Chinese preoccupation with the synthesis of extremes. Many observers have noted the traditionally strong Chinese emphasis on the need to control conflict in order to achieve a harmonious way of life. The contemporary official Chinese preoccupation with the synthesis of dialectical opposites through struggle is but a modern expression of this long-standing cultural value. In this connection, it may be hypothesized that the well-known Chinese cultural sensitivity to polarized tendencies and the quest for an acceptable resolution of such opposing forces may have their roots in the Chinese infant's struggle to resolve the contradiction between extreme freedom in bodily and motoric functions and the need to submit and conform to strict, externally imposed standards of discipline—that is, the struggle to resolve the latent tension between private, inner freedom and public, outward behavioral control.

It is also interesting to speculate what might happen to this cultural theme in the future, since many urban Chinese children who are currently being raised in group-care institutions are not permitted the traditional exploratory freedoms of motility and control over bodily functions. For these urban children, the traditional conflict between private freedom and public conformity appears to be largely suppressed, rather than behaviorally induced.

At a less psychologically primitive level, the traditional Chinese preoccupation with conflict resolution may also be a cultural reflection of certain personal dilemmas confronted from the earliest years of life. Almost from the beginning, the Chinese child must learn to achieve a tolerable balance between personal, private needs and the ever-present expectation that he/she must conform to the demands of the group.

On the basis of a thorough study of the Chinese communist educational curriculum from the earliest years of primary schooling, Ridley et al. observed that "'Communist morality' is . . . primarily a social ethic (a collective conscience) rather than a personal ethic (an individual conscience). The standard for judgment of a person's behavior becomes how closely it conforms to the principles of 'communist morality,' or in other words, how well it conforms to the essential requirements of the collective interest."[44]

Historically, the Chinese have believed and continue to believe that the root of patriotism is the child's love and devotion to the family.[45] However, the inculcation of "proper" values and behavior begins long before the child's formal exposure to indoctrination in the elementary school. During the earliest period of childhood, the socialization process involving the communication of values operates—largely unconsciously—through adult socializers. Continuity of values is maintained through the unconscious transmission of adult attitudes to off-spring, who in turn later—and also unconsciously—transmit the same (or similar) values through their behavior toward their own children. Hence, the lack of stimulation of individualized infant personality traits, together with the demand that the toddler learn to curb outward expressions of overly aggressive or assertive behavior, sets the stage for the future development of the group-oriented adult.

One particular method employed to curb the aggressive impulses—and shape the personalities—of very young children in China is of crucial relevance during the toddler period. This is the method of shaming, which is applied via the threat of literal or figurative abandonment. During the child's normal developmental struggle to separate, individuate, and achieve a rudimentary sense of autonomy, this threatened withdrawal of love would be expected to have an enormous impact on the immature psyche. Thus, in his comparative study of Mainland and Taiwanese youngsters, Wilson found that "The most frequently utilized injunction of both parents and teachers is the phrase, 'If you do that, I will not like (or love) you.'"[46] This threat of withdrawal of affection is intimately related to the traditional Chinese disciplinary technique of shaming. Wilson describes this relationship in the context of current Chinese political socialization practices:

> Chinese socialization practices develop anxieties with regard to interpersonal relations in which fear of abandonment (loss of affection or approval by significant others and the group) is accentuated. Explicit moral precepts reduce ambiguity about appropriate and inappropriate behavior and function powerfully as guides which can help the individual to secure the goals of approval of others and avoidance of anxiety about shaming. One's own behavior becomes a matter of acute concern, and the behavior of others is subjected to continuing scrutiny.[47]

According to Gerhard Piers, shame anxiety in children is frequently—and often unconsciously—triggered by the fear (or threat) of parental abandonment. In his words, it is "based on the fear of the parent who walks away 'in disgust.'" Such fear "draws its terror from the earlier established and probably ubiquital separation anxiety."[48]

Since the manipulation of shame anxiety has been and continues to be a basic method of Chinese childhood socialization, it is assumed that this method colors the fabric of parent-child interactions during the toddler stage of development; for it is during the toddler stage, as has been seen, that all human beings begin the normal struggle to achieve a sense of individual autonomy without developing an overwhelming sense of shame. This early quest for autonomy has been etiologically linked to the subsequent development of certain adult depressive syndromes:

> As the child begins to assert his autonomy and sense of will, some parents become threatened by such early assertions. . . . Control may be instituted using the threat of withdrawal of love and parental nurturance. Of course, this would mean "death" for a child at this age. Against such overwhelming forces, the child often goes down in defeat. He may become overly compliant to please the parents, gaining their acceptance and sacrificing his autonomy. He is left with a strong sense of self-doubt and shame.[49]

It has also been hypothesized that the "shamed" individual is likely to fall prey repeatedly to the demands, wishes, and expectations of others, trying to "live up to these foreign expectations as best he can, in order not to lose the protection and love of his surroundings."[50]

While it is critically important not to confuse what is considered psychopathology in one culture with what is regarded as "normal" in another, the above hypotheses concerning the making of an overly compliant, self-doubting personality may have relevance in this attempt to understand one widely noted element of the "modal" Chinese personality. It should be remembered, however, that these hypotheses were formulated in the context of extreme and discrete symptoms of individual neurosis, and they may therefore not be wholly or mechanically applicable to the analysis of an alien cultural milieu. Hence, they are presented here as merely suggestive, rather than as definitive in a cross-cultural sense.

In this connection, it must also be remembered that many American parents utilize an implicit threat of abandonment when they inhibit their toddlers from stubbornly running off by invoking the possibility that they will "let him go" or, more drastic still, that they will "leave without him." In the Chinese cultural context, however, it is the combination of such parental threats with the high value placed on conformity to group norms that ostensibly contributes to the Chinese style of maintaining the appearance of outward behavioral compliance. Moreover, it is this combination of cultural traits that gives rise to the widely noted Chinese concern over "losing face"—that is, fear of being ostracized by one's primary group of significant others. While such fear is by no means unique to Chinese culture, it is nevertheless a central element of that culture, in both its traditional and contemporary forms.

Closely related to the Chinese concern with "saving face" is the fact that Chinese society has never been child-centered in the same way as, for example, American society. In American culture, families are conceived of as having come together primarily to produce—and insure the protection of—children. In China, however—and this is true of both traditional and modern China—children are conceived primarily to insure the protection and survival of the adult and elderly members of the family. Lamenting this lack of child centeredness in Chinese society, Mao Zedong in 1953 made an impassioned plea on behalf of the rights of children:

> We of the older generation were deprived of our due, for adults simply didn't bother themselves about their children. Adults had a table to eat their meals at while children had to do without one. Children had no say in the family, and if they cried they were sure to get slapped. In the new China of today we must change our approach and think more in the interest of our children and youth.[51]

Despite such exhortations, however, the social utility of children in China continues to be defined largely in terms of service to others, though the state (or "the people") has replaced the family as the primary object of loyal devotion. Thus, visitors to contemporary China almost uniformly note that the standard response of Chinese children to the question, "What do you want to do when you grow up?" is a variant of the formulaic "serve the people." The fact that one's social value in China is thus predicated on one's usefulness to others (the family, the state, or the people), combined with the powerful socializing tool of shaming (with its concomitant underlying fear of abandonment) produces, for the child, a highly contingent—as opposed to an unconditionally secure—status in the family and society.

One primary function of parents and family is to provide young, vulnerable children with a sense of safety both from their own instincts and from external danger. This protective function is one of the most basic requisites of human survival. If, as appears to be the case in China, the child's continued acceptance by his significant others (family or state) is contingent upon his ultimate utility to these "others" (rather than upon their utility to him), he will normally learn to behave in socially accepted ways, doing whatever is necessary to maintain his sense of safety and security as a "favored" group member. Thus, Wilson has noted that "during the socialization of the Chinese, great stress is placed upon learning and internalizing an appropriate set of ideals concerning proper behavior. Failure to behave in terms of these ideals will subject the individual to a loss of positive identification about himself—to a loss of face."[52]

Conformity, therefore, becomes a prime requisite of psychic survival. Since the loss of face (or shame) triggers the fear of abandonment (based on the most primitive separation anxiety), it is not difficult to understand why Chinese children are typically, at least on the surface, highly compliant; for if the child's basic sense of security is derived within a context of contingent supportive relationships within the family (or society), then the costs (both psychic and, in extreme cases, physical) of nonconformity are simply too great.

Consciously or unconsciously, contemporary Chinese Communist propaganda makes effective use of this ubiquitous fear of abandonment through the technique of recounting endless tales of the family's extreme vulnerability to external vicissitudes in the preliberation period, under feudalism and under Kuomintang rule. Tales of suffering (and danger) experienced in the "bitter past"—always contrasted with the relative security of the "benevolent present"—are not lost on Chinese children. As Ridley et al. noted in their thematic study of elementary school curricula in the PRC, "The two most important subcategories of this theme [i.e., 'benevolence of the new society'], 'improved conditions under the new society' and 'modernization under the new society,' occur more frequently during the first three grades than in higher grades. . . . As can be seen, this theme often involves a direct or implicit comparison with past evils."[53]

Ridley et al. also note that primary school textbooks in the PRC frequently picture Mao Zedong as the "father," the Party as the "mother," and the PLA as "wholeheartedly devoted to the welfare of the common people."[54] Additionally, where the Kuomintang is discussed in school textbooks, themes of oppression and exploitation are predominant. Thus, the message is clear: the Party, the Army, and Chairman Mao—the new "extended family"—protect the impotent and highly vulnerable biological family from the ravages of ruthless enemies. Moreover—an extremely critical factor—this new surrogate family is portrayed as eminently more able to provide needed safety and security from a hostile environment than the child's own biological family.

Added, therefore, to the Chinese child's traditional culturally induced compulsion to exhibit "acceptable" behavior (as a means of insuring primary security within the biological family) is the contemporary and equally compelling message that without the Communist state, the family itself was (and is) as vulnerable as the child.

In this connection, it is important to bear in mind that it is during the toddler period that the issue of autonomy and the formation of a rudimentary sense of separate identity become crucial. Thus, during the toddler stage a socializing tool that emphasizes conformity as the primary means of ensuring one's safety within the family will have the most powerful—and in terms of a reactive mechanism, long-lasting—effect. Because the fear of abandonment is believed to underlie the affective experience of shame, it follows that the use of shaming as a technique for controlling children's behavior will be most effective when the struggle of autonomy versus shame and doubt is developmentally most intense—that is, during the toddler years.

Just as the internalization of shame provides a powerful motive for Chinese children to conform to external behavioral norms, so too can shame be redirected and externally projected onto others as a defense mechanism. Thus, Wilson notes that

> where negative identity characteristics are perceived, anxiety will be engendered; and where this anxiety is intense, then inwardly directed or outwardly projected hostility are possible and plausible responses. . . . The imputation of shameful behavior to others may

be used as a cover for other motives, but even in those instances where this is the case, the preference for this mode of stigmatization (for which there is a distinctive phraseology) reveals the "legitimacy" in Chinese culture of citing behavior as shameful as a justification for hostility.[55]

To understand the frequency with which the projective defense is encountered in Chinese culture, one must bear in mind the powerful impact exerted by shaming and separation anxiety during the toddler period of human development.

Another defense mechanism closely related to projection is "splitting." This defense was described by the Kleinian school of psychoanalytic theory in relation to the earliest development of infantile ego-defense mechanisms. According to this theory, splitting (that is, separating objects into "good" and "bad" categories)

> allows the ego to emerge out of chaos and to order its experiences. This ordering of experience which occurs with the process of splitting into a good and bad object . . . orders the universe of the child's emotional and sensory impressions and is a precondition of later integration. It is the basis of what is later to bcome the faculty of discrimination, the origin of which is the early differentiation between good and bad.[56]

The ego-defense mechanisms of projection and splitting allow the young child to deny the bad within himself and to project such badness onto the world around him. Adults do not normally employ these mechanisms in their extreme infantile forms, but the adult's sense of badness and its opposite, idealization, clearly originate in these early and crude infantile sensations. Again according to Kleinian theory, "With splitting are connected persecutory anxiety [projection of the bad onto persecutory objects] and idealization. . . . Idealization persists in many situations such as falling in love, appreciating beauty, forming social or political ideals, . . . emotions which . . . add to the richness and variety of our lives."[57]

It is during the later stages of the toddler period that the child becomes fully aware that the mother (or parenting figure) can be physically elsewhere— that is, has an independent, separate existence. It is also during this period that the mechanism of splitting the object world is frequently employed as a defense against separation anxiety, which has become heightened by the toddler's recent discovery that he is not in control of his caretaker's comings and goings.[58]

Applying these insights to our analysis of Chinese socialization styles and practices may help us illuminate the oft-noted Chinese dualistic proclivity to idealize the "good object" (for example, the working class, the Party, Chairman Mao, and various revolutionary heroes and martyrs) and to defend against anxiety and self-doubt by vilifying the shameful conduct of the "bad object" (for example, the "five black categories," the "Gang of Four," or the "bourgeois power-holders"). Such projective and splitting mechanisms may help to account for the well-known Maoist preoccupation with "dividing one into two." Indeed, the dialectical method itself, which the Chinese Communists seem to have adopted more comfortably than any other Marxist-Leninist regime, is wholly syntonic with the Chinese cultural emphasis on the mechanisms of splitting and projection.

In Chinese society, manipulation of shame anxiety during the toddler stage (when shaming engenders intense fears of separation and abandonment) heightens the normal human tendency to seek security by attempting to become what is ideal (and therefore safe) and to deny in oneself (and project onto others) that which is subject to disapproval or ostracism.

This underlying mechanism may also shed light on the widely noted Chinese Communist political propensity for changing positions regarding good and bad objects. Thus, Lin Biao spoke of Mao Zedong's tendency suddenly to turn against those whom he had previously favored:

> Today he is saying sweet things to one group and tomorrow he condemns them to death for a non-existent crime; today he treats them as honored guests, and tomorrow they are cast into prison. For the past several decades, has there been anyone whom he has pulled up who has not been sentenced to death later on? . . . Once he has decided to offend someone, he never stops halfway. And for this he always lays the blame on others.[59]

Without necessarily affirming the objectivity of the above argument (for, after all, Lin Biao was not exactly a detached observer), it does nevertheless appear that extremes of good and bad have been frequently and quite rapidly interchanged in postliberation China. It is suggested that such apparently facile interchangeability has its cultural origins in the primitive projective and splitting defenses engendered by a shame-oriented style of early childhood socialization. Metaphorically speaking, once good becomes frustrating to a young child, it changes into bad. And if bad should become gratifying or security-enhancing, it reemerges as good. (The checkered, up-again/down-again political career of Teng Xiaoping may be another relevant case in point.)

This is not to imply that Chinese adults react to the stress of shame anxiety in exactly the same manner as do young children. Rather, it is suggested that this style "flavors" the perceptions of Chinese adults and appears odd to American eyes only because the socialization mechanisms are quite different. Unlike Chinese, Americans cling rather more tenaciously to their heroes—even when, as often occurs, they are shown to be less than ideally virtuous. (In this regard, it may be noted that our deep-seated wish to idealize our political leaders was only recently undermined by the revelations contained in the Watergate tapes—revelations that deeply shocked a naive American public unaccustomed to the idea that a president could lie or utter undeleted expletives in the Oval Office.)

We do not wish to imply that either cultural style, American or Chinese, is necessarily pathological. All cultures emphasize certain ego defenses and deemphasize others in the socialization of their children. (The English and American cultures, for example, have frequently been typified as "obsessive-compulsive," due to the extreme emphasis on cleanliness and early hygienic approaches to bodily functions.) The point here is simply that adult behavior frequently—and necessarily—reflects the dominant cultural modalities of early childhood socialization. As Hanna Segal put it,

> No experience in human development is ever cast aside or obliterated; we must remember that in the most normal individual there will be some situations which will stir up the earliest anxieties and bring into operation the earliest mechanisms of defense. Furthermore, in a well-integrated personality, all stages of development are included; none are split off and rejected.[60]

Viewed in this light, certain elements of the contemporary Chinese cultural mode of adult political and social behavior become more readily explicable as latent functions of early socialization practices. This is not to say that adult behavior is totally predetermined by socialization styles; but rather it is to point out that in a culture that emphasizes certain types of ego defenses at crucial stages of childhood development, one should not be surprised to see adults evidencing these same defense mechanisms, particularly under conditions of stress.

NOTES

1. René A. Spitz, *The First Year of Life* (New York: International Universities Press, 1965), p. 286.

2. John Bowlby, *Attachment and Loss* (New York: Basic Books, 1973), especially Vol. I. On the impact of Bowlby's work, see Jane Kessler, *Psychopathology of Childhood* (Englewood Cliffs, N.J.: Prentice-Hall, 1966); and Mia Pringle, *The Needs of Children* (New York: Schocken Books, 1975).

3. See, for example, Sheldon Glueck and Eleanor Glueck, "Working Mothers and Delinquency," *Mental Hygiene* 41 (July 1959): 321–37; and John G. Howells, *Modern Perspectives in International Child Psychiatry* (New York: Brunner/Mazel, 1969), pp. 256ff. For secondary analysis of the literature on the "bad mother" syndrome, see Carolyn Lee Baum et al., "Value Inconsistencies in Therapists' Attitudes toward Mothers," especially Ch. 2. Master's thesis, School of Social Welfare, University of California, Los Angeles, June 1977).

4. See Rochelle Paul Wortis, "The Acceptance of the Concept of the Maternal Role by Behavioral Scientists: Its Effects on Women," *American Journal of Orthopsychiatry* 41 (October 1971): 735.

5. See Alice Rossi, "Equality between the Sexes: An Immodest Proposal," *Daedalus* 93 (Spring 1964): 616–17.

6. See Wortis, "The Acceptance"; Ruth Sidel, *Women and Child Care in China* (Baltimore: Penguin Books, 1972), especially Ch. 5; and Jerome Kagan, "The Parental Love Trap," *Psychology Today* 12 (August 1978): 54–61.

7. Margaret S. Mahler, Fred Pine, and Anni Bergman, *The Psychological Birth of the Human Infant* (New York: Basic Books, 1975), p. 44.

8. Ibid., p. 54.

9. Spitz, *The First Year*, pp. 35–36, 152–232, and passim; see also Mahler et al., *Psychological Birth*, p. 42.

10. Seymour S. Kety, "Psychiatric Concepts and Treatment in China," *China Quarterly* 66 (June 1976): 315–22.

11. Erik H. Erikson, "The Concept of Identity in Race Relations: Notes and Queries," p. 233. Mimeographed.

12. Erik H. Erikson, *Childhood and Society* (New York: Norton, 1950), pp. 111–86, passim.

13. Richard W. Wilson, *Learning To Be Chinese* (Cambridge, Mass.: MIT Press, 1970), p. 5.

14. See William Parish and Martin K. Whyte, "Village and Family in Contemporary China," 1977, Ch. 11, especially pp. 21–22, 43–46. Unpublished manuscript.

15. Charles P. Ridley, Paul Godwin, and Dennis Doolin, *The Making of a Model Citizen in Communist China* (Stanford: The Hoover Institution, 1971), pp. 33–40.

16. Richard W. Wilson, "Shame and Behavior in Chinese Society," *Asian Profile* 1 (December 1973), p. 434.

17. Richard W. Wilson, "A Comparison of Political Attitudes of Taiwanese Children and Mainlander Children on Taiwan," *Asian Survey* 8 (December 1968), pp. 995–96.

18. Parish and Whyte, "Village and Family," p. 49.

19. Ibid., pp. 46, 48–49.

20. Sidel, *Women and Child Care*, p. 99.

21. See Mahler et al., *The Psychological Birth*, p. 5; also, Saul L. Brown, "Family Experience and Change," Department of Child Psychiatry, Cedars-Sinai Medical Center, Los Angeles, n.d., p. 7. Mimeographed.

22. Bruno Bettelheim, *The Children of the Dream* (New York: Avon Books, 1970), pp. 211–16.

23. Ibid.; also, Sidel, *Women and Child Care*, p. 99.

24. William Kessen, ed., *Childhood in China* (New Haven: Yale University Press, 1975), p. 25.

25. Ibid., p. 6.

26. Ibid., p. 55.

27. Sidel, *Women and Child Care*, p. 93.

28. "Women at Work," *Newsweek*, December 6, 1976, pp. 68–81.

29. Mahler et al., *The Psychological Birth*, p. 76.

30. Ibid., p. 72.

31. Erikson, *Childhood and Society*, pp. 251–54.

32. Richard Solomon, *Mao's Revolution and the Chinese Political Culture* (Berkeley and Los Angeles: University of California Press, 1971), pp. 44–47.

33. Olga Lang, *Chinese Family and Society* (New Haven: Yale University Press, 1946), p. 239.

34. Parish and Whyte, "Village and Family," pp. 50–51.

35. Kessen, *Childhood in China*, pp. 53–70.

36. Ibid., p. 55.

37. Mahler et al., *The Psychological Birth*, p. 74.

38. Ibid., p. 3.

39. Sidel, *Women and Child Care*, p. 102.

40. Ibid., p. 96.

41. Parish and Whyte, "Village and Family," p. 51.

42. Sigmund Freud, *Civilization and its Discontents* (Garden City, N.Y.: Doubleday Anchor Books, 1958).

43. Jerome Kagan and Robert E. Klein, "Cross-Cultural Perspectives on Early Development," *American Psychologist* 28 (November 1973): 949–50.

44. Ridley et al., *Making of a Model Citizen*, p. 55.

45. Ibid., pp. 39–40.

46. Wilson, "Shame and Behavior," p. 438.

47. Richard W. Wilson, "Political Authority as Moral Entrepreneur in China," in *Proceedings of the Fifth Sino-American Conference on Mainland China* (Taipei: Institute of International Relations, 1976), p. 479.

48. Gerhart Piers and Milton E. Singer, *Shame and Guilt* (Chicago: Charles C. Thomas Publishers), pp. 5–6; see also Wilson, "Shame and Behavior," pp. 432–33.

49. Kenneth Miya, "Autonomy and Depression," *Clinical Social Work Journal* 4, (1976), p. 263.

50. Ibid., p. 263.

51. Mao Tse-tung, "Take the Characteristics of Youth into Consideration," in *Selected Works of Mao Tse-tung*, Vol. 5 (Peking: Foreign Language Press, 1977), p. 97.

52. Wilson, "Shame and Behavior," p. 433.

53. Ridley et al., *The Making of a Model Citizen*, p. 106.

54. Ibid., pp. 87–161, especially p. 107.

55. Wilson, "Shame and Behavior," pp. 441–42.

56. Hanna Segal, *Introduction to the Work of Melanie Klein* (New York: Basic Books, 1964), p. 22.

57. Ibid., p. 23.

58. Mahler et al., *The Psychological Birth*, pp. 98–99.

59. This quotation is contained in the remarkable "Outline of Project 571." See Michael Y. M. Kau, ed., *The Lin Piao Affair* (White Plains, N.Y.: International Arts and Science Press, 1975), pp. 89–90.

60. Segal, *Introduction*, p. 22.

5

MODELS AS AGENTS
OF CHANGE IN CHINA

Betty B. Burch

All societies use models in one form or another as part of their socialization process. Models are used to perpetuate traditional values and to infuse new ones, to provide social cohesion by establishing a shared body of beliefs, and to adapt society to new needs and situations. They provide social stability but may also be active agents of social change. Models provide vivid, concrete examples to the people of each society, especially their young, and it is anticipated that the values and norms represented by models will be internalized by others and lead to emulative behavior. In most societies the process of model emulation is informal and achieved largely through unstructured, random suggestions by parents and teachers, through peer group interaction, or through popular literature and other media. For example, George Washington, who refused to tell a lie, according to Parson Weems's cherry-tree story, became a folk hero for the young, and in due time, when American society became more complex, he became the model-symbol of the whole nation as the revered Founding Father. In such cases individuals informally catch the popular eye for some special quality, enter the cultural stream, and are perpetuated because of their social utility.

Some societies, however, under certain circumstances deliberately create models in a formal, organized, and planned way. This is likely to take place in authoritarian systems with a new set of ideological beliefs or in societies, not necessarily authoritarian, that are in the process of economic and social modernization or of building a new state. Under these conditions state systems are more concerned with change than older, stabilized societies whose primary purpose is social stability. They have found emulation of models, who have been set up and publicized under state or official auspices, to be a very effective means for discrediting dysfunctional traditional values, making known new ones, and encouraging popular behavior consistent with new ideologies or new political and economic goals.

China has gone farther than other societies in institutionalizing the selection and publicizing of models as vehicles of socialization and as a means of social control. It exceeds others in the degree of organization, frequency and ubiquity of use, and in the political importance given to modeling in the governing system. It is an exaggerated case of human engineering for purposes of social, political, and economic change, but also for stability once the desired change has taken place. An examination of the Chinese case is therefore useful for throwing light on the socializing role of models wherever found, and in particular for understanding in part how change has been possible in a society of 900 million people. Before discussing why China more than other states has looked to model emulation as a primary vehicle for change, what is unique about the system, and how effective it has been, the prior question of who are models must be considered.

WHO ARE MODELS?

A model is a person or group held up to others as an example of a quality or behavior that others should emulate, that is, imitate. The term as used in this discussion will refer exclusively to those Chinese models who have been so designated by a formal or official process of selection. This will exclude mythical or historical hero/models, individuals who are simply admired by those around them, and even widely revered leaders—including Mao Zedong himself—who have not been formally selected as models by their peers.

The number of individuals who are formally chosen to be models is perhaps the most important reason for their effectiveness in producing change. A rough estimate would be that at any given time there are probably three to five million models. This is only an approximate number because no official count has been given, and in all probability the national leadership itself has no precise idea, because the number is determined largely by many separate units on the local level. Furthermore, the number fluctuates considerably according to political conditions and the intensity of campaigns for emulation that accompany them. In any case, the number of models in proportion to the total population is sufficiently great to be influential.

The number is large because individuals are elected models by their basic units and because models multiply themselves. Basic units consist of a very large number of rural production teams and brigades, industrial plant subdivisions, neighborhood committees, local units of state and party bureaucracies, and the basic units of the various mass organizations such as the Communist Youth League (YCL), trade unions, Womens Federation, and the like. A single, local unit is small, probably 15 to 20 members. Again there is no official count of such units, nor of how many models each may elect on a routine basis. The number of three to five million may be extrapolated from numerous local accounts of figures such as that given by the Canton press in 1965, which reported a meeting of provincial heroes in industry, commerce, construction, trade, and finance that was attended by more than 2,000 model collectives and 60,000 model workers.[1] In 1960 Hupei reported that 3,227 model persons were elected to Party membership, representing 84.6 percent of the total.[2] Furthermore, the number rises geometrically because the purpose of a model is to produce other models by stimulating others to emulate them. This self-multiplication has been called a "crystallizing" effect, "igniting the fuse of a chain reaction," a "capillary" effect, or what Mao Zedong has said to be "the spark that lights the prairie fire." A major model like Lei Feng produces successive generations of models. He was killed in 1962 and a "learn from Lei Feng" campaign began in 1962, became national in scope in 1963, and by 1965 had led to a second crop that included Ouyang Hai and Wang Jie, who in turn led to a third generation in 1966, including Liu Yingjian who lost his life saving children from a runaway horse. The campaigns to emulate these submodels and sub-submodels were carried on simultaneously. The result is that these two factors—election by basic units and self-multiplication—provide models in very large numbers, a situation that distinguishes the Chinese system from others, and that makes it uniquely possible for models to have a wide and pervasive influence.

Another important aspect that makes models effective as agents of change is that they are ordinary people who have been chosen by their associates in their local units as outstanding in qualities that all people can emulate. Collectives or groups such as a PLA (People's Liberation Army) squad or production team can also be models. All ages, sexes, occupations, racial minorities, and geographical localities are represented by models. A labor-heroes conference in 1962 was attended by more than 1,000 model workers including "machine building and textile workers, steel personnel, shop assistants, truck drivers, cooks and local opera singers."[3] Models have no unique aptitudes except boundless will power and determination, and they have no innate genius. They are not individuals who have won the spontaneous and unstructured admiration of their peers, but have been chosen by a carefully planned and regularized process, one that insures in most cases that the model is known to his fellow workers or neighbors, and through personal, daily, face-to-face contacts can readily communicate and explain in appropriate terms the messages and directives sent down from above.

Models are part of the everyday, normal environment and every person has some form of contact with them. Local newspapers and wall posters eulogize them, photographs identify them beyond their own units, forums and meetings discuss them. An individual's work period is spent with them, and his leisure hours are filled with literature, speakers, broadcasts, and dramas and films portraying them if they reach national eminence. His education, formal and informal, presses home their lessons. His small group discusses them and how to be like them. By now the Chinese masses are thoroughly model-conscious, a fact that enables the leaders to use model emulation easily and effectively for introducing and publicizing new values, new goals, and new policies.

SOURCES

Emulation of models in Communist China has many roots, the combination of which made it natural for the regime to continue to use emulation for introducing social and political change. Roots may be found in the Confucian heritage, Marxism-Leninism, China's historical experiences, and the thoughts of Chairman Mao. These sources merged to provide continuity and durability to model emulation, so that its political institutionalization by Communist leaders and its internalization by the people came quickly and easily under the new regime. The unique strength of emulation as a social phenomenon in China rests on the continuity of tradition and its adaptability to new revolutionary goals.

The emulation of models was an important Confucian principle. Donald Munro, in speaking of the early Chinese concepts of man, says that "For the Confucian model emulation was not just one way of learning; it was by far the most efficient way, and one could inculcate any virtuous behavior in people by presenting the right model."[4] This observation about early thought is paralleled by a contemporary Communist comment on the nature of models: "To conduct education by positive example among the worker masses is by far the most effective way to educate them."[5] Furthermore, Confucius and Mao both believed that models are efficacious because man is malleable and capable of change. He is like a lump of clay that can be shaped by exposure to virtuous examples. To Mencius, man had a natural propensity for the good if exposed to moral influences, and Mao characterized models as vanguards who show the masses the correct revolutionary path and lead them on it. China may be "poor and blank," but "a clean sheet of paper has no blothces and so the newest and most beautiful words can be written on it."[6] The concept of malleability lies at the heart of model emulation, the purpose of which is to change the behavior of men. Mao and the Chinese leaders, of course, rejected those aspects of Confucianism that were incompatible with revolutionary change, such as filial piety, and preferred the dynamics of struggle over the quiescence of harmony.

The inputs of Marx and Lenin were not antithetical to the use of heroes and models to hasten change. Both Marx and Mao believed that men's attitudes and behavior could be altered by changing the means of production, although Mao gave increasing priority to subjective factors as the cause of objective change.[7] Lenin's belief that the proletariat needed a vanguard to lead them was accepted by China's leaders, and Mao spoke of models as vanguards.[8] The institutionalization of models is based largely on Lenin's theory of organization; that is, the process of choosing models and the setting up of emulation campaigns follow Lenin's insistence on careful planning and structural coherence. In the 1950s, Chinese leaders were aware of Russian Stakhanovite models and were influenced by them, but the Chinese soon rejected the Russian emphasis on heavy individual competition to become a Stakhanovite, material rewards for outproducing others, and the single function of raising production. Chinese models are chosen for their productivity, but also for moral values and political activism.*

China's historical experience also helped to prepare the way for the institutionalization of models as agents of change. In addition to Confucian beliefs about man and his susceptibility to the influence of good examples, certain institutions had appeared that involved models such as the ceremonial virtuous widow's arch and the Ch'ing dynasty *xiangyue* (*hsiang-yüeh*) system of imperial lectures which praised good men for the edification of the masses.[9] Furthermore, the climate for the changing of values and institutions had been accelerating since the late nineteenth century with its reform movements, the 1911 revolution, the ferment of the May 4th movement, and in the early 1920s the long exposure of peasants in areas such as Kwangtung to propaganda for social change. Yenan leaders had these precedents to work with when they began to use models to educate the masses and to increase production in the beleaguered area, and in the process developed most of the techniques and structural forms still in use today.

> On November 26, 1943, the first labor-heroes congress was held in the Shensi-Kansu-Ninghsia border areas, in which the experiences of the previous year of the border-areas production movement were summarized and exchanged, and the policies and methods for further developing production in 1944 were fixed. Chairman Mao in this meeting gave his famous report entitled "Let's Organize," and indicated that organizing the popular forces was the policy for developing production. This meeting was the first in our country's history of a large scale labor-heroes congress. The more than two hundred labor heroes and model workers who came to the congress from all areas of the border regions played an important part in raising the production enthusiasm of the masses and extending the experiences of mutual aid and cooperation.[10]

The uses to which models were put at Yenan and the innovative techniques became standardized: using workers and peasants as models in contrast to old military heroes, election of models by their peers, conferences of models, publicity by mass media, rewards of status and public acclaim, and the organization of models, both individuals and units, to stimulate production and arouse enthusiasm among the masses. The use of models at Yenan and the development of these techniques were a response to the problems raised by the Kuomintang and Japanese blockades, and their purpose was to mobilize and unify the peasants to shift popular attitudes from fear to hatred of the enemy, and to depict the

---

*In the early 1960s the Chinese rejected what they called "crass" individual competition for "socialist" competition under the slogan of "compare with, catch up with, overtake the advanced, and help those lagging behind."

bright new future. It was at Yenan that emulation of models was rationalized, organized, and institutionalized, and became a major component in the Communist style of government after 1949.

Finally, a major influence in shaping and molding model emulation for revolutionary purposes were the thoughts of Chairman Mao, expressed in his speeches, writings, and directives. Although it is not possible to discuss fully his ideas, some points particularly relevant to models may be made. "Mao has always placed a concern with changing man at the very core of his conception of revolution."[11] His whole vision of a New Society is predicated on the creation of the New Socialist Man, involving an optimistic view of the perfectability of man. Following the Confucian tradition, Mao believed that if men understand the good they will follow it, and that the best way to teach men is by giving them virtuous models to emulate. The traditional theory of learning from models" and that "most people are definitely attracted to and consciously seek to emulate virtuous models."[12] A contemporary comment makes the same point: "The masses like to emulate good examples set by good people and good deeds, and find them much easier to learn."[13] Differences of ability are sublimated in the ultimate equality of all men, because present differences result merely from the fact that some men are slower to grasp the proper spirit and need more help to do so. Mao said that the people are composed of the advanced, the intermediate, and the backward; the advanced act as models for the intermediate and the intermediate for the backward, and through emulation the whole society moves forward. Once the creative energy of the masses is harnessed and released, "miracles can be accomplished." The significant factor according to Mao is changing men's attitudes. Behavior proceeds from and reflects attitude, and positive behavior is the natural function of a positive attitude; and only by observing an individual's behavior is it possible to tell if he has a correct attitude. Theory and practice are inseparable. Mao has been ambivalent about how to change men's attitude. In the 1950s he followed the orthodox Marxist doctrine that attitudes could be changed only by a change in objective factors—that is, in the means of production—but increasingly after 1960 he shifted his priority to subjective reform.

> Mao has long been convinced that the real key to successful revolution is a spiritual transformation of values, a revolution in men's minds. Creating "new socialist men" is even more important than building new social institutions, although of course the two tasks are linked. Some would argue that Mao has turned traditional Marxism-Leninism on its head. Marx, and most subsequent classical Marxist-Leninist ideologues, asserted that human values are fundamentally shaped by the nature of the social base of history, and that revolutionizing society's institutions, modes of production, and patterns of social relations is a prerequisite to lasting change in "the superstructure" of society.[14]

Mao, on the contrary, became increasingly preoccupied with the superstructure—that is, with virtue and virtuous men who act with revolutionary zeal, and with educational reforms to produce such men.

Change in man according to Mao does not occur spontaneously but must be motivated and directed by external sources. Change in attitude, and therefore behavior, is not self-generated by the individual himself. Once motivated, there must be an input of will and determination on the part of the individual, but motivation comes from outside. "The ordinary people become advanced personalities because they receive education and encouragement from advanced personalities."[15] "Young shoots can grow, blossom, and bear fruit only with the diligent labor of the gardener."[16] According to Mao "the vast majority of men are good," and they will therefore respond better to persuasion and education by advanced personalities than to force and coercion. He says:

> To be able to carry on their production and studies effectively and to lead their lives in peace and order, the people want their government and those in charge of production and of cultural and educational organizations to issue appropriate administrative regulations of an obligatory nature. It is common sense that without them the maintenance of public order would be impossible. Administrative regulations and the method of persuasion and education complement each other in resolving contradictions among the people. In fact, administrative regulations for the maintenance of public order must be accompanied by persuasion and education, for in many cases regulations alone will not work.[17]

In accordance with the mass line, right attitudes as preludes to right action can be obtained only after the people have thoroughly understood the ideology or the issue involved. Mao said that the Chinese masses are poor and blank, which is good because the finest pictures can be painted on them. This imprinting can be accelerated by using models who vividly illustrate virtuous attitudes and behavior. In this way coercion can be minimized.

If the masses are to understand, then they must be taught and persuaded by those who are more advanced in understanding the course of the revolution, or the "continuing" revolution. Models are more advanced because they stand above others in some respect, such as production or political activism, and being more advanced they act as leaders of the masses. Mao, in his "Some Questions Concerning Methods of Leadership," June 1, 1943, laid down three principles that he considered key points in his general theory and practice of leadership, each of which has particular relevance for models as leaders.[18] The first principle is the essential interrelatedness of the general and the particular. This is derived from his theory of the unity of opposites, which finds the universal in the particular and the particular in the universal in a never-ending dialectical series of contradictions. In practice, this principle indicates that models are particulars illustrating universal socialist values, and must also be living, real persons rather than abstractions, so that the masses seeing the particular will understand the universal. The second principle is the necessity of a breakthrough at one point. Procedurally it is more effective to concentrate available force at one particular point than to make a broad attack on a problem. "At any one time there can be only one central task, and the art of leadership is to view the whole and determine the particular point for making a breakthrough."[19] Models may be used to focus public attention on one aspect of a problem as well as to show how a breakthrough can be accomplished. For example, if the problem is to increase agricultural production, a model may pinpoint the particular problem in a particular place as salinity of the soil, and then demonstrate techniques for overcoming that condition. The third principle is the need for typical examples to show the masses the path opened by the breakthrough. Here models clearly play a role. If the problem is saline soil, a model peasant fortuitously appears who knows how to overcome salinity, and he both publicizes the problem and shows how to solve it. In this way a model demonstrates in a living way that his solution constitutes a breakthrough which may be followed by all peasants coping with salty soil, and so the behavior of a particular individual becomes the behavior of many, once they have understood the problem and that the result of a breakthrough is higher production. Models are essentially problem solvers, and they can be aimed at specific targets such as youth or peasants; they can be used to publicize new policies, to refer to particular problems of a particular place, or they can illustrate general procedures for problem solving, such as proper analysis of a given problem.

These principles were announced and put into practice at Yenan, and on January 10, 1945 at another conference of model workers in the border region, Mao went on to discuss the roles that models play in the continuing revolution.

THE ROLE OF MODELS

Mao said that models play three roles: as leaders, hardcores, and bridges.[20] All of these are political roles, and taken together explain the function of models in the political system. However, before discussing roles it is essential to understand that these roles are strictly informal, that models are not personnel of any state, party, or other bureaucracy (although they are used as unofficial agents by them), that they have influence but no authority, and that they fulfill their roles in an undefined area between officials and the people. Model emulation may be institutionalized, but there is no formal structure or organized body of models; they are only a collectivity of individual models linked to officials and the people, but not to each other. They are used as agents for change, but they have no part in determining the substance of any change.

According to Mao, the first role is that of leader. "This is because you have exerted special efforts and made many creations; your work has become an example for the people in general, raised the standard of work, and induced all others to learn from you." The general term "leader" has subsequently been paraphrased as "guide," "compass," "forerunner," but the most frequent is "vanguard," which is used in the Leninist sense of individuals who are in the forefront of history, but which in this case is not confined to Party members. Models "walk ahead of the era." They show the way of the future and open up the path to the masses.

> To the proletariat and other working masses, heroes are outstanding figures who can only emerge from the people's revolutionary struggle, who represent the interests of the masses, and who, in line with the direction in which history develops, help propel history forward. . . . Compared with the rank and file, they aim higher and are more far-sighted.[21]

However, the ideal must become real. In practice, models act as vanguards or vehicles through whom new policies are made known to the people. They are "living" edicts. Mao said that the Chinese revolution is like fighting a war, and after winning one battle, new tasks must be put forward. New tasks mean new policies, and shifts in policy are heralded by a model or series of equivalent models who make known the task and its solution. For example, when the Soviet technicians left abruptly in 1959–60, a general call was issued for indigenous Chinese technical innovations, and soon models appeared, like old Shang Shun who invented a portable potato digger that enabled one man to do the work of 15, and like He Jisheng, a young peasant who invented a mechanical rice transplanter. In the prelude to the Cultural Revolution total devotion to the thoughts of Chairman Mao was called for, which soon was epitomized in the person of Liu Yingjian who gave his life stopping a runaway horse from injuring some children, and was able to do so because he had diligently studied, faithfully carried out, and enthusiastically propagated the works of Mao as the supreme guide.

The second role is that of hard cores, also known as "pace setters," "energizers," or "tough-boned." If models as vanguards make known to the masses the path of the future, as hard cores they make sure that the people move along that path. They maintain and sustain the task of carrying out the new guidelines. As Mao said "With you, the work can be properly activated." Pace setters, as the name implies are essentially activists, and activism is a common characteristic of all models. Among their fellow workers they are more energetic, lively, and productive in carrying out tasks. They are not only exceptionally active and hard-working, but they must go among the masses in a "deep and penetrating way" to activate others, set the pace, and maintain momentum. If this were their only role, Chinese labor models would have much in common with the Soviet Stakhanovites, but the Chinese workers are urged to avoid crass competition in outstripping each other, though this quality is not totally absent, and to make every effort not only to catch up with the advanced, but having done so, to help those lagging behind.

The third role according to Mao is that of a bridge. "You are a bridge between the leadership above you and the broad masses below. The masses' views are transmitted to the upper levels through you, and the upper levels reach the lower levels through you." The terms "link" and "intermediary" are also used. According to the mass line, a cardinal error in leadership is to become divorced or separated from the masses, because if the masses are left to themselves they may go forward in the wrong direction. Acting as links is undoubtedly the most important function of models. It is this role that enables them to be potent factors in change. They are part of the complex mechanism for passing down to the people information that the leaders want them to know. They pick up the messages from the press, from local party and state cadres, from "exchange of experience," and from conferences of advanced persons, and pass them on to their fellow workers, friends, and associates in a form relevant to local conditions and the level of understanding of their listeners. Transmitting information informally on a daily, face-to-face basis while working or sharing leisure moments has been found to make a deeper impact than bureaucratic efforts or the mass media.

The roles of leader, hard core, and bridge—as defined by Mao—indicate the multiple functions models are expected to play as agents of social change. However, the purpose of models is above all to be emulated, for only through emulation does the single spark start the prairie fire and particular behavior become mass behavior.

EMULATION AND COMPLIANCE

Emulation as an explicit precept reaches far back in Chinese cultural history. Confucius said that when one sees a worthy person, one should think of equaling him. Emulation is the attempt on the part of a person to replicate the desirable behavior of another. It involves, therefore, interaction between the emulator and the model to be emulated, and is a process by which an individual responds to another in such a way that the former is motivated to equal the attitude and behavior of the latter. In theory, if not in fact, this is the way it should work and it is the way it is officially said to work.

The relationship between emulator and model is complex and has four different aspects that may be expressed prepositionally. These are imitation of, inspiration by, competition with, and emanation from. The first two are characteristic of model emulation wherever found. The third is unique to China, not in its nature but in the quantity and extent of its use and the degree of organization involved. The fourth has a uniquely Chinese quality, though not absolutely so. In China, models are never imitated as persons because they are not charismatic; it is their behavior or their "spirit" that is to be emulated. It is "the spirit of Dazhai" that is followed. They are like charismatic figures because they provide leadership of an intensely personal nature, but they deviate from Weberian charismatic figures because they are not the source of a bright vision of the future, but only transmit the vision of others who determine what is to be exemplified. They are examples of desirable behavior, but they do not determine what is desirable. They are both leaders and led. "Spirit" to Mao meant "attitude," and during the Cultural Revolution he became more and more preoccupied with instilling correct attitudes as a basis for carrying on the revolution.

Imitation of a model is taking the latter as an example to be followed. This is the cognitive, didactic, instrumental aspect of emulation. Imitation of a worthy example is inherent in all emulation. Lenin recognized the value of imitating models and said: "We have to give the peasant who . . . is a practical man and a realist concrete examples to follow to prove that the 'Kommunia' is the best possible thing." In order to be imitated, models must be publicized, and care is taken not to present models whose behavior is so sublime that although they are deeply admired, the ordinary man feels it is beyond his capacity.

> Targets of the emulation drives should not be too high or too low. Experience proves that if the targets are too low, they can be fulfilled without effort and can in no way stimulate the enthusiasm of the masses to compete. On the other hand, if the targets are too high, they cannot be fulfilled even with great effort and in this way can dampen the enthusiasm of the masses. For this reason, targets of emulation drives must be based neither on the "advanced" levels nor on the backward levels; instead they should be based on the general production levels of the masses so that they can be reached by the masses with a certain amount of effort.[22]

Models are everywhere and are adapted to various circumstances and levels of achievement, and consequently each individual has before him an example that he is capable of imitating.

Inspiration by a model provides the motivation to imitate him and activates the will to do so. It is the link between being aware of a model and translating that perception into behavior. This aspect is emotive, affective, and consummatory rather than cognitive. The individual, by comparing and contrasting his behavior with that of a model, naturally wishes to catch up. This is something like Socrates' principle that to know the good is to do it, and the Mencian doctrine that good men respond naturally to the good. For example, a campaign was set up to emulate Men He, a five-good soldier who fell on a rocket to save his comrades, which held that his spirit and action acted as "the greatest inspiration, education and stimulus" to the masses.[23] Those who were inspired by his heroic deed were told that they did not have to fall on rockets, but could emulate his spirit of acting selflessly in situations of smaller dimensions. This was because "the masses like to emulate good people and find them easier to learn from."[24] Ideally emulation is inspired by knowledge about a model, but to reinforce this natural reaction campaigns are promoted to whip up enthusiasm for emulation and to incite imitative action.

Competition is another important factor, as used in China. The term for emulation, *jingsai*, is literally translated as "compare two sides and one will win." Imitation and inspiration involve a one-to-one relation between model and emulator, but competition introduces another dimension. It socializes emulation in the sense that individuals and units not only try to equal or surpass a model, but compete with each other to become models by outproducing others or showing greater activism. They compete with models to surpass them, and this is done by comparing themselves with the more advanced and finding out the causes of their backwardness; and by overcoming their weaknesses they can outstrip and become even more advanced than the model. The term "advanced" model means outstripping others, which creates a competitive upward spiraling "stage by stage," "bit by bit." As early as 1950–51, units, factories, and enterprises competed with each other to become advanced models, which in those days entailed bonuses as well as honor.[25] When the Hehenzheng brigade in Hupei became a model production brigade and the "key point" for the whole province, all other brigades in the province then entered into stiff competition with each other to raise their production to the Hehenzheng level with the ultimate goal of surpassing it.[26] Competition thus also adds to motivation for emulation, and is peculiarly Chinese in the sheer quantity of officially organized and sponsored competitive emulation drives.

The first three aspects of emulation are comprehensible to Western experience; emanation is not, yet it supplies an answer to the question of why emulation is so deeply engrained in Chinese culture and behavior. It is elusive, mystical, Taoist in its ineffability, but Confucian in its belief in the power of virtue (*te*). Emanation refers to the ability of virtue in itself to directly affect, without the intervention of will on the part of the model or those exposed to him, the attitudes and behavior of others. It is the rubbing off on others of some of the virtue of the model, by what Munro calls the "unintentionality of effect." More precisely, pure virtue directly activates virtue in others. Virtue is contagious; it has a potency, and a radiation effect. It is close to but goes beyond inspiration that is derived from knowledge about good men and their deeds, because its source is virtue itself. Emanation differs from charisma because in charisma it is the person or his personality that affects others strongly, but in emanation it is the pure virtue itself (the person being but a carrier or container) that affects others. It is the idea that pure virtue has its own direct potency that is presently alien to Western thought. The concept of emanation can be found in various cultures such as *darshan* in India (derived from *darshana*, "being in the presence of truth"). It appears in Mark 5:30 when a woman was healed by touching the garment of Jesus, and "Jesus, immediately knowing that virtue had gone out of him, turned him about in the press, and said 'Who touched my clothes?'" However, this tradition was later rejected in the West as magic but not science. It appeared in early China as the Doctrine of the Mean, which expressed both the point of virtue and the unintentionality of its effect. It is this tradition of emanation that may explain the special vitality of emulation. It also explains that the call is to emulate "the spirit" of the model, not the model himself. "Catching the spirit" immediately makes it possible "to do miracles."* The fact that virtue must be "pure" may explain why literary figures must be portrayed as totally evil or totally good, but never "grey" or "middle" characters.† Pure virtue in this case consists of the revolutionary virtues inherent in Marxism-Leninism-Maoism, and when found in a high-virtue model may radiate a spirit to which others respond by themselves becoming more virtuous. Emanation subtly permeates the whole phenomenon of emulation. It lies outside the realm of conventional Western psychology, but within that of traditional Chinese beliefs.

Imitation, inspiration, competition, and emanation explain the general nature of emulation of models on which the leaders rely heavily to secure compliance with changed values and changing policies. But the question remains of why people are willing to modify their behavior in this way. Emulative behavior and compliance are almost identical, because models controlled by the Party or state are recognized by the people as authoritative in their expression of official directives, so that by emulating they are complying. It is probable that almost every one in China has reacted emulatively to a model at some time, to some degree, and for different reasons.

Emulation must be expressed in overt action which may vary from zealous imitation of the model's behavior in order to become a model to cynical verbal expressions of admiration for the model, but between these extremes emulative behavior consists of routine compliance because it is expected and because failure to comply calls forth peer pressure. On the whole, there is little overt resistance to accepting the norms and directives expressed through models. Zeal in emulation varies according to motivation, which is determined by objective and subjective factors. Objectively, there may be a period of intense political activity, such as occurred in 1962-66 when zealous, even frenzied emulation was stimulated, but in 1966-69, when political disorder disrupted the normal procedure for choosing models, little was heard of models. In periods of political calm, such as the early 1970s, models are routinely chosen and citations and photographs are posted on bulletin boards, but zeal in emulation is muted and citations act largely as merit rewards and as a mild stimulus to others to increase their production. Publicity is minimal and emulation campaigns almost disappear. Zeal also depends heavily on local leadership. If plant managers or Party cadres are indifferent to model emulation or too busy to give it priority, then response is limited or even nonexistent. An informant during a Hong Kong interview said that if the leaders organize a meeting to choose models in a proper manner, the individuals will be respected, but if it is done in a rigid or biased manner so that good people are not chosen, then no one will pay much attention to them.

---

*Mao, as stated above, also used "spirit" in the sense of "attitude," but the mystical and psychological interpretations are not incompatible because the emanating spirit of virtue produces virtuous attitudes in others by direct effect.

† "Grey" figures were justified by some in the early 1960s as more realistic, but this point of view was rejected by Jiang Qing when she controlled cultural outputs.

The subjective factors that motivate emulation may be negative or positive.* Hatred, anxiety, and fear are powerful motives. Communist models from the beginning have been used to change attitudes toward landlords and capitalists, arousing hatred by bitterly recalling their former mistreatment by the feudal class and by contrasting their former state with the much better life they are now enjoying. Hatred of opponents who attempt to subvert the masses by their ideological errors is aroused by models chosen especially for their activism in denouncing class enemies, as in the case of Liu Shaoqi, Lin Biao, and the Gang of Four. These class enemies are presented as negative models of what not to do. Mao in his *Talks at the Yenan Forum on Art and Literature* in 1943 says that "all dark forces which endanger the masses of the people must be exposed while all revolutionary struggles of the masses must be praised."[27] Negative models are useful for exposing the enemy, highlighting the good, and focusing on the object of hatred. Anxiety also motivates. When filial piety and Confucian father-authority figures ran counter to revolutionary needs and were denounced, the anxiety caused by the loss of traditional sources of guidance was relieved by models who made quite clear what behavior was acceptable and what was to be done. They became father-authority substitutes, educating and persuading young and old to follow the right path.[28] Fear is very basic and although overt force is avoided as much as possible, semicoercion is inherent in the system. Everyone knows that models are authoritative, not in having power to punish but because they have official backing. They know that emulation is expected of them, and self-preservation dictates behavior at least overtly consonant with that of the model presented to them. Failure to conform may lead to group pressures, criticism and self-criticism meetings, or even attacks in the more feared struggle meetings. Fear leads at least to overtly voluntary compliance. This compliance through voluntary or semivoluntary pressures to adopt the official line by emulation is a very important component of the Chinese style of indirect rule.

However, individuals genuinely and enthusiastically emulate models for positive motives as well. Perhaps the strongest motivation is found in group identity and group consciousness. Strong self-identification with a group such as clan, family, or village had long been a traditional norm, but as these groups were weakened by the impact of modernization or Communist ideological policy, personal loyalties and obligations were increasingly transferred to new social groups such as "the people" or the Party in general, and to particular personal groups such as school, work unit, neighborhood, or study group. It is in the personal groups that models have their greatest influence, because they are members of them and were chosen by them. Consequently, the group as a whole

*The following discussion is based on Western psychological concepts. The Chinese look at behavior more in terms of Confucian interpersonal relations than of Western behavioral science. Relatively little concern is shown about human motivation, but rather it is assumed that to know the good is to do the good with no intervening layer of motivation.

is likely to respond in positive action to the message of its models, and individuals participate in group activities because it gives them a sense of belonging, and prevents fear of alienation, isolation, of being left out. Individuals who do feel alienated from the group and its emulative activities are brought into line by fear of making their alienation conspicuous. However, more important than fear of exclusion is the sense of security and social acceptance derived from being within the group, a sense accentuated by the Chinese tradition of group rather than individual orientation. Inclination is toward collective rather than independent behavior, and consequently toward cooperation rather than deviance. Other positive motivations include response to the appeals made by models for altruism, self-satisfaction in supporting the revolution, patriotism in making China the leading nation once again, raising production so that all may live better. Youth find outlets for their idealism in emulating models, and may solve their normal crisis of identity by becoming models themselves, though it should be pointed out that many do not want to be models because being a model is too arduous, with its heavy calls on time and energy. More self-serving as motivation is the attempt to emulate enthusiastically in order to be chosen as a model, because becoming a model is often the first step in upward mobility to Party membership or to becoming a lower-level official. It may also open the way to better housing, better jobs, and preference in school admissions.

In conclusion, the Chinese Communist regime has found that widespread use of models is politically useful in publicizing intended changes, disparaging old attitudes and institutions, inculcating new values, gaining support for innovative structures and procedures, and motivating the masses to emulate them—that is, to comply with what the leadership wants. The Chinese people under Communism have continuously accepted such drastic changes as the various stages of collectivization of land or the oscillation of education policy, with remarkably little overt opposition. All has been done largely by persuasion and education and with a minimum of direct force, though semicoercion through group pressure is not absent. Models are not the sole agents for educating and motivating the people but they are an important factor, and the emulation of models is an excellent example of the Chinese style of getting people to do what is wanted by indirect, participatory means.

NOTES

1. *Survey of the China Mainland Press (SCMP)*, No. 3550 (October 4, 1962), p. 2.

2. "Over 40,000 Superior Elements Join the Party in Hupeh Province," *SCMP* No. 2230 (April 4, 1960): p. 5.

3. "Tientsin Labor Heroes Meet," *SCMP*, No. 2694 (March 9, 1962), p. 21.

4. Donald J. Munro, *The Concept of Man in Early China* (Stanford: Stanford University Press, 1968), p. 96.

5. *SCMP*, No. 2991 (June 4, 1963), p. 20.

6. From an article written by Mao in 1958 for the first issue of the Party paper, *Hung Ch'i*. In Stuart R. Schram, *The Political Thought of Mao Tse-tung* (New York: Praeger, 1969), p. 351.

7. Benjamin Schwartz and Stuart Schram discuss the development of Mao's ideas in Dick Wilson (ed.), *Mao Tse-tung in the Scales of History* (London: Cambridge University Press, 1977), pp. 9–34, 35–69.

8. *SCMP*, No. 2623 (November 21, 1961), pp. 15–16.

9. See Hsiao King-ch'uan, *Rural China: Imperial Control in the Nineteenth Century* (Seattle: University of Washington Press, 1967), pp. 184–208, for a discussion of *xiangyue*.

10. "Let's Organize the Labor Force," quoted in Franz Schurmann, *Ideology and Organization in Communist China* (Berkeley: University of California Press, 1970), p. 419.

11. Stuart R. Schram, ed., *Authority, Participation and Cultural Change in Communist China* (London: Cambridge University Press, 1973), p. 27.

12. Munro, *Concept of Man*, p. 96.

13. *SCMP*, No. 2991 (June 4, 1963), p. 20.

14. A. Doak Barnett, *Uncertain Passage, China's Transition to the Post-Mao Era* (Washington, D.C.: The Brookings Institution, 1974), p. 13.

15. *Joint Publications Research Service* (JPRS), No. 261 (February 16, 1965), p. 57.

16. Kan Wei-min, "Grasp Typical Examples Properly," *Selections from China Mainland Magazine (SCMM)*, No. 667 (1969), p. 8.

17. "The Correct Handling of Contradictions among the People," *Selected Works of Mao Tse-tung* (Peking: Foreign Language Press, 1977), Vol. 5, p. 389.

18. Ibid., Vol. 3, pp. 117–22.

19. Ibid.

20. *SCMP*, No. 2623 (November 21, 1961), pp. 15–16.

21. *Peking Review*, No. 29 (July 21, 1972), pp. 8–9.

22. "Socialist Emulation Drives are the Motive Power that Promote Production Increases and Economy," *SCMP*, No. 2885 (December 21, 1962), p. 2.

23. *British Broadcasting Corporation, Far East*, No. 2788 (June 6, 1968), p. 9.

24. *SCMP*, No. 2991 (June 4, 1963), p. 20.

25. See William Brugger, *Democracy and Organization in the Chinese Industrial Enterprise* (London: Cambridge University Press, 1976), pp. 162–67, for a discussion of production competitions.

26. Silas H. L. Wu, "The Experience of My Native Village," *Eastern Horizon* 13, No. 4 (1974): 19.

27. *Selected Works of Mao Tse-tung*, Vol. 3, pp. 69–97.

28. See Lucian W. Pye, *The Spirit of Chinese Politics* (Cambridge, Mass.: MIT Press, 1968), pp. 107–24, for further discussion of father-authority substitutes.

PART 2

VALUE CHANGE IN DIVERSE CHINESE SETTINGS

In this section, attention is focused on specific areas of value change. The first two studies explore changing Chinese values as they relate to ecological concerns. In the first of these, value orientations regarding traditional agriculture are compared to the values that inform modern Chinese industry. The second study examines variations in domestic architecture and how these various architectural forms reflect changing values in regard to lifestyle and outlook. The last two studies analyze the ways in which values differ by sex, thereby revealing how value orientations and rates of value change are not distributed uniformly throughout the population. Since some of the material presented in this section is derived from analysis of survey data or from unrestricted observation, readers will note that research for three of the essays was done in Taiwan.

6

AGRICULTURAL AND INDUSTRIAL VALUES IN CHINA

Lynn T. White, III

Values are not easy to define. It is polite to presume that everyone has them, but that much is not social science. Values are something less than culture, something similar to attitudes, something more than norms. Each of these closely allied categories can be explored in terms of its logical relations with other concepts, or can be examined in terms of examples of people's behavior. Such studies may prove to be more revealing than generalized definitions. Several basic approaches to the topic are distinguished by the degree to which they rely on material constraints as the basic generators of values. To begin, three such approaches will be described, for the purpose of showing how arbitrary any choice among them is.

The first approach is boldly philosophical. Socrates stands in contrast to most social scientists, with his stunningly direct questions about "the good." This style has undeniable attractions. It treats values only insofar as they can be expressed intellectually, even if it abstracts them from behavior patterns. This approach is especially good in efforts to find the expressed intentions of important social actors, particularly those who can write. It is direct in its search for the inherent, logical relations between values, which is something that behavioral scientists tend to do only after apologizing by saying that minimal amounts of such activity are unavoidable in framing the questions of empirical research. In the philosophical approach, ideal categories are asserted or quoted, shown to be consistent or inconsistent, and thrown up against other ideas. In the contemporary Chinese field, the most prominent philosopher is Donald Munro.[1]

A second approach relates values to concrete communities of people. Joseph Levenson in the Chinese field is often misread as a philosopher, but actually he was less interested in "thought" than in "men thinking."[2] Max Weber also insisted that values (whatever their logical relations might be) are always linked to specific groups of men and women. Ideas do not exist apart from communities. Weber saw that value systems derive from both the ideal traditions and the material conditions of particular groups.[3] This approach incorporates the philosophical one, but it is more relativistic and more specifically designed to treat value change. Empirical theory of this sort can deal with dynamic societies that have tensions between subgroups within them. Alterations of ideas over time can be correlated with other social things that change simultaneously. New insights from new leaders or from external cultures, changes in physical resources or in the whims of nature—these things are made relevant to abstract values by the postphilosophical method. Social and ecological factors both become important in this most comprehensive kind of analysis of values.

A third approach to values—the one that will be used in this brief study—is less ambitious and multipurpose than either of the first two. It deals with values insofar as they can be related to the environmental conditions under which they arise. This ecological method is an arbitrary, conveniently restricted subtype of the second procedure described above. It can refer to only some of the values that might be approached by less narrow paths into this perilous realm of ideals. The aim here is to look at what most Chinese have been doing with their environment most of the time, and to see whether such activities conduce to particular values. Marxists have explored this kind of problem to a limited extent in the past, but the current project certainly need not adopt their particular philosophy.

The task divides naturally into two parts. First, one can look at traditional agriculture, which has long engaged the majority of China's people, to see what general norms that activity may foster. Second, one can look at the specific resource arrays and material conditions that constrain China's new industrial development, to see how they may affect values in the modern, more complex, and even international contexts. By the nature of this project, the results are more likely to be hypotheses than conclusions; the study is an experiment. The main theme of the paper is that some obvious, current Chinese values (for example, communalism, the self-reliance of groups, self-consciousness above planning and above ecological optimism, frugality, faith in the value of enthusiastic mobilization campaigns) are connected at least loosely with the traditional and modern ways in which Chinese people have worked daily to sustain themselves.

TRADITIONAL AGRICULTURE

The Chinese traditional economy, which is still predominant in most parts of the country, is based on rice and wheat. The inherited technologies for these products require mass mobilization of labor at several stages in the growth cycles of crops. Communitarian values, which justify this mobilization and enable it to take place, have long been important in China.

Mencius, for example, wrote a good deal about the economics of conservation. He stressed the need to preserve the productivity of fisheries and forests, and he advised kings to make sure their peasants would join together to plant diversified crops and keep enough hogs for fertilizer.[4] Fear of shortage led to an emphasis on planning and a prescriptive optimism that resources could in fact be planned. The Communists, while criticizing Mencius on many grounds, follow similar farm policies. They stress that agriculture is the "root" of a developing economy, and their main kinds of agriculture are inherently conservationist and collective.

This was not always the case. The basic, aboriginal method of raising food in all parts of the world is slash-and-burn culture. This technique exploits natural environments without changing them. An individual can remove natural plants from an area, and then sow seeds whose growth differs from the original forest plants only in the sense that men can eat the fruits. This method is productive only for a short time (often just one or two crop cycles) in a given spot, because it depletes soil fertility.[5] It is not conservationist and does not become much more efficient if cultivators cooperate with each other.

Wet rice culture, especially, creates a whole new ecology, not at all like this "state of nature." It contrasts sharply with slash-and-burn techniques. Fertility can be maintained indefinitely under a wet regime. The excavation of flat terraces and the introduction of water allow stable calorie yields from the land year after year. The reasons are specific and several:

Water transports and distributes soluble nutrients to plant roots more efficiently than solid soil can do.

The surface of shallow, sun-warmed water develops a green algae scum which captures solar energy to fix nitrogen from the air.

Weeds are inhibited by terrace water, the depth of which can usually be made to accord with the height of rice rather than of other plants. The gooey, yielding consistency of the wet soil permits farmers to remove useless plants easily.

The slow flow of flat water helps aerate the soil; but at the same time, its moderate speed helps to prevent the physical erosion and chemical laterization of this standard platform for rice roots.

The wet terrace environment tends to make acid soils more basic; this allows ionized ammonium, phosphate, and other radicals to be more available in solution to the plants.

If the terrace is properly cared for, its fertility and yield will be reasonably high and predictable on a permanent basis.

Paddy agriculture meshes better with some social values than with others. One of these tenets is communitarianism. Rice yield responds elastically to labor inputs because of the importance for plant growth of certain stages in the crop cycle. During the transplantation of rice sprouts, for example, if seedlings are moved from small nursery terraces to larger fields too early, they will be weak and subject to damage by weather. If they are transplanted too late, there is insufficient time for the side stalks to grow. In either case, rice yield will be below maximum. To harvest the largest amount of grain, peasants must transplant all their seedlings quickly. Transplantation is thus a crash campaign, mobilizing all available labor, but because fields at such high levels of production can in fact support a large population, the necessary labor is available. Later in the crop cycle another crash campaign is necessary for harvesting the rice.

In most wheat areas, yield is similarly responsive to labor inputs, especially during summer months and other periods when China's particularly high-yield, mixed-crop farming practices are used. On most of the north China plain, wheat is harvested in summer, and fields must immediately be prepared for sweet potatoes or other tubers or legumes. In autumn, when the potatoes and peanuts are harvested, winter wheat must be quickly sown before the first snow falls. This constant shifting of crops, typical of China's wheat areas, requires vast amounts of work; but it also conserves soil fertility better than constant planting of the grain would do. Also, effective irrigation of wheat requires firm collective authority to mediate water disputes between cultivators. The communal effort needed to sustain such a labor-intensive agriculture, in both the rice and wheat areas, deeply structures peasants' lives. In the several weeks each year when the fields need tending most, everyone must go and work long hours. Traditional values help organize these essential tasks. Parallels to communitarian values and campaign styles in the People's Republic should be obvious. It is no accident that this is the country that makes so much of long marches, the Great Leap Forward, the Cultural Revolution, and many other recurring civilian mobilizations, while nonetheless emphasizing a frugality and practicality that seem less excessive than these campaigns. Perhaps the context of general values, by which ordinary Chinese people understand these movements, was laid down long ago.

The old field culture permitted substantial human control over most determinants of crop yield. Unlike slash-and-burn techniques, it was an artificial, planned agriculture. Weather was not controlled, and droughts and floods could have disastrous effects.[6] Some years were unavoidably bad, and peasants' fear of indebtedness only reinforced their hope of effective resource planning. The traditional technology for paddy was sensitive, above all, to undersupplies or oversupplies of water: too little meant that paddy culture was impossible; too much meant that rice plants on flat land would be killed. Nonetheless, paddy has a very high calorie-per-acre yield (about six times the yield of most dry rice, for example). Also, it is relatively easy to store after it is harvested, in comparison with many other foods. Although there were some unavoidably bad years, long strings of several bad years together were rare. Starvation was usually the result of maldistribution and maladministration, not of the traditional agricultural technology.

Total population in most areas was determined by the lower ranges of output over several-year periods. Harvests, being more directly subject to weather, varied more radically on an annual basis than population, which could depend for a while on stored grain. In flat rice regions, because the wet terrace is physically and chemically so efficient in using all agricultural inputs except labor, population was usually maintained at very dense levels.[7] In wheat areas, people could scatter into the hills somewhat more, but large populations accumulated also in the north.

In most years, China's particular types of agriculture created yields that were high and reasonably stable on a long-term basis, but these kinds of cropping both required and supported huge amounts of labor.[8] Much work was put, for example, into irrigation systems; China contains about 40 percent of the planet's heavily irrigated land—which is nearly twice her portion of the world's people, despite the size of that latter statistic. This high amount of irrigated land per capita is congruent with values that mobilize work and conserve resources, and also with a gigantic population that emerged from particular sorts of agriculture as surely as the proverbial chicken comes from the proverbial egg. None of the elements of the unified syndrome "came first," but the country's unique demography and its labor-responsive cropping practices form a single story with its conservationist-collectivist values.

In modern times the story has changed somewhat. China's careful, labor-consuming, and necessarily planned agriculture still constitutes the world's foremost example of a "spaceship economy." However, this pattern also affects human lives. Its labor-intensiveness makes for much simple drudgery, of a sort that is no more likely to be seen as a value in modern times than it was before.

MODERN INDUSTRY

China now has a developing culture, as well as a traditional paddy culture. Modernization is in some tension with the old ecological and social resourcefulness. The benefits of traditional communalist values for modern change are moot. Some countries that have agricultures broadly similar to China's, notably Japan, have gone through long periods of strenuously enforced national unity, so that a grand communal march to modernization was made possible. Others, for example Indonesia, have not had any such experience. As Clifford Geertz concludes, ecological traditions alone will give only some clues to predicting styles of modern change.[9] Other social and political factors are important, too.

In China old agricultural values are certainly not yet overwhelmed by more "modern" ideals, and they continue to influence the development process. Many practical examples of conservationism and collectivism could be cited. Chinese farmers have been wary of using DDT, because that poison washes easily into ponds where it kills fish that are needed for food and other purposes. They shy away from using too much inorganic fertilizer, which can burn roots and reduce yields when water supplies are uncertain. They have sound economic reasons to be conservationists. Their work in production teams (mostly in natural villages) is done on assignment by the leaders of small collectives.

In most respects, however, modern Chinese have a straightforward and optimistic attitude about natural resources. Concern about shortage has led to a compensatory hope in planning for plenty. Posters adorning the walls of China have often shown the current chairman (once Mao, now Hua) surrounded by cornucopias, wheat sheaves, oil derricks, baskets brimming with oranges, and plump peasant children. The Chinese do not, officially, think they will face any ultimate resource shortage. They do not predict ecological doom. The need for planning and social cooperation in traditional fields may encourage their optimism that even the modern environment can be managed.

This sanguine view, born of China's field culture that was usually but not always efficient, is reflected in the fact that many articulate Chinese elite members have become Marxists. They believe history is the record of the release in progressive stages of society's productive powers, of ways of exploiting resources, and are confident that such history will continue. The human race, they believe, will not face any material depletion it cannot prevent or make up in other ways. The Chinese even explain the origins of the current obvious shortages in the West on this basis, claiming that these problems have been caused in the world capitalist economy—precisely because it is capitalist. They say the West has bungled things, that a greed for quick profits has led to mismanagement. Valuable minerals became slag, which should have been used. A source of energy as important as natural gas has been flared off at wellheads in past years, without consideration of its potential uses. Inadequate distribution and marketing arrangements have prevented materials from being placed where their value to humans might be maximized.[10] The Chinese tend to associate these problems with non-Socialist political structures, but their specific critiques are usually expressed in organizational terms. They even think that maladministration can be basically cured—a proposition that has been held duly suspect in liberal countries. The Chinese retain their traditional belief in the usefulness of artificial human planning and mobilization, saying that more forethought can go into economic arrangements. Substitute raw materials can be lined up before old supplies have nearly disappeared.[11]

This faith—that it is feasible to plan the use of materials in the long term—is basic to Chinese statements on natural resources. They speak and write these precepts repeatedly, whether or not their practice follows suit, and even if an implicit basis of this emphasis lies in China's past and present poverty. How can the Chinese be so optimistic, even smug, about the practicability of planning against basic depletion? The answers to this question are several. Faith in planning derives more from Chinese than from Marxist precedents. Its connection with old Confucian rationality, and with related agricultural traditions, is only somewhat obscured by recent criticisms of the Sage. Statesmanly traditions of policy making among old imperial bureaucrats, like the reformer Wang Anshi in the Sung, are a common and famous heritage of all educated Chinese.[12] Mandarins long held a hopeful trust in the efficacy of consistent policy sets. Long-range resource plans can be understood by Chinese as echoes of traditional land and tax reforms.

Faith in planning, derived largely from the experiences of family organizations with the requisites of work on productive fields, has long been advertised by Chinese governments, because it implies concurrent faith in the hierarchy of the planners. At most times in China, there has been an officially sponsored confidence that everything will work out well if young people respect those who are experienced, if sons heed fathers, and little bureaucrats obey big bureaucrats— because the leaders at the top really have more information than anybody else, and they are said to be doing their best for the collective group. Sometimes this confidence has been challenged for short periods. But even during cultural revolutions, at least some of the helmsmen were said to be good navigators.

MATERIALS RESERVES AS SUPPORTS FOR ECOLOGICAL OPTIMISM

Another cause of Chinese optimism about resources lies in the abundant array of raw deposits that China actually enjoys. This is a huge continental area, with a staggering population to use its resources, but also much space in which to look for them. A quick inventory of Chinese industrial supplies will lead directly to considerations of specific policies.

In the field of metals, China is the world's leading producer of tungsten.[13] During some recent years, she has accounted for one quarter of world exports of that metal. Because no available substitute has been discovered for tungsten in its most important use as a steel alloy, inelastic international demand puts China in a strong position to influence tungsten prices. Among certain other nonferrous metals, such as tin, mercury, antimony, molybdenum, and manganese, China also has current surpluses for export, which may persist even as her own industrialization picks up speed. There also seem to be sufficient national reserves of lead, zinc, aluminum, and uranium—enough to supply the Chinese economy for a long time.

Above all, China is well endowed with iron ore, widely distributed in various parts of the country. The largest mine is at Maanshan, Anhwei, and major deposits have long been worked in Liaoning Province. This sufficient supply of iron ore is a central pillar of Chinese plans for further industrialization.

Copper may well become the most troublesome specific resource shortage as China modernizes. Small amounts of the red metal are currently mined in several southern provinces,[14] but no large Chinese deposits that might ameliorate the situation have been discovered. However, China is the world's fastest growing importer of copper. (For some electrical uses, but not all, aluminum is a substitute.) This specific shortage helps explain some aspects of China's foreign policy. It is no accident that the People's Republic has taken particular initiative in building the railroad to the Indian Ocean from Zambia and southern Zaire. When President Salvador Allende's government in Chile fell to a violent anti-Communist coup, the Chinese retained diplomatic relations. China clearly wants to maintain her copper trade options with both the African and Andean sources of supply.

China's most important energy resource is coal. Bituminous deposits are widely spread throughout the populated parts of the country. There are particularly rich concentrations in the north near Peking, and in northeastern and eastern China not far from iron mines. Anthracite and lignite are available on a smaller scale. The excellent Chinese coal supply may even affect the country's future soil fertility, because wherever coal can be provided, the peasants can leave rice and wheat stalks to rot in the fields, rather than burn them to keep warm in winter. China is currently the world's third largest producer of coal, after the Soviet Union and the United States. Over two-thirds of the nation's marketed power comes from this source, which will continue for many years to be the main fuel of China.

Another kind of energy, recently risen to supply about one quarter of the nation's fuel, is petroleum oil. No one knows how much or little oil there is under China, but guesses based on geological structures suggest that considerably more is there than people previously thought. Selig Harrison has speculated that China might even have 30 billion barrels onshore, and possibly the same amount again under stretches of the East and South China Seas, which will fall under the People's Republic sovereignty after the Law of the Sea Conference completes its work.[15] China in 1976 was already producing more than 80 million metric tons, half from the Tach'ing field in Heilungkiang.[16] In the future, she will reach much higher levels, although large amounts of this oil will probably remain within the country for energy and petrochemical uses. Despite certain technical problems, at least some oil can be refined for the thirsty Japanese market; and Japan already accounts for eight-tenths of China's oil sales abroad.[17] The large Chinese coal deposits, discussed above, will permit more oil to be exported—and to earn foreign capital—than would be possible if there were no coal. This circumstance may give the Chinese somewhat more incentive to interdependence in their foreign policy than would be expected on the basis of ideological or cultural considerations alone.

Nonfossil sources of machine power are still of minor significance. Hydroelectric potential in China, as measured by the average discharge of streams and gross head sites, is probably the world's second largest after that of the Soviet Union. However, practically none of this potential has been developed, because the types of dams required to tap it on great rivers like the Yangtze are very expensive. In any case, none of the world's large economies relies on hydroelectricity for as much as a tenth of its energy needs. In no modern country is water power of great importance.

"New" forms of power generation—solar and nuclear plants especially— are insignificant in China. This situation will continue, because no present or prospective technology in the fusion, fission, or solar fields can compete with Chinese coal in terms of cost, at least for many years to come. As has been seen, paddy algae and grain plants are the main means for tapping direct solar energy in that country.

The most interesting kind of Chinese energy, which must now be considered alongside the others, is the food people eat. These calories come mainly from grains, about half from rice. The production of such energy depends on many natural conditions that are not commonly considered energy resources, such as soil types, seeds, and weather. It also depends on fertilizers, and thus on organic compost and manure as well as inorganic nitrogen and phosphorus oxide. China is able to produce nearly all the phosphate she uses, with current irrigation facilities, but in some recent years she has imported nearly half of her relatively small consumption of inorganic nitrogenous fertilizer. Recently, major foreign credits have assisted the construction of more fertilizer factories, although inorganic compost will be important for a long time.

Human energy, based on food, has specific characteristics that distinguish it from the other types mentioned above. From a narrow engineering viewpoint, the "machine" to use such energy is inefficient: men require more calories than they put into strictly economic work. But the energy actually used for this purpose is steered with a flexibility that few real machines can match. Above all, a system that relies on large amounts of this particular kind of animate power is a system of drudgery. China has a poor economy on a per capita basis, and understandably the Chinese want to change that as quickly as they can. China is low in energy consumption, if energy is measured in the usual way—which does not count human or other animate power—but this low energy consumption is the opposite of ideal. So long as an average peasant consumes about 2,000 calories per day and his field produces about 2,000 calories per day (this figure is approximately accurate, counting all persons in peasant households), then the agrarian economy is making no progress from the viewpoint of most of its members.[18]

COLLECTIVE NATIONALISM VERSUS SLOW-GROWTH CONSERVATIONISM: APPLYING MOOT VALUES TO INTERNATIONAL ECONOMIC POLICY

In the traditional environment, values that encouraged the collective mobilization of work were complementary to values that encouraged the frugal conservation and recycling of resources. In modern times, the union of these two values has not exactly been dissolved, but it has become moot. The reason is that the main modern collective is the nation-state, which is much larger than any family. This huge unit now lays claim to the previous kind of strong collective loyalty, even more surely than ever before. Other nations, trading in China and sometimes occupying parts of it in treaty ports, grew in strength by pursuing exploitative and very nonconservationist modes of economic progress.

Furthermore, the value of collectivism in the modern context could be used to argue either for quick collective growth (often this means interdependence with foreign sources of capital and technology) or else for collective independence. The operational meanings of old beliefs have become uncertain. Faced with pressure from the international environment, China has had to re-orient (so to speak) its inherited values to meet a new external situation.

No stable transformation of the old collectivism and conservationism has yet been approached in the modern era, much less achieved. Government officials, because of their administrative roles, make the relevant statements on this. To a large extent they have been able to postpone and circumnavigate many immediate problems implying value conflicts. Reliance on arbitrary (and often temporary) official "lines" is a convenience to the uncertain and the busy.

For cadres, simple optimism about China's munificent reserves of raw materials and powerful collective organizations is altogether a more congenial topic than concern about the possibilities of pollution and the costs of conservation in an industrial economy without much spare capital. Nationalistic leaders naturally prefer public styles of self-confidence to gloomy attitudes, warning that the environment will become more difficult to use for purposes of progress. National development is everywhere of more interest than national depletion. A Chinese spokesman has put this into ambiguous metaphysical language, and then into hopeful policy language: "Developing industrial production and protecting the environment are a unity of opposites. Though the two are mutually contradictory, they promote each other. . . . A planned Socialist economy provides the possibility for rational distribution of industries and effective environmental protection."[19]

The inputs needed in a modern industrial state are vastly more complex than the water, seed, fertilizer, planning, work, and luck that the fields have always required. But despite changes in the tasks to be accomplished and the size of the community to accomplish them, the new national group has a sense of identity, a will to choose its own values on internal rather than external grounds, as surely as the old households did. The new unit, like the old ones, will try to retain its independence at work. As Wang Yaoding, chairman of the China Council for the Promotion of International Trade, wrote:

> We have never been cowed by the imperialists' "blockade and embargo." Nor did we yield to the political and economic pressure put on us by the social-imperialists [the Soviets]. . . . On the contrary, these temporary difficulties only served to increase the Chinese people's determination to build their Socialist motherland at a faster pace through self-reliance and hard struggle.[20]

This determination to decide conflicts of values independently has practical implications. For example, if China has the resources to supply herself with more primary materials through an upcoming period of industrialization, then there is no reason for her to make long-term international commitments that might restrict her future freedom of action. Many specific instances of this inclination to autarky are evident in China's policy toward Third World international cartels. These have now been established for petroleum, coffee, rubber, bauxite, copper, tungsten, cocoa, phosphate, oilseeds, timber, mercury, iron, bananas, and sugar. While heartily supporting their establishment, China has not actually joined any of them. To do so might confine her future sovereign freedom in ways that could not be specified at the time of commitment to the cartel. For example, the new tungsten cartel and China (as the world's leading producer of that metal) clearly have interests that coincide. Consultation between them on short-range goals is natural. But the People's Republic has not joined the organization set up by Bolivia, Peru, Thailand, and the other tungsten producers, presumably because she wants to prevent the possibility of ever finding herself in a position such as Saudi Arabia faced recently at Vienna, when a major producer had to apply pressure on allied states for the purpose of assuring a price that could clear the market.

Other reasons for China's official emphasis on the value of economic autonomy can be found in the guerrilla heritage of the Communist movement and in a generalized dislike of foreigners, which the history of the past century has exacerbated. The Chinese party leadership is intensely proud of the self-sufficiency it achieved in wartime base areas during the 1930s and 1940s, when most of its organization and populace were blockaded into hill and marsh regions by the Nationalists and Japanese. Guns, mortars, and many other new products were produced in scattered boondock locations. Xenophobia, especially against Westerners and Japanese, has understandable historical causes in modern Chinese history. This legacy somewhat discourages even the current strong government from letting many foreign people or goods back into the country now, despite the fact that China's plans for modernization are in practice aided by such trade when it is allowed. The broad, cultural impulse to autarky is furthered by the government's desire for administrative convenience. The Communists are trying to run a Socialist, planned economy, and that effort is easiest when there is no dependence on decisions made elsewhere.

Apparent resource abundance, the guerrilla tradition, xenophobia caused by historical events, and administrative convenience—all these tend to justify independent Chinese policies on resource issues in the development of modern industry. But these factors, even in combination, do not predetermine any practical decision. They are counterbalanced by the benefits that China can reap from interdependence. That big country's comparative advantage does not always lie in immediate use of its own resource reserves; in fact, the current government of Kua Kuo-feng has increased trade, albeit from a low base and with more circumspect restrictions than apply in most countries. The Chinese say they approve of foreign trade only if it does not weaken the potential production of the importing country in similar commodity lines; otherwise, such trade is unequal. China herself has in some years imported wheat, but at the same time she claims to have exported rice of equal value; so the purpose of the exchange was allegedly to add variety to the people's diet while taking advantage of some favorable terms of trade.[21] International dependence is, in this sometime-official view, an unmitigatedly bad thing. When it occurs, it must be described in terms of national independence. Under present circumstances, how else can collective pride be squared with collective growth?

Chinese spokesmen have expressed contempt for multinational corporations (MNCs), and especially for Third World countries that give them any local freedom on a long-term basis. The Chinese do not universally condemn specific, limited agreements between less developed countries (LDCs) and MNCs; but for many purposes they have regarded the corporations as being subject to no one, anarchic, unplanned fly-by-night institutions, not usually to be trusted, without general responsibility to any nation, wasteful of landscapes around the world. However, China has dealt with many MNCs on its own terms, with guarantees to conserve its future options and resources, insofar as possible.

International credit to finance trade has until recently been suspect in official Chinese thought. The People's Republic claims to have paid off all outstanding international debts. Increasingly in the mid-1970s, its corporations have signed contracts that call for payment of foreign bills on an extended, postponed basis. This creates a debt in fact if not in appearance, and prices may be higher than if the contract had provided for quick payment. Direct international bank loans have even been mooted as a possibility. The Chinese, however, are loath, as a rule, to contract a debt that is labeled as such. They pay interest, but they often avoid calling it by that name. Many of the attitudes described above are in conflict with the present Chinese leadership's desire to import more modern technology to speed economic growth. Nonetheless, these attitudes suggest that recent relaxations of autarkic practice in China may reach a limit. Economic nationalism, a new and expanded form of age-old collectivist ideals, is still alive and well in China.

Examples from trade have dominated the discussion of applied values in the modern era, but instances from many other fields could just as easily be cited, and obviously, no full inventory of the possible types of examples is possible here. Even if restricted to international affairs, many others can be noted. At the Law of the Sea Conference, Chinese delegates have emphasized each nation's right to collective sovereignty, especially as regards environmental problems. They have favored coastal state jurisdiction over a 200-mile exclusive economic zone; and this position only expands strict PRC policies regarding its own coast[22] and the "Informal Single Negotiating Text."[23] The Ch'iungchou Strait, ten miles wide, between Hainan Island and the mainland of Kwangtung, is an international shipping route to Haiphong from all points north and east. A sovereign Chinese veto power over use of the strait is maintained. This is a more exclusivist position than even the "Single Negotiating Text" implies for international straits in territorial seas.

Chinese positions on economic aid, and on the problems it is ostensibly designed to solve, also follow from this same strong feeling for the importance of collective national sovereignty. The Chinese insist that the international food problem, to which much past aid relates, will likely recede in the future, since they say it has been caused by imperialist countries' exploitation of the agricultural resources of poor countries.[24] The optimism behind many Chinese resource policies makes pleasant assumptions about the ease with which new raw materials can be found and population growth rates controlled. Faith in the efficacy of planning helps rationalize many hopes in this area—and may possibly help to realize some of them.

Population affects most of the resource issues listed above in ways that have not been given much attention in China. Is that country really rich in resources, relative to her staggering supply of people? At one point in the mid-1960s, Vice Premier Li Xiannian admitted frankly that nobody in China knew what the country's population was, even within a margin of error several times the size of that of most nations.[25] The Communist forte has always been to mobilize people, rather than to count them.

CONCLUSION: MIXED VALUES

The modern examples do not suggest that practical work in the industrial era has generated as consistent a set of values as was inherited from work in the fields in traditional times. This should scarcely be surprising, both because modern work takes more varied forms than was usual before, and also because most of the Chinese population still lives by the rhythm of the crop cycles. Was a less mixed model expected now from the world's largest wet rice culture, from the populous nation that has been recycling resources in tight communities not just for centuries, but for millennia? Cannot an old ideal of conservation survive the will to change in China, and perhaps even appear a feasible value for others too? The answer is that it cannot. The main input to the traditional Chinese ecology is back-breaking human work. This is no goal for the future in the People's Republic, or anywhere else. Recycled traditional ideals concerning natural resources will not solve the world's problems. All the oil wells will probably run dry some day. But this is an issue the Chinese do not think they have to face yet. They have some time to worry about development first. For most resources, and for a few years to come, they are probably right, despite their huge population. An answer to their development problems implies a new set of values, which differs in many ways from their tradition.

A large bed of raw asbestos was found in Szechwan, and a work town was built there to house the miners. The new city was dubbed "Asbestos" (Shimian, literally "rock cotton"). In the United States, people used to found towns and name them Leadville (Colorado) or "Oil City" (Louisiana) or Carbondale (Colorado, Georgia, Illinois, Kansas, and Pennsylvania) but this practice has now stopped. One does not call a place Leadville if one thinks the lead is going to run out a few years later. In China, most people do not worry about resource depletion. What will happen when the development culture ends? The Chinese do not know, nor anyone else.

NOTES

1. Donald J. Munro, *The Concept of Man in Early China* (Stanford: Stanford University Press, 1969); and *The Concept of Man in Communist China* (Ann Arbor, Michigan: University of Michigan Press, 1977).

2. Joseph R. Levenson, *Modern China and its Confucian Past: The Problem of Intellectual Continuity* (Garden City, N.Y.: Doubleday Books, 1964).

3. Reinhard Bendix, *Max Weber: An Intellectual Portrait* (Garden City, N.Y.: Anchor Doubleday, 1962).

4. Mencius, *Mencius*, trans. C. D. Lau (Baltimore: Penguin Books, 1970).

5. Lucien M. Hanks, *Rice and Man: Agricultural Ecology in Southeast Asia* (Chicago: Aldine-Atherton, 1972).

6. William K. Kapp, *Environmental Policies and Development Planning in Contemporary China and Other Essays* (Paris and The Hague: Mouton, 1974).

7. E. N. Anderson, Jr., and Marja L. Anderson, "Modern China: South," in *Food in Chinese Culture: Antropological and Historical Perspectives*, ed. K. C. Chang (New Haven: Yale University Press, 1977).

8. Clifford Geertz, *Agricultural Involution: The Process of Ecological Change in Indonesia* (Berkeley and Los Angeles: University of California Press, 1971).

9. Ibid.

10. Kapp, *Environmental Policies*; and Norman Myers, "China's Approach to Environmental Conservation," *Environmental Affairs* 5 (1976): 33–63.

11. Kuo Huan, "Accent on Environmental Protection," *Peking Review* 45 (November 8, 1974): 9–11.

12. Wang An-shih, "Memorial to the Emperor Jen-tsung," and "In Defense of Five Major Policies," in *Sources of Chinese Tradition*, vol. 1, ed. William Theodore deBary (New York: Columbia University Press, 1960), pp. 413–49, 123–25.

13. K. P. Wang, "Natural Resources and Their Utilization," in *China: A Handbook*, ed. Yuan-li Wu (New York: Praeger, 1973), pp. 71–84.

14. Hsieh Chiao-min in *Atlas of China*, ed. Christopher L. Salter (New York: McGraw-Hill, 1973).

15. Selig S. Harrison, "China: The Next Oil Giant," *Foreign Policy* 20 (Fall 1975): 3–27; see also Park Choon-ho and Jerome Alan Cohen, "The Politics of the Oil Weapon," *Foreign Policy* 20 (Fall 1975): 28–49.

16. U.S. Government, Central Intelligence Agency, *China: Economic Indicators* (Washington, D.C.: C.I.A., 1977), p. 28.

17. Ibid., p. 41.

18. Vaclav Smil, "Food Energy in the PRC," *Current Scene* 15 (1977): 1–11.

19. Kuo, "Environmental Protection," pp. 9–11.

20. Wang Yao-ting, "China's Foreign Trade," *Peking Review* 41 (October 11, 1974): 18–20.

21. Hao Chung-shih, "China's Views on Solving World Food Problem," *Peking Review* 46 (November 15, 1974): 9–12.

22. Cheng Tao, "Communist China and the Law of the Sea," *American Journal of International Law* 63 (January 1969): 47–73.

23. United Nations, Document A/conf. 62/WP. 8 (New York: United Nations).

24. Hao, "Solving World Food Problems."

25. Leo A. Orleans, "China's Population: Can the Contradictions Be Resolved?" in *China: A Reassessment of the Economy*, ed. U.S. Congress, Joint Economic Committee (Washington, D.C.: Superintendent of Documents, 1975), pp. 69–80.

7

DOMESTIC ARCHITECTURE IN TAIWAN: CONTINUITY AND CHANGE

Emily M. Ahern

Anthropologists have found it fruitful to understand the use of space in the houses of many people—among them the Antoni, Temne, and Trobrianders— in terms of notions about such things as family structure, sex role division, and links to the wider society.[1] This tradition will be followed in dealing with the Taiwanese case, arguing that when Taiwanese draw distinctions among kinds of domestic architecture—one primarily rural and one primarily urban—they are talking indirectly about different attitudes they have toward two kinds of livelihood: farming on the one hand, commerce and industry on the other. Approaching the problem of attitudes toward different occupations by looking at architectural form has two advantages. First, one can at least guess at aspects of attitudes expressed in this way that people do not commonly articulate directly. Second, in Taiwan's state of rapid social and economic change, the spread of urban styles of housing into the countryside gives an unusually clear index of changes in occupation, and of concomitant changes in attitudes about how households are connected to the outside world.

THE VOCABULARY OF DOMESTIC SPACE: TRADITIONAL AND RURAL

One prominent feature of domestic spatial organization is what might be called axiality. In its simplest form, a traditional rural house (*dacu*, big house) is a rectangular structure, usually with five rooms. There is one major axis, along

---

Fieldwork on which portions of this chapter are based was carried out in Sanxia Township in northern Taiwan, especially in the village of Qinan. The author has used Mandarin transcriptions of Taiwanese terms and place names.

the long side of the rectangle. Orientation along this axis is talked about from the vantage point of the ancestors and gods whose tablets and images face out the door of the central, ceremonial room, called *keting* (Guest hall), or *zhengting* (main hall). The left side of the long, rectangular table on which their tablets and images rest, as these spirits would look at it, (stage left to the viewer) is the most honorable side, and this space is correspondingly occupied by the gods (all of whom rank higher than the ancestors).[2] The ancestral tablets occupy the stage-right half of the table: if there are tablets for peripheral ancestors (uxori-locally married men or the parents of an in-marrying woman, for example), they are placed farther stage right than tablets for agnatically central ancestors.[3]

The same principle of orientation applies to living people. The room to stage left of the central room is called the *dafang* (big room), and is occupied by the parents unless there is a married son. When the *dafang* is occupied by a married son, the parents take the "second room" or *erfang*, located to stage right of the central room.[4] Similarly, when several tables of guests are seated in the central room, it is the tables on the stage-left side of the room that have the place of honor.

The uses to which rooms are put also follow along this same axis. The central room is the place for presentation of offerings to ancestors and gods and for formal entertainment of guests. The family may display there any valuable objects they own, and make special efforts to decorate it: it is the public face of the household. This room is flanked by bedrooms, which are private in comparison to the central room, and used for family life by both sexes. Finally, the two end rooms are the most "miscellaneous" of all, as the author's informants explained it. They may include space for a kitchen, storage, livestock pens, or toilets.[5] One could summarize the general pattern by saying that the central room is oriented toward public display and group entertainment. As such, it houses both the family's most eminent members (the ancestors) and their resident guests (the gods). It is outfitted as beautifully as the family can manage and is the proper domain of the men in the family, who are usually in evidence on important public occasions. As one moves away from this room along the axis in either direction, one enters the relatively private domain of the family. In the end rooms, in contrast to the central room, women are in evidence, individuals may eat separately, at separate times, baths are taken and toilet facilities used, and animals are raised and slaughtered.[6] (See Figure 7.1.)

When perpendicular wings are added to the original rectangle, forming a U-shaped house, it is the distance away from the original house, or more exactly the central room, that may effect both architecture and use. As a villager expressed it, in the side wings "each room is built lower than the next, all lower than the central room. Things that can go into these rooms are kitchen facilities, servants, cows, and agricultural implements. The lower down the room, the more motley are the things kept there."[7]

Something of this pattern can be seen in published accounts. Wang Sung-xing describes a U-shaped house in which the far room of each wing houses a

FIGURE 7.1

Dacu in Qinan Village

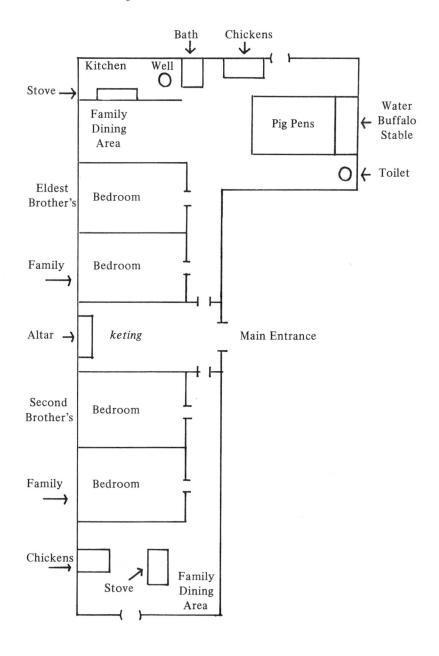

Source: Prepared by the author.

FIGURE 7.2

Compound in Taqi, Taiwan

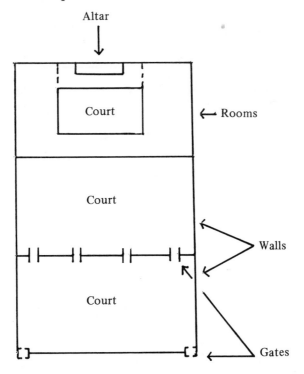

Source: Prepared by the author.

kitchen.[8] Myron Cohen describes a house with two wings on each side, and although the kitchens are the first room in each wing (perhaps lining up with the kitchens on the end of the original house), "motley" things—toilets, storage rooms, animal sheds—are still housed farthest away from the central hall, in the side rooms paralleling the second wing.[9] (See also Figure 7.2.)

Distance from the center can also be combined with the predominance of the stage-left side over the right. If there are four brothers who wish to divide the space in a U-shaped house, for example, they usually take, in order of birth and therefore precedence, the *dafang* and adjoining side room, the *erfang* and adjoining room, the left wing, and then the right wing. The central room is kept in common.[10]

Another important feature in spatial organization is relative height, the greater height associated with greater honor. Numerous examples can be cited:

the altar for ancestors' tablets and gods' images is higher than any other table in common use; the incense pot for *Tiankung*, the highest god, hangs by the door in the central hall, higher than other gods' images; as already noted, the roof of the central room is built higher than the roofs of the adjoining rooms.[11]

Yet another feature of domestic architecture is interiority. By the construction of walls enclosing courts, the entrance to the central hall can be protected and its central position emphasized. In rural Taiwan, this is seldom carried farther than the construction of a wall to enclose the court formed by the wings of a U-shaped dwelling. But more elaborate constructions can be found, with more barriers between the outside and the central hall. In a village in Taqi Township in northern Taiwan, the former outlines of a once magnificent compound can still be discerned. The central hall with its ancestral altar was preceded by no less than three courts, each walled. (See Figure 7.2.) The former magnificence of this compound was clearly related to the former stature of the lineage that occupied it: some of its members had been officials in the Ch'ing dynasty. Similarly, the wealthy Lin family of Wu-feng, Taiwan, lived in houses with a series of forecourts. "The several successive courts and receiving rooms gave the greater ceremony needed by a wealthy family or by government and allowed a hierarchy of privacy not seen in the more egalitarian farm house."[12]

The creation of multiple interior barriers in front of the main hall is a mark of high status or wealth elsewhere in China too. D. H. Kulp includes a floor plan of a compound with two courts in front of the hall, which is clearly one of the "larger and finer houses of the wealthy families" in Phoenix Village.[13] In addition, Martin Yang presents plans of upper class families' houses with two courts in front of the room used for ceremonial purposes.[14] (See Figures 7.3 and 7.4.)

The use of interior barriers to reflect hierarchy reached its apex, of course, in the dwelling of the highest ranking person in the country, the emperor. The "Forbidden City," the inner core of the government buildings in Peking, had a "complex of audience courtyards and halls extending in a narrow, deep rectangle up the grand axis (the counterpart of the front court and reception hall in the city residence of any Chinese gentlemen)."[15]

The final feature of domestic architceture discussed here is expandability. In Taiwan a simple rectangular house is often built with bricked-in but not mortared-in doorways at either end, anticipating the addition of wings. This architectural feature clearly reflects the common desire of a family to expand its numbers and to keep its members residing under the same roof. It has already been seen how houses are enclosed, not by walls but by functional living space.[16]

THE VOCABULARY OF DOMESTIC SPACE: NEW AND URBAN

In Taiwan's major urban centers and small villages alike, there are other forms of housing beside the U-shaped compound. Most ubiquitous is the *yanglou*,

FIGURE 7.3

Diagram of House with Multiple Courts

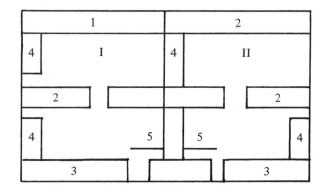

Note: 1. Main house or *cheng-wu* where the parents, the unmarried daughters, and the first married son live; 2. Middle house or *ch'ien-wu*, where the second married son or other junior members live; 3. Front house or *nan-wu*, where hired laborers live (also for house and farm implements; 4. Small houses for keeping the domestic animals; 5. Spirit wall, or *yung-pei*.

Source: Martin C. Yong, *A Chinese Village: Taitou, Shantung Province* (New York: Columbia University Press, 1976).

or "foreign-style building." In its simplest form it is a rectangular structure of one story with its main entrance in one of the narrow ends, facing a road or highway. (The significance of this will be seen later.) Normally *yanglou* are built in rows, sharing their long walls in common, and with no presumption that adjacent houses are occupied by related families. Given the great physical differences between this form of housing and the U-shaped compound, it is striking that a number of general features are common to both. *Yanglou* of one story almost invariably have the finest room, the room for entertainment of guests and installation of ancestral tablets, if any, immediately inside the front door. Other rooms behind this one are often oriented to it axially, much as if they formed one side of the base rectangle of a U-shaped compound. Bedrooms are often located behind the front guest hall, and the kitchen, bath, toilet, and animals behind them. Just as in the rooms stretching away from the central hall in a

FIGURE 7.4

Plan of House with Multiple Courts

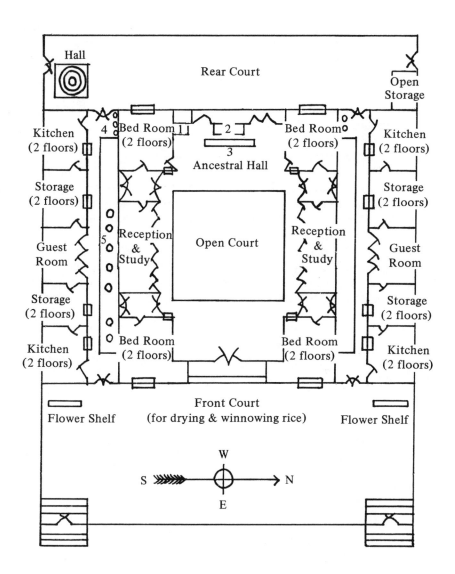

Source: D. H. Kulp, *Country Life in South China* (New York: Teachers College, Columbia University, 1925), p. 153 (Figure 5).

compound, the more "motley" and private functions are farthest away from the guest hall. Virtually all of the more than 10 *yanglou* in Qinan Village follow this general floor plan: one such is illustrated in Figure 7.5. Out of a sample of 13 *yanglou* located in Taipei and its urban environs inhabited by relatives, friends or classmates of Qinan villagers, eight follow this plan. One other in the sample, a third-floor dwelling, has its guest hall located in the middle of the house, so that the visitor enters it directly from the staircase. This preserves one feature of the ground-floor *keting*; the visitor enters it first, but changes the spatial relationship of other rooms to it.

In addition to axiality, the association of height with honorific position is found in *yanglou*, but in a new way. In four of the sample of 13 *yanglou*, families are occupying more than one story. In three of these four cases, the ceremonial altar with ancestral tablets and gods' images is located on the topmost occupied floor. In the fourth, the tablets remain on the ground floor, in the front room. In *yanglou* there is no equivalent to the many layers of courts possible in compounds, because they cannot be extended front or back, in most cases. Still, it should be noted that *yanglou* do often have an interior court, open to the sky. (See Figure 7.5.)

It has been seen that the architecture of compounds seems to prefigure the expansion of families. This feature is found (in altered form) in *yanglou*. A *yanglou* is essentially a rectangular concrete box. Its floor, walls, and roof are poured concrete, reinforced with brick, and at the corners, steel rods. Compounds expand sideways through additional wings; *yanglou* expand upward through additional stories. Compounds indicate the intention to expand by the construction of unmortared doorways; *yanglou* indicate the same intention by leaving the roof unfinished. Typically, the steel rods at the four corners are left sticking out, ready to form the base for the corners of the next story.

In sum, most of the features of old-style compounds that relate to the growth of families and the presentation of their public face are preserved in new-style houses. One cannot argue that lack of change in these architectural features means that people's notions about the family are not changing, but at least it is clear that there is no explicit association between increasing numbers of *yanglou* and alteration in people's notions about the growth of families or what constitutes their public face. As will be seen below, people explicitly recognize that other aspects of *yanglou*, however, do mark changes in the way families relate to the outside society.

THE ORIENTATION OF BUILDINGS

It is obvious that *dacu* are suited to places where there is room to expand laterally, and *yanglou* to places where lateral expansion is unfeasible or prohibitively expensive, leading to upward expansion. As Arthur Smith said of U-shaped compounds, "in cities this type is greatly modified by the exigencies of the contracted space at their disposal."[17] The fact that land values are often at a

FIGURE 7.5

Yanglou in Qinan Village

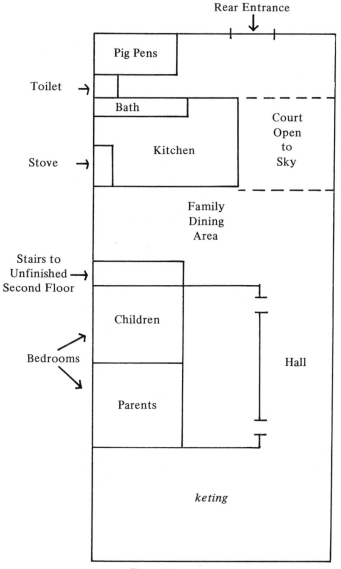

Source: Prepared by the author.

premium in commercialized urban centers means that *yanglou* are characteristically found there. There is still in Taiwan a dichotomy between rural areas devoted primarily to agriculture where *dacu* are common, and commercial, urban, industrial areas where *yanglou* are common.

This opposition is a key to understanding an important difference between *dacu* and *yanglou*: when *dacu* are built, they must be carefully oriented to the environment according to the principles of geomancy, known in Taiwan as *dili*. Normally a professional geomancer is hired to make sure the house faces in the most propitious direction, given the configuration of shapes in the surrounding landscape, the lie of the land, the flow of water, and so on.[18] If the fortunes of the inhabitants are going poorly, one strategy they may adopt is to alter the shape of the landscape or even change the orientation of the house. In sharp contrast, *yanglou*, the author was told, are not oriented according to the principles of *dili* when they are built. One house builder said, "It's a bother to build a *dacu* because you have to be so careful about the *dili*. With *yanglou* you do not have to build according to the *dili*; *yanglou* are built according to the road."[19] Although *yanglou* are not oriented according to *dili*, they are built at propitious *times*. Just as with *dacu*, a propitious time for breaking ground, building a stove, and setting up an altar must be found, usually by a geomancer. The only difference is that a *dacu*'s central roof beam must also be set at a propitious time: since *yanglou* have no beam, this is obviously not a matter of concern.[20]

The many people who spoke about this distinction between *dacu* and *yanglou* seemed to have in mind two paradigms. On the one hand, for a farming household located in a rural, relatively unpopulated area and dependent for its livelihood on its own labor and the natural workings of rain and sun, the *dacu* will be oriented according to geomantic principles, stressing this reliance on the natural order of things. On the other hand, for a household engaged in commerce, located in a densely populated, highly commercialized central place and dependent for its livelihood on its business judgment and the fluctuations of the market, the *yanglou* is oriented not according to geomancy but according to the road, stressing reliance on the man-made environment of market demand. The reason for the stress on roads is immediately apparent: they not only provide the physical means by which customers reach one's door, but are also a primary determinant in whether a commercial area will be able to intensify its commercial activity.[21] The two paradigms are relevant not only in the present: informants were sure to stress that even far back in Taiwan's development *yanglou* in towns were built "according to the road."

The two paradigms as presented so far are overly simple, largely because of the extreme commercialization that exists in Taiwan.[22] One aspect of this is that commercial establishments are common in the countryside;[23] another is that a great proportion of farming families also engage in some market activity.[24] The growing existence of commercial establishments in rural areas is marked vividly on the first and second, and fifteenth and sixteenth days of the lunar month. According to tradition, farmers pay respect to *Tudi Gong*, the minor territorial god, on the first and fifteenth, and those in business do so on the second and sixteenth. Nowadays firecrackers for *Tudi Gong* can be heard going off on the second and sixteenth days of the month in rural villages as well as in towns and cities.

One concomitant of the growth of market-oriented activity is the increase in numbers of *yanglou* in rural areas. In Qinan Village, there were three *yanglou* in 1969, occupied by two village stores and a ritual paper-house manufacturer. By 1975 there were five more, occupied by a third village store, a carpenter's shop, two households engaged in a variety of commercial activities, and one primarily farming household. All these were oriented "to the road" in contrast to the *dacu* around them. Similarly, Cohen notes that in Yen-liao in southern Taiwan, families who settled there after 1950 did not, as did earlier settlers, build U-shaped compounds. All these had nonagricultural businesses and all located them on the roadside.[25] One can only assume they built *yanglou*. Fittingly, the two families settling after 1950, who were farmers, built compounds.[26] Although the general trend is for *yanglou* to be increasingly built in the countryside, occasionally urban centers overtake old *dacu*. San-xia town includes within its limits a *dacu* with two wings. People explained the contrast between this house and its *yanglou* neighbors by saying the family occupying the *dacu* had once been farmers. The court yard, now used as an area for washing taxicabs, was once an area for drying rice.

Just because *yanglou* are not oriented according to *dili*, it does not follow that they do not have a geomantic orientation. A geomancer told the author, "You can't consider *dili* when you build a house onto a row of *yanglou* in a town, but the house *has* a *dili* anyway. Some have good *dili*, some bad. You can tell by whether the business is going well or poorly. If you get a house with a bad *dili*, there is no way to fix it. All you can do is move out."*

The architecture of *yanglou* and *dacu* in and of itself implies nothing about differences between the families of farmers and those of businessmen, as has been seen; but the different way the houses relate to *dili* may imply something about different attitudes to the outside world in each case. It could be that people say *yanglou* cannot be oriented or reoriented according to *dili* simply because the form of architecture (houses in contiguous rows) makes it difficult to change their alignment with the compass, and the small size of the plots they are built on makes changes in the surrounding environment impractical; but even very small changes in alignment or in the immediate surroundings could in theory affect the *dili*. Yet people declare that bad *dili* in a *yanglou* cannot be fixed; one can only move out. Hence it seems possible that what people say about the *dili* of *yanglou* is an indirect way of talking about something else.

---

*Taiwan informants did not speak of the *dili* of whole towns; but numerous mainland sources show this was a possibility. If this were the case, all inhabitants of the town might share in its *dili*.[27]

Perhaps what they are saying is that if one lives in a *yanglou*, assuming one engages in commerce, one has a different kind of control over one's fate than if one lives in a *dacu*, assuming one engages in farming.

If a farmer's life goes poorly, he can, on the one hand, change the *dili* of his *dacu* and, on the other, alter his cultivating techniques or plant a different crop. Of course, he might perceive the activity of farming itself to be a failure, sell the land, and switch to another livelihood entirely. But before resorting to that, there would be ample room for changing his methods of dealing with the same raw material, land. Land, after all, can always produce something, especially in Taiwan's generally favorable climate. In contrast, a small industrialist or businessman who found himself without a market for his goods might well have no recourse but to cut his losses and switch to some other line of business. Machinery and raw materials are often more specialized than land: if *tatamis* went out of style or the overseas market for sweaters declined, the machines and materials for their production could not readily be put to another use.

Perhaps this is the parallel in the world of business to the *yanglou* whose *dili* cannot be altered, but only abandoned. In this connection, it is of the greatest relevance that failure in the small business sector is very common in Taiwan, partly because of the increasing extent of commercialization and concomitant competition.[28]

So far, this study has followed Taiwanese informants in stressing the distinction between *dacu* and *yanglou*. They mentioned no other form of domestic architecture (except apartments, *gongyu shi*) and insisted that urban houses had always been called *yanglou* as far back as the Chinese settlement of Taiwan. Even at that early time, they maintained, *yanglou* had been built according to the road instead of according to the dictates of geomancy. But the very name *yanglou*—*foreign*-style building—should make one wonder whether these structures have not been rather more recently introduced into the Chinese scene. Is it not likely that there was another form of domestic architecture before *yanglou*, one that was an urban place of business and residence for merchants? One source refers to "merchant houses" (*shangdian zhuzhai*), which can be found in the early coastal trading cities of Lugang and Danshui in Taiwan. These were similar in some ways to *yanglou*, having a short frontage on the street and a very long depth, and often being built in two stories. Unlike *yanglou*, they were enclosed by walls on either side.[29] If there were in fact merchant houses in Taiwan's cities before the existence of *yanglou* (contrary to the author's informants), an interesting question arises: Were these merchants' houses oriented geomantically or not?

Some light is shed on this question by material from the New Territories, Hong Kong. First, attention must be drawn to a major difference between rural domestic architecture in the New Territories and in Taiwan: whereas in Taiwan, as we have seen, rural farmhouses are isolated entities, differently oriented to its surroundings, houses in New Territories' villages are arranged in rows along lanes or streets.[30] Geomancy is important in house construction, but it seems to play a smaller role in orienting the house to the environment than in governing the placement of openings such as windows and doors.

Yanglou were seemingly introduced in the New Territories by emigrants to foreign countries, who invested some of their earnings in elaborate two-story houses, partly for the prestige this brought to them and their kinsmen.[31] Aside from the addition of one or more stories, New Territories' *yanglou* differ from traditional houses in other ways, the most important of which for present purposes is that they ignore the dictates of geomancy. In a letter negotiating the construction of two *yanglou*, one emigrant in Manila speaks directly of his desire to build a geomancy-free house in spite of the possible objections of local people:

> Your letter mentions the Provisional Constitution of the Republic as a guarantee of liberty and freedom, and contends that I need not be afraid of coercion on the part of our kinsmen at home in the event of our building new houses. But you must remember that our kinsmen have a deep-rooted belief in geomancy and that this has more than once prevented us from realizing our desire to build ourselves new houses.
>
> Fortunately, A and B have recently agreed not to interfere with each other's affairs. This is a rare opportunity which we should not allow to pass. Our kinsmen in Manila have lately discussed the available building land of B and G, and have decided to build two foreign-style houses thereon. Meantime, they have appointed H and I to be responsible for the building operations.[32]

In the New Territories' case, ignoring geomancy means the addition of many windows: traditional houses have few or none.[33] In the Taiwan case, it means orienting the house to the road instead of the geomantically significant environment. In the New Territories, traditionally styled houses built with geomancy in mind (lacking windows) mark rural farming households whose livelihood comes from the local Chinese economy; foreign-style houses built in disregard of geomancy (with windows) mark households whose livelihood comes at least in part from the international economy through overseas members. In Taiwan traditionally styled houses built with geomancy in mind (oriented according to its dictates) mark rural farming households primarily engaged in farming; foreign-style houses built in disregard of geomancy (according to the road) mark households primarily engaged in commerce, whether its scale be local, national, or international. In the New Territories, abandoning geomancy goes along with abandoning the local economy; in Taiwan, abandoning geomancy goes along with abandoning a farming economy. This shows us that the disappearance of geomancy as a concern can be a way of talking about a variety of contrasting attitudes about how households relate to the means of their livelihood.

Returning now to the questions of whether pre-*yanglou* urban houses existed in Taiwan and whether or not they were built according to geomantic concerns, it can be imagined that one of at least two situations could have been possible.* (1) There were pre-*yanglou* urban dwellings built according to geomantic dictates. (Even if these were oriented according to the road, the New Territories' case shows that other elements, such as the placement of windows, could have been significant geomantically.) These came to be called *yanglou* and to be built without reference to geomancy as, in the course of Taiwan's industrialization, specialized mechanization of industry increased. The move away from geomancy would then have marked, as suggested above, recognition of a loss of ability to adjust the means of one's livelihood to changing circumstances. (2) Whatever form of urban houses existed before *yanglou*, or before they came to be called *yanglou*, were not built in accord with geomancy. The contrast between urban houses built in commercial centers without geomancy and rural houses built in farming areas with geomancy would have marked a simple distinction between commerce and small-scale industry whose success is determined largely by the market—emphasized by orientation to the road—and farming, whose success is determined largely by the physical environment—soil, water, weather—emphasized by orientation to geomantic forces in the landscape.

Ironically, despite the obvious and visible physical differences between *dacu* and *yanglou*, the physical shape of *yanglou* permits almost all the same principles of construction that relate to family structure in *dacu* to have a place. One must look elsewhere for clues to changes in attitudes toward family size, growth, or composition. But the less obvious and visible difference between *dacu* and *yanglou*—the *dili* of the first can be manipulated, whereas the *dili* of the second is unalterable—indirectly gives a strong clue about peoples' different attitudes toward farming and commerce as livelihoods. They seem to be saying that aside from the great potential for wealth and success commerce has, when one abandons a base of agricultural land, one incurs the risk of total failure because one's ability to respond flexibly to changing conditions is reduced. Or in other words, farmers may be prey to the vagaries of the climate, but over time they can recoup their losses; businessmen are even more prey to the vagaries of the market, and as a consequence may be unable to repair the damage caused by a crisis, just as they are unable to repair the *dili* of their houses.

NOTES

1. Clark E. Cunningham, "Order in the Atoni House," in *Reader in Comparative Religion*, ed. William A. Lessa and Evon Z. Vogt (New York: Harper and Row, 1965), pp. 116–35; James Littlejohn, "The Temne House," in *Myth and Cosmos*, ed. John Middleton (New York: National History Press, 1967), pp. 331–47; Bronislaw Malinowski, *Argonauts of*

*The author has no evidence to suggest which of these situations, or perhaps others, existed, but further research into the history of domestic architecture in Taiwan could presumably settle the question.

the Western Pacific: An account of Native Enterprise and Adventure in the Archipelagoes of Melanesian New Guinea (New York: Dutton, 1922), pp. 55–57.

2. Wang Sungxing, "Taiwanese Architecture and the Supernatural," in *Religion and Ritual in Chinese Society*, ed. Arthur P. Wolf (Stanford: Stanford University Press, 1974), p. 184.

3. C. Stevan Harrell, "The Ancestors at Home: Domestic Worship in a Land-Poor Taiwanese Village," in *Ancestors*, ed. William H. Newell (The Hague: Mouton, 1976), pp. 382–83.

4. Wang, "Taiwanese Architecture," p. 184.

5. See Rudolf Kelling, *Das Chinesische Wohnhaus* (Tokyo: Deutsche Gesellschaft für Natur- und Völkerkunde Ostasiens, Supplement 13, 1935), p. 59, on the proximity of animal quarters to the kitchens.

6. This pattern can be seen in Bernard Gallin, *Hsin Hsing, Taiwan: A Chinese Village in Change* (Berkeley: University of California Press, 1966), p. 28, Figure 1; note the "original house," Wang, "Taiwanese Architecture," p. 185; D. H. Kulp, *Country Life in South China* (New York: Teachers College, Columbia University, 1925), p. 153. The pattern is altered in northern areas, where the necessity of winter heating makes it advisable to locate stoves centrally. See Martin C. Yang, *A Chinese Village: Taitou, Shantung Province* (New York: Columbia University Press, 1965), p. 39.

7. Personal communication.

8. Wang, "Taiwanese Architecture," p. 185.

9. Myron L. Cohen, *House United, House Divided: The Chinese Family in Taiwan* (New York: Columbia University Press, 1976), p. 22.

10. Wang, "Taiwanese Architecture," p. 184.

11. See Yingdao Wu, *Taiwan Minsu* (Taipei: Guding Shuwu, 1970), p. 207.

12. Reed Dillingham and Chang-lin Dillingham, *A Survey of Traditional Architecture of Taiwan*, (Taichung, Taiwan: Center for Housing and Urban Research, Taichung University, 1971), p. 131.

13. Kulp, "Country Life," pp. 14, 153 (Figure 5).

14. Yang, *Chinese Village*, p. 39 (Figure 6).

15. Laurence Chalfont, Stevens Sickman, and A. C. Soper, *The Art and Architecture of China* (Baltimore: Penguin, 1956), p. 286.

16. See Yang, *Chinese Village*, p. 39 (Figure 3).

17. Arthur H. Smith, *Village Life in China* (Boston: Little, Brown 1970), p. 12.

18. See Stephan D. R. Feuchtwang, *An Anthropological Analysis of Chinese Geomancy* (Vientiane: Vithagna, 1974); and Maurice Freedman, *Chinese Lineage and Society: Fukien and Kwangtung* (London: Athlone Press, 1966), p. 118ff.

19. Personal communication.

20. See G. Endemann, "Hausbau und Hausweihe bei den Hak-ka," *Der Ostasiatsche Lloyd* 25 (1911): 79–80, on various rituals associated with house building.

21. Larry Crissman, "Marketing on the Changhua Plain, Taiwan," in *Economic Organization in Chinese Society*, ed. W. E. Wilmott (Stanford: Stanford University Press, 1972), p. 246.

22. Ibid., p. 218.

23. Ibid.

24. Ibid., pp. 248–49; Ramon H. Myers, "The Commercialization of Agriculture in Modern China," in *Economic Organization in Chinese Society*, ed. W. E. Willmott (Stanford: Stanford University Press, 1972), pp. 177, 181.

25. Cohen, *House United*, pp. 24, 26. On the mainland, too, urban-style houses might be built in the countryside. J. E. Spenser, "The Houses of the Chinese," *Geographical Review* 37 (1947): 256, Figure 1, notes that a rich family with urban connections might build a version of an urban-style house (one with multiple interior courts) in a home village.

26. Ibid., p. 24.

27. See Feuchtwang, *Anthropological Analysis*, pp. 207–9.

28. Donald R. DeGlopper, "Doing Business in Dukang," in *Economic Organization in Chinese Society*, ed. W. S. Willmott (Stanford: Stanford University Press, 1972), p. 304.

29. Dillingham and Dillingham, *Traditional Architecture*, p. 132.

30. H. G. H. Nelson, "The Chinese Descent System and the Occupancy Level of Village Houses," *Journal of the Hong Kong Branch of the Royal Asiatic Society* 9 (1969): 113–14.

31. See Rose Hun Lee, *The Chinese in the United States of America* (Hong Kong: Hong Kong University Press, 1960), p. 83; and James L. Watson, *Emigration and the Chinese Lineage* (Berkeley: University of California Press, 1975), pp. 159–60.

32. Chen Ta, *Emigrant Communities in South China* (Shanghai: Kelly and Walsh, 1939), p. 112.

33. Ibid., p. 111; Watson, *Emigration*, p. 161.

8

CHANGING FAMILY ATTITUDES OF TAIWANESE YOUTH

Nancy J. Olsen

INTRODUCTION

The process of industrialization, as outlined by William Goode,[1] Talcott Parsons,[2] and others, involves a breakdown of economic control of the larger kin group over its members, and the emergence of the conjugal family as an "ideal type." The conjugal or nuclear family is said to "fit" the needs of an industrial society by permitting geographical and social mobility, encouraging the hiring and promotion of individuals on universalistic rather than kin-based criteria, and serving as a haven of emotionality and acceptance in an increasingly impersonal and achievement-oriented industrial order. One concomitant of actual changes in family behavior is, according to Goode, a "conjugal family ideology." This ideology asserts the worth of the individual, as against kinship-controlled elements of wealth or position. It "proclaims the right of the individual to choose his or her own spouse, place to live, and even which kinship obligations to accept. . . . One principle in this family ideology is egalitarianism, and the spread of the conjugal family is accompanied by a trend toward 'egalitarianism' between the sexes."[3]

Empirical studies in developing nations have generally found that family attitudes* are indeed highly correlated with other aspects of traditionalism-

---

*In this paper the terms "attitude" and "ideology" are used in what is believed to be their commonly accepted usages. "Attitude" refers to an individual's beliefs or feelings

---

The research on which this chapter is based was supported by grants from the National Institute of Mental Health and the Social Science Research Council. The paper owes much to the careful criticisms of earlier drafts by Sally Hacker and Stephen Olsen.

modernism. The "modern man" of Joseph Kahl's study in Brazil and Mexico,[4] for example, subscribes to a philosophy that accords women the right to disagree with their husbands and to take work outside the home, and men the right to place occupational advantage over close ties with relatives.

Similarly, valuing equal rights for women and the limitation of obligations to kin beyond the nuclear family was found by Alex Inkeles and David Smith[5] to be one component of a general syndrome of "personal modernism." This personality/attitudinal complex is viewed as emerging in much the same way in all developing nations, as increased levels of education, factory employment, and exposure to mass media models create a cross-culturally similar "modern man." Although Inkeles and Smith have, in fact, studied only males, it is their belief that the modernization of women's attitudes occurs to the same degree and in response to the same processes that affect men.

Alternative formulations see change in family-related behaviors and attitudes as more complex. For example, Michael Anderson[6] argues that norms and values grow out of the process of economic reciprocity, as individuals attempt to maximize long-term benefits to themselves within the constraints of the various opportunities open to them. Since relationships of economic exchange vary among groups of individuals located at different positions within the differentiated social structure of a developing nation, the process of attitude change will not be a uniform one.

This alternative approach would seem to apply most particularly to sex differences in the modernization of attitudes toward family relationships. An extensive literature has recently developed documenting and analyzing shifts in male-female reciprocities as nations move from agrarian to industrial economies,[7] but there has been little concomitant research into the possible effects on family attitudes of men and women.

Taiwan is a nation engaged in the process of industrialization and urbanization. At the present time just over half the labor force is employed in nonagricultural occupations. This study is an attempt to discern the extent to which urbanization-industrialization has affected the family attitudes of Taiwanese youth, and in particular to determine whether the forces of modernization have influenced the sexes equally.

---

about a specific object or class of objects. As such, attitudes include both cognitive and evaluative components. An "ideology" is an organized, integrated set of attitudes that characterizes not an individual but a group of individuals. Ideologies, furthermore, may be seen as linked to the sociopolitical and economic interests of groups, delineated on such bases as gender, social class, nation, and so forth.

METHOD

The data on which this analysis is based were collected in Taiwan in 1974, as part of a larger study of family relationships. Young people in the eighth and ninth grades of two junior middle schools completed a questionnaire that included a number of items concerning family attitudes. Three of these items dealt with preference for traditional versus modern family organization, and four with attitudes toward the role of women.

Family preferences
1. When I get married I would rather
   a. live together with my parents or in-laws in a large family.
   b. live alone with my spouse in an independent family.
2. When I get married I would rather
   a. have my parents help me select a suitable spouse.
   b. choose my spouse completely on my own.
3. When I get married, the number of children I think would be ideal is _____.

Sex-role attitudes
4. Generally speaking, women are less capable than men of making important decisions.
   a. mostly agree
   b. mostly disagree
5. No matter what they say, most women these days will feel bad if they don't give birth to a son.
   a. mostly agree
   b. mostly disagree
6. It's wrong for women with young children to work outside the home.
   a. mostly agree
   b. mostly disagree
7. When a woman disagrees with her husband, she should keep silent rather than speak up.
   a. mostly agree
   b. mostly disagree

These questions were selected as representative of those employed in previous studies of "individual modernization," and thus assumed to be universal indicators of traditional versus modern family attitudes. The voluminous ethnographic literature on Chinese family patterns, however, would suggest the use of a very similar set of items to indicate adherence to or rejection of traditional Chinese practices.

For each question, the traditional response is represented by the first alternative. In the case of ideal family size, a stated preference for three or more children is defined as traditional, two or fewer as modern. (Education for birth planning had apparently been successful by 1974 in that the majority of students said that the ideal family consisted of two children. Thus, although three children can hardly be called a traditionally large family, this response was of necessity so definted for purposes of analysis.)

Intercorrelations among the two sets of items are presented in Table 8.1. It is worth noting that the four sex-role items are all intercorrelated and in that sense may be said to constitute a single attitudinal dimension. In other words, a pupil who agreed to one item was likely to agree to the others. However, this is somewhat more the case for girls than for boys, as shown by an average inter-item correlation of .11 for boys, .15 for girls. This suggests that these four discrete items, touching on quite different aspects of women's role and, as will be seen, differentially related to rural versus urban residence, nonetheless constitute a cognitive "package" for youth of both sexes, but more so for girls than boys.

The same cannot be said of the family preference items. The wish to live in an extended family is correlated with a preference for help with mate selection for both boys and girls, but with a large ideal family size only for boys. The remaining items are either uncorrelated or negatively correlated.* Altogether, then, although there are some relationships among the responses to these items, "the traditional Chinese family" does not appear to be a unitary phenomenon that youth either accept or reject in its entirety. Rather, the component parts seem to be cognitively separable, and as such amenable to differential influence by factors associated with modernization.

The students who answered these questions were enrolled in junior middle schools in two locales in Taiwan. The urban sample came from Ch'eng-yuan School in the Ta-t'ung District of Taipei. This school was selected because of its relatively high proportion of Taiwanese (rather than mainland) pupils, and because it drew from an area representing a wide range of types of urban occupations. The rural students were from Hsin-p'u, a marketing center for an agricultural area in the heavily Hakka region of Hsinchu County.

These two communities may be said to serve as representatives of the modern and the traditional in contemporary Taiwanese life. Although urban occupations may be of a traditional as well as a modern sort, it seems reasonable to imagine that the modernizing effects of life in the capital city will be felt to some extent by all who live there. Similarly, despite the fact that Hsin-p'u fathers are employed in a variety of occupations in addition to farming, the town is at the center of a traditional rural way of life. Additional information about the sample is summarized in Table 8.2.

---

*It is also the case that family preference and sex-role items are uncorrelated. These data are not presented.

TABLE 8.1

Intercorrelations of Family Attitudes of Boys and Girls in Two Taiwanese Communities

	Boys			Girls		
	Item 2	Item 3	Item 4	Item 2	Item 3	Item 4
Family preference items						
1. Extended family	.07	.15		.21	.02	.14
2. Mate choice	—	-.07		—	.01	.09
3. Large family	—	—		—	—	—
Sex-role attitude items						
1. Less capable	.19	.11	.10	.24	.18	.14
2. No son	—	.10	.17	—	.15	.09
3. Work outside	—	—	.08	—	—	.12
4. Keep silent	—	—	—	—	—	—

Note: Kendall's tau was used. For a sample of this size, a correlation of approximately $\pm$ .06 is significant at the .05 level.
Source: Compiled by the author.

TABLE 8.2

Characteristics of Sample

	Urban	Rural
Sample size	1,181	211
Percent living in nuclear families	53	43
Mean number of children	4.6	5.2
Father's occupation (percent)		
Farmers	0	43
Workers	20	15
Small businessmen	44	17
White-collar employees	15	12
Professionals, managers	21	13
Father's education (percent)		
High school graduates	33	21
Elementary school or less	47	58
Mother's employment (percent)		
At home only	79	73
Part-time or intermittent outside	6	12
Full-time outside	16	15

Source: Compiled by the author.

RESULTS

Most theories of individual modernization, as reviewed above, would predict a decline in traditional family attitudes as individuals move from rural to urban environments. The figures presented in Table 8.3 support this prediction to a limited extent for family preferences, but not at all for sex-role attitudes. With regard to the former, urban young people indicate a modernization of attitudes in the areas of mate selection and ideal family size, but not with regard to nuclear versus extended family living. In terms of sex-role attitudes, only the item that asks about the importance of having a son shows a change in the predicted direction, whereas the belief that women should not disagree with their husbands is more prevalent among urban than rural youth.

Although it might be possible to construct a post-hoc theory that could explain these results, it seems more profitable to turn to a comparison of the responses of boys and girls as these are affected by area of residence. This information is presented in Table 8.4.

The most notable conclusion to be drawn from this table is that girls are markedly more modern in their family attitudes than are boys. Girls, it is true, are more likely than boys to want parental help in finding a suitable spouse, but for all the remaining items, and for both samples, girls are consistently less likely to subscribe to traditional beliefs and practices. Since traditional attitudes support a kinship system based on female subordination, the general rejection of these attitudes by girls is not surprising.

TABLE 8.3

Family Attitudes of Youth in Two Taiwanese Communities (percent)

	Urban	Rural
Family preferences		
Prefer extended family	42.2	37.9
Prefer parental help with mate choice	19.2	33.0
Want large number of children (3+)	19.6	25.3
Sex-role attitudes		
Women less capable than men	44.5	44.7
Women feel bad if no son	35.1	46.2
Wrong for mothers to work outside	46.1	46.2
Keep silent if disagree with husband	54.1	41.9

Source: Compiled by the author.

More interesting and theoretically relevant, therefore, is the way in which the modernization experience differentially affects the attitudes of boys and girls, especially those attitudes that concern sex roles. In general, the movement from rural to urban life is associated with a modernization of attitudes for boys, but not for girls. On the contrary, for some items the urban girls are more traditional than their rural counterparts.

This pattern is most clearly and dramatically evident in the responses to the item, "In general, women are less capable than men of making important decisions." Of the boys in the farming community, 76 percent agreed with this statement, but only 23 percent of the girls did so, a difference of over 50 percentage points. In the urban sample, however, the percentage of boys agreeing dropped to 58, while the percentage of girls accepting this statement as true *rose* to 29. Although girls remain more modern in this respect than boys, the difference between the sexes is sharply reduced. A similar pattern holds with re-

TABLE 8.4

Family Attitudes of Boys and Girls in Two
Taiwanese Communities
(percent)

	Urban		Rural	
	Boys	Girls	Boys	Girls
Family preferences				
Prefer extended family	55.7	26.7	55.3	25.5
Prefer help in mate choice	14.5	24.8	18.3	44.0
Want many children	25.2	13.0	28.9	22.6
Sex-role attitudes				
Women less capable	57.9	28.7	75.6	22.6
Feel bad if no son	43.5	25.2	60.0	36.5
Wrong to work outside	50.6	40.7	58.0	37.9
Keep silent	57.7	49.8	49.4	36.4

Source: Compiled by the author.

spect to the belief that it is wrong for mothers to work outside the home. Urban boys are less likely, urban girls more likely, than their rural counterparts to accept this statement.

For the remaining two sex-role items, a slightly different but not inconsistent pattern emerges. Urban youth of both sexes are less likely than those living in rural areas to believe that women will feel bad if they do not have sons, but the decline in adherence to this attitude is greater for boys. In other words, urban residence does have a modernizing effect on girls, but to a lesser degree than it does for boys. Similarly, both boys and girls in the urban sample are less modern than those from the rural samples in believing that women should keep silent rather than disagree with their husbands, but the increase in acceptance of this attitude is greater for girls. Again, urban residence appears to promote traditionalism rather than modernism in young women.

A different pattern emerges when considering family preferences. As has already been shown, urban youth are more modern in their preference for free mate choice and a small family size, and Table 8.4 shows that this generalization holds true for both boys and girls. For the boys, however, the degree of attitude change is small, while for the girls it is more pronounced. For family preferences, then, urban residence appears to have a greater modernizing effect on girls than on boys.*

If it is true, as the analysis so far has suggested, that modernization affects the attitudes of boys and girls differently, it might be possible that these differential effects exist within the heterogeneous population that makes up Taipei City. It has been argued that it makes sense to treat the urban sample as a single entity in making comparisons with youth from the rural community. However, an index of exposure to modernizing influences within the city might reveal a pattern of findings similar to that which exists between the rural and urban samples. This strategy is similar to that of intrasocietal replication of cross-cultural findings.[8]

Level of education is a widely used measure of exposure to modern attitudes. Although at the time of the study, the young people in the sample had all been educated to the same degree, they came from homes that varied markedly in the level of parental education, and thus presumably in the extent to which family influences might be directed toward the more modern or the more traditional. The father's educational level was thus selected as a rough index of family modernization and, by extension, of the exposure of urban youth to modernizing influences.

In Table 8.5 the family attitudes of boys and girls in the city sample are correlated with the educational level of their fathers. This table offers some weak support for the idea that modernization affects boys and girls differently. For the first two of the four sex-role items, boys exposed to more modern influences (as indexed by father's educational level) have more modern attitudes, while this relationship does not exist for girls.

On the other hand, one correlation approached significance for girls—the belief that it is wrong for women to work outside the home—and this shows girls from more highly educated homes to be more traditional rather than more modern. (Again, it needs to be emphasized that for all subgroups, whether based on parental education or area of residence, girls are more likely than boys to subscribe to modern sex-role attitudes. It is not the case, for example, that within highly educated families girls are more likely than boys to believe mothers

---

*A two-way analysis of variance was performed on the data presented in Table 8.4. The main effects analysis showed the differences between the attitudes of boys and girls (rural and urban communities combined) to be significant for all seven questionnaire items, whereas the differences between rural and urban youth (boys and girls combined) were significant for only three items—preferring help in mate selection, believing that women feel bad if they do not have sons, and believing that women should keep silent rather than disagree with their husbands. (The last, as has been mentioned, was a difference in the opposite direction from that predicted.) The interaction effects of sex and community were found to be significant for one item, the belief that women are less capable than men, with several other items approaching but failing to reach conventional significance levels.

TABLE 8.5

Correlation of Father's Educational Level and Family Attitudes of Boys and Girls, Urban Sample

	Boys	Girls
Family preferences		
Prefer extended family	−.02	.11
Prefer help in mate choice	.01	−.03
Want many children	.04	−.06
Sex-role attitudes		
Women less capable	.07	−.03
Feel bad if no son	.06	.01
Wrong to work outside	−.03	−.05
Keep silent	.01	.02

Note: Kendall's tau was used. Positive correlations indicate that higher educational levels are associated with modern family attitudes.

Source: Compiled by the author.

should remain at home. Girls from such families are, however, more likely than girls from less educated families to accept such a belief.)

This analysis also shows differential effects of parental education for the family preference of boys and girls, although not of the same sort as the cross-sample analysis. Here it is seen that, as family educational level increases, the preference for nuclear family living increases among girls, but that girls from more educated families have a weak tendency to prefer a larger number of children. The family preferences of boys are unaffected by level of parental education.

Combining the findings of Tables 8.4 and 8.5, one may say that there is considerable evidence that increased exposure to modernizing influences is associated with more modern sex-role attitudes for boys but more traditional sex-role attitudes for girls. The evidence concerning family preferences, however, is ambiguous.

DISCUSSION

Had this study been based on the responses of Taiwanese boys only, the results would have supported those theories of "modern man" that see a modern family ideology as emerging in a relatively uniform way in response to or as a concomitant of the process of urbanization and industrialization. Taiwanese boys are apparently much like their counterparts in other developing nations. Urban boys were found to be more likely than those in rural areas to prefer free mate choice and small families, and to subscribe to egalitarian norms concerning the role of women. Similarly, within the capital city, boys from more highly educated families showed a weak tendency to be more modern in their family attitudes.

The picture for girls was quite different. Although the move from rural to urban residence brought with it a preference for free mate choice and a small number of children for girls as well as boys, urban girls were less egalitarian in their sex-role attitudes than their rural counterparts. Among the girls in Taipei, those from more highly educated families were more apt to express a preference for nuclear family organization, but for other items, higher levels of parental education tended to be weakly associated with more traditional attitudes.

The urban girl in contemporary Taiwan thus expects to choose her own husband freely and to have a modern small family, but she is less likely than a rural girl to see herself in an egalitarian relationship with her spouse. Recent research by feminist anthropologists in Taiwan offers insight into this seeming paradox.

Ethnographic studies of both middle-class housewives and unmarried female factory employees suggest that the options available to urban women in Taiwan are extremely limited. For the less well-educated, factory employment offers dreary working conditions, long hours, and low wages.[9] Among the middle class, education is prized for girls as well as boys, but not in order that a girl may pursue an independent livelihood. She is expected to use her training to educate her own children.[10]

For both categories of women, then, economic security and a sense of accomplishment are more likely to be achieved via a good match than by independent activity. And in both cases, although for slightly different reasons, the ideology that emerges is one that emphasizes both modern romanticism and sex-role inequality. Norma Diamond describes this ideology as a Taiwanese version of the "feminine mystique" that dominated American thinking in the years following World War II. Like the Americans of that era, contemporary middle-class Taiwanese picture the ideal wife as one who is devoted to her family and who finds fulfillment in domestic pursuits. In contrast to the situation of the post-World War II American suburbanite, however, the home-bound urban Taiwanese mother has relatively little contact with neighbors and friends, and cannot expect much in the way of family involvement from her husband. Physical living arrangements typically isolate each family behind the concrete wall surrounding its small garden, or within its unit of a modern apartment complex. The unemployed married woman frequently suffers from intense feelings of loneliness, and is thus highly dependent on her husband for what limited companionship he can provide, as well as for financial support.

The urban family ideology described by Diamond was also found to be prevalent among the young women factory workers studied by Linda Chen.

Here, however, it was the desire to escape from the grim, dead-end conditions of factory employment that formed the basis for the romantic idealization of domesticity and female dependency. Marriage is the only other option open to most of these young women, and in order to make herself attractive in the competition for desirable husbands, Chen argues, a woman must cultivate excellence in domestic skills, personal beauty, and a charming dependency on the opinions and guidance of men. This orientation stands in bold contrast to the realities of life in rural Taiwan, where women take price in economically productive work and in the establishment of cooperative relationships with other women.[11]

From this point of view, then, the relative lack of egalitarianism present in the attitudes of urban girls does not represent an acceptance of the Chinese patriarchal tradition at all, but rather is an adaptation to life in an industrializing society. The stress on domesticity and dependency may be justified by reference to Chinese tradition,[12] but this is not the origin of such an ideology. Rather, this belief system arises in response to the changing options available to women in an early industrial economy.

It is interesting, then, that the attitudes of boys do not change in a similar fashion. Indeed, as has already been shown, it is characteristic of industrializing nations that men more exposed to modernizing influences have more egalitarian sex-role attitudes. What this analysis seems to suggest is that the values of women (and girls) may correspond more closely to behavioral reality than do the values of men (and boys). The rural male may enthusiastically assert an ideology of male dominance, in the face of an economy in which women play an important part, and a domestic life in which women are quite assertive and powerful.[13] At the same time, middle-class urban men are likely to grant women ideologically an equality that is denied in reality. Goode makes this point generally,[14] and research on family decision making documents this relationship. For example, studies in the United States[15] have consistently found that the higher a man's educational level, occupational status, and income, the more likely he is to dominate family decision making, despite the fact that high-status men are less likely to subscribe to norms of male dominance.

In general, the results of this study of Taiwanese youth are not as paradoxical as they first appeared. One theoretical approach to the effects of modernization on family attitudes, the "modern man" approach, in fact seems to apply very well to the young men of Taiwan. On the other hand, the recent work of feminist anthropologists, analyzing the effects on family attitudes of changing economic realities, applies with equal precision to the young women in the study.

Modernization theory, and particularly the theories of attitude change proposed by Goode, Parsons, Kahl, Inkeles, and others, represents an important step toward understanding the dynamics of social change. But the unidirectional and optimistic view of "progress" inherent in these theories needs to be tempered by the recognition that modernization affects different groups of people differently, and not always for the better.

NOTES

1. William J. Goode, *World Revolution and Family Patterns* (New York: Free Press, 1963).

2. Talcott Parsons, "The Kinship System of the Contemporary United States," *American Anthropologist* 45 (January-March 1943): 22–38.

3. Goode, *World Revolution*, pp. 19–20.

4. Joseph A. Kahl, *The Measurement of Modernism* (Austin: University of Texas Press, 1968).

5. Alex Inkeles, and David H. Smith, *Becoming Modern: Individual Change in Six Developing Countries* (Cambridge, Mass.: Harvard University Press, 1974).

6. Michael Anderson, *Family Structure in Nineteenth Century Lancashire*. (Cambridge: Cambridge University Press, 1971).

7. As examples, see Esther Boserup, *Women's Role in Economic Development*. (London: George Allen and Unwin, 1970); Laurel Bossen, "Women in Modernizing Societies," *American Ethnologist* 2 (November 1975): 587–601; Susan Carol Rogers, "Female Forms of Power and the Myth of Male Dominance: A Model of Female/Male Interaction in Peasant Society," *American Ethnologist* 2 (November 1975): 727–56.

8. For a discussion of this procedure as used in relation to the cross-cultural survey method, see Charles Harrington and J. W. M. Whiting, "Socialization Process and Personality," in *Psychological Anthropology*, ed. F. L. K. Hus (Cambridge, Mass: Schenkman, 1972), pp. 469–507.

9. Linda Gail Chen, "The Gender Ideology of Unmarried Taiwanese Working Women." Mimeographed. Stanford, Calif.: Stanford University, 1976; Lydia Kung, "Factory Work and Women in Taiwan: Changes in Self-Image and Status," *Signs* 2 (Autumn 1976): 35–58.

10. Norma Diamond, "The Middle-Class Family Model in Taiwan: Women's Place Is in the Home," *Asian Survey* 13 (September 1973): 853–72; and Norma Diamond, "The Status of Women in Taiwan: One Step Forward, Two Steps Back," in *Women in China: Studies in Social Change and Feminism*, ed. Marilyn Young (Ann Arbor: Center for Chinese Studies, University of Michigan, 1973), pp. 211–242.

11. Chen, "Gender Ideology"; see also Margery Wolf, *Women and the Family in Rural Taiwan* (Stanford, Calif.: Stanford University Press, 1972).

12. Diamond, "The Middle Class "; and "The Status of Women in Taiwan."

13. Rogers, "Female Forms of Power."

14. Goode, *World Revolution*, p. 21.

15. The classic work is by Robert O. Blood and Donald M. Wolfe, *Husbands and Wives* (New York: Free Press, 1960).

APPENDIX

Chinese Version of Questionnaire Items

Family Preferences

1. 當我結婚時，我希望

　　____ 和我 的父母或公婆住在一個大家庭裏

　　____ 和我 的配偶（丈夫或妻子）住在一個獨立的小家庭裏.

2. 當我結婚時，我希望

　　____ 讓我父母幫助我選擇一個合適的對象（丈夫或妻子）.

　　____ 完全由我自己選擇我的對象.

3. 當我結婚時，我希望我最理想的小孩子數目是 _____ 個.

Sex-Role Attitudes	大體上同意	大體上不同意
4. 通常女人較男人沒有決定重要事情的能力.	____	____
5. 不管人家怎麼說，現在大部分的女人都覺得她們不能夠生一個男孩，就感到難過.	____	____
6. 一個有小孩的家庭主婦在外面工作是不對的.	____	____
7. 當一個太太和她丈夫的意見不一致時，她應該保持緘默，不要說出來.	____	____

9

SEX, VALUES,
AND CHANGE ON TAIWAN

Sheldon Appleton

Despite the world-wide surge of interest in the social roles and values of women, very little data-based work has appeared on the values held by men and women in Taiwan.[1] The reasons for this are not difficult to find. Because survey research is in its infancy in Taiwan, surveys dealing with the values of individuals have been conducted relatively infrequently.[2] Since even these were designed primarily to probe ethnic (that is, Taiwanese-Mainlander) or status differences rather than sex differences, value differences between men and women often have not been reported at all or have been merely mentioned in passing.* Some of these surveys, moreover, suffer from a number of methodological deficiencies.[3]

METHODS

In this chapter an effort will be made to take another look at some of the studies relevant to values, which have been carried out on Taiwan, to see what they can tell us about the relationship between sex and values among the island's

---

*Because this chapter is based on analysis of parts of a number of surveys, the term "values" as it is used here includes both generalized goals (freedom, social recognition, inner harmony) and more specific ones (having a respectable job, being a good family person). The questionnaire items most frequently used are those designed by Milton Rokeach, whose definitions are given in the notes to Table 9.2, p. 189.

The term "Mainlander" is used here to refer to Chinese who have emigrated to Taiwan from the mainland of China since the end of World War II, and to their descendants. The term "Taiwanese" is used to refer to Chinese whose ancestors emigrated to Taiwan before 1945, and usually before the period of Japanese administration of the island (1895–1945). About 85 percent of Taiwan's more than 16 million residents are "Taiwanese"; about 13 percent "Mainlander"; and the rest aborigines, living mainly on the mountainous east coast.

residents. This will be done both by reviewing and reinterpreting previously published data, and, in some cases, by reprocessing the original data sets in search of further insight into the changing values of men and women on Taiwan. These techniques of analysis have advantages as well as disadvantages. The principal disadvantage, of course, is that the surveys cited were not designed specifically to explore sex-based differences in values, and therefore did not include a number of questions that would have been very helpful to the present analysis. The main advantage is that by using a number of independently conducted surveys findings emerging from one survey can often be tested against those from another. Especially in view of the methodological problems involved in these surveys, it is necessary to look for patterns supported by more than one survey whenever possible, and to view with caution interpretations suggested by only a single survey.* Some of the surveys involved—virtually all of them conducted over the decade from 1966 to 1975—focus on Taiwan's student population, constituting more than a quarter of the island's more than 16 million residents, or on residents of the capital city alone, rather than on the population of the island as a whole.

The only available survey that attempted to inquire about the values of almost all of the residents of Taiwan was conducted by a missionary, Wolfgang Grichting,[4] in 1970.† This was an islandwide stratified sampling of households rather than individuals, which probably underrepresents some population groupings—notably soldiers and young people. Since it was carried out with government cooperation, the responses given by those interviewed no doubt reflected a good deal of caution. Few of the responses that will be reported, however—mostly those dealing with simple demographic information and with values—seem so politically sensitive as to be susceptible to major distortion on this account. In any event, the results can be compared with responses to paper-and-pencil questionnaires administered by several investigators to students whose anonymity appears to have been credibly guaranteed.

---

*These problems include, in some instances, samples that are not fully representative, and in others, the possibility that respondents may not have been completely candid because of fear of government involvement in the conduct of the survey.

†This study was supported by mission funds, and the commentary and analysis it contains are primarily oriented toward the missionary effort on the island. Three quarters of the book consist simply of tabular presentations of the responses to each question by a series of demographic groupings. A number of the statements and tables that appear further on in this chapter are based on interpretations of Grichting's tables or on computations made from them by the author. Statements based on these data are footnoted accordingly. The original data set for this survey was obtained by the present writer through the Inter-University Consortium for Political Research and reprocessed extensively with the aid of a grant from the Oakland University Research Fund. Neither Grichting nor the Consortium bear any responsibility for the analyses or interpretations presented here. References to Grichting's data not supported by citations to particular page references may be assumed to be based on this secondary analysis.

Probably the most direct question regarding values posed to this island-wide household sample utilized an adapted version of Rokeach's "terminal values" inventory.[5] Respondents were asked to rank nine values in order of how important each was as a guiding principle in their lives. The results are given in Table 9.1. From this table can be inferred two main themes that will appear re-

TABLE 9.1

Rankings of Values by Men and Women in Taiwan

Values	Average Rank	
	Men	Women
Family security	2.6	2.3
A world at peace	2.7	3.1
Inner harmony	3.4	3.2
A comfortable life	4.1	3.7
True friendship	4.7	5.3
Social recognition	5.7	5.9
Faith	7.0	6.8
Religion	7.0	6.8
Happy afterlife	7.7	7.8

Notes: The highest possible ranking is 1; the lowest is 9. Rho = .98. The sample consisted of 973 men and 901 women.

Source: Computed from Wolfgang Grichting, *The Value System on Taiwan*, 1970 (Taipei: privately printed, 1971), pp. 356–65.

peatedly in the data. First, the stated value preferences of male and female Taiwan residents are very much alike—more so, for instance, than the preferences of those in differing ethnic or level-of-education groupings. Second, such differences as do appear seem to involve the traditional *nei/wai* (inside/outside) distinction in sex roles among Chinese: the woman's role centering on home and family and matters within the household; the man's on matters outside of the home.* Thus, the women in Grichting's sample assigned a marginally more im-

---

*A similar role differentiation has been observed in American society.[6] Male-female differences were much smaller among American students, however, than among their parents. William Rodd reports the results of administering the Allport-Vernon Study of Values

portant role to "family security," and the men to "a world at peace." Men also ranked "friendship" and "social recognition" slightly higher, though in these cases the differences are too small to be conclusive.*

FINDINGS

Young men—as might be expected, since many of them are unmarried— place less emphasis than their elders on "family security" and more on "friend- ship" and "inner harmony."[9] (Only 2 percent of the women in this household sample, as compared to 7 percent of the men, had never been married.) Both young men (under 30) and old (over 55) put greater stress on "social recogni- tion" than do the middle-aged. Younger women, too, value "family security" a bit less than their seniors, but for them, unlike the men, this value comes first at every age. Younger women also put more value (though still less than young men) on "friendship" and give less priority to "a comfortable life" than do older women, more heavily involved in family raising. Beyond these relatively small variations, differences in value rankings by age group for each sex are not large (though they are a bit greater than the differences between the sexes). The limitations on the data available make it impossible to discover to what extent these differences may be attributed to generational or "life cycle" effects, re- spectively.[10]

Responses to a different version of the Rokeach terminal and instrumental values inventories, administered to college and vocational high school students on Taiwan by the author,[11] are quite similar to those of Grichting's sample. (See Tables 9.2 and 9.3.) Again, and especially among the high school students, who

---

to Taiwan high school students and Japanese and U.S. college students in the 1950s.[7] In all three cases, men scored higher on "theoretical" and "economic" interests, women on "aesthetic" and "religious" interests. The Taiwan and U.S. women students scored higher than their male counterparts on "social" interests, and there were no consistent differences on the test of "political" interests. In addition, Rodd found Taiwan male students scoring higher than their female counterparts on tests of mathematics, science, and critical thinking. These findings seem consistent with the role differentiation suggested by the Taiwan surveys cited here and later in this chapter. See also the chapter in this volume by Emily Ahern.

*A very different (18-item) version of the Rokeach Values Inventory was adminis- tered to a U.S. national sample. For two of the values used by Grichting ("social recogni- tion" and "religion/salvation"), sex differences were in the same direction in both samples. For two others, the direction of the differences was reversed: Taiwan men and U.S. women gave higher rankings to "a world at peace"; and lower rankings to "a comfortable life." There were no sex differences in the U.S. sample on "family security," ranked higher by Taiwan women, or "true friendship," ranked higher by Taiwan men. "Inner harmony," ranked higher by U.S. women than men, was valued about equally by both sexes on Tai- wan.[8] In view of the differences between the two inventories and the problem of compara- bility of items because of translation, it does not seem useful to attempt to interpret these cross-national differences in response.

TABLE 9.2

Rankings of Values by Vocational High School
Students in Taiwan

	Average Rank	
	Men (N = 249)	Women (N = 146)
Terminal values[a]		
A world at peace	3.5	3.6
National security	3.8	3.6
Freedom	4.2	4.1
Equality	5.0	5.5
A meaningful life	5.5	5.5
True friendship	5.8	5.6
Wisdom	6.4	6.1
Respect for others	7.5	7.3
Respect from others	7.8	7.1
A comfortable life	8.5	9.0
Maturity	10.0	10.5
Salvation	10.1	10.0
Instrumental Values[b]		
Responsible	4.4	4.6
Clean	5.1	5.5
Honorable	5.6	5.3
Trustful	5.7	5.8
Polite	6.2	5.6
Broadminded	6.3	7.0
Cooperative	6.4	7.1
Courageous	6.8	6.3
Forgiving	7.1	6.5
Self-Disciplined	7.4	7.8
Tender	7.8	7.3
Intellectual	9.1	8.9

[a] Defined as "an idealized goal or end-state of existence."
[b] Defined as "an idealized mode of conduct."

Notes: Data are for combined groups of students from the same school surveyed at two different times, three years apart. The sample consisted of 249 men and 146 women. The highest possible ranking is 1; the lowest is 12. For the terminal values, Rho = .98; for the instrumental values, Rho = .91.

Sources: Survey data collected by the author; Milton Rokeach, *The Nature of Human Values* (New York: Free Press, 1973).

TABLE 9.3

Rankings of Values by College and University Students in Taiwan

	Average Rank	
	Men (N = 450)	Women (N = 304)
Terminal Values[a]		
National security	4.1	4.9
Freedom	4.2	4.5
A meaningful life	4.6	4.4
A world at peace	5.0	5.3
Equality	5.5	6.3
Wisdom	5.5	4.4
True friendship	5.5	4.8
Respect from others	7.2	6.2
Respect for others	7.5	7.6
A comfortable life	7.5	8.3
Salvation	10.4	9.8
Maturity	10.8	11.1
Instrumental Values[b]		
Responsible	3.8	3.9
Honorable	4.7	4.9
Trustful	5.1	4.9
Clean	6.3	6.2
Forgiving	6.8	6.5
Polite	6.8	6.5
Cooperative	6.9	7.3
Self-Disciplined	7.1	7.4
Broadminded	7.2	8.2
Courageous	7.3	8.5
Tender	7.4	6.0
Intellectual	8.4	7.6

[a] Defined as "an idealized goal or end-state of existence."
[b] Defined as "an idealized mode of conduct."

Notes: The highest possible ranking is 1; the lowest is 12. For terminal values, Rho = .79; for the instrumental values, Rho = .77.

Sources: Survey data collected by the author; Milton Rokeach, *The Nature of Human Values* (New York: Free Press, 1973).

are less atypical than the college students of the population at large, the value rankings assigned by male and female students correspond closely to one another. There are somewhat greater differences between the rankings of high school and college students of the same sex, and between those of two groups of students at the same high school surveyed three years apart. The main differences in terminal values between the two sexes are the slightly higher rankings assigned to "equality," "a comfortable life," and "maturity" by the men, and to "respect from others" by the women. The last of these may have a sex-related connotation for these young women—that is, it may include respect for their conformity to traditional sexual mores which are strongly affirmed on Taiwan.

Among the college students, women again value "respect from others" slightly more, while men clearly place a higher value on "equality" and "a comfortable life." Some other differences show up as well. The male students put a higher value on "national security" and "freedom," consistent with the *nei/wai* distinction. The women's higher ranking of "wisdom" and "friendship" seems related less to sex-role differences than to their particular position in life—what is sometimes called the "life cycle" effect. Many fewer women than men get as far as universities in Taiwan.

The following table, computed from Grichting, shows the levels of education of respondents in his household sample:[12]

	Under 35		Over 35	
	Men (N = 139)	Women (N = 278)	Men (N = 834)	Women (N = 623)
Percent with more than 6 years schooling	44	25	32	14
Percent with more than 12 years schooling	12	4	8	1

Women who do get as far as the university are likely to be from higher status families, and to put a special value on learning (note also their higher ranking of "intellectual" among the instrumental values). They also may have a special need for friends (usually fellow students) to help them navigate their way through the basically male university world. The high school women also valued "wisdom," "friendship," and "intellectual" slightly more than their male counterparts. After they have married and become involved in raising families, however, Grichting's data show that women put a lower value on "friendship" than men, and report having fewer friends as well.[13] After age 55, this difference on the value assigned to "friendship" diminishes.

The higher rankings assigned to "tender," "polite," and "forgiving" by both college and high school women, and to "courageous" by the college males are certainly consistent with traditional sex roles. The greater male preference for "broadminded" is largely a function of Mainlander/Taiwanese differences rather than sex differences per se. Mainlanders ranked "broadminded" last among these twelve instrumental values, while Taiwanese ranked it eighth, and at both the high school and college levels a much greater proportion of the female than of the male students were Mainlanders. The self-selection process involved in the choice of the high school women to attend a vocational school may be reflected in the relatively high value they put on "courageous." The higher rankings of "a comfortable life" by *male* high school and college students and by the *women* in Grichting's islandwide sample are not as inconsistent as they seem. For this value, the key explanatory variable is socioeconomic status (SES). The higher the SES, for both students and the general population, the lower the ranking of "a comfortable life." Women, as noted, have higher status than their male fellow-students at the high school and college levels, but somewhat lower status in the population at large. Finally, women, especially higher-status Mainlander women, are more likely than men to be Christian. Thus the greater emphasis on "salvation" among the college women.[14]

Other findings from surveys of adult Taiwan residents seem consistent with the pattern described above. There was a close correspondence between the responses of men and women to Grichting's questions on the goals of a college education and the meaning of success. Both groups were likely to cite specialized skills as the main thing to be gained from college, though women were a bit more likely to mention earning power and men to cite personal qualities or good citizenship. Similarly, both groupings defined success primarily in terms of education itself, with women more likely to refer to career success, while men were a bit more likely to mention development of individual talents, good citizenship, and independence. The differences in each case, however, were very small, and are accounted for largely by the generally higher status and educational levels of the men. In accordance with Maslow's theories, lower-status groups on Taiwan seem to put more emphasis on lower-order needs (money, career, family security, a comfortable life), while higher-status groups, having achieved a greater measure of these, put more emphasis on "self-actualizing" values (world peace, inner harmony, citizenship, personal development).The greater emphasis by men on good citizenship, however, remains even when education is controlled.[15]

Ronald Inglehart reports similar findings for the United States, Western European nations, and Japan. Men are more likely to have "post-industrial" values, such as protecting freedom of speech, and women to have "materialist" values, such as fighting crime and inflation. The differences by sex are smallest in the United States, largest in Japan. Except in the United States, women were also found more likely than men to vote for conservative political parties.[16]

These findings seem related to the tendency previously noted for women to be somewhat more traditional than men in their outlooks. Thus the women in Grichting's islandwide sample were more likely to say that obedience should be emphasized most in child rearing, while men were more likely to stress independence.[17] Analysis of the data shows that this difference is a function of educational differences, however, and is virtually eliminated when level of education is controlled.

Studies of schoolchildren point in the same direction. Richard Wilson found minimal differences in the value orientations of third, fifth, and seventh grade boys and girls with respect to autocentricity (inner-directedness) versus heterocentricity (other-directedness). Girls were slightly more inner-directed, but differences were very small.[18] Analyzing the responses of a large, randomly drawn, islandwide sample of 11- to 19-year-old students, Gerald McBeath found women students less likely to identify failure to recover the mainland as Taiwan's most urgent national problem, and more likely to cite social disorder.[19] The responses of lower-status students on these items were similar to those of the women. The author found women students less likely than men to follow public affairs in the media or discuss them with others. Grichting found the same to be true among his islandwide household sample.[20] These behavioral differences reflect the *nei/wai* distinction referred to earlier.

MECHANISMS

The pattern noted here—very similar responses by men and women, except for differences in attitudes toward appropriate sex-role behavior—appears also in responses by residents of the city of Taipei to Robert Mitchell's questions concerning what gives them the most satisfaction, what people must have in order to be looked up to and admired, and what they worried about most. Thus, though both sexes said their children gave them the most satisfaction, women (39 percent) were more likely to give this response than men (27 percent), and to mention their spouse (25 percent of the women; 14 percent of the men). Men more often (17 percent, to 3 percent of the women) said that work gave them the most satisfaction. Men worried most about jobs and money, women about their children. And though both men and women agreed (44-45 percent) that being willing to help others was most important in winning the admiration of others, men more often mentioned having a respectable job (15 percent, to 6 percent for women), and women being a good family person (12 percent, to 5 percent of men).[21]

Some of Mitchell's questions to Taipei residents help in understanding something of the consequences of these differences in values. Women were much more likely to hold lower-status jobs, and to earn less. But they were no more likely than men to say they were unhappy, or to score high on an index of hostility. Men were more likely to feel it was personally important to them to be successful, and to be dissatisfied with their present living situations and with what they had achieved in life. Thus the very fact that they seemed to set higher goals for themselves than did women seemed to lead men to greater disappointment. Women, on the other hand, appeared to internalize their frustrations. They were more likely than men to feel they could not control the course of their own lives (57 percent of the women and 41 percent of the men expressed this feeling), to withdraw from both home and work roles, to have low self-esteem, to worry, and to report poorer physical health and symptoms of emotional strain.[22]

BEHAVIORAL EVIDENCE

Behavioral evidence of the influence of traditional sex roles in Taiwan can also be found in government-issued statistics on educational enrollments and employment. At every educational level, more males than females are enrolled as students and employed as teachers. The higher the level, and in the universities, the higher the rank, the greater the ratio of males to females. Thus, in 1973, 49 percent of primary-school students, and 45 percent of the teachers were women, while at the college and university level only 37 percent of the students and 25 percent of the full-time faculty (9 percent of the full and associate professors) were women.[23] Of the small number of graduate degrees (fewer than 1,000) awarded in 1972, only 12 percent were received by women.[24] It is also worthy of note that unemployment has been higher among women than among men at every educational level.[25] Table 9.4 shows the percentage of women enrolled in various subject fields in colleges and universities and in vocational high schools. Women were grossly overrepresented in the humanities, nursing, home economics, and commerce (often secretarial), and grossly underrepresented in the natural sciences and enginnering and in industrial programs.

However, the same educational statistics that give evidence of the continuing strength of traditional sex roles yield evidence as well of gradual change. Over the nine years from 1964 to 1973, the percentage of enrolled female students increased from 37 to 43 percent in high schools, from 29 to 37 percent in colleges and universities, and from 28 to 40 percent in the prestigious national universities. Over the same period the percentage of women teachers went up from 38 to 45 at the primary level, from 23 to 39 at the secondary level, and from 18 to 25 at the college and university level. In absolute terms, the number of women obtaining higher levels of education is even more dramatic. In 1965, fewer than 3,200 women graduated from colleges or universities. In 1972, just seven years later, 17,800 graduated.

This change in educational and job opportunities for women is reflected also in responses to the surveys previously cited. The younger respondents in Grichting's islandwide sample, for instance, were more likely to discuss a variety of matters with their spouses and to share in the making of family decisions. Both men and women considered level of education an important factor in choosing a wife as well as a husband; and both sons and daughters were widely expected to play an important role in selecting their own marriage partners.[26]

Even in personality characteristics, change was apparent. Kenneth Abbott administered the California Personality Inventory to samples of adolescents and their parents in a district of Taipei. On almost every scale, males of both genera-

TABLE 9.4

Women Enrolled in Various Courses of Study in College
and Universities and in Vocational High Schools, 1973

Course of Study	Percent Women
College and university	
Humanities	64
Education	42
Social sciences	34
Law	29
Agriculture	29
Fine arts	25
Medical science	21
Natural sciences	16
Engineering	2
All courses	37
Vocational high school	
Home economics	100
Commerce	88
Nursing and midwifery	79
Agriculture	21
Marine products	9
Industry	4
All courses	45

Source: *Chung-hua Min-kuo Chiao-yu T'ung-chi, 1974* [*Educational Statistics of the Republic of China, 1974*], (Taipei: Ministry of Education, 1974).

tions scored higher than females. But the differences between adolescent men and women were in almost every case smaller than sex differences in their parents' generation on scales measuring poise, self-assurance, personal adequacy, sense of responsibility, achievement potential, intellectual efficiency, and so on.[27]

ATTITUDES TOWARD SOCIAL CHANGE

Table 9.5 shows the responses of men and women in Grichting's island-wide sample to a series of questions asking them, first, to assess the changes in a number of relationships over the last ten years; second, to indicate their view of expected further changes in these relationships over the following decade; and, finally, to compare Taiwan with the United States with respect to each of these relationships. For each of these nine relationships, more people thought there

TABLE 9.5

Attitudes of Taiwan Men and Women toward Changes in Social Relationships

Relationship	Attitude Toward Change Over Past 10 Years[a]		Attitude Toward Change Over Next 10 Years[b]		Comparison of Taiwan to the United States[c]	
	Men	Women	Men	Women	Men	Women
Husband-wife	22	27	18	27	70	65
Father-children	9	20	17	22	74	75
Mother-children	14	24	20	24	75	77
Siblings	11	22	17	20	73	74
Boys-girls	14	18	12	16	63	63
Neighbors	4	10	10	14	66	70
Teacher-student	3	8	11	13	60	63
Employer-employee	10	10	13	15	55	58
People in general	-1[d]	5	7	11	61	63

[a]Percentage seeing favorable change in relationships, minus percentage seeing unfavorable change.
[b]Percentage predicting favorable change in relationships, minus percentage predicting unfavorable change.
[c]Percentage rating Taiwan better on relationships, minus percentage rating the United States better.
[d]Minus sign indicates a plurality of negative responses.

Note: Sample consisted of 843 men and 738 women.

Source: Wolfgang Grichting, *The Value System on Taiwan, 1970* (Taipei: privately printed, 1971), pp. 231, 239–41, 274–78.

had been some change than felt that matters had remained the same; and a majority of those who saw a change believed it to have been a change for the better. The same was true for expectations of future change. And in every case, about two-thirds to five-sixths of those responding said Taiwan was superior to the United States with respect to these relationships.

In almost every case, women were more positive than men about the changes that had taken place over the past ten years, and more optimistic about the changes expected over the next decade. Both men and women were most positive—women even more so than men—about changes in the relationships between husbands and wives; and the women, but not the men, were more hopeful about likely future changes in this relationship. The other relationships viewed most positively and hopefully by women also involved the family—relationships between mothers and children, fathers and children, and among siblings. In particular, men were far less positive than women about both past and anticipated changes in relations between fathers and their children. There were actually slightly more men who felt that relations among "people in general" had changed for the worse than for the better—the only negative entry in the entire table—whereas at least a small plurality of women believed the reverse. Since this was the most general relationship inquired about, it is perhaps the one most likely to tap vague misgivings over the trend of developments. Only a very small plurality of men were hopeful about expected future changes in relations among "people in general."*

In all but two cases, women were at least slightly more likely than men to feel, on balance, that Taiwan is superior to the United States with regard to these relationships. The two exceptions are boy-girl relations, where there is no sex difference in the responses, and husband-wife relations—the only instance in which women show more receptivity to the American model than men. Men were also more likely than women to believe that the United States had something to offer Taiwan in every one of the ten areas inquired about by Grichting: morality, art, law, religion, medicine, education, industry and technology, economics, political ideas, and social welfare.[29] Though consistent with a greater *wai* orientation on the part of men, these differences are largely attributable to men's higher educational levels.

An interpretation consistent with these figures would suggest that some change is taking place in relationships between men and women on Taiwan and among other family members—change in the direction of the more equalitarian

---

*A 1977 Gallup survey covering 70 nations shows pluralities of those responding in every area of the world believing that the role of women in their country is changing "a great deal" or at least "a fair amount." The greatest perception of change in women's role was in North America and secondarily in African countries, the least in Asia. Overwhelming majorities in all regions also said that women now have equal educational opportunities in their countries (again the smallest majority being in Asia), but respondents were almost evenly split on whether women now have equal job opportunities.[28]

Western model. This change seems to be received fairly well, though perhaps with some misgivings, by men, and for the most part quite favorably by women.

The surveys of Martin Yang in rural Taiwan, and the studies by Mitchell and Abbott already cited, have documented some of these changes in the structure of the Chinese family under the impact of modernization. "There has been a . . . displacement of the most intensive relationship in the family from father-son (ideal) or mother-son (actual) to husband-wife," Abbott reported.[30] The change in class status of many families also leads to changes in family influence and communication patterns, since these seem to be class-based. The traditional misery of young women's situations is somewhat mitigated, and the emotional distance between fathers and sons lessens, leaving more room for emotional warmth between them. Nevertheless, these changes have created some problems for the personality development of Chinese young people, somewhat akin to those felt by Western youth.[31]

A similar set of questions asked of a group of vocational high school students by the author offers some striking support for this interpretation. In the same year that Grichting's survey was conducted, these students were asked to compare contemporary Taiwan with the United States and traditional China on a number of dimensions.[32] Table 9.6 gives men's and women's responses to these questions. As noted earlier, the women in this group are somewhat more "select" than their male fellow students, simply because it is less likely that a woman will continue her education as long as a man. These students, both men and women, are above average in educational attainment for their age group (less than a sixth of Grichting's sample [a fifth of those under 35] had received *any* senior high school education),[33] though, as vocational high school students, they are scarcely candidates for membership in the island's socioeconomic or educational elite. Their value choices have been discussed above in some detail (see Table 9.2). The main difference between the value rankings of these students and those of a group surveyed at the same school three years before was the greater emphasis placed by the later (1970) students—and especially the women—on "a meaningful life" and "broadminded," at the expense of such traditional virtues as "polite" and "courageous."[34] Note that "a meaningful life" was rated even higher by the college students surveyed (Table 9.3), and highest of all—at the very top of their rankings—by college women.

Perhaps the most striking difference revealed in Table 9.6, consistent with the analysis of Grichting's data, is the tendency of women to be more positively oriented to the present, and less positively oriented toward the traditional model, on 10 of the 11 dimensions included (the single exception is commercial abilities). For a number of the dimensions, including human relations and life aims, the size of the difference is quite large.

In comparing their own society with that of the United States, both men and women preferred the Chinese pattern of interpersonal relationships (father-son relations; teacher-student relations; friendship relations; and human relations in general). Both preferred the Western (U.S.) model in business-related

TABLE 9.6

Vocational High School Students' Comparisons of Their Own Society (Taiwan) with Traditional China and the United States

Dimension	Taiwan Compared with Traditional China		Taiwan Compared with the United States	
	Men	Women	Men	Women
Father-son relations	−28	−3	86	90
Teacher-student relations	−61	−28	38	20
Friendship relations	−34	−16	49	42
Superior-subordinate relations	11	29	−24	−9
Commercial abilities	63	54	−30	−59
Ability to manage large organizations	69	77	−65	−78
Life aims	46	74	18	−11
Civic-mindedness	−3	16	−45	−29
Human relations	−43	3	51	41
Group cooperation	5	28	−25	−21
Relations between government officials and the people	14	37	−36	−22

Notes: For each dimension, figures show percentage preferring contemporary Taiwan, minus percentage preferring traditional China or the United States, respectively. Minus signs indicate a plurality of responses favoring traditional China or the United States. The sample consisted of 183 men and 78 women.

Source: Survey data collected by the author.

and civic areas (commercial abilities; ability to manage large organizations; superior-subordinate relations; civic-mindedness; group cooperation; and relations between government officials and the people). All of this is consistent with the *ti yong* model of nineteenth-century Chinese reformers: Western values for practical use, Chinese values for fundamentals. One of the sharpest divisions shows up on the dimension most relevant to values—life aims. A majority of the male students felt that life aims on Taiwan today are better than what they believe those aims to be in the United States. A majority of the women, on the other hand, believed that American life aims were preferable to those in their own society.

Similarly, women were likely to feel even more distant from traditional China's life aims than men. Two-thirds of the men, but almost nine-tenths of the women, believed that life aims in Taiwan today were better than those in traditional China, and women were almost twice as likely (39 percent to 22 percent) to say contemporary life aims were *much* better. This is particularly interesting because, as noted, survey responses show women to be generally most traditional and less "Westernized" or "modern" than men. For this reason, it seems quite probable that the responses described in the last several paragraphs are indications of a positive response on the part of many women—especially the young—to the gradual opening-up of greater educational and career opportunities for women on Taiwan, and to the development of somewhat more equalitarian relations between the sexes in familial and personal relationships in general.

SUMMARY AND DISCUSSION

A review of available empirical studies and educational statistics has led to a number of inferences and interpretations concerning the relationship among sex, values, and change on Taiwan. The expressed values of men and women on Taiwan were found to be very similar, with such values as "family security," "a world at peace," and "inner harmony" near the top of their value hierarchies. Marginal differences were largely consistent with traditional sex-role expectations and the distinction between *nei* and *wai*: women gave higher priority to home and family, men to matters outside the home—friends, the community, the nation, the world at large.

There were some indications that the results of these value differences and the social context in which they are embedded created emotional strains of somewhat different types for women and men. While neither sex seemed clearly happier than the other, the higher value put by men on the achievement of success outside the home appeared to make them more subject to disappointment in themselves and feelings of failure. Women, in contrast, seemed more likely to resign themselves to the difficulties inherent in their role expectations and to turn their frustrations inward in the form of low self-esteem, poorer physical health, symptoms of emotional strain, withdrawal from home and work roles, and feelings of inability to control the course of their lives. Some evidence was presented, however, that sex roles have been gradually changing on Taiwan in the wake of rapid economic growth and Westernization. These changes have opened up somewhat greater—though still far from equal—economic opportunities for women, and have led to more equalitarian relations between the sexes in the family, at school, and in the society as a whole. Especially among young people, there were indications that women were more receptive to these changes than men and more hopeful of continued change in a positive direction—that is, in the direction of Western models of relationships between the sexes. The young also showed some tendency, with increasing education, to emphasize self-actualizing values ("inner harmony," "a meaningful life") more, and material values less, than their elders.

One disquieting factor in the course of social change in Taiwan has been the more negative response to social change on the part of the best educated, most elite (and disporportionately male) segment of the population. This elite seems uncomfortable not only with the prospect of future changes, which might jeopardize their places at the top, but even with many of the changes that have already taken place, and, in fact, often have been instrumental in their attainment of elite status. This group seems to have passed through the initial stages of Westernization, when rising living standards, growing career opportunities, and the loosening of rigidly hierarchical social ties bring new satisfactions. They have begun to experience some of the negative aspects of Western social life as well—disruption of family ties, uncertainty in social relations, the perils of urban life, lessened "respect" from others, and some general alienation from traditional moorings. At the same time, in accordance with Maslow's theories, their achievement of basic material needs has led them, as noted, to place a new emphasis on "self-actualizing" values that involve states of inner being and are less readily fulfilled on Taiwan.[35] As women increasingly gain entry to this elite, the form their reaction to this dilemma will take remains to be seen.

In the longer run, the gradual changes in relations between the sexes that have been described here are bound to continue to affect the dynamics of the family system, the personality development of children, and the attitudes of Taiwan's residents toward their political system. These changes, in turn, are likely to pose serious social and political problems for Taiwan, its government, and its people. Material needs, after all, are more easily met by governmental and social action than the "self-actualizing" values that seem to emerge in industrializing societies.

All that is certain is that these changes are already in motion, and that given the unwillingness of the populace to return to the living standards and personal constraints of traditional times, the old ways cannot be expected to return. The impact of Western modes of interpersonal relations on Taiwan's society and values are only beginning to be felt. Whether the island's people will be able to work out a distinctive and viable response to the clash of Chinese and Western values—and whether the vicissitudes of international politics will permit them to do so—remain very much open and fascinating questions as the decade of the 1980s comes into view.

NOTES

1. A number of revealing studies of women's lives and roles on Taiwan have appeared, however, including Margery Wolf, *Women and the Family in Rural Taiwan* (Stanford: Stanford University Press, 1972); Norma Diamond, "The Status of Women in Taiwan: One Step Forward, Two Steps Back," in *Women in China*, ed. Marilyn Young (Ann Arbor: University of Michigan, Center for Chinese Studies, 1973), pp. 211–42; the chapters by Arthur Wolf, Margery Wolf, and Emily Ahern in *Women in Chinese Society*, ed. Margery Wolf and Roxane Witke (Stanford: Stanford University Press, 1975), pp. 89-141 and 193–214; and, based partly on a survey of urban middle class women, Norma Diamond, "The Middle-Class Family Model on Taiwan: Woman's Place Is in the Home," *Asian Survey* 13 (September 1973): 853–72.

2. See Sheldon Appleton, "Survey Research on Taiwan," *Public Opinion Quarterly* 40 (Winter 1976–77): 468–81.

3. Ibid., p. 469.

4. Wolfgang Grichting, *The Value System on Taiwan, 1970* (Taipei: privately printed, 1971).

5. This inventory was taken from a preliminary version presented in Milton Rokeach, "Attitudes, Values and Political Behavior," a paper presented at the 62nd Annual Meeting of the American Political Science Association, September 1966. The conceptual foundations of this inventory, and results from its administration to a national sample in the United States and to college students in four Western countries, are discussed in Rokeach's books: *Beliefs, Attitudes and Values—A Theory of Organizational Change* (San Francisco: Jossey-Bass, 1968); and *The Nature of Human Values* (New York: Free Press, 1973).

6. M. Kent Jennings and Richard Niemi, *The Political Character of Adolescence* (Princeton: Princeton University Press, 1974), pp. 305-9.

7. William G. Rodd, "Cross-Cultural Use of 'The Study of Values,'" *Psychologica* 2 (1959): 157–64.

8. See Rokeach, *Nature of Human Values*, pp. 57–59.

9. Grichting, *Value System*, p. 75.

10. On the methodological problems involved, see M. Kent Jennings and Richard Niemi, "Continuity and Change in Political Orientations: A Longitudinal Study of Two Generations," *American Political Science Review* 64 (December 1975): 1317–19.

11. Reports by the present writer on the results of these surveys include "Taiwanese and Mainlanders on Taiwan: A Survey of Student Attitudes," *China Quarterly* No. 44 (October-December 1970): 38–65, which includes the Chinese-language version of the questionnaire; "Surveying the Values of Chinese College Students," *Asian Forum* 2 (April–June 1970): 75–88; "The Political Socialization of College Students on Taiwan," *Asian Survey* 10 (October 1970): 910–23; "Regime Support Among Taiwan High School Students," *Asian Survey* 13 (August 1973): 750–60; and "The Social and Political Impact of Education in Taiwan," *Asian Survey* 16 (August 1976): 703–20.

12. Grichting, *Value System*, pp. 109–10.

13. Ibid., pp. 280, 364.

14. Ibid., pp. 59, 72.

15. On "self-actualizing" values, see Abraham Maslow, *Toward a Psychology of Being* (Princeton: Van Nostrand, 1962). See also the discussion, and the citations of studies conducted in Western Europe and Japan, in Appleton, "Social and Political Impact of Education," pp. 710–13.

16. Ronald Ingelhart, *The Silent Revolution: Changing Values and Political Styles Among Western Publics* (Princeton: Princeton University Press, 1977), pp. 90–92, 110–11, 228–29. See also Appleton, "Social and Political Impact of Education," pp. 710–13.

17. Grichting, *Value System*, p. 252.

18. Richard Wilson, *The Moral State: A Study of the Political Socialization of Chinese and American Children* (New York: Free Press, 1974), pp. 141–44, 152, 174, 208, 240.

19. Gerald McBeath, "Death of the Leader: Perceptions of Isolation and Self-Strengthening at the Onset of the Successor Regime in Taiwan." Paper presented to the 30th International Congress of Human Sciences in Asia and North Africa, August 1976, p. 16.

20. Grichting, *Value System*, pp. 232, 285, 290, 313, 319.

21. Robert Mitchell, *Levels of Emotional Strain in Southeast Asian Cities*, 2 vols. (Taipei: Orient Cultural Service, 1972), pp. 286–90.These findings are based on interviews with a stratified sample of Taipei residents, consisting of 495 men and 505 women, interviewed in 1968.

22. Ibid., pp. 22–30, 27, 42, 58, 135–36, 191, 128, 246, 293. See also Kenneth Abbott, *Harmony and Individualism: Changing Chinese Psychosocial Functioning in San Francisco and Taipei* (Taipei: Orient Cultural Service, 1970), p. 190.

23. Statistics in this and the succeeding paragraphs are taken or computed from *Chung-hua Min-kuo Chiao-yu T'ung-chi, 1974* [Educational Statistics of the Republic of China, 1974] , (Taipei: Ministry of Education, Government of the Republic of China, 1974), and from prior editions of this report.

24. Ibid.

25. See Frank Young, "Problems of Manpower Development on Taiwan," *Asian Survey* 16 (August 1976): 723.

26. Grichting, *Value System*, pp. 221–26. See also the results of a survey of college students conducted by Albert O'Hara, reported in Abbott, *Harmony and Individualism*, p. 154; and David Schak, *Dating and Mate Selection in Modern Taiwan* (Taipei: Orient Cultural Service, 1974).

27. Abbott, *Harmony and Individualism*, pp. 219–20.

28. The Gallup Poll, News Release, January 9, 1977.

29. Grichting, *Value System*, p. 294.

30. Abbott, *Harmony and Individualism*, p. 143.

31. Ibid., pp. 160–63; and Martin Yang, *Socio-Economic Results of Land Reform in Taiwan* (Honolulu: East-West Center Press, 1970), pp. 446–55.

32. These items were based on similar ones administered to Chinese college students in 1961 by Robert and Ai-li Chin. See their "Comparative Evaluations of Aspects of Contemporary Chinese Culture by College Students in Taiwan," *National Taiwan University Journal of Sociology* (Taipei) No. 1 (December 1963): 41–57.

33. Grichting, *Value System*, pp. 109–10.

34. See Appleton, "Regime Support," p. 758, which, however, does not give a breakdown of the rankings by sex.

35. See the discussion in Appleton, "Social and Political Impact of Education," pp. 713–20.

PART 3

VALUE CHANGE WITHIN SPECIFIC SETTINGS IN THE PEOPLE'S REPUBLIC OF CHINA

In this final and concluding section, the studies deal with the value orientations of specific settings in the People's Republic of China. The studies demonstrate not only the differences in value orientations but also the tension that derives from these conditions. The studies discuss how particular value orientations can be used as justifications for varying methods of social control and for the occupancy of leadership positions. In addition, attention is focused on some explicit mechanisms that are utilized by leaders to foster value change.

10

TRADITIONAL, MODERN, AND REVOLUTIONARY VALUES OF NEW SOCIAL GROUPS IN CHINA

Gordon Bennett

"Value" remains an inchoate concept in political science, used more often (in the plural) in the sense of "acts, customs, institutions, etc., regarded in a particular, especially favorable, way by a people, ethnic group, etc."[1] One exception, David Easton's famous systems analysis of politics as "the authoritative allocation of values for a society," still gives "value" the very broad meaning of any material good or symbolic reward that is scarce, yet desirable, thereby creating a distribution problem.[2] In addition to being considered an untidy concept, values have come to be regarded by some scholars as a force corrosive to the scientific foundation of the discipline of political science. A recent generation of behavioralists launched a search for neutral methodologies by which investigators, regardless of any kind of bias or ideology, could replicate one another's professional results, and issued a call for a "value-free" science of politics. The next wave to hit the beaches has been the "public choice" theorists who take people's values, renamed "preference schedules," as a given rather than as a suitable subject for study. Almost forgotten now is the "political culture" approach of the 1950s which came closest to examining values seriously, but ultimately spent its strength trying to uncover psychological variations across the world's major nationalities. Consequently, in the scholarly literature on modern China, where the concept of political values appears at all, it typically stands undefined and is rarely used in explicit hypotheses.[3]

It will be argued here that "value" is not a hopelessly vague notion for political analysis: several interesting interpretations of latter stages of the Chi-

---

The valuable criticisms and suggestions of the conferees, and especially the careful critical reading by the three editors, have led to substantial revisions in the original draft of this paper.

nese revolution can be framed, using values as a concept. Several assertions are briefly defended: that values, understood as relative general preferences, have an autonomous existence in political life; that "revolutionary" values are distinguishable from "traditional" and "modern" values; and that each type of value has an identifiable following. Finally, there is an analysis of several "new social groups" in China since 1949 and their attachment to traditional, modern, and revolutionary values, respectively, as value "constituencies" that have been taken into account by political elites constructing coalitions.

VALUES IN POLITICAL ANALYSIS

An air of drama fills Milton Rokeach's assessment that in shifting our focus from other concepts to values "we would be dealing with a concept that is more central, more dynamic, more economical, a concept that would invite a more enthusiastic interdisciplinary collaboration."[4] Yet Rokeach also succeeds in making a forceful assertion of the utility of "values" for political analysis. He affirms their reality, however one might choose to define or elaborate them.

Values in sociology and political science can best be understood as *relative general preferences* governing the countless choices that people must make, day in and day out. They function much like habits to simplify social interaction. A general inclination, for example, to place family interests before community interests may influence individuals' political participation, leadership style, and/or policy preferences. Scholars of these particular issues in a cultural setting could benefit greatly from an appreciation of general values prevailing there, involving the relationship between family and community.

Values in the sense of relative general preferences are not norms (standards for behavior or achievement), attitudes (durable opinions), or beliefs (confidence in certain truths). They are general preferences in situations where clear alternatives are evident. "A spirit world exists that must be appeased to avoid harm" is a belief. "The kitchen god is unreliable" is an attitude. "A good village chief honors the kitchen god" is a norm. But "properly observing expensive rituals is more important than building up family wealth" is a value. Nor are values in this sense equivalent to interests (awareness of specific benefits expected to follow from favorable decisions). A farmer can have a concrete interest in lower agricultural taxes while at the same time adhering to a value that public welfare should prevail over private welfare, or even that all members of the community ought to support communal institutions in proportion to their wealth. At first glance, the generality attribute might strike readers as a weakness of the concept; if preferences must be vague and fuzzy and subject to several interpretations in practice to qualify as values, then how can this category form the basis of scientific propositions suited to nonarbitrary investigation? Looking more closely, however, the apparent vulnerability can be seen to be a strength. As broad preferences disengaged from the day-to-day, hurly-burly world of concrete choices, values can have an undisturbed autonomous existence. And different values can blissfully coexist even while derived positions on immediate problems are in conflict. For example, a general predilection to attach higher prestige to civilian careers than to military ones may be held by people who also value strong state defenses to bar inroads from culturally alien lands; in times of threat, arguments embodying the latter value may be heard more loudly, even though the former value suffers not at all and reemerges unsullied in later peaceful times. Values as relative general preferences are real, unmeasurable, autonomous, and durable.

Values, of course, not only exist as abstractions in the intellectual history of a society, or of a political culture; they also may have "constituencies" of people who adhere to them. For any population, variations may be observed in the distribution of values, in the intensity with which they are espoused, and in patterns of change in distribution and intensity over time. Typically, analysis of any one group will reveal a number of values accepted to different degrees; newer values will be found to have been added onto older ones without necessarily displacing the older ones, and concern for value change will be evident in intergenerational dialogue.

TRADITION, MODERNITY, AND REVOLUTION

Chances for a better understanding of the phenomenon of revolution have suffered under the major approaches to the study of political values—universal, cultural, and developmental. In universal approaches, "mankind" as a passenger on spaceship earth faces common dangers and opportunities and shares common interests. Some proponents of universalism, such as Milton Rokeach, strive to identify salient values inductively and to identify patterns in people's pursuit of them. Other proponents, notably missionaries and prosyletizers of global human rights, assert the appropriateness of certain values for all people in all cultural or historical circumstances. Analysts who adopt this latter variant tend to view revolution as leading merely to infringements of human rights, or to denials of political or religious freedom.

Cultural approaches emphasize cultural uniqueness. In some of them the stress is on "Chineseness," often from a psychological perspective. "To a Chinese," according to one cultural study, "an important aspect of social identity, of self-discipline and self-respect, is the control of emotions rather than of actions. Self-control means restraining improper feelings more than improper behavior, especially where one has been taught to depend on external authority for guidance as to what is correct or incorrect behavior."[5] Scholars following this approach have little to say about revolutionary values per se. Rather they stress key factors, such as Chinese ambivalence about authority, that produce characteristic responses to revolutionary instability and change. Others who use cultural approaches emphasize regional and class variations, usually from an anthropological perspective. Their work questions the meaningfulness of categorical statements about the Chinese people, and about the reality of "dominant" values in China.

Developmental approaches assume that all states are in a process of becoming more modern, and developmental writers proliferate dichotomies intended to bring into focus fundamental contrasts between premodern and modern society (Table 10.1). In development approaches, revolution is analyzed as one variety of transition from tradition to modernity, that is, as one

TABLE 10.1

Dichotomous Attributes of Tradition and Modernity in Developmental Approaches

Premodern Society	Modern Society
Rural	Urban
Agricultural	Industrial
Primitive	Civilized
Static	Dynamic
Sacred	Secular
Gemeinschaft	Gesellschaft
Status relationships	Secular, rationally determined, contractually negotiated relationships
High degree of self-sufficiency	Highly specialized division of labor
Ascriptive status, diffuse roles, particularistic values, collective orientation, affectivity	Achievement status, specific roles, universalistic values, self-orientation, affective neutrality
Fused society	Diffracted society

Source: Adapted from James A. Bill and Robert L. Hardgrave, Jr., *Comparative Politics: The Quest for Theory* (Columbus, Ohio: Merrill, 1973), pp. 50 ff.

path to the modern world. This conceptualization leads directly to two conclusions: all traces of revolution disappear once modernity is reached; and revolution is a cancerous consequence of the failure of other, more desirable transition paths. In Walt Rostow's famous phrase, communism is a "disease of the transition."[6]

A very serious scholarly problem can now be isolated. China has experienced, and still is experiencing, what many scholars believe to be the most intensive revolution in history. Thus analyses of Chinese politics that downplay the revolutionary experience and its far-reaching impact on political culture and values sacrifice a crucial vantage point. The literature on modern China contains far too few explanations for the appearance of radical episodes like the Great Leap Forward, the Cultural Revolution, and the political maneuvers of the "Gang of Four," while it contains an overabundance of explanations of why each of these resurgences of revolutionary themes "failed" or "could not last." Analytical approaches that take revolution more seriously are crucial. Yet none of the major approaches to studying political values reviewed here gives much explicit attention to revolution. The problem is conceptual. Thus, abhorrent as new concepts may be in a discipline already fat with jargon, the introduction here of "revolutionary values" is unavoidable, since no present concept in political science affords them a permanent home.

The danger one faces by introducing a new concept like "revolutionary values" is that one may only be drawn more deeply into the bog. If revolutionary values are neither traditional nor modern, then one is obliged to reject familiar developmental dichotomies (Table 10.1) and to replace them with what amounts to a trichotomy. Moreover, revolution suggests style as well as content—not only the substance of values but the manner and intensity with which they are pursued. Related to this, the term "revolutionary" has a relativistic connotation—what is revolutionary today (say, equality between the sexes) may not be so tomorrow. One could reasonably argue that many traditional and modern values today were once revolutionary.*

Without presuming to revise two centuries of Western sociology in a paragraph, there are grounds for believing that application of the "revolutionary values" concept can yield significant insights. First of all, most dichotomies suffer from imbalance between the two aspects; usually one side is defined clearly and the other is left as a residual catchall. In developmental sociology, the "modern" side is more often brought sharply into focus while the "traditional" side must span a spectrum of premodern experience. Second, addressing the point about style and content, revolutionary values no less than traditional and modern values include both desired "terminal" states (such as Rokeach's "equality—brotherhood, equal opportunity for all") and "instrumental" means for getting there (such as "honest—sincere, truthful"). Revolutionaries who are committed to the values of freedom, equality, high political participation, and the smashing of exploitative social relationships, view these as terminal, not instrumental values. And third, while the term "revolutionary" suggests relative discontinuity with the present order more than it suggests fixed values drifting down through time like Platonic ideals, an equal measure of relativity inheres in

---

*The author's thinking on all three of these points has benefited from correspondence with Professor James Townsend of the University of Washington.

the terms "traditional" and "modern." The 1891 Benz was a modern apparition on the turnpikes of its era but now is part of automotive tradition. All three of these concepts are historically relative, and one of them, tradition, is even infinitely expandable. The categorization of prevailing values as traditional, modern, or revolutionary, in a concrete case such as China at mid-twentieth century, must be according to historically specific criteria.

Enumeration of traditional values is most usefully restricted to a late premodern subset in order to avoid cluttering the analysis with traditions tied to extinct social institutions. In the list below for China (Table 10.2) the century from 1840 to 1949 is regarded as "late premodern China." But otherwise, any broad preference from an earlier era that still attracts a constituency would be appropriate to include. Because of cultural differences, great variation in the nature of late premodern values is typically found among traditional societies.

Modern values, by contrast, are more universal. Intellectual, technological, and organizational innovations have been diffused throughout the world with increasing ease until today a modern American and a modern Chinese may share more interests and perspectives with one another than they do with their more tradition-minded countrymen. Such modern developments as citizens' rights, computers, and labor unions have permeated all modernizing cultures in one form or another. The idea of modernization implies humankind's increasing control over elements of its natural and social environment,[7] a quest that is global in scope. Still, some important differences from one modernizing society to the next are destined to survive, no matter how far the forces of convergence may lead. Chinese cities, like all cities, will expand and incorporate adjacent areas of countryside as new suburbs, face problems of old neighborhood blight, and confront increasing demands for mass transit. Yet Chinese urbanism may never yield as unplanned a history of settlement, as distinct a subculture, as elegant or cosmopolitan a lifestyle, or as dominant a political force as has been the case elsewhere in the world, nor need China be any less modern for its partial uniqueness.

Revolution as a source of values has many meanings. At minimum it can be a doctrineless revolt against conditions large numbers of people feel are no longer tolerable. Under favorable circumstances, and with adequate leadership, it can become a seizure of state power in some measure. At most it is a dramatic transformation of institutions and values. In this last and highest form, a most difficult issue facing revolutionary leaders and students of revolution alike is the identification of the limit of feasible transformation—that is, the drawing of a boundary beyond which revolutionary authority falls to anarchy or intervention and the movement loses ground or even fails. In Chinese rhetoric this line is said to divide the genuine Left from the ultra Left. As Mao Zedong wrote in his essay, *On Practice*, "The thinking of Leftists outstrips a given stage of development of the objective process; some regard their fantasies as truth, while others strain to realize in the present an ideal which can only be realized in the future. They alienate themselves from the current practice of the majority of the people and from the realities of the day, and show themselves adventurist in their actions."[8] Revolutionary values in the abstract crowd this boundary but do not cross it; however. empirically rejecting a value on this ground (as "Left" in form but "Right" in essence) is an impossible task for external observers. One can only record whether revolutionary values are appealed to in support of arguments favoring "mobilization"—a further transfer of political resources to the revolutionary coalition—or arguments favoring "consolidation"—the protection of gains in authority and policy already achieved.

The list of Chinese values given below, broken down by category—traditional, modern, and revolutionary—is by no means exhaustive, nor does it stem from an empirical procedure. The values are merely an informal and suggestive elaboration of relevant examples falling into each of the three categories. Construction of a more complete and careful inventory should be a priority in contemporary Chinese studies. Such an effort must be multidisciplinary.

Late Premodern Chinese Values

Age should be respected over youth.

Established authority is preferred over innovation.

Scholarship should emphasize the study of Chinese tradition. Ideas from abroad are unimportant.

Criticism of Zhu Xi's Neo-Confucianism should uphold the classics and the imperial institution.

Moral superiority should be pursued through self-cultivation.

Moral individuals should be recruited to hold public office, to achieve good government.

Official careers are the most respected of all.

Officials who exploit their public positions for limited private gain should be tolerated.

The public welfare (*gong*) should be placed ahead of individual welfare, but the meaning of *gong* is very abstract.

Family loyalties are most important: all others are secondary. Family rituals should be performed properly and conscientiously.

Expenditures intended to appease a spirit world to avoid harm should not be neglected, even when money is short.

The welfare of one's region should be maximized, even at a cost of other regions.

Chinese contributions to civilization, especially from the Han, Tang, and Ming golden ages, are preferable to any additions to Chinese life by conquest dynasties ("culturism").

Social classes and severe inequality are desirable if not natural.

Conspicuous consumption and material possessions should be taken as leading indicators of status.

Favors must be repaid equivalently; otherwise one is under obligation.

The building block of interpersonal relationships should be *guanxi* ("connection"), a confident feeling of reliability arising from accumulated obligations.

Men should go out and work to support their families; women should stay home and take care of household duties.

Verbal obligations must be honored as fully as written ones.

Decisions should be made by consensus.

Modern Chinese Values

No old cultural norms are sacred. When in conflict, a modern value always should prevail over a traditional value.

National unity and independence ("nationalism") are worth great personal sacrifice and, if necessary, war.

Military strength should be built to whatever level is required to defend national independence.

Individual identity and dignity should be respected without reference to the group to which a person belongs.

Everyone should have an opportunity to become literate.

Political channels should be devised to maximize public participation.

The channels of public participation should allow as much influence as possible to flow upward into authoritative decision-making bodies ("democracy").

The scope of impartially administered law should be expanded.

Workers and students should be promoted on the basis of merit.

High standards of technical education and professionalism should be emphasized to achieve rapid economic growth.

Production should be capital-intensive.

Division of labor should be promoted to maximize comparative advantage and economies of scale.

The state should insure through welfare policies that disadvantaged individuals' living standards do not fall below a recognized floor.

Revolutionary Chinese Values

Everyone should be conscious of his or her social class origin and of its relationship to exploitation ("class consciousness").

Proletarian dictatorship over class enemies is preferable to liberalism.

Single-party rule is preferable to party competition.

Ideological coherence and orthodoxy are desirable to bolster single-party rule and proletarian dictatorship.

The ruling revolutionary party should continue to pyramid political resources even after military victory over the old regime is won and state power is seized.

The leadership core should be rectified continuously by mass line methods to contain the growth of bureaucratic power centers.

Mass campaigns are desirable and effective.

Egalitarianism is desirable to eliminate the root cause of exploitation.

The welfare interests of the individual, the collective, and the state should all be promoted. *Gong* has a more concrete meaning.

"External" costs of rapid industrial growth should be controlled by enterprises themselves or by the state.

Revolution should be encouraged elsewhere in the world to insure its ultimate success in China.

NEW SOCIAL GROUPS

An argument has been made above for the reality of political values—enduring, abstract, relative general preferences people draw upon to help them organize the complexities of everyday life. A value put to work in a worldly decision situation, either as a ground for one's own choice or as a building block for an argument intended to sway the choice of another, contributes to the formation of attitudes or opinions. In much the same way Franz Schurmann has interpreted the Thought of Mao Zedong as an application of fundamental truths of Marxism-Leninism to practical problems of the Chinese revolution.[9] A particular derivative attitude may not survive the challenge of competing values or hostile interests and be short-lived, but values themselves attenuate only gradually as a result of repeated failures in practice.

The next step is to inquire into value constituencies in China. If new values are to take hold as additions to or substitutions for old ones, then some groups or sectors of the population must espouse them. When a value, such as the idea that people should make most of what they use with their own hands, no longer attracts a constituency, then that value retains only historical significance. A value no longer appealed to is not even a traditional value for present purposes. It is the interplay between value and constituency that holds promise for political analysis.

The informal assessments below of self-interests and of traditional, modern, and revolutionary values among seven new social groups in China since liberation are a first cut at analyzing this interplay. The groups selected are only a sample of all new social groups (see Table 10.2), and new social groups in the first place are only one possible category. But one must begin somewhere, and these groups are intrinsically interesting. Most of them are "new" in the sense that the people who belong to them enjoy (or suffer) a significantly altered status under the Communist regime, compared with their lot before 1949.

Collective Farmers—Former Elites (CFEs)

Collective farmers who used to be landlords or other rural elites before the Communists took power suffered sharp loss of status in the revolution. Some of

TABLE 10.2

New Social Groups Under Chinese Communist Party Rule

Group	Abbreviation Used
Farmers living and working in collectives	
Former landlords and other elites	*CFE
Former rich peasants	CFR
Former middle peasants	*CFM
Former hired laborers	*CFP
Others	DFO
Workers belonging to a union of the official labor federation	*UW
Women who participate in public affairs	*WP
Nonintellectual, educated youth (most of whom would have remained uneducated before the Communist period)	NY
Returned "Overseas Chinese"	RO
Chinese Communist Party (CCP) members (with the Party in power)	
Upward mobiles	PMU
Local elites	*PML
People's Liberation Army (PLA) members (after victory in revolutionary civil war)	
Commissioned officers of military regions	LAOR
Commissioned officers of central service arms	LAOC
Noncommissioned officers and ordinary soliders	LAN
Writers and artists who must serve socialist politics	WA
Scientific and technical specialists	*ST

*Indicates the groups analyzed in this chapter.
Source: Compiled by the author.

them, insofar as they had taken advantage of their status to behave exploitatively or cruelly toward their poorer neighbors, or had even collaborated with Japanese occupation forces, should not have been surprised by their fate. Others felt, often with justification, that their wealth and advantages had been relatively small, and that they had behaved humanely in the old days. Much of what they had expected of life, and what many of them had largely achieved, was suddenly taken from them. They plummeted from the top of rural society to the bottom. This fall in itself left feelings of resentment, but the situation later worsened. Class labels assigned during land reform in the countryside (and during the democratic reform of industry and commerce in cities) proved nearly inflexible. The only new category introduced that allowed some to avoid their debilitating label was "Overseas Chinese" (1955). Hopes arose after the Great Leap Forward that good behavior might lead to a change of label, but these hopes were dashed by Chairman Mao's 1962 call to "never forget class struggle." The "five black elements," *di fu fan huai you*, began with *di*, "landlord," and *fu*, "rich peasant." CFEs along with CFRs (former rich peasants) were frequent and easy targets for criticism and struggle during mass campaigns. Red Guards persecuted them during the Cultural Revolution. And the later movement to clean up the class ranks exposed new landlord elements, some within the CCP (Chinese Communist Party) itself.

Many production teams in the 1970s still treat CFEs with reserve; some team members will not talk to them or have any other social dealings with them. CFEs enjoy few civil rights. They are prohibited from voting, and they may not hold office in their teams or brigades. Particularly severe is the extension of the class-label stigma to their children. Sons and daughters of landlords are also considered landlords and suffer much of the same discrimination. It is almost impossible for them to attain higher education, or even to be sent by their teams or brigades to a local technical training course. Families with better class backgrounds are reluctant for their children to marry CFE children. This aspect reinforces CFE resentments, and of course it leaves their offspring deeply ambivalent toward the type of system that denies them opportunities to overcome presumptions of their having an antisocial nature.

As persons atop the list of "bad elements," CFEs find themselves continuously under the microscope. Any misdeed is magnified, and its origin allegedly found in the miscreant's bad class background. Seldom do extenuating circumstances temper the community's judgment. CFEs would like to leave China, were emigration only practical for them, and to live in a nonrevolutionary society. Short of that, they would prefer to have their class label changed and be able to shrink into anonymity. Thus they favor political leaders who would mute the "class struggle" theme, and fear most young and intensely ideological activists who thrive on reaffirming the class basis of the revolution. CFEs despise mass campaigns, and find little with which to identify in the thought of Mao Zedong.

In the absence of political changes that might allow them some opportunity and room for maneuver, CFEs must choose between strategies of passivity and modest participation in narrow, approved channels. Strategies of passivity cause them to put survival first, and to become withdrawn within themselves, much like inmates in a penitentiary. All their hopes are pinned on the future and the chance of ameliorative political change, though many years have passed with little change and their optimism is progressively harder to arouse. This has the effect of resigning them to their destiny and transferring their aspirations to the next generation. Thus the restrictions they see strangling their children are especially depressing, and they long to see their children escape the pariah status.

CFEs enjoy the degree to which folk customs are still honored in village life under socialism. Old people are still venerated, relatively expensive wedding celebrations still occur, holiday feasting is still common, and significant expenditures are still made on funerals. Since these vestiges of older culture are not popular with CCP leaders, CFEs take heart in their continued popularity as an indication that the Party is not all-powerful and cannot always have its way.

The effectiveness of alternative strategies of limited participation in approved channels depends upon several local factors, most importantly local people's attitudes toward the CFEs' behavior before liberation, the recent prosperity of the production team, and the need of the team for production skills of the CFE. There is some documentation of teams, for example, in which CFEs are denied all observable status but are given a crucial role as behind-the-scenes advisors to more politically orthodox formal officeholders. Presumably CFEs benefit from opportunities to help their teams or brigades become more prosperous, in good times or bad. While prosperity lasts, a CFE who is making such a contribution, even if behind the scenes, is safer. Therefore, CFEs who choose the strategy of limited participation value general economic progress in the countryside. At the same time they have little control over developments that affect their welfare. They cannot be self-assertive on their own behalf. They are "nonpeople," and even "people" must act circumspectly when seeking to advance their private interests. Their only legitimate move for self-improvement has been to seek a change of class label, on grounds of original error, during times when a policy of limited reclassification has been in effect.

CFEs have another calculation to make when policies like "three guarantees and one reward" and "paddy field management responsibility system of reward for production in excess of quota" of the early 1960s come along. Because they had experience in operating their own farms before liberation, they are in a superior position to benefit from such policies. On the other hand, if they alone benefit while CFMs (former middle peasants), CFPs (former poor peasants), and others do not, then the ultimate effect would be to kill the goose that lays the golden egg. Thus CFEs value policies such as the ones Deng Zihui and Tao Zhu advocated in the early 1960s, but they prefer that such policies have collective benefits and also some selective benefits for people from a wider range of classes.

CFEs' attitudes toward technology and professionalism are the most ambivalent of all. On the one hand, CFEs are denied opportunities for higher education and even for lesser training in agricultural technical specialities. Thus, in the short run, they stand to gain little from the promotion of professional and technical values. On the other hand, technological progress cuts across class lines, and in the longer run the promotion of such values might very well benefit the CFEs. Political overtones in debates over the advance of professionalism in China have caused these debates to be most acrimonious. People who are good at technical subjects, irrespective of their politics, are promoted when technological values are prized in public life. This dilemma can be solved in the long run by educating politically favored classes to be good at technology, which passes the problem back to the education system. Thus, technical capacity in the short run must be given up to get nonelitist technology in the long run.

Collective Farmers—Former Middle Peasants (CFMs)

Middle peasants of the old society worked their land. They neither rented out part of their acreage nor hired labor, nor did they generally work others' land as tenants. They owned most of their own animals and equipment, and they were minimally self-sufficient. They were a large class, comprising as much as one-third of the population in some areas and owning as much as one-half of the cropland. Their level of education was generally low, if they were literate at all, although some were quite skilled at traditional farming techniques. They were not able to obtain agricultural credit easily. Also they were very vulnerable to unexpected shifts in the weather and, because they were small, the market. Middle-peasant status was unstable. CFM families yearned for greater security through upward mobility, but lived in fear of losing what they had at any time through a turn of bad luck. The new government's initiatives that won their most willing response were policies designed to stabilize rural markets and thus increase the security of the small producers buying and selling there. In good times, of course, they were disappointed at having to sell their produce at artificially low official procurement prices, but government welfare and protection in bad years made up for it.

The frequent mention of a "middle peasant problem" in Party documents underscores the low revolutionary consciousness of this class. CFMs are not antagonistic to revolutionary values; they simply have no natural attachment to them. The only reliable CFM in Party eyes is a "lower middle peasant" whose former status was closer to poor than rich. Party doctrine neither advances CFM interests nor stands in their way. CFMs cannot get ahead easily, a situation that appears to some of them a little worse than their status in the old days, but they also cannot fall into poverty, which is a much more secure situation than before. Only those possessed of a gambling mentality prefer the old system to the new. CFMs are still eager to get ahead, whether by Communist criteria or traditional. Those who find they can succeed by attaining a production skill, higher education, Youth League or Party membership, or recruitment into the People's Liberation Army, do so while appropriately disparaging the backwardness of old values. Others seek greater prestige among their fellow villagers in traditional value terms through calculated selection of marriage partners, conspicuous consumption on ritual occasions, expansion of profitable household production, development of *guanxi* and collection of obligations, and even through entering the shadowy world of factions.

Party leaders regard CFMs as fickle revolutionaries who adhere to revolutionary values only as long as they feel they derive some benefit from them. Ironically, this position has a positive aspect. Marxist revolutionary doctrine, Chinese statements of it offering no exception, eschews utopian calls for single-minded altruism in favor of respect for "the interests of the individual, the collective, and the state." CFMs are an important political weather vane when individual interests are being overlooked. Whereas CFMs may be publicly attacked for their "rich peasant" or "petty bourgeois" deviations, *in camera* real policy changes to redress the imbalance are proposed. Correspondingly, when CFMs uphold revolutionary values, the leadership has a sign that present policy is effective. This is the real significance of the "middle peasant problem."

CFMs are similarly ambivalent toward modern values. They see their immediate self-interest reflected in the impartial administration of law, in the wider use of inanimate energy, and in a rise in overall living standards through industrialization. Other modern values they may take or leave. As a group, they are neither a force for diffusing modern values nor a barrier to their progress.

Collective Farmers—Former Poor Peasants (CFP)

Poor peasants in the old society, comprising over half the population in some areas and owning about one-fourth of the cropland, rented some or all of the land they worked, and may also have hired out their labor part time. By no standard can their life in these times be said to have been good. Most of them barely survived. Their income left little or no surplus for saving; going into debt was more common. Their diet and housing were poor, their access to medical care was minimal, most were not educated, and their cultural level was low. Life offered little in the way of hope—theirs was a "culture of poverty." In fact, the early investigations of class background conducted during land reform, which required a family to have held "poor peasant" status for three generations to qualify for that highly prized label, uncovered a sobering reality: literally no one qualified in some villages because poor peasant boys had been unable to support wives and hence could last only one generation.

Poor peasants, perhaps because they assessed their situation as desperate, gave strong support to the Red Army during the revolutionary civil-war years. What they expected in return for their support in the way of land reform or other government policies is not well understood. What they got, ultimately, probably benefited them the most. The initial redistribution of institutional, landlord, and rich peasant holdings to poor households often left the recipients vulnerable. If they were not short of skills needed to manage their own farms, they lacked adequate credit, labor, and tools. Many failed, and a tendency toward recombination of larger landholdings in the hands of more successful farmers appeared.

Households that were victimized by this recombination tendency greeted collectivization eagerly, and were even willing to go along with most features of the early communes. The CCP proved quite sincere in its professed class line and its redistribution policy. In rural China "poor and lower middle peasants" were given subsidies to allow them to join agricultural production cooperatives as full members, given preference in school admissions, and generally made to embody virtue in rural life. All policies were to "serve" them. Poor and Lower Middle Peasant Associations were formed down to the production brigade level to give organizational muscle to the redistributive programs. CFP life is still far from bounteous, but it is much better than it was before the revolution.

Changes in CFP status since the early 1950s are more difficult to plot. Rural standards of living for all farm families have more than doubled, and CFPs seem to have enjoyed most of their share of the improvement. Other changes are less dramatic. While entrance exam standards and grading were relaxed to raise the proportion of poor and lower middle peasants in universities, special tutoring and other remedial programs could not overcome their lack of academic preparation, and compromises with the ideal of "putting politics in command" of education have been necessary. In many brigades CFP families are relatively small, their diet is simple, they have the most members who suffer from a disease or disability, they have minimal education, and bring in comparatively low household incomes. Thus, they stand to benefit most from the welfare aspects of the commune system—co-op health plans, five guarantees, controlled consumer prices, minimum food distribution, practically free education, and more. All this numbers them among those who value collective institutions most highly, and among those who least enthusiastically support policies that discriminate among individual households.

CFPs as a whole have not stood out in political participation or as cadres, despite laudable examples to the contrary that have been widely publicized. Culturally CFPs are used to deferring to their higher-income and higher-status "betters," not to asserting themselves in adversary or leadership roles. Persistence of status differentials from the beginning of the Communist regime is a contributing factor. Also everyone, including CFPs themselves, knows that the masses are not always right. Sometimes the interpretation of a political episode emerging with official hindsight is that "hoodwinked" masses were manipulated by deviant cadres. Political participation to CFPs appears full of mysteries, dangers, and discomforts of unnatural status relationships, especially if an individual is not able to speak coherently in public. They do not value political participation highly, however much they might value its effects. The Dazhai workpoint system and other innovations pinned on continuous mass participation have tended to decline into formalism. CFPs are among the least threatened by "sent-down youth" who take positions of responsibility in their teams and brigades. Campaigns to teach ideology to the masses, such as the recent one to "train mass contingents of Marxist theoretical workers" (one of the Cultural Revolution's "newborn things") are designed to combat their culture of deference. At the very least CFPs continue to prize many other late premodern values; for them these values sum up the Chinese way of life. They and others in their village know the values, they understand what behavior is appropriate to them, and they regard them as familiar foundations or guideposts during a time of rapid social change.

CFPs are not able to respond easily to the introduction of modern values, and social science has yet to learn why. Hypothetical explanations abound, among them fears grounded in superstition, fear of the unknown, systemic effects (one change, such as draining wet rice three times during maturation, may dictate others—in this case termination of fish breeding in flooded paddy fields and the consequent removal of the chief natural enemy of mosquitoes), interference with existing status hierarchies, and others. Some modernization occurs gradually, such as building rural, small-scale industries and shifting to chemical fertilizer, while other modernization occurs almost overnight, such as the replacement of water buffalo with hand tractors in Taiwan in the mid-1970s. CFPs can readily accept greater reliance upon inanimate energy that relieves them of drudgery. And they have shown an inclination to place high value on military strength, national unity, and independence, probably because they well remember it was they who suffered the most when China was torn by invasion and civil war.

Revolutionary values mostly strike agreeable chords with CFPs. Though they provide only weak leadership for promoting these values, they do make up a strong constituency for them.

Unionized Workers (UWs)

The Chinese revolution is famous as a rural movement. Mao Zedong rejected the urban-based leadership of Li Lisan in the late 1920s, and led a peasant army from the hills of Kiangsi and Yenan to fight a guerrilla resistance against Japan and to drive Chiang Kai-shek's forces from the coastal cities in the late 1940s. This stereotype is not completely accurate, but it is reasonable. After takeover, the CCP had to build labor unions almost from scratch.

The new system of official enterprise unions, joined into a general national union after a few years, resulted in an organization that, in addition to its intended purpose of helping to transform capitalist industries into thoroughly socialist ones, acted to protect unionized workers' privileges. This result is associated with the growth of a dual labor market. Only half of the members of China's industrial labor force belong to a union and enjoy job security and welfare benefits. The other half are not eligible for union membership, usually because they are apprentices or temporary workers recruited from nearby communes. The CCP wants to reward the key urban class of its ruling coalition-workers, but also wants to discourage migration from farm to city. Nonunion workers absorb the effects of this contradiction while union members enjoy a favored status. Despite the many policies of recent years to develop agriculture and build up the quality of life in the countryside, the standard of living in most city neighborhoods is still higher than in most villages.

UWs probably have a lower attachment to traditional values than any other new social group. Their work is not traditional, nor is their political position. UW attachment to modern values, on the contrary, is very strong. Working conditions in Chinese factories are vastly superior to conditions before the revolution, even if many factories must improve greatly before the sources of Marxian alienation are removed. Workers believe that progress will be most likely to continue if individual dignity, literacy, participation, democracy, and merit systems are highly valued. Worker families have the closest recollections of foreign pressure in the old treaty ports and are most easily mobilized around nationalistic themes. And workers' self-interest is advanced by industrialization and further technical education.

UW commitment to revolutionary values is real but qualified by a desire to preserve their relative position of privilege. They benefit, for example, from mass campaigns that promote worker democracy but not campaigns attacking labor unions as conservative (as happened in 1966-67). And they benefit from CCP advocacy of a degree of egalitarianism but not from elimination of the eight-grade wage system that preserves higher pay for more skilled and experienced workers.

Women Who Participate in Public Affairs (WPs)

Women's position before the revolution was for all practical purposes subservient. China was ruled by men, and men believed that women should stay home and tend to family duties. Some women joined in the socialist revolution over male opposition, thus effectively asserting their right to equal political participation. The new Communist government passed a progressive marriage law in 1950; the CCP has a Women's Work Department; a National Women's Federation and its local affiliate is an organizational vehicle for the women's movement; and propaganda outlets including artistic and literary productions give unusual emphasis to women in nonfamily roles. But many barriers to real equal participation remain, as the intensive organization and propaganda in this area suggest. WPs are still considered progressive.

The women's movement since takeover has gone through distinct stages. The first attempt to implement the new marriage law in the 1950s met with severe resistance from men in farm families. The Great Leap Forward brought women into public life on an unprecedented scale. The years after the Great Leap saw a return to idealization of more traditional family life. And in the

1970s a more subdued struggle for equal pay for equal work has been under way.

WPs hold little attachment to traditional values, and such attachment as they do display may be more realistic compromise than sincere espousal. In rural areas they must contend not only with the objections of men but also of traditionalist women who themselves feel threatened by modern women who belittle family responsibilities and want to "go out." Women who hold to specifically elite traditional values could do so only vicariously through sons and families, since even in late premodern China women could not be a part of official and scholarly life.

WPs attachment to modern values is selective. Their self-interest is served by modern values that are individualistic, such as personal dignity, literacy, impartial law, and merit systems. Their self-interest is less directly related to modern values that are nationalistic or developmental.

WPs have a strong stake in revolutionary values because the CCP has regularly advocated greater equality for women. This is a far cry from saying that the Party has done much to advance many feminist causes current in other countries, but in the Chinese context, especially considering its other political obligations, the CCP has been a progressive force. WPs experience some ambivalence toward arguments using the concepts of class and class struggle. On the one hand, such arguments underpin ideologically the revolutionary authority that has benefited them. On the other hand, class arguments can be used to justify postponement of strictly feminist issues.

Chinese Communist Party Members—Local Elites (PMLs)

Most of China's 35 million Party members (1977 figure) fall into the category of the Party member local elites. In rural areas, where about 2 percent of the people belong to the Party, "local" extends as high as responsible cadres in commune or county organizations; in urban areas, where 5 percent or more of the population may belong, it extends as high as neighborhood or district organizations. While promotions to higher office are made regularly, at least through the middle reaches of the hierarchy (the fact that most top leaders began their political careers at the bottom is a hallmark of Chinese government), the promotion ratio is very small as a proportion of all local Party members and cadres. The basic PMLs' position is astride a gulf between friends and neighbors whose respect they seek and whose interests they are expected to represent, and higher leadership levels whose demands may conflict with local sensitivities. That is, PMLs must serve two masters. They may adopt one of three broad strategies to reconcile the conflicting pressures—competence, activism, or factionalism. Pursuing the competence strategy is safest for the individual, but yields the least political leadership; higher levels cannot be satisfied to have all PMLs taking this approach. Activism is the hardest strategy, but potentially the most successful in the eyes of higher authorities; the chief danger is the appearance of false moral superiority and opportunism at the expense of others. Engaging in factional activities is the most tempting but also the most dangerous strategy in the long run, because factionalism is highly illegitimate in Chinese political thought, however common it may be in practice.

PMLs are close to local traditional values because they are local people. In fact they are tempted to favor their local identity over their elite responsibility when they realize the Party can offer rewards for organizational loyalty only to a few upward mobiles. When dividing local customs into good "heritage" and bad "superstition," PMLs are inclined to be flexible and tolerant. They are restrained only by an awareness that higher Party leaders cannot brook the performance of basic-level personnel who exemplify "localism" or display cultural backwardness.

PMLs are strong on technological modern values but not necessarily on political ones. Not only do some modern political values collide with revolutionary values (for example, democracy versus proletarian dictatorship over class enemies), but they also directly threaten PML status. Individual dignity, democracy, impartial law, and merit systems are not highly valued by PMLs. Within the CCP these values lead to policies such as annual "open door" rectification, and expulsion of "stale" members to make room for "fresh" ones. Insecurities derived from modern policies like these merely reinforce insecurities caused by the propensity of higher leaders to make local cadres scapegoats for mistakes implied by shifts of Party line. The pressure can be so intense that many otherwise qualified persons share the attitude of "not wanting to be a cadre."

Revolutionary values legitimate the elite status of Communist Party members, so we might expect PMLs to uphold them vigorously. The cross-pressures that they feel, however, mute the anticipated effect. PMLs envision themselves as transmission belts for priorities decided above them, or as enforcers who have little choice but to implement decisions taken elsewhere. This position naturally conflicts with their desire to minimize differences between themselves and their peers.

Scientific and Technical Specialists (STs)

China's scientific establishment, now much larger than it was before 1949, is stratified into three distinct generations. The senior scientists compose a small elite of first-rate scholars with degrees from European or American universities. They head the academies and institutes and direct the principal research projects. A middle-aged generation trained in China before the Cultural Revolution is much larger in number. Many of them have carried out high-quality research and authored significant papers in their disciplines, although they have had to work with less up-to-date instruments and facilities than their colleagues elsewhere in the world. The Cultural Revolution cut a decadewide political swath through scientific recruitment and training in China; many of the graduates of that period are not competent. Just now a fourth generation is beginning its education. Scientists as a breed share some common values irrespective of generation, but in China these generational groups also have somewhat distinctive orientations on important issues.

China has followed the Russian practice of training young scientists in institutes rather than universities. University departments stand last in line for equipment and do little significant research work. With a few exceptions the institutes themselves have equipment manufactured in China with 10- to 30-year-old foreign designs. Chinese creativity and design have been focused on the defense sector—namely, nuclear power and rocketry—and on a small number of priority projects where Chinese accomplishments would be recognized worldwide as frontier contributions. This approach has led them to emphasize empirical work in fields like seismology, where they have access to superior data, and to emphasize theory in fields like astronomy, where their less refined instruments prevent them from competing in empirical studies. The institutes subscribe to foreign scientific journals and acquire excellent collections of English-language technical publications. They are not tied into international circles of specialists in different research areas, who regularly exchange papers and preprints, meet one another at conferences, and lecture at each other's institutions. All these forms of communication have become very important, but China's scientists can keep up only with published work abroad. A tiny proportion of Chinese scientists enjoy opportunities for foreign travel and study. Mao Zedong's successor in 1976, Chairman Hua Guofeng, has been promoting the "four modernizations," one of which is modernization of science and technology, as a key policy of his administration. Accordingly, research institutes have been promised higher levels of funding, entrance examinations have been restored (1977) to select university students, and the mandatory two years of labor on communes before proceeding from middle school to university has been lifted.

Many traditional values do not threaten scientists or their work and hence are not an active concern of scientists. The only late premodern values toward which scientists feel actively negative are the ideas that age should be respected over youth, that established authority is preferred over innovation, that the study of Chinese tradition should prevail over the absorption of scholarship from abroad, and that official careers are the most respected of all.

Of all groups in China, STs are probably the most receptive to modern values, technical and political. These values reward their talents, advance their careers, and elevate their status.

Scientists' relationship to revolutionary values is complicated. They are not naturally inclined to adhere to revolutionary values for their own sake; science always comes first. But they may regard revolutionary values as instrumental to their professional interests to the extent that revolutionary authorities promote scientific achievement as a means of achieving the goals of national prestige and military self-sufficiency. The greatest conflicts arise when political authorities criticize the "pure professional viewpoint" and call for "politics in command." Scientists' response to strong political currents is basically defensive.

They tactfully acknowledge the significance of practical applications of scientific findings and mass involvement in these applications, even though they really may belittle the value of popular science and resent the diversion of resources to it. They yearn for greater respect and larger budgets. Their formula for success has been to incline toward both modern and revolutionary values, even though in specific situations these two types of values might be in conflict.

These informal assessments of the relative strength of traditional, modern, and revolutionary values among these seven groups is summarized in Table 10.3.

TABLE 10.3

Summary of Hypothesized Political Values for Seven New Social Groups in China

Group	Value Category		
	Late Premodern Traditional	Modern	Revolutionary
CFE	1–	3	5
CFM	3	2	3–
CFP	3+	5	2
UW	5+	1	2
WP	4	3	2
PML	3	3	2–
ST	4+	1	3

Note: Groups are assessed on a scale of 1–5 with 1 indicating most values in the category held relatively strongly; 2, values in the category generally adhered to; 3, ambivalence or cross-pressure; 4, values in the category weakly adhered to; and 5, few if any values in the category held.

Source: Compiled by the author.

CONCLUSION: TEN HYPOTHESES

In the early part of the chapter a rationale for introducing a new concept called "revolutionary values" was presented. In the following part the author experimented with this concept by applying it informally to assess the significance of several new social groups in China since 1949 as constituencies for traditional, modern, and revolutionary values. What remains is to fulfill the promise put forth at the outset, and reiterated subsequently—the promise to use the "revolutionary values" concept to frame new interpretations of the latter stages of the Chinese revolution.

1. The mere existence of a revolutionary movement, however well it succeeds on its own terms, introduces revolutionary values to society which may then attract constituencies.

2. Once a revolutionary movement is successful in seizing state power, revolutionary values begin to attract wider constituencies. The values of the winners inevitably gain a following at first.

3. The more intensive a revolution (measured by scope of change, pace of change, level of violence, amount of elite displacement, and degree of foreign intervention), the longer the period, following a successful seizure of power, during which revolutionary values will hold or expand their constituencies.

4. As long as a revolutionary value continues to hold or expand its constituency, the probability remains high that it will be drawn into political debate.

5. Following a successful seizure of power by a revolutionary movement, all appeals to revolutionary values will be to solicit support for one of two broad revolutionary strategies: "mobilization"—a further transfer of political resources to the revolutionary coalition; or "consolidation"—the protection of gains in authority and policy already achieved.

6. The more intensive a revolution, the more forcefully mobilization arguments are pressed. Consolidation arguments are always strong.

7. The more intensive a revolution, the wider the range of policy issues that become tied to the mobilization/consolidation cleavage. Never is debate on all issues restructured by this cleavage. The "two-line struggle" in Chinese political discourse is an example. It has been energized by a salient mobilization/consolidation conflict since 1949, but not all issue areas have been equally affected, public rhetoric aside.

8. The more forcefully mobilization arguments are pressed, the longer the mobilization/consolidation cleavage restructures at least some policy debates. As mobilization arguments subside, consolidation arguments also subside.

9. The ultimate success of a revolution can be measured by the strength of the revolutionary values added to political culture.

10. The more salient a mobilization/consolidation conflict, the greater the likelihood of a secondary "revolution from above" after a decade or more.

NOTES

1. *Webster's New World Dictionary of the American Language*, College Edition (Cleveland and New York: World Publishing Company, 1966), p. 1609.

2. David Easton, *A Framework for Political Analysis* (Englewood Cliffs, N.J.: Prentice-Hall, 1965), p. 50.

3. Among the more prominent articles in the field that contain interesting discussions of values are: John Israel, "Continuities and Discontinuities in the Ideology of the Great Proletarian Cultural Revolution," in *Ideology and Politics in Contemporary China*, ed. Chalmers Johnson (Seattle: University of Washington Press, 1973), pp. 3–46; Michel Oksenberg, "The Chinese Policy Process and the Public Health Issue: An Arena Approach,"

Studies in Comparative Communism 7 (Winter 1974): 375–408; Tang Tsou, "The Values of the Chinese Revolution," in *China's Developmental Experience*, ed. Michel Oksenberg (New York: Praeger, 1973), pp. 27–41.

4. Milton Rokeach, *Beliefs, Attitudes, and Values* (San Francisco: Jossey-Bass, 1968), p. 159.

5. Richard H. Solomon, *Mao's Revolution and the Chinese Political Culture* (Berkeley: University of California Press, 1971), p. 72.

6. Walt W. Rostow, *The Stages of Economic Growth* (Cambridge: Cambridge University Press, 1960), p. 162.

7. James A. Bill and Robert L. Hardgrave, Jr., *Comparative Politics: The Quest for Theory* (Columbus, Ohio: Merrill, 1973), p. 67.

8. Quoted in Hua Tse, "Left, Ultra-'Left' and Fake Left," *Peking Review*, No. 15 (April 14, 1978), p. 6.

9. Franz Schurmann, *Ideology and Organization in Communist China*, new enlarged edition (Berkeley: University of California Press, 1968), p. 30.

11

MOBILIZATION VERSUS WELFARE IN MASS ORGANIZATIONS: A CONFLICT OF VALUES

Amy Auerbacher Wilson

Two important values from within the Chinese symbolic order—mobilization and welfare—are the focus of this study. The analysis explores some of the significant changes that have occurred with respect to each of these two values and, in addition, probes the nature of the relationship between the two. Logically and empirically, mobilization and welfare seem to manifest a considerable degree of interdependence, both as general ideological constructs and as specific organizational guidelines.

This study proceeds from the general to the specific, with the first two sections commenting on mobilization and welfare as societal standards in New China and tracing the translation of these broad social ideals into narrower ones, in particular into the pragmatic rationales associated with China's major mass organizations. The third and major section provides further detail on the specification of mobilization/welfare values in mass organizations. These hypotheses are tested that predict values from social structure, using data on mass organization goals and elites. At each level of generalization the question of conflict is noteworthy: To what extent do mobilization and welfare represent a potentially—if not actually—contradictory set of objectives in Chinese society?

MOBILIZATION AND WELFARE AS VALUES IN CHINESE SOCIETY

Despite the conceptual imprecision associated with values, a difficult social science issue that Richard Wilson wrestles with in his Introduction to this volume, there is probably reasonable lay consensus on a commonsense meaning for value. In everyday terms, values are generally understood to be ultimate ends or goals, to be collective standards or ideals. As abstractions that refer to desired outcomes, values nevertheless function as the bases on which choices are made and conflicts resolved.

Both mobilization and welfare are collectively held goals of the contemporary Chinese social system that quite adequately fit popular notions of values. Moreover, they are significant symbolic elements in the official Chinese world view. In this study mobilization, as a value, connotes active participation as an end in itself, in accordance with official ideology and with the commonsense meaning. The term mobilization, used broadly here, gives a positive valence to collective endeavors that may be predominantly economic or political in nature. In this research mobilization as a value subsumes a wide range of energizing efforts, whether initiated by authorities at the center or sparked by the masses at the periphery of society. The critical factor, definitionally speaking, is that the very marshaling of human resources is deemed desirable. (And here, too, the author is in basic agreement with Lynn White's use of "mobilization" in his contribution to this work.)

Similarly, welfare constitutes a value insofar as the well-being of China as a nation and/or that society's component parts is perceived of as an ultimate good. With welfare subscribed to as an ideal, the life chances of citizens are to be enhanced, their interests and needs given positive consideration. Here, too, welfare is broadly conceptualized and encompasses the distribution of both material and nonmaterial benefits. Neither welfare nor mobilization is limited in this analysis to strictly empirical outcomes. Mobilization and welfare goals for the betterment of New China include the creation and harnessing of new modes of consciousness.

There is a sense in which mobilization and welfare values can reasonably be conceived of dualistically, as a pair of opposing orientations. Certainly several of the more obvious analogs to mobilization versus welfare evince such a polarity: production versus consumption; inputs versus outputs; responsibilities versus rights; or obligations versus benefits. Gordon Bennett, in the chapter he has written for this volume, makes a related distinction between mobilization and consolidation as two broad revolutionary strategies. And, less succinctly, the relationship between mobilization and welfare values seems to mirror the potential contradiction in the classic Communist dictum: from each according to abilities, to each according to needs.

As will be noted, a tidy dualistic view of mobilization/welfare breaks down, however, with the introduction of specifying categories: level of analysis, from society to subsocietal collective to individual; a time framework, such as short versus long-run considerations; the distinction between instrumental and terminal values (alternately distinguishable as intermediate versus ultimate values); or the rank order of values within a value hierarchy.

First, with regard to level of analysis, explicit attention to level appears to be a necessary clarifying step when referring specifically to welfare. Ideally, who is to benefit? Society at large? Some lower-level collectivity? Individuals? Not only are levels of analysis important methodologically, but also they emerge as prominent substantive issues in the Chinese political arena. The ideologically orthodox in the People's Republic of China have repeatedly averred that collective or public interests and needs are to take precedence over individual or private ones.

In an examination of mobilization versus welfare values in Chinese society, a second factor to be considered is time. If the simplest of temporal distinctions is made, that between short-term and long-term goals, what, then, is the implication of the respective emphasis upon mobilization or welfare goals? Which of the two values is given priority and therefore promoted as the more pressing objective? Overall, it appears that Chinese authorities have imparted a greater sense of immediacy and urgency to mobilization. Clearly, mobilization ends have been primary during active mass campaign phases, those collective outbursts of human energy programmed by the regime periodically since 1949.[1]

A third analytic category relevant to an empirical study of mobilization and welfare values distinguishes between instrumental and terminal values and is closely allied to the temporal dimension noted above. Here, however, the contrast is one of means versus ends—or of intermediate versus ultimate values—presumably determined at one point in time. The parsimony and clarity of means-ends theoretical schemes are appealing in the abstract but difficult to apply to real-life situations. In the Chinese context, breaking down the relationship between mobilization and welfare values in terms of means versus ends can be a thorny problem. For a given social setting, the problem involves ascertaining whether welfare operates as a terminal goal, with mobilization functioning as an instrument for goal attainment or, conversely, whether welfare objectives are intermediate values, serving to effect the ultimate value of active involvement in societal tasks. The rub is that whatever means-ends relationship exists at one particular point in time and/or at one level of analysis may not exist at another.

Fourth, the idea of value hierarchy is also useful for scrutinizing the interaction between mobilization and welfare values in Chinese society. Social scientists suggest that values frequently cluster together, forming an ordered set of discrete symbolic elements for which a ranking system or hierarchy exists. In the case of the Chinese mobilization/welfare value nexus, mobilization ends have quite consistently been granted official precedence over welfare objectives. The degree of primacy afforded mobilization, however, has by no means been constant but rather has varied significantly over time and across diverse sectors of society.

The official line of the Chinese Communist Party (CCP) that periodically sets forth the correct "mix" of mobilization versus welfare values is not political sentiment created in a vacuum. Rather, the ideology that establishes the proper balance between the two goals does so in response to perceived social realities and reflects the continuous overarching struggle to realize the joint aims of modernization and of socialist transformation.

The reality of scarcity in China is a good case in point, for the regime has found it necessary to restrict welfare and to place limitations on material rewards and benefits in the short run in order to concentrate on the longer-run objective of transforming Chinese society. Labor, however, is a plentiful resource in China, and its relative abundance has meant a rational stress on labor-intensive methods of production, methods that depend on effective mobilization procedures. The Chinese leadership has consequently, and not surprisingly, promoted active participation as a societal value, relying, moreover, on moral incentives to supplement material ones in fostering mobilization as a goal. Now that certain basic levels of well-being have been achieved and the most blatant ills and the major injustices of the old society eradicated, many observers have been wondering whether a zealous commitment to mass mobilization will be dissipated. How long can repeated spurts of mobilization be sustained, using predominantly normative means for securing participation?

This study is not intended to be a general discourse on mobilization and welfare values in Chinese society. Instead, further analysis of these constructs is to be "grounded" in a particular slice of Chinese social reality, namely, mass organizations. The choice of mass organizations as units of analysis is felt to be especially apt, for these organizations were created by the CCP leadership and designated as the very mechanisms whereby mobilization/welfare ideals could be communicated and translated into action. Insofar as ideological tenets involving mobilization and welfare were to be operationalized in terms of these organizations, at least until the Cultural Revolution in the mid-1960s, they offer a rather unique vantage point from which to observe the dynamic interplay between these two values.

MASS ORGANIZATIONS AND MOBILIZATION/WELFARE VALUES: THE TRANSMISSION BELT FUNCTION

Mass organizations are a type of large-scale formal organization characteristic of China and other socialist nations. James Townsend uses the term "mass organization" to refer to "those secondary associations that recruit their members on the basis of common interests, characteristics, or occupations and have national as well as local organizations."[2] In a related vein, Chalmers Johnson has found the notion of "pre-emptive organization" useful in comparing Communist societies. He cites the practice of setting up official organizations for youth, women, occupational groupings, and so on, to serve the regime's mobilizational goals and also, he believes, to preclude the formation of autonomous groups with private loyalties.[3]

In the People's Republic of China mass organizations were set up to serve quite explicitly as intermediary structures, joining the political center with selected target groups in the Chinese population. Since Lenin's time mass organizations in the Soviet Union and other Communist societies have been referred to as "transmission belts," organizational links between the Communist party and the people. Party policies and orders from the center are transmitted downward via the mass organization to the particular constituency that is to be served, and, in theory at least, the masses also initiate communication upward to the center. The extent to which the transmission belts actually operate in the latter direction—from the masses to the Party—is problematic, especially, it would appear, in the Soviet case. Chinese adherence to a "mass line" technique of leadership, however, would seem to indicate a significant degree of two-way flow. Corresponding to the two-directional manner in which mass organizations may function as transmission belts (center to masses versus masses to center), it is suggested here, is the distinction between mass organizational goals that stress mobilization of members to carry out official Party policy versus goals that emphasize member welfare and interests. What is being assumed then, is that mobilization measures generally proceed from the top down, whereas welfare aims are normally initiated by the masses and hence operate from the bottom up.

The focus here is on three of China's principal mass organizations: The All-China Federation of Trade Unions (ACFTU); the All-China Youth Federation (ACYF);* and the Women's Federation of the People's Republic of China (WFPRC). These three organizations are comparable in size, with memberships in the millions (either direct or through affiliated suborganizations), and scope, or range of activities. Moreover, each has had a multiple-level formal structure, extending from national office to local-level units. Each of the three federations has, furthermore, ostensibly represented a social aggregate—women, workers, or youth—that tends in most social systems to rank low on the major dimensions of stratification: power, prestige, and property. The Chinese Communist revolutionary movement has made some notable, although admittedly variable, attempts, however, to impart a leading role in Chinese society to these aggregates. In research on the structure and functioning of the three mass organizations, the author questions the extent to which these attempts have been realized and examines the degree to which mass organizations have drawn their respective memberships into central societal processes, spotlighting the issue of mobilization versus welfare goals. Of special importance is whether the welfare ideals of mass organizations are sufficiently fostered to term these organizations "interest groups." David Truman has given a widely adopted definition of interest group: "any group that, on the basis of one or more shared attitudes, makes certain claims upon other groups in the society for the establishment, maintenance, or enhancement of forms of behavior that are implied by the shared attitudes."[4] For mass organizations to fit this definition, they must be genuine two-way transmission belts, not merely sending orders from the Party to the masses but also promoting mass interests. Evidence of interest-group behavior in the operation of mass organizations would also, of course, raise further doubts about the

---

*In the case of mass organizations serving youth, the more prominent and prestigious Communist Youth League (CYL) has been omitted, focusing instead on the inclusive All-China Youth Federation, with which the CYL is affiliated. Because of the CYL's unique role in preparing future CCP members and its consequent intimate ties to the Party, inclusion of the CYL with the women's and trade-union organizations presented serious problems of comparability.

validity of totalitarian or monolithic paradigms of the People's Republic of China (PRC), formerly so prevalent (and by no means yet dead), and would suggest alternatively that a relatively pluralistic, participatory model may more accurately reflect the structure of Chinese society.[5]

This examination of mass organizations in terms of welfare goals as indicative of interest-group functions uses a social structural approach to values. More specifically, a viewpoint familiar to demographers is adopted, whereby social structure is seen as a "crystallization of past processes."[6] With such a demographic perspective, a compositional view of a population provides a proximate description of social structure.[7] For each of the three federations under study, however, the constituent population has necessarily been limited to national-level elite members who can be properly identified and for whom a reasonable amount of information exists. Fortunately, it has been possible in each instance to identify all members (full and alternate) of three consecutive Executive or National Committees, newly elected in 1948/49, 1953, and 1957/58, thus assuring a complete sample of mass organization elites over a ten-year span. Inferences about the structure of a particular mass organization qua organization are to be made, therefore, on the basis of compositional information about its respective elite subpopulation, those individuals who have undergone differentiating processes of recruitment, retention, and exist from 1948 to 1958.

Compositional information on the elite populations of these three organizations is derived from social background data and from more abundant career information. It is especially from the latter type of data that it has been possible to construct three indexes of elite structure that, in turn, give a cogent summary of organizational structure: expertise, autonomy, and stability. As the next section of this chapter demonstrates, these indexes are employed to test hypotheses about the relationship between mass organization structure and mobilization/welfare values, and thus to reach relatively objective conclusions about Chinese mass organizations both as transmission belts and as interest groups.

MASS ORGANIZATION GOALS AND ELITE STRUCTURE: PREDICTING A CONFLICT OF VALUES

Examination of mass organizations from the standpoint of value conflict is limited here to the decade or so after liberation, a time that might well be called the heyday of such organizations. Although the relationship between mass organization goals and elites is viewed within this circumscribed temporal framework, some cautious extrapolation and interpretation of findings for more recent years would appear feasible. Standard biographical sources, cross-checked for reliability, were used to obtain data on mass organization elites: approximately 1,000 national-level Committee members of these three associations. Raw data on the experiences of these leaders were recorded, coded, and ultimately incorporated into three indexes of organizational structure in the following manner.

Expertise has two essential components in the context of Chinese bureaucracies. First, there is what is commonly referred to as the red-versus-expert distinction, the extent to which ideological or technical criteria are associated with elite bureaucratic status. One might also substitute here the terms reliability versus competence.* A second distinction, closely allied to the first component of expertise but analytically separable, is that made between specialist and generalist. How broad or narrow is the range of skills, experience, and so on, typically allied with elite organizational positions? For the red-versus-expert pole an index has been constructed using information about two characteristics of mass organization elites: intraorganizational functional specialization and extraorganizational functional specialization. In doing this the author has relied on the important Chinese notion of functional system, or *xi tong*, classifying positions held by the elite in addition to their Committee roles accordingly: political/legal; propaganda/education; rural work; industry/communications; finance/trade; United Front work; foreign affairs; women's work/youth work; military affairs; organization/personnel. Functional specialization is thus equated with supplementary women/youth work roles in the case of Women's or Youth Federation leaders (such as a position in the Propaganda Department of the respective federation, in a regional branch of the federation, or in relevant Party work). For Trade Union Federation members functional specialization is seen as further industry/communications experiences (such as Party secretary in a factory).

The generalist/specialist continuum makes a second subindex of expertise and is derived by combining two types of elite data: number of extraorganizational functional system affiliations and number of extraorganizational institutional affiliations. The Chinese concept of institution, which coincides with concrete organizational sectors and is transversed by the more abstract bureaucratic principle of functional system, is broken down in the following manner: state; Chinese Communist Party; military; worker/peasant; symbol manipulation; mass organization; economic; scientific/academic/intellectual; democratic parties. In either a functional or institutional sense, individuals with no more than one outside affiliation were defined as specialists; those with more than one affiliation, generalists. For a summary expertise index, the red/expert and generalist/specialist subindexes were combined.

Autonomy is defined here in terms of the degree of interlocking between a mass organization and other organizations, especially the Communist party. There is ample evidence that at all levels of contemporary Chinese society

---

*The Chinese themselves speak of a red-versus-expert distinction, yet earlier in this volume Tu Wei-ming convincingly raises some serious questions about the validity of a red-versus-expert dichotomy in either traditional times or the contemporary setting.

individuals have frequently occupied positions simultaneously in more than one organization. Elite data indicating range of extraorganizational affiliations for individuals is employed here as an inverse measure of organizational autonomy, high autonomy being indicated by a relatively low degree to which interlocking appointments are characteristic of the elite. Specifically, the index of organizational autonomy resulted from combining available elite data on two types of extraorganization experiences: proportion of members with no known CCP institutional affiliation and proportion of members with no known institutional affiliation in organizations other than the Party.

The third component of mass organization structure that is examined is stability, in which elite stability is seen as critical to overall organizational stability. Stability is therefore measured according to elite turnover: proportion of holdovers versus newcomers in successive Committees. Reflecting an assumption of more substantial organizational inputs from those in more responsible positions, double weights were assigned to members of "officer" rank (those with the status of honorary official, chairman, vice-chairman, secretary general, member of the Secretariat, or member of the Standing Committee or Presidium) as distinct from mere full or alternate members of the Executive or National Committees.

A crucial general question that is addressed concerns the impact of elite members upon organizational operations. It is assumed that elites can and do exercise some independent influence upon the functioning of their respective mass organizations despite the patently firm hand of Party control over internal matters. In this particular test of elite effects, the focus is upon the consequences of certain elite configurations for the value orientations of the three federations. Hypotheses are derived from expectations that, all else being equal, mass organization elites who are more specialized in terms of experiences within the same functional system and/or in terms of the range of coterminous affiliations would, by virtue of their greater expertise, have a greater investment in the mass organization and its mission and hence be more likely to promote member interests and welfare. Similarly, the more mass organization leaders are characterized by organizational autonomy—particularly, the fewer the positional ties to the Party—the freer they can be expected to be in supporting the claims of mass organization members. And, in like fashion, the higher the degree of mass organization stability (that is, the lower the rate of elite turnover), the more apt are incumbent elites—especially those in superior officer positions—to manifest strong feelings of identification with and commitment to the organization and its membership and, subsequently, to espouse welfare values. The obverse of these assumptions states that the less the elite expertise, autonomy, and stability, all else being equal, the more likely leaders are to fall in line with Party-inspired demands for enhancing mobilization values and for dampening undue expression of member interests. In short, it is hypothesized that the degree of mass organization expertise, autonomy, and stability, as manifested in elite structure, is directly related to organizational goals promoting member welfare and is inversely related to goals aimed at the mobilization of members for officially approved projects.

Mass organization documents and publications, particularly those published during the first decade or decade and a half of the new regime, are an abundant source of written material related to values. In this instance the author was especially interested in publications issued by the mass organizations, house organs as it were, written for their respective mass audiences. These mass organization publications are taken at face value in the sense that their messages are seen as conveying current organizational aims and policies from the national federation leadership to the membership at large. Content analysis was an obvious methodological choice for dealing with this considerable body of documentary data. For purposes of hypothesis testing, content analysis categories were limited to two: desired organizational ends that incorporate values emphasizing member welfare and interests and those emphasizing mobilization of members. In the procedures used to select units of analysis, the first step was to sample randomly among available journal issues—five issues per year for the period 1949 through 1960—and then to select one article from each issue, making a possible total of 60 articles for each organization over a 12-year span.* In each issue the article chosen for analysis was an editorial whenever one was published, the assumption being that the editorials would, in general, be the articles most reflective of organizational goals.

Once a sample of articles had been assembled for content analysis, a frequency count was made of total mobilization and welfare "mentions" per article—the number of times either of these goals was cited. For a mobilization regime such as the People's Republic of China, the public communications of mass organizations are likely to express mobilization values with greater absolute frequency than welfare values. Significant changes in welfare-oriented goals can thus be signaled by an increase or decrease in the relative frequency with which they are openly advocated. For each of the three federations an index of welfare goals was therefore constructed, which represents the proportion of welfare mentions out of total welfare and mobilizations mentions per year (W/M + W). The annual index figures for each organization were also weighted and summed to produce a welfare index for each of the three consecutive periods that correspond basically to the tenure of the three national-level Committees: 1949-1952; 1953-1957; 1958-1960.†

---

*It was, in fact, possible to obtain 60 journal articles for the Women's Federation and for the Youth Federation. For the Trade Union Federation some substitutions from other trade-union publications were made because of gaps in library holdings of its journal.

†In the author's larger study of mass organizations the following period designations are used: Period 1 (P1)—pre-1948; Period 2 (P2)—1948-52; Period 3 (P3)—1953-57; Period 4 (P4)—1958-62. This present analysis of values focuses more narrowly on 1949-60, omitting P1, the pre-1948 era; 1948, the first year of P2; and the post-1960 years of P4.

Analysis of the data for the three federations points up a striking degree of similarity by virtue of the indexes of elite structure, summarized in Table 11.1. (For a more comprehensive look at the elite data see Appendixes A through C.) In all three organizations, stability increased steadily over time, as might be expected for associations of such recent vintage, and the interorganization differences that exist are thus ones of degree, not direction. The fact that among the three federations the Youth Federation was lowest in stability in all periods is not surprising, for a relatively high elite turnover rate would be in keeping with an organization for youth that places upper-age restrictions on its members. By contrast, the Trade Union Federation eventually became the most stable of the mass organizations by Period 4. For autonomy, too, identical patterns characterize the three organizations, with the greatest proportion of autonomy found in Period 2 and the least in Period 3, followed by a slight upturn in Period 4. Moreover, all autonomy figures fall within a narrow range and vary little across organizations. With regard to expertise, however, the three organizations are found to diverge. Whereas the Women's Federation and the Trade Union Federation were in general correspondence, with expertise in those two organizations increasing from Period 2 to a high point in Period 3 and followed by a decrease in Period 4, the Youth Federation, on the other hand, experienced a steady decline in elite expertise from Period 2 to Period 4. Nevertheless, all three organizations were in agreement in one respect: the direction of change from Period 3 to Period 4, marked by a decrease in expertise.

Despite the remarkably high degree of consistency in elite structure for all mass organizations, the three elite structural variables analyzed do not apparently have the kind of predictive strength that was hypothesized. The reason for this incapacity of structural features to predict values is in the nature of welfare/mobilization goals expressed in publications of mass organizations. As Table 11.2 demonstrates, the W/M + W ratio evinces wide annual variations, which are obscured when period rates are calculated. Given the extent of intraperiod fluctuations in the ratios, welfare and mobilization mentions were then plotted individually in order to ascertain the degree to which ratios are dependent on W or on M. For all three organizations the resultant graphs similarly depict a substantial number of "outliers," or widely dispersed points, but since the correlations between the organizations in terms of their ratios are low, each organization will be discussed separately below.

For the Trade Union Federation the W/M + W ratio correlates quite strongly with W (.63) but weakly with M (.18). Both welfare and mobilization show sharp annual variations, with W having its highest peak in 1960, followed by 1951, 1953, and 1955. Mobilization is also highest in 1960, with lower peaks in 1950, 1953, and 1955. There are two years when W is absolutely greater than M: 1951 and 1958. Because the M figure for 1960 is an extreme outlier, however, the trade union data were subsequently analyzed both with and without that particular high year. When 1960 is included, M, summed, increases sharply overall from Period 2 to Period 3 to Period 4, and W, summed,

TABLE 11.1

Federation Elites: Autonomy, Expertise, and Stability Indexes, by Period

	All China Federation of Trade Unions			All-China Youth Federation			Women's Federation of the People's Republic of China		
	Autonomy	Expertise	Stability	Autonomy	Expertise	Stability	Autonomy	Expertise	Stability
Period 2 (1948–52)	86	48	24	89	49	6	88	34	25
Period 3 (1953–57)	80	54	42	83	40	29	80	46	32
Period 4 (1958–62)	83	49	79	86	38	36	85	40	46

Source: Compiled by the author.

TABLE 11.2

Federation Goals: Ratio of Welfare/Mobilization Plus Welfare Mentions, 1949–60 (W/M + W)

Year	All-China Federation of Trade Unions	All-China Youth Federation	Women's Federation of the People's Republic of China
Period 2 (1948–52)			
1949	38	33	41
1950	25	0	28
1951	94	18	40
1952	29	0	27
Rate = 46			
Period 3 (1953–57)			
1953	41	14	38
1954	29	11	57
1955	41	11	25
1956	0	40	38
1957	0	0	30
Rate = 35			
Period 4 (1958–62)			
1958	67	0	30
1959	8	25	50
1960	30	78	25
Rate = 29			

Source: Compiled by the author.

dips in Period 3. By contrast, omitting 1960, one sees, more accurately it seems, W declining steadily from Period 2 to 3 to 4, and M increasing in Period 3 but decreasing in Period 4.

Within the Youth Federation the W/M + W ratio correlates much more strongly with W than with M (.94 versus .21). Moreover, over the 12-year span surveyed, welfare mentions show much less annual variation than mobilization. There are sharp upswings of M in 1951 and 1955, whereas W has smaller peaks, occurring in 1951, 1956, and 1960. Only in 1960 are welfare mentions absolutely greater than mobilization.

In the Women's Federation the annual plot of the ratio shows for the 1949 to 1960 time span a slight downward trend. Correlations of the W/M + W ratio with W and M are .61 and .44, respectively. Even more than in the Youth Federation, W goals of the Women's Federation display very little annual fluctuation in comparison with M. For this mass organization the high points of mobilization occur in 1950, 1959, and 1960. Welfare mentions, which run somewhat higher in 1950, 1954, and 1959, are absolutely greater than mobilization in 1954, but only by a small margin.

Because of the irregular patterns in the expression of mobilization and welfare goals, the hypothesized links between social structure and values examined in this research on mass organizations remain uncorroborated. In order to make an independent evaluation of the value postures of mass organizations, the author reverted to historical evidence, which has often been the basis upon which China scholars have made their relatively subjective judgments about social structure in the People's Republic.

In Paul Harper's study of the ACFTU, for example, generalizations about union policies and practices emerge from a careful reading of extant documentary materials.[8] The prominent periods of "economism," according to Harper, were during the Li Li-san debates of 1950–51 and the 1957 battle over Party-union relations culminating in the purges of union leaders of 1957–58. By contrast, Harper found the interests of union members to have been less an issue in the intervening years 1952-57 and the mobilization of members for political and economic activities more accepted. Harper's conclusions with regard to mobilization and welfare values are in basic agreement not only with the author's qualitative analysis of historical materials but also with the quantitative measurement of these factors. The objective information collected on W/M values of the Trade Union Federation show, first of all, welfare exceeding mobilization in 1951 and again in 1958, when the union was accused of economism. Moreover, the advocacy in the union media of welfare values, while not absent, was less vocal in the 1953-57 period.

Townsend has conducted a qualitative study of published messages to Chinese youth over the period 1949-65.[9] Among the highlights of youth policy cited by Townsend were the focus in 1951 on national mobilization and sacrifice; a deemphasis in 1956 on youth work and more attention to individual interests and expression; and a revival in 1959 of youth work with a new stress on abstract ideological issues. Townsend concluded that through 1956 China's youth movement was not a particularly salient national issue and was granted a certain amount of autonomy from Party control, whereas by 1959 the movement had become a prominent political concern. Content analysis of youth publications is in fundamental agreement with Townsend's findings. Throughout most of Period 2 and 3 (1948-57) welfare was mentioned in a sporadic and essentially subdued fashion, in keeping with the low profile of the Chinese youth movement. An exception was 1951, when the high tide of mobilization seems to have been backed up by welfare concessions. The year 1956 was also idiosyncratic, as Townsend found too, with an abrupt and substantial increase in the proportion of welfare-oriented messages that is in keeping with the relaxed tenor of the Hundred Flowers Campaign. Interestingly, in the years thereafter, when Townsend saw the youth movement becoming a matter of national concern, one might have expected mobilization values to show an increase as welfare declined. Instead, welfare values remained quite steady. Two possible explanations for this unanticipated strength of welfare values are that overarching Party attempts to mobilize youth were tempered by the demands of a relatively specialized and entrenched mass organization elite, operating on behalf of the membership at large; and/or that the Party recognized the necessity of attending to the needs of youth in order to insure the success of mobilization programs involving youthful participation.

The author's historical treatment of the women's movement indicates that the 1948-52 period was one with a major emphasis on mobilization values that advocated women joining the labor force, and with a significant minor stress on the rights and general well-being of women. When the First National Congress of the Women's Federation met in April 1949, the basic theme was one of unity, of bringing together the disparate assortment of existing women's organizations to form a truly national federation. During the subsequent tenure of the First Executive Committee of the WFPRC (1949-53), a number of national policies that profoundly affected Chinese women were propounded and administered by the CCP, often with the assistance of the federation, the most outstanding measure being the Marriage Law of 1950. Although the law was ostensibly to benefit both sexes, intermittent criticism in the early 1950s suggested it had gone too far in protecting women's interests.

By 1953-57, the years of the First Five Year Plan, however, the balance seems to have shifted more to mobilization, particularly for economic tasks, with the dominant motif of the Second Congress of the WFPRC in 1953 being one of female participation in agricultural and industrial production. Realistically, the importance of domestic duties performed by women in addition to "real" labor was recognized and even glorified on occasion. The outset of the 1958-62 period, by contrast, marked a potentially new stage of the Chinese women's movement. Integral to the Great Leap Forward was the utilization of the productive power of women, to be freed by collectivization and concomitant socialization of housework. The heightened attention to mobilization goals of the economic variety in the late 1950s subsided within a few short years, how-ever, when it became necessary to retract from the high tide of the Great Leap and to repair the considerable harm done by overexuberant policies. Broadly speaking, from liberation into the 1960s the historical evidence shows vacillating but ample consideration given to the welfare of the female half of the popula-tion, and the Women's Federation publications analyzed are similarly, and per-haps even more consistently, favorable to women's interests. Furthermore, a pervasive official preference for mobilization values, rising to a crescendo in the late 1950s, which is communicated in historical documents, has a numerical counterpart in the journals sampled.

In conclusion, having compared quantitative findings on mobilization and welfare values with results obtained through more subjective historical methods, one is assured, in terms of reliability, by the agreement between the two modes of analysis. Despite this congruence, however, the picture of values that emerges is indeed a complex one. Among the principal observations to be made about values and value conflict in China's principal mass organizations is the fact that mobilization and welfare are not mutually exclusive end-states, nor do they fol-low a cyclical pattern. Departing from G. William Skinner and Edwin Winckler's model, welfare and mobilization goals—constructs quite analogous to remunera-tive versus normative and coercive means of compliance—tend to peak simul-taneously, especially so with the Trade Union Federation and to a lesser extent with the Youth and Women's Federations.[10] The co-occurrence of high points in the expression of these two values demonstrates that mobilization and welfare are not polar entities operating in a zero-sum manner.

A second notable observation is that several mobilization campaigns waged by the mass organizations have been accompanied by significant welfare conces-sions, granted either coterminously or by the following year. The implication here is one of trade-offs, of negotiations in actual political processes that are also reflected on a symbolic level. In short, it appears that when mobilization ends are sought, welfare goals are instrumental in attaining the desired end-state.

Thirdly, the year 1960 turns out to be an especially interesting vantage point from which to view the relationship between mobilization and welfare values. It emerges as a time of crisis, one characterized by a veritable state of value conflict. Great Leap Forward mobilization messages continued to bom-bard mass organization audiences in 1960, yet policy misjudgments created a situation that seemed to require reassurances about the validity of mass inter-ests. Here, then, is an example of tension between values at the societal level (or what Franz Schurmann has called ethos) being played out within an or-ganizational context as a conflict between ideologies.[11] Organizations are, by definition, goal-directed, and in the PRC they are to be oriented, above all, to national exigencies. However, in return for functioning as intermediary struc-tures and mobilizing selected mass groupings, mass organizations are also allotted substantial welfare incentives.

Fourth, one is struck by how precarious the mobilization/welfare balance has been in the three federations. An orthodox balance has normally been maintained, skewed in the long run well in favor of mobilization. Nevertheless, in keeping with the "mass line" as a tenet for bureaucratic behavior, a reasonable-- albeit secondary—degree of attention has also been paid by mass organizations to the interests and demands of the individuals and groups they serve.

Contrary to hypotheses, the mobilization/welfare goal content of mass organization publications was too variable to be readily predicted from prominent elite structural features. However, some speculative interpretations can be made of the impact of these particular social structural features on values. Within the context of Chinese organizations, although broad aims are generally formulated by the Party, these abstract goals apparently come to be translated by the leadership elements within an organization into concrete operative programs. Thus, insofar as bureaucratic elites in the PRC necessarily clarify value stances and then implement the resultant policies, room exists for initiative and for negotiation of organizational ends. Strong potentials for maneuverability and discretionary power appear to have been the case for the Trade Union, Women's, and Youth Federation elites. Especially within the Trade Union Federation, keeping limits on actual elite discretionary power seems to have posed a persistent problem. On a number of occasions the ACFTU was faulted for having gone too far in asserting its independence from Party control, and its alleged "economism," syndicalism," and so on were openly criticized. By contrast, in the WFPRC the patent commitment to women's welfare was less problematic. What is, to be sure, less clear is how much of this commitment is attributable to the success of WFPRC leaders in exerting influence on behalf of their members, and/or to Party approval of the federation engaging in interest-group behavior.

Given the nature of changes in mass organization leadership in the course of the 1950s, one should not be surprised to find tensions mounting, even to the point where all three federations were ultimately dispensed with, early in the Cultural Revolution. For the potential contradiction between mobilization and welfare values to have evolved into an actual value conflict of such magnitude is not an unreasonable prediction, given the degree of autonomy and expertise associated with elites that were becoming more and more entrenched. With such leadership in command, the mass organizations could perform interest-group functions and operate as genuine transmission belts, with considerable (and unequal) two-way flow between the center and the masses. The extent to which interest-group claims of the three federations were honored would, therefore, seem to call for a modification of Johnson's conceptualizing mass organizations as preemptive organizations and, more broadly, of totalitarian paradigms of the Chinese political system that overlook participatory elements. Methodologically, in the case of these three bureaucracies, elite careers have served as warning signals, indicating when value conflicts might erupt. Lest one overemphasize the uniqueness of mass organizations, however, one should also be reminded that the conflict between mobilization and welfare values documented here is but part of a societywide struggle between two lines that has existed for years in the People's Republic of China and has certainly yet to be resolved.

NOTES

1. Mass campaigns have been judiciously analyzed by Charles P. Cell in his *Revolution at Work: Mobilization Campaigns in China* (New York: Academic Press, 1977).

2. James R. Townsend, *Political Participation in Communist China* (Berkeley and Los Angeles: University of California Press, 1968), pp. 150–51.

3. Chalmers Johnson, "Comparing Communist Nations," in *Change in Communist Systems*, ed. Chalmers Johnson (Stanford: Stanford University Press, 1970), p. 19.

4. David B. Truman, *The Governmental Process: Political Interests and Public Opinion* (New York: Knopf, 1951), p. 33.

5. A not untypical example of writings that categorize the PRC as a totalitarian state is the oversimplified and emotionally charged account by Peter L. Berger, *Pyramids of Sacrifice: Political Ethics and Social Change* (New York: Doubleday, 1976).

6. Norman B. Ryder, "Notes toward a Model of Societal Transformation." Unpublished manuscript, 1961, p. 5. Ryder is now with the Sociology Department, Princeton University.

7. Leo F. Schnore, "Social Mobility in Demographic Perspective," *American Sociological Review* 26 (June, 1961): 411.

8. Paul Frederick Harper, "Political Roles of Trade Unions in Communist China." Ph.D. dissertation, Cornell University, 1969.

9. James R. Townsend, "Revolutionizing Chinese Youth: A Study of *Chung-kuo Ch'ing-nien*," in *Chinese Communist Politics in Action*, ed. A. Doak Barnett (Seattle: University of Washington Press, 1969).

10. G. William Skinner and Edwin A. Winckler, "Compliance Succession in Rural Communist China: A Cyclical Theory," in *A Sociological Reader on Complex Organizations*, ed. Amitai Etzioni (New York: Holt, Rinehart and Winston, 1969).

11. Franz Schurmann, *Ideology and Organization in Communist China*, 2nd ed. (Berkeley and Los Angeles: University of California Press, 1968), p. 6.

APPENDIX TABLE 11.A.1.

All-China Federation of Trade Union Elites: Autonomy, Expertise, and Stability Indexes, by Period

Elite Index	Period 1 Pre–1948	Period 2 1948–52	Period 3 1953–57	Period 4 1958–62
Autonomy				
CCP affiliation: proportion without known affiliation	95	93	88	91
Non-CCP affiliation: proportion without known affiliation	94	79	71	75
Mean autonomy index	94	86	80	83
Expertise				
Red/expert				
Intraorganization experience, functional system, proportion specialized	89	64	71	80
Extraorganization experience, functional system, proportion specialized	15	27	26	20
Generalist/specialist				
Extraorganization experience, functional system, proportion with one or no affiliation	63	47	60	(56)
Extraorganization experience, institution, proportion with one or no affiliation	74	55	61	(60)
Mean expertise index	59	48	54	(49)
Stability				
Proportion held-over from previous Committee, double weight to officers	– [a]	(24) [b]	42	79
Stability index		(24)	42	79

[a] P1 represents the pre-1948 period; there are no figures on holdovers from an earlier time.

[b] Estimate based on proportion known to have ACFTU or other relevant labor work experience in P1, prior to liberation.

Note: Parentheses indicate estimate, necessitated by missing data.

Source: Compiled by the author.

APPENDIX TABLE 11.A.2.

All-China Youth Federation Elites: Autonomy, Expertise, and Stability Indexes, by Period

Elite Index	Period 1 Pre-1948	Period 2 1948–52	Period 3 1953–57	Period 4 1958–62
Autonomy				
CCP affiliation: proportion without known affiliation	97	98	96	98
Non-CCP affiliation: proportion without known affiliation	90	80	70	73
Mean autonomy index	94	89	83	86
Expertise				
Red/expert				
Intraorganization experience, functional system, proportion specialized	100	100	24	40
Extraorganization experience, functional system, proportion specialized	00	21	28	18
Generalist/specialist				
Extraorganization experience, functional system, proportion with one or no affiliation	89	44	44	(52)
Extraorganization experience, institution, proportion with one or no affiliation	89	36	50	(52)
Mean expertise index	61	49	40	(38)
Stability				
Proportion held-over from previous Committee, double weight to officers	—[a]	(06)[b]	29	36
Stability index		(06)	29	36

[a] P1 represents the pre-1948 period; there are no figures on holdovers from an earlier time.

[b] Estimate based on proportion known to have relevant youth-work experience in P1, prior to liberation.

Note: Parentheses indicate estimate. necessitated by missing data.

Source: Compiled by the author.

APPENDIX TABLE 11.A.3.

Women's Federation of the People's Republic of China Elites: Autonomy, Expertise, and Stability Indexes, by Period

Elite Index	Period 1 Pre-1948	Period 2 1948–52	Period 3 1953–57	Period 4 1958–62
Autonomy				
CCP affiliation: proportion without known affiliation	97	95	96	96
Non-CCP affiliation: proportion without known affiliation	92	81	64	74
Mean autonomy index	95	88	80	85
Expertise				
Red/expert				
Intraorganization experience, functional system, proportion specialized	100	39	71	83
Extraorganization experience, functional system, proportion specialized	05	07	07	01
Generalist/specialist				
Extraorganization experience, functional system, proportion with one or no affiliation	65	41	58	(55)
Extraorganization experience, institution, proportion with one or no affiliation	70	50	67	(62)
Mean expertise index	57	34	46	(40)
Stability				
Proportion held-over from previous Committee, double weight to officers	—[a]	(25)[b]	32	46
Stability index		(25)	32	46

[a] P1 represents the pre-1948 period; there are no figures on holdovers from an earlier time.

[b] Estimate based on proportion known to have relevant woman-work experience in P1, prior to liberation.

Note: Parentheses indicate estimate, necessitated by missing data.

Source: Compiled by the author.

12

VALUES, CHANGE, AND CHINESE HEALTH-CARE POLICIES

AnElissa Lucas

There is an international value-change movement in process within the health-care policy field. The issue of evaluative concern is equity. Whether critically focused upon inequitable distribution of health-care services between urban and rural sectors in developing nations or upon the failure of developed nations to serve more equably both urban poor and suburban elites, the issue of evaluative concern—equity in health-care services—remains the same. Given this concern, it should not be surprising that one of the current symbols of change or one of the national models for more equable health reform policies is the People's Republic of China, the nation that has most recently and vociferously issued value injunctions to its medical personnel to serve all the people, whether urban political elite, industrial laborer, or rural peasant.[1]

The type of change under discussion here is change in the values, attitudes, and behavior of Chinese medical personnel and the society they serve, not concrete changes in the objective realities of health standards in China, such as declining infant mortality or national morbidity rates. In terms of these latter types of statistical measurements, there is no question that improvements in Chinese health and health care have indeed occurred over the last half century. However, just as gross national product statistics represent national averages and are not descriptive of income distribution patterns within any nation, so national health statistics fail to describe inequities in the distribution and quality of health and health-care services between different regions or sectors within nations. While the leaders of the People's Republic of China (PRC) have rightfully exhibited national pride in publicizing progressive changes in China's national health statistics, there has also been concern on the part of Chinese policy elites with inequities between the urban and rural sectors of their population. This concern over inequable distribution of health-care services led to a number of changes in Chinese health-care policies after 1965. These policy changes emphasized not merely the physical redistribution of medical manpower and material, but also the need for changes in the values, attitudes, and behavior of Chinese medical personnel toward rural patients. It is the value goals and injunctions stated in these Chinese health-care policy changes, and the question of how and to what extent these evaluative policy changes may have effected value change among Chinese medical personnel, that are the focus of analysis here.

Answering this question about the interrelationships between national values, policy changes, and individual value change requires, however, a much broader analytic perspective than merely reconstructing a chronology of reported changes in Chinese national health-care policies and identifying the evaluative content of such policies. If a study of value change within the Chinese health-care system is to be useful as a partial indicator of value change processes within Chinese society and of the nature of value change generally irrespective of cultural values, several conceptual problems must be confronted.

First, it is necessary to understand the limitations inherent in existing value-change theory. One of the as yet unresolved problems in the theoretical literature on the nature of value change is the difficulty of verifying with any certainty whether expressed values and attitudes and/or observed behavior represent actual "internalized" or personally accepted value change or merely the pretense of change. As will become apparent, this limitation of certainty created problems both for Western health-care reformers interested in reports of change within the Chinese health-care system and for Chinese policy elites attempting to assure compliance with health-care policy changes.

The current focus on health care in the PRC as a symbolic international model for more equable health-care reform has also created several additional problems related to understanding value change in the Chinese health-care system and the society it serves. The equity value change movement in process within the health-care policy field is an international movement that has been affecting changes over the last decade in the health-care policies of a number of diverse developing and developed nations, not only the PRC.[2] Yet published perceptions about change in Chinese health care currently available in the West have to date been restricted both geographically and chronologically to the PRC alone, with little or no reference to similar equity concerns and health-care policy changes occurring simultaneously within other nations. In the search for present and future policy solutions to current universal problems and concerns about distributing health-care services more equably, national and international health-care reformers not only have failed to maintain a comparative perspective, but have in addition suffered from historical amnesia and forgotten lessons which should have been remembered from past international health-care reform movements. It was only a half century ago, in the late 1920s and early 1930s, that another nation, the Soviet Union, was being lauded as the model for more equable "sociomedical" services in a similar concern on the part of the international health reform movement about rural health-care inequities following the Depression. However, it is now generally accepted that the Soviet Union has yet to implement many of its 1930s redistributive rural health policy goals and has consistently encountered resistance from Soviet medical personnel unwilling to accept the personal sacrifices involved in "serving the people" in the rural sector. As in the 1930s, current health-care reformers have forgotten the need, especially when reporting on Marxist-Leninist systems, to distinguish national policy goals and injunctions to implement approved policy goals from evaluative reports of actually implemented policy.

As will become apparent, these problems of theoretical uncertainty, non-comparative perspective, historical amnesia, and policy stage misperception have confused rather than clarified the understanding of values, change, and Chinese health-care policies.

VALUE CHANGE IN THEORY

In order to understand analytically the interrelationship between value change and Chinese health-care policies, it is useful to define the current concern about equity as an evaluative policy goal, conceptually separate from the behavioral changes of Chinese medical personnel that reportedly followed policy-implementing injunctions to put equity into practice by serving all the people. The distinction drawn here relies upon the work of Milton Rokeach, one of the leading theorists in the field of value definition and value change.[3]

In brief, Rokeach argues that behavior and behavioral change are a function of the interaction between an "attitude-toward-object" (in this study, the attitude of an urban physician toward a rural patient) and an "attitude-toward-situation" (in this study the organizational situation for the delivery of health-care services by the physician to rural patients).[4] An attitude, according to Rokeach, is a collection of beliefs concerned with both "matters of fact and matters of evaluation" cognitively organized so as to predispose a person to behave in a preferential manner to specific objects and/or situations. While an attitude represents several beliefs, the evaluative component of an attitude is a single belief—a value—which Rokeach sees as the basic imperative to all action or behavior. Because of this general role given to values, it is important to understand Rokeach's conceptualizations about two types of values—instrumental values and terminal values. An instrumental value is an evaluative belief that a particular "mode of conduct . . . is personally and socially preferable in all situations with respect to all objects." A terminal value is an evaluative belief that a particular "end-state of existence . . . is personally and socially worth striving for." According to Rokeach, "once a value is internalized, it becomes, consciously or unconsciously, a standard or criterion for guiding action . . . and for comparing self with others."[5]

The most crucial part of the Rokeachean theory for this study—the question of how values and hence behavior or action change—relies upon the above definitional relationships among behavior, attitudes, beliefs, and values, but adds an important theoretical assumption that human beings will generally prefer to change or adapt when confronted with conflict or inconsistency. Hence, according to Rokeach, an individual will undergo value change or "cognitive reorganization" and "internalize" new or modified values when "cognitive dissonance" or "a felt state of inconsistency" is experienced "between two values, or between a value and an attitude or between one's values and a reference group's values."[6] Rokeach argues that such cognitive dissonance is most likely to occur when two terminal values are perceived as being in conflict because of the central position terminal values are thought to hold in any value-attitude-behavior system.[7]

There are difficulties, however, inherent in these Rokeachean propositions. One of the as yet unresolved limitations in the value-change research field is the dependency upon outwardly observable behavior and/or a subject's explicit statements of attitudes. Neither source of data enables scientifically controlled cross-checking on conscious withholding or distortion of unarticulated attitudes or repressed behavior. While Rokeach acknowledges that changes in expressed opinion or behavior may be observed as acts of public conformity or compliance, when an individual is subject to reward or punishment and conditions of surveillance without actual change having occurred in the individual's personal underlying values or attitudes,[8] such circumstances are treated by Rokeach as uncommon and not central to his theory of value change. As will become apparent, however, these Rokeachean propositions about value change are even more difficult to identify and verify in the Chinese case than in controlled clinical experiments.

Before turning to the specifics of the Chinese case, clarification is required of the linkages being drawn here between Rokeach's definitional vocabulary and theoretical concepts about value change and the vocabulary and concepts of public policy. The nature of Rokeach's terminal and instrumental values can perhaps be most clearly understood by thinking of the impact of values upon attitudes and behavior as a process of decreasing generalized ambiguity or increasing specificity of acceptable individual behavior. Equality or equity is defined in the Rokeachean rubric as a universal end-state worth striving for, or a terminal value. Hence, the universal goal or terminal value of equality between nations and between citizens within nation-states has become an international policy goal that has been further specified into what might be termed functionally specific terminal value concerns, or specific evaluative policy goals. Because observed patterns of inequity between the development of urban industrializing and rural agricultural sectors have been seen as frustrating achievement of the goal of equality in developing nations, the general terminal value has been subdivided into specific functional problems or public policy issues, such as the goal of correcting inequities in the distribution of health-care services. The same process of increasing specificity applies also to instrumental values. For example, the instrumental values or policy implementing injunctions to practice "self-sacrifice" and "self-reliance," to "learn from the masses" and "serve the people" that have appeared repeatedly in the media of the PRC. These evaluative standards for guiding the attitudes and actions of Chinese citizens have been generally espoused as modes of conduct that should be individually and collectively practiced in all situations toward all members of the society, whether one's functional specialty is teaching, engineering, or health care and whether one works in the countryside or the city.

If an individual is to avoid cognitive dissonance, as Rokeach argues, the more broadly such instrumental values are accepted within a society as applicable to different, functionally specific, public policy issues, the more likely a member of that society is personally to put into practice the espoused instrumental values in their functionally specific situations. There is, then, a mutually reinforcing mechanism between generalized terminal and instrumental values and the application of these general values to individual behavior in response to specific problems or situations. Theoretically, a Chinese physician transferred from a well-equipped urban research hospital to a one-room rural health clinic without indoor plumbing and modern medical equipment *might* be more likely to undergo value change and internalize the espoused generalized terminal and instrumental values to pursue equity by practicing "self-sacrifice," "self-reliance," and "serving the people," *if* similarly transferred teachers, accountants, and sanitary engineers appeared from their attitudes and behavior toward rural peasants to be practicing such modes of conduct or instrumental values in the belief that the end-state of urban-rural equity is worth striving for as a terminal value. However, this hypothetical Chinese physician could also according to Rokeachean theoretical allowances merely appear to comply without personally undergoing actual value change. As will become apparent, the theoretical difficulty of ascertaining actual value change from apparent compliance became in Chinese practice an issue of bitter political debate.

THEORY AND REPORTED CHINESE PRACTICE

Official reports from the PRC about change within the Chinese health-care system have differed significantly since the mid-1960s. In the decade prior to Mao Zedong's death in 1976, progress in Chinese health care was attributed to changes achieved because of the Cultural Revolution in 1967. More recent 1977–78 reports following the purge of the Cultural Revolution "Gang of Four" leadership, however, claim that the Cultural Revolution sabotaged many of the progressive changes made in the Chinese health-care system between 1949 and 1967.[9] Despite these changing reports, enough details have been provided to compare Rokeachean theory about value change with Chinese reports of policy and value change.

For example, Rokeach's concept that an individual is most likely cognitively to reorganize value priorities when a felt sense of inconsistency or dissonance between two terminal values is experienced. As already noted, equality or equity is defined in the Rokeachean rubric as a universal end-state or terminal value. Striving for "self-fulfillment," "comfort," and/or "prestige" are also among the 18 terminal values identified by Rokeach.[10] During the criticisms in the mid-1960s of Chinese urban medical personnel for failing to serve the rural masses, such terminal-value pursuits were repeatedly contrasted in a manner that suggests a deliberate political attempt to create value dissonance and value-behavior change among individual Chinese medical personnel. Politically sanctioned, model "revolutionary" health workers were depicted in the Chinese media as those who pursued the collective value goal of equity and overcame individualistic predilections for cosmopolitan comfort or prestigious research by cheerfully treating and teaching the peasants, despite the cultural deprivations and physical hardships they suffered in the countryside. Such positive or politically sanctioned models for medical personnel behavior were repeatedly contrasted and reinforced by examples of undesirable behavior or negative models. The urban medical specialists who cared more for their expensively equipped research institutes and the prestige of erudite publication than for the suffering of the rural peasants were vilified as "lordly" and "bourgeois." The contrast between such collective equity and individualistically oriented terminal values was further reinforced by being closely linked with instrumental value injunctions to "serve the people" by practicing "self-sacrifice" and "self-reliance."

Discussion of problems in urban and rural health services appeared in the Chinese media and health policy organs prior to the mid-1960s. In June 1965, however, Mao Zedong's criticisms of the Public Health Ministry intensified the value emphasis on collective equity by contrasting urban privileges with rural problems and by calling for the implementation of redistributive health-care policies.

> Tell the Ministry of Health that its work caters only to 15 percent of the national population, and that, moreover, the greater part of this 15 percent are lords. The broad masses of peasants are not provided with medical care; they are denied doctors and medical supplies. The Ministry of Health is not one belonging to the people; it is . . . the urban lords' ministry of health.
>
> Medical education has to be reformed. . . . The prevailing set of methods of diagnosis and treatment in hospitals are basically unsuited to the training of rural doctors; they are designed for the cities. . . . Huge amounts of manpower and material resources are devoted to the study of difficult and uncommon diseases, while little or no attention is given to the prevention and treatment of common diseases, . . . It is not that the advanced subjects should be ignored but that lesser amounts of manpower and material resources should be devoted to them. Large amounts of manpower and material resources should be devoted to the . . . masses.
>
> Urban hospitals should retain some doctors who have graduated for one or two years and who are not very experienced. All the others should go to the countryside. . . . The center of gravity of medical and health work should be in the countryside.[11]

In the next two years, between Mao Zedong's June 1965 redistributive health directive and the June 1967 Cultural Revolution attack on the Ministry of Health, reports of health work in the Chinese media and the *Chinese Medical Journal* clearly contrasted undesirable elitist attitudes and behavior with the positively sanctioned instrumental and terminal values of learning self-sacrifice and self-reliance from the peasants in order to serve the rural masses more equably.

> Public health authorities and medical institutions are taking radical measures to make medical and public health work face the country-side. . . . City hospitals are carrying out reforms and medical colleges have begun to modify curriculums in line with the principle of study for practical use . . . [and are] sending personnel and equipment to set up rural and mobile medical bases and units.[12]
>
> Large numbers of medical workers have changed their stand-point and class consciousness after study of Mao's works and participation in country medical teams. . . . However, adverse influences are still fairly strong [among] workers who believe that "one who has technical skill has all."[13]
>
> Medical departments at all levels and revolutionary medical workers must resolutely implement Mao's instruction of "practicing economy in making revolution," humbly learn from former poor and lower-middle peasants, and solve difficulties of shortage of equipment and appliances by adopting means appropriate to local conditions and by using materials obtained locally. Under no circumstances should they "seek after a big scale and demand Western supplies" and waste public money.[14]

Several aspects of these 1965-67 reports on Mao's redistributive health directives and the later post-1967 Cultural Revolution criticisms of elite Chinese urban medical specialists can be related to additional Rokeachean theoretical concepts about value change. Rokeach argues that although cognitive reorganization of value priorities is most likely to occur when inconsistency or dissonance is experienced between two terminal values, value change could also result from a felt sense of inconsistency between an individual's own values and some reference group's values. Consider, for example, the coverage given in the *Chinese Medical Journal* to a special urban medical team organized in Peking and sent to work in three Hunan rural communes in 1965. Both the composition of and the coverage given to this special medical team would seem to epitomize an ideal reference group for medical professionals. Led by the president of the national Chinese Academy of Medical Sciences (CAMS) who reportedly authored the *Journal*'s account of "Our Medical Team in the Countryside," the team consisted of 30 nationally, and in many cases internationally, known medical specialists from the CAMS and from China's leading research-oriented medical college, the Chinese Medical University in Peking and its affiliated training hospital, the Peking Union Hospital. According to the *Journal* account, this was the first trip into the countryside for almost all the team's medical specialists. After reportedly living in the homes of former poor peasants for more than four months and learning how to treat economically and communicate effectively with the rural population, the team members were prominently displayed as happily working among the masses in four pages of accompanying *Journal* photographs.[15]

Considering the extent of coverage given between 1965 and 1967 to Mao's redistributive rural health-care policies and the apparent terminal and/or reference group dissonance inducements for value change noted in that coverage, value-behavior change should have occurred within the Chinese health-care system according to Rokeachean theory. It would appear, however, from Cultural Revolution criticisms of the Ministry of Health in June 1967 that not all Chinese medical personnel perceived their national leader, official Party organs, or leading professionals to be value-change-inducing reference groups.

Although the Ministry of Health was not the only central ministry to come under attack during the Cultural Revolution, it was one of the 9 out of 49 central ministries existing in the mid-1960s to have more than half of its personnel criticized and removed from policy positions.[16] Accused of conspiring with Lui Shaoqi and others to sabotage rural health organizations by dividing the central Party "line" into "two lines," the minister of health, Qian Xinzhong (Ch'ien Hsin-chung), and all six vice-ministers were personally named as "counter-revolutionary revisionists . . . taking the capitalist road" and were "removed from office" by the spring of 1967. The choice of language in the Cultural Revolution Red Guard accusations against the Ministry of Health underlines the theoretical problems already noted in verifying internalization of value change in Chinese practice.

For over ten years . . . Lui Shaoqi, Qian Xinzhong and others were *ostensibly submissive, but inwardly adamant and defiant* toward the Chairman's criticism and . . . call to push development of health services in rural villages. . . .

[They were] *secretly recalcitrant* . . . in executing their assignment of preventing and exterminating the five body parasites . . . and other infectious diseases . . . .

The "lordly" Ministry *for sake of show* detailed some medical teams to villages. First, they made a show of some experts and professors in the villages, to create news and publicity *for fooling the Party Center*. Then, they let the doctors be substituted by nurses, laboratory workers, technicians and even administrative personnel . . . retaining the majority of experienced personnel in the cities.[17]

In the Ministry of Health a handful of Party persons in authority taking the capitalist road . . . *only feigned compliance . . . deceived the masses . . . and made superficial gestures* of improvement in vain attempt to gain some political capital so as to achieve

> their *object of opposing the Party Center, deceiving Mao, and protecting the Ministry of Health.*[18] (Emphasis added)

The accusation that the Ministry of Health was opposing the Party Center and protecting the ministry clearly involves other complex issues that cannot be covered in detail here, but relate to the question of changing values, attitudes, and behavior of Chinese medical personnel. Redistributive policies tend to generate conflicts of interest and debate within any nation. In a developing nation struggling to accumulate trained manpower, materiel resources, and surplus capital, such as the PRC, attempts to implement redistributive policies will often involve substantial trade-offs or policy choices as to who gets what and when. According to Marxist-Leninist theory, such difficult policy choices are said to be correctly resolved through the deliberative processes of "democratic centralism" under Party leadership and unanimously articulated to administrators and the people through the Party's "central line." Contrary to theory, however, historical practice in a variety of Communist nations suggests that conflicts of interest and competition for scarce resources often continue between particular local and functional interest groups after policy formulation or the direction of the Party's "central line" has been officially articulated.

One analyst who has studied changes in post-1949 Chinese health care from the perspective of Western bureaucratic organization theory has suggested that the similar educational backgrounds and functional administrative responsibilities of technical experts in the Ministry of Health tended to separate the medical bureaucrats from political decision makers, such as Mao Zedong who advocated mass political mobilization over technical leadership.[19] Bureaucratic organization theory emphasizes the impact of technical education, functional division of expertise, and organizational purposes or responsibilities upon individual and group behavior. Value change theory in contrast emphasizes the impact of shared experiences and values upon the formation of reference group identity and individual value internalization and reinforcement.[20] Both theoretical approaches are useful in understanding the Cultural Revolution attack on the Ministry of Health and the changes in Chinese health-care policies that reportedly followed the Cultural Revolution.

By labeling the technical medical specialists in the Ministry of Health as "counter-revolutionary revisionists" who divided the Party's "central line" into "two lines" and by removing this group from leadership positions in a nationally publicized campaign lauding "red" over "expert" policies and behavior, the Cultural Revolution radicals appeared to achieve several objectives. Any reference-group identification among Chinese medical personnel with the technical policies and professional values of former Ministry experts should have theoretically been publicly, if not personally, discouraged. Discrediting the "lordly" and "bourgeois" attitudes of ministry experts provided nationally known negative models which could be contrasted with the politically sanctioned "Red revolutionary" health workers who were to "serve the people." This discrediting was both symbolically and selectively focused on a handful of persons in authority in order to contrast sanctioned from unsanctioned policies and in order to encourage value-behavior change on the part of the majority of urban medical personnel who were assumed to be potentially "Red experts" if provided with the correct political leadership. Selective discrediting of medical policy experts is evident from the following figures. Over three-quarters of the medical experts personally named and criticized in the Chinese media during the Cultural Revolution held administrative policy positions in the central ministry or in provincial- or municipal-level health departments. In contrast, urban-based medical specialists holding elected positions in the Chinese Medical Association were not personally criticized, except for four who simultaneously held policy positions.[21] By removing the "handful of persons in authority" in the Ministry of Health who were "ostensibly submissive, but inwardly adamant and defiant" about developing health services in rural villages and who purportedly "only feigned compliance . . . and made superficial gestures," the Cultural Revolution appeared to legitimate both policy change and the changed value-behavior means thought necessary to implement mass political mobilization policies within the Chinese health-care system.

With the passing of the high tide of Cultural Revolution criticisms by the early 1970s, Chinese reports on health work emphasized the rapid changes and "new-born Socialist things" that had reportedly been developed in Chinese rural health care since the post-Cultural Revolution implementation of Mao's revolutionary thought and mass line health policies. A July 1970 report on health work in Yan-qing (Yen-ch'ing) *hsien*, a suburban county within the municipality of Peking, is representative.

> The Yen-Ch'ing county revolutionary committee has come to understand that there must be a backbone force in medical work . . . loyal to Mao and both red and expert so that the mass movement for the cooperative medical service can be sustained and take deep root. This is the central question determining whether poor and lower-middle peasants can hold power over medical services in rural areas, [and whether] the new-born cooperative medical system can be consolidated and . . . developed along Mao's direction. . . .
>
> Every commune [within the country] has its own clinic, every production brigade a medical station, and every production team part-time medical assistants. . . . Some communes and brigades have established indigenous [medicinal herb] pharmacies . . . [which] has helped cut the cost of the cooperative medical service. . . .[22]

CHANGING INTERNATIONAL PERCEPTIONS

Surveying such Chinese media reports on health work in 1970, the president of one of America's larger medical philanthropic foundations concluded that "China is in the midst of radical reforms in both medical services and medical education . . . [with the] emphasis on improvement of medical care in rural areas and training of a new type of medical assistant—the 'barefoot doctor.'"[23] Following the first post-World War II official exchanges of medical delegations between the PRC and the United States in 1971–72, interest in Chinese health work increased and published perceptions in the West began to describe changes in the Chinese health-care system in much the same terms as the Cultural Revolution period Chinese media. Articles appeared in a number of leading American and international scientific and medical publications,[24] followed by a rapid increase after 1972 in the number of English language books in print on Chinese medicine and health-care policies.[25]

An American physician and a psychiatric social worker, following their 1971–72 visit to the PRC, offer one of the more comprehensive and accurate examples of how Western published perceptions about change in Chinese health care reflected the then current "line" in Chinese health-care policies.[26] In brief, changes in the Chinese health-care system were described as a great effort to redistribute current resources according to Cultural Revolution "principles." Each person, family, village, and health unit was to be transformed and strengthened by implementing self-sufficiency programs to collect and process local efficacious herbs, learn traditional cures for treating local diseases, and train local health workers, with the assistance of transferred urban medical specialists. The powers inherent in the people, both individually and collectively, were to be organized through health education, community volunteer work, and mass mobilization to fulfill the ideological goal of providing opportunities for each person to "serve the public first, self second."[27] By combining redistributive policies with injunctions to "serve the people," China has been perceived as having apparently

> had considerable success in approaching the urban-rural distribution problem, a problem that remains unsolved, not only in poor countries and countries such as the United States, but even in the Soviet Union, which theoretically has the power to assign its vast number of doctors to areas where they are needed. . . . This [Chinese] technique of transferring manpower rather than money from urban to rural areas avoids . . . some of the difficulties rural areas would have in recruiting doctors, even if they had the money to do so. . . . [28]

As has already been noted, however, the "central line" in Chinese health care has recently changed. Since the death of Mao Zedong in September 1976 and the purge of the Cultural Revolution "Gang of Four" leadership in October 1976, reports from China have criticized the Gang of Four for "concocting poisonous films and articles" during the Cultural Revolution which "painted a black picture" of progress made in Chinese health work from 1949 to 1967. Contrary to Cultural Revolution reports that radical steps forward were made in Chinese health care after 1967 because of Cultural Revolution criticisms and changes, the current post-Gang of Four "line" attributes existing problems in medicine, public health, and birth control work to interference and sabotage by the Gang of Four and their "sinister henchmen" who "slanderously claimed doctors were bourgeois and nurses revisionists." Not only did the Gang of Four, according to current reports, seriously damage China's urban hospitals by their "counter-revolutionary 'two assessments'" policies, but they also opposed rural health work by trying to disrupt the "technical training" of barefoot doctors in order to "strangle this new-born Socialist thing in its cradle."[29]

Will international perceptions of change within the Chinese health-care system now change to take this new current health-care policy "line" into account? Questions were raised at the beginning of this inquiry as to how changing international evaluative concerns have historically affected international perceptions of change within symbolically selected model nations. In order to understand the current international concern with health-care inequities, it is useful to recall the more generalized concerns and criticisms about post-World War II economic development theories and policies, which began to be articulated in the late 1960s. As more and more developing nations began to experience increasing gaps in economic development between themselves and more advanced nations and, similarly, increasing inequities between their own industrializing urban and rural agricultural sectors, impatience with "trickle-down" theories of development and disillusionment with the inappropriateness of Western modernization models increased. This disillusionment generated a number of studies by Western social scientists that challenged the previously accepted paradigm that traditional societies were static and resistant to change, while modernization was the sole historical basis for change.[30] One analyst of this period of disillusionment and its so-called "revisionist" social science literature has suggested that although these critiques of the late 1960s were a corrective reaction to the impatient optimism of modernization theory in the 1950s and early 1960s, there was also inherent in these critiques a "traditional, romantic opposition" to modernization as a process that "sacrifices human, personal and spiritual values to achieve mass production and mass society."[31]

One of the consequences of this general disillusionment with the human costs of modernization has been the search for new models or policies for providing more humane and equable health care. The more generalized concerns and criticisms of post-World War II economic development began in the late 1960s with a focus on problems within developing nations and expanded over the next decade to doubts about the future possible directions of postindustrial societies and international patterns of development. Similarly, the literature in the health-care policy field began in the late 1960s by positing proposals for more humane and equable health care in developing nations, and expanded in the last decade to question the "scientific medicine" policies held up as an international model after World War II by the more advanced industrialized states.[32] The substance of this current critique against the post-World War II emphasis on solving mankind's health problems through the DDT- and antibiotic-type miracles of scientific medical research has been that the "scientific medicine" model is technologically inappropriate to developing nations and insensitive to the need for human services in both developing and developed nations. In the process of rationalizing this critique, however, current health-care reformers have suffered from historical amnesia and forgotten that their current espousal of "serve the people" health-care-reform policies is not new but rather very similar in both evaluative policy goals and in implementing means to pre-World War II, Depression era, health-care concerns and policies.

The international impact of these "new" concerns with gaps in development and the search for more equable and appropriate health-care policies has been even more recently reflected in the 1977 World Health Organization (WHO) policy announcemment that the organization plans to

> slash its staff and to divert the resulting savings to programs aimed at narrowing the health gap between the industrialized and developing countries . . . to emphasize programs that its officials say will have immediate "social relevance" to the hundreds of millions of people who suffer from the parasitic, bacterial and other diseases that were virtually wiped out in the United States and other industrialized countries years ago.[33]

The current focus on Chinese health-care policies as an international symbol of change from which other developing nations could model more technologically and socially relevant health-care reforms has been most explicitly stated in the first health-policy paper of the World Bank, published in 1975.

> Recently several countries have initiated health service programs that rely on very low levels of technology, and focus broadly on community activities rather than exclusively on personal services. These programs have recruited indigenous service providers, systematically building on public trust and social discipline to implement impressive programs of vector control, sanitation, health education and public health. The most notable of the programs has been developed in the People's Republic of China.[34]

Chinese reports published since this World Bank appraisal of the PRC's "impressive" and "most notable" health-care program have been, however, much more self-critical. In contrast to post-1967 reports that radical changes had taken place in Chinese health care following the Cultural Revolution, the repeated theme in recent 1977–78 Chinese health-policy reports is of the need to consolidate progress made since 1949 and to do "a better job," whether the task is medical research or health personnel "work style."

> [We must] do a better job of consolidating and building rural medical and health networks as well as medical and health establishments in factories and mines and in the cities, . . . we must fight . . . to raise

the health standards of the people. We must energetically conduct scientific research, speed up the pace of combining Chinese and Western medicine and conduct medical education well. We must do a better job of family planning and maternal and child care. In order to carry out these tasks, the Ministry of Public Health and health departments at all levels must resolutely reform their work style, go down to grassroots units and among the masses . . . and do our work in a down-to-earth way. In short, under the firm leadership of the party Central Committee headed by Chairman Hua, we must fight in unity, ... and strive to achieve marked success in health work.[35]

Although it is still too early to fully appraise the exact direction these recent policy changes will take, it would appear that current Chinese health-care policy intends to deemphasize the redistributive Cultural Revolution programs that "put stress on the countryside" and emphasize instead doing "a better job" in *both* the urban and rural sectors. Rather than relying upon the transfer of urban medical personnel to solve inequities between the urban and rural sectors, rural Chinese health care will upgrade the technical training of the more than 1.3 million part-time "barefoot doctors" and 3.6 million part-time "health workers" and midwives reportedly working in the Chinese countryside.[36] This apparent deemphasis of urban personnel redistribution also appears to be linked with a deemphasis of the Cultural Revolution campaign to reeducate "bourgeois" urban medical personnel by sending them to the countryside to learn from the poor and middle-level peasants. Although the current policy line urges "health departments at all levels" to "resolutely reform their work style" and do their work "among the masses . . . in a down-to-earth way," the current policy line at the same time criticizes the Cultural Revolution Gang of Four because they "slanderously claimed doctors were bourgeois and nurses revisionists." During the Cultural Revolution it appeared that a handful of medical experts in the Ministry of Health were selectively discredited in a national campaign in order to symbolically contrast sanctioned and unsanctioned policies and encourage value-behavior change on the part of the majority of urban medical personnel, who were assumed to be potentially "Red experts" willing to "serve the people" if provided with the correct political leadership. Now, Chinese medical personnel and the Chinese people are told that the Cultural Revolution Gang of Four leadership was not the "correct political leadership" and that "health departments at all levels must resolutely reform their work style . . . under the firm leadership of the party Central Committee headed by Chairman Hua." Detailed evaluative and behavioral descriptions or sanctioned models of "a down-to-earth . . . work style" have, however, not yet appeared in the Chinese press. As a consequence, it is not yet possible to compare in detail how the characteristics of "a down-to-earth . . . work style" may or may not differ from the Cultural Revolution value injunctions to "serve the people."

Inferences, however, can be made about how the current leadership is likely to treat the previously drawn contrast between "Red" and "expert" health-care personnel. Given the overall national policy concerns of the current leadership with scientific and technological development as part of their new 10-year plan for Chinese economic modernization, and the nature of the criticisms that have been published against the Cultural Revolution Gang of Four leadership for trying to disrupt the technical training of barefoot doctors and sabotage urban hospitals, it would appear that the current leadership intends to emphasize the importance of technical skills or expertise over political attitudes and behavior. If, as also appears to be the case, urban medical personnel will be retained in their urban health facilities as part of the program to do "a better job" in the cities and correct Cultural Revolution "sabotage" of urban hospitals, rather than be rotated or "sent down" (*xiafang*) to train indigenous rural health workers, the Chinese health-care system will resemble in many respects the policy format of the Soviet post-World War II health-care system. In the Soviet Union a dual or double-track medical education system exists. Research-oriented medical colleges supply more highly trained personnel for the specialized urban health facilities, while intermediate medical schools with shorter curricula supply medical personnel and auxiliary health workers for the rural health-care service facilities.[37]

This similarity in policy format between the Chinese and Soviet health-care systems is interesting for a number of reasons. Some Western observers had published perceptions in the early 1970s as to how the PRC apparently "had considerable success in approaching the urban-rural distribution problem, a problem that remains unsolved, not only in poor countries and countries such as the United States, but even in the Soviet Union, which theoretically has the power to assign its vast number of doctors to areas where they are needed."[38] Prior to the publication of such perceptions as part of the current international health equity movement, the last time urban-rural distribution problems and questions of "social relevance" were concerns of international health-care reformers was in the late 1920s and 1930s.[39] In this Depression era of concern about "socio-medicine," the Soviet Union's national health-care policies that were perceived as offering the most equable model for health-care reform and were characterized as the "wave of the future." It was in this Depression era that English-language publications on Soviet medicine and public health policies rapidly increased in number and popularity. It was also in this period that the Soviet Union obtained foreign recognition from Great Britain (1921) and the United States (1933), attempted to more effectively court Western trade unions (1928-33), belatedly entered the League of Nations (1934) as part of Soviet "Popular Front" attempts to contain fascism in Europe, and relaxed travel restrictions for foreign visitors. Between 1928 and 1937 a number of books were published in England and America by first-hand "expert observers" ranging from a British trade-union nurse,[40] to an English physician who had assisted Pavlov in his research in Leningrad,[41] to the first commissar of the Soviet Commissariat of Public Health (1918-30),[42] to several prominent Western public health specialists and historians of medical science who visited Soviet Russia in the early 1930s.[43]

Given the emphasis during the 1967–76 Chinese Cultural Revolution on "serving the people," the nature of Chinese perceptions of the Soviet health-care system during this earlier Depression era international health reform movement should be noted. One of the primary sources for Chinese perceptions of Soviet Russia in the early 1930s was Zuo Tao-fen (Tsou T'ao-fen),[44] whose journal, *Life Weekly*, carried articles on his four-month visit to the Soviet Union in the summer of 1934 and whose Life Publishing Company had translated at least 14 books on conditions in Soviet Russia by 1935.* As perceived and described by Zuo in his journal articles and book reviews, it was "The Soviet model . . . [with] its system of economic planning and the 'spirit of self-sacrifice evidenced by the leadership and party personnel of the Soviet Union in struggling for the masses' . . . [that was] most relevant to China."[46] Zuo was particularly impressed during his visit to Soviet Russia with "the medical care provided the workers by salaried doctors . . . [who] 'serve the masses' . . . [and who have the] willingness to suffer hardships and to make a sacrifice!"[47] Despite this international attention given to the Soviet health-care system in the 1930s and despite improvements in Soviet health care since the 1930s, it is now generally accepted that the USSR has yet to implement many of its 1930s redistributive rural health policy goals and has encountered many of the same problems as other developed and developing nations in equably redistributing health-care personnel between its urban and rural populations.[48]

CONCLUSION

It is clear from the above surveys of changing international perceptions about Chinese and Soviet health-care policies that each of these nations has attracted attention from international health-care reformers as a model for constructing more socially relevant health-care services. Although international attention has focused on these two nations as symbols for health-care reform during two entirely separate international health reform movements—the USSR in the 1930s and the PRC in the 1970s—there have been similarities between these two movements as well as between the health-care policies in the USSR and PRC during these two periods of concern about more equable health-care reform. Both the 1930s and 1970s international health reform movements were

---

Sheng-huo zhou-kan (*Life Weekly*) rapidly exceeded the circulation of the leading May 4th periodical *Xin Qing-nian* (*New Youth*) to become the foremost publication in China in the 1930s. The Books on Russia "were popular among student readers because the success of the Five Year Plans, the disappearance of unemployment, and the stern simplicity of the Soviet official contrasted impressively with the conditions in the capitalist world especially during the years of the economic depression of 1929–31."[45]

concerned with finding low-cost means for improving health care among agricultural populations lacking the economic and technological capacities of more industrialized and urban populations. In the 1930s, this concern began because of the impact of the Depression upon poorer European rural populations. In the 1970s, this same concern was first raised by developing nations disillusioned with "trickle-down" theories of modernization. In both international movements low-cost means were seen as most likely to result from policies that emphasized powers inherent in the people themselves, rather than scientific and technological means, which were more expensive, usually unavailable, and often inappropriate to the needs of differing rural localities. In both international movements, specially organized state programs and rotating urban medical teams were seen as the most economical and effective means for redistributing health-care resources and more equably serving rural populations. Both the 1930s Soviet and the 1970s Chinese models for health-care reform utilized mass mobilization campaigns to redistribute medical personnel, to conduct public-health education programs emphasizing prevention over curative treatment, to organize locally available and seasonally underemployed rural peasants in self-help village sanitation clean-up and construction campaigns, and to train rural laborers as part-time indigenous health workers.[49]

Although both the Soviet Union in the 1930s and the PRC in the 1970s attempted to implement health-care policies along these lines, they were not the only nations pursuing such policies in those years. The basis of attraction as international models for health-care reform seems to have been the timing and vociferousness of both Soviet and Chinese articulation of their "serve the people" health-care policies, rather than the content or orientation of national health-care policies. For entirely unrelated political reasons both the Soviet Union and the PRC relaxed previously existing travel restrictions for Western visitors several years after their "serve the people" rural health-care programs had been begun. As a consequence, the first Western observers to visit Soviet Russia in the late 1920s and early 1930s, and the PRC in the early 1970s, toured these nations and their model health-care facilities when the political mobilization campaigns to implement redistributive rural health-care policies were still prominent in the national media and the public political rhetoric of both nations.

As foreign analysts of Soviet and Chinese policy changes are all too painfully aware, it is often necessary to wait for the next change in central Party policy "line" before it is possible to determine which if any of the injunctions to implement policy were in fact successfully followed and what difficulties were encountered in implementation. There is no question that the published perceptions of medical and public-health observers following their tour visits to Soviet Russia in the 1930s and the PRC in the early 1970s provided new insights into previously closed societies for general readers as well as for health-care reformers in the West. However, many of these reports on then current health-care policy in these two nations failed to explain to their readers that current policy in Marxist-Leninist party systems is most often a statement of policy goals and injunctions to act upon and implement policy, rather than a report of implemented policy outcomes.

The Cultural Revolution value injunctions to Chinese medical personnel to practice "self-reliance" and "self-sacrifice" and "serve the people" were just that—injunctions to act upon and implement redistributive policy goals. The extent to which these sanctioned value-behavioral means—apparently considered necessary means by the Cultural Revolution leadership for implementing their redistributive rural health-care policies—were in fact internalized as conscious or unconscious value changes by Chinese health-care personnel cannot, however, be effectively determined from such national and/or international policy reports. The difficulty here is a reflection of the as yet unresolved limitation in the theoretical literature of the value-change research field, which in its dependency upon outwardly observable behavior and/or a subject's explicit statements of attitudes, cannot completely control for conscious withholding or distortion by test subjects of unarticulated attitudes or repressed behavior. Even first-hand Western health-care observers, who have marveled at the prevalence of "serve the people" concerns expressed by the Chinese medical personnel and people they have met during their visits, cannot know to what extent the expression of such values may or may not have been "ostensibly submissive, but inwardly adamant and defiant" about the social and political pressures during the Cultural Revolution to express such values and attitudes and conform to the sanctioned behavior in practice.

Value-change theory does suggest, however, that the age-cohort of Chinese health-care personnel now in their late 20s and early 30s, educated during the Cultural Revolution, is more likely to have internalized Cultural Revolution value injunctions than the older generations of Chinese medical personnel which were given a more technically oriented education during the 1950s in Eastern European and Soviet medical schools, or in pre-Revolution elite Chinese medical schools in periods emphasizing different evaluative concerns. Given the tendency of older personnel to dominate decision-making positions within Chinese governmental institutions, and given the recent policy changes emphasizing the importance of technical training within the Chinese health-care system, it remains to be seen to what extent professional competition and value-behavioral dissonance between generational subgroupings of Chinese medical personnel may or may not frustrate implementation of future health-care policies, and/or diminish whatever service-oriented values may or may not have been internalized by the Cultural Revolution generation of Chinese health-care personnel.

Such limitations of certainty, however, should not be taken as a basis for dismissing either the possibility of value-behavior change among some Chinese medical personnel, change within portions of the Chinese society they serve, or the usefulness of attempting to study value change generally within Chinese society. Close examination of the value content of changing Chinese health-care policies, from the perspective of both national and international reports of such policy changes and from the perspective of value-change theory, has helped in several respects to clarify the interrelationships among values, change, and Chinese health-care policies.

First, the too often forgotten role of values in both national and international public policy processes has been noted—whether the process step of analysis is the agenda setting of public policy goals or the implementation of specifically formulated policies. Second, attention has been called to the problems inherent in doing comparative public-policy studies involving Marxist-Leninist party systems, which require distinguishing between reports of mobilizing injunctions to implement policy goals and reports of actually implemented policy outcomes. Finally, although such an examination has not enabled any certain measurements to date of the extent to which value change may have been internalized by Chinese health-care personnel and the society they serve, it has provided a basis for more clearly understanding possible future value differences between different generations and different administrative levels of Chinese health-care personnel and health-care policy formulators. According to value-change theory, it is such value differences that are the basis for the individual dissonance that generates individual, group, and eventually societal value change. The future course of Chinese health-care policies may well be determined in the long run as much by individual urban and rural patients in the general Chinese public, who were inculcated during the Cultural Revolution with expectations that Chinese health-care personnel *should* "serve the people," as by competing generations of medical personnel or Party policy formulators debating whether politics or technique should be in command.

NOTES

1. For example, see Victor W. Sidel and Ruth Sidel, *Serve the People: Observations on Medicine in the People's Republic of China* (Baltimore: Port City Press for the Josiah Macy, Jr. Foundation, 1973), pp. 203-27; Susan B. Rifkin and R. Kaplinsky, "Health Strategy and Development Planning: Lessons from the People's Republic of China," *Journal of Development Studies* 9 (January 1973): 213-31; "Learning From the Barefoot Doctors," Boston *Globe*, July 9, 1973, p. 13; H. T. J. Chabot, "The Chinese System of Health Care," *Tropical and Geographical Medicine* 28 (1976): S87-134.

2. See John Bryant, *Health & the Developing World* (Ithaca and London: Cornell University Press, 1969); Odin W. Anderson, *Health Care: Can There be Equity? The United States, Sweden and England* (New York: Wiley, 1972); Jan Howard and Anselm Strauss, *Humanizing Health Care* (New York: Wiley, 1975).

3. Milton Rokeach, *Beliefs, Attitudes and Values: A Theory of Organization and Change* (San Francisco: Jossey-Bass, 1970).

4. Ibid., pp. 135-41.

5. Ibid., pp. 159-60.

6. Ibid., p. 173.

7. Ibid., p. 167.

8. Ibid., p. 142.

9. See *FBIS* (Foreign Broadcast Information Service) (Hong Kong: U.S. Consulate General, December 1977-February 1978).

10. Ibid., p. 161.

11. Chairman Mao's Directives on Health Work," (June 26, 1965) in *Xin Ren Wei* (*New People's Health*) (Peking: People's Health Press, June 3, 1967); Selections from Chinese Mainland Magazines (SCMM) Supplement No. 22 (Hong Kong: U.S. Consulate General, April 8, 1968), p. 15.

12. Editorial, "Medical Services in the Countryside," *Chinese Medical Journal* (December 1965): 799.

13. "News and Notes: Ministry of Health Conference on Political Work," *Chinese Medical Journal* (May 1966): 345–46.

14. *Guang-ming Ri-Bao* (*Enlightenment Daily*), Peking, Survey of China Mainland Press (SCMP): 3910, March 22, 1967, p. 23.

15. *Chinese Medical Journal* (December 1965): 800–26.

16. Donald Klein, "The State Council and the Cultural Revolution," *China Quarterly* 35 (July-September 1968), p. 85.

17. "Monstrous Crimes of Urban 'Lords' Health Ministry in Opposing June 26 'Directive'," in *Hong-yi Chan-bao* (*Red Medical Battle Bulletin*) and *Ba-yi-ba Chan-bao* (August 18 *Battle Bulletin*) (Peking: Revolutionary Committee of Grand Alliance of Peking Medical and Health Circles and August 18 Joint Headquarters of Peking Medical College, Red Guard Congress, June 26, 1967) (SCMP Supplement: 198: 30–35) pp. 31, 32, and 34.

18. "Mayflies Lightly Plot to Topple Giant Tree," written by Red Flag Commune, Chinese Medical University, Red Guards Congress, in *Chuan-wu-di* (*Invincible*) (Peking: Revolutionary Committee of Metropolitan Medical Circles and Health Bulletin, Yenan Commune, June 26, 1967) (SCMP Supplement: 290: 14–23), pp. 14 and 15.

19. David M. Lampton, *The Politics of Medicine in China: The Policy Process, 1949-1977* (Boulder, Col.: Westview Press, 1977).

20. See William A. Scott, *Values and Organizations: A Study of Fraternities and Sororities* (Chicago: Rand McNally, 1965), pp. 56–59.

21. AnElissa Lucas, "Legitimate Criticism or Cultural Revolution Rhetoric? An Analysis of Mao's Indictments Against the Ministry of Public Health." Unpublished research paper on file in the Harvard East Asian Research Center Library, Cambridge, Mass., pp. 21–22.

22. *New China News Agency* (NCNA), Peking (SCMP: 7030, July 19, 1970), pp. 93–95.

23. John Bowers, President of the Josiah Macy, Jr. Foundation, "Medicine in Mainland China: Red and Rural," in *Current Scene* 8, (June 15, 1970): 1–11.

24. For example, E. Gray Dimond, "Medical Education and Care in People's Republic of China," *Journal of the American Medical Association* 218 (December 6, 1971): 1552–63; "Medicine in China," *Medical World News*, (January 14, 1972): 51–62; "Chinese Doctors to Visit the United States," *Science* 178 (October 6, 1972): 42; Victor W. Sidel and Ruth Sidel, "The Delivery of Medical Care in China," *Scientific American* 230 (April 1974): 19–27; *World Health* (Geneva: World Health Organization, September 1974), pp. 11–13.

25. Shahid Akhtar, *Health Care in the People's Republic of China: A Bibliography with Abstracts* (Ottawa: International Development Research Centre, 1975).

26. Sidel and Sidel, *Serve the People*.

27. Ibid., pp. 191–207.

28. Ibid., p. 193.

29. "Gang's Fallacy on Barefoot Doctors Criticized," *Guangdong Daily*, December 10, 1977, p. 1 (*FBIS*, December 19, 1977), pp. E10–12; "Progress in Health Work," *Guangdong Daily*, January 7, 1978, p. 1 (FBIS, January 23, 1978), pp. E14–15.

30. For example, Wilbert E. Moore, *Order and Change: Essays in Comparative Sociology* (New York: Wiley, 1967), pp. 23–25; Lloyd Rudolph and Susanne Rudolph, *The Modernity of Tradition* (Chicago: Chicago University Press, 1967), pp. 6, 10; S. N. Eisenstadt, *Tradition, Change and Modernity* (New York: Wiley, 1973), esp. pp. 99–126; A. R. Desai, ed., *Essays on Modernization of Underdeveloped Societies* (Bombay: Thacker, 1971).

31. Samuel P. Huntington, "The Change to Change: Modernization, Development and Politics," *Comparative Politics*, 3 (April 1971): 290–93.

32. See Maurice King, ed., *Medical Care in Developing Countries: A Primer on the Medicine of Poverty* (Nairobi and London: Oxford University Press, 1966); Bryant, *Health*; Anderson, Health Care; Howard and Strauss, *Humanizing Health Care*.

33. W. H. O. to Cut Staff in Shift of Goals," New York *Times*, January 30, 1977, p. 1.

34. World Bank, *Health: Sector Policy Paper* (Washington, D.C.: World Bank, March 1975), p. 39.

35. "Progress in Health Work," *Guangdong Daily*.

36. *China Reconstructs* (February 1976): 3.

37. See I. I. Rozenfel'd, *Curative and Preventive Aspects of Public Health Services for Rural Population*, translated from the Russian, *Lechebnosprofilakticheskoe obsluzhivanie sel'skogo naseleniya* (Moskva: Gosudarstvennoe Izdatel'stvo Meditsinskoi Literatury, 1955) by Israel Program for Scientific Translations for NSF, Washington, D.C., 1963.

38. Sidel and Sidel, *Serve the People*, p. 193.

39. See Andrija Stampar, "On Social Medicine," "Five Years of Socio-Medical Work in the Kingdom of Serbs, Croats, and Slovenes," "Health and Social Conditions in China," and "A New Spirit in America: Socio-Medical Observations," in *Serving the Cause of Public Health: Selected Papers of Andrija Stampar*, ed. M. D. Grmek (Zagreb: Andrija Stampar School of Public Health, University of Zagreb, Monograph Series No. 3, 1966). Several of these chapters were originally published as League of Nations Health Section documents: for example, "Health and Social Conditions in China," League Document No. C. H. 1220 (October 15, 1936).

40. Anna J. Haines, *Health Work in Soviet Russia* (New York: Vanguard Press, 1928).

41. W. Horsley Gantt, *A Medical Review of Soviet Russia* (London: British Medical Association, 1928).

42. Nikolai A. Semashko, *Health Protection in the USSR* (London: V. Gollancz, 1934).

43. Sir Arthur Newsholme and John A. Kingsbury, *Red Medicine* (New York: Doubleday, Doran, 1934); Henry Sigerist, *Socialized Medicine in the Soviet Union* (New York: Norton, 1937).

44. Margo S. Gewurtz, *Between America and Russia: Chinese Student Radicalism and the Travel Books of Tsou T'ao-fen, 1933-37* (Toronto: University of Toronto-York University Joint Centre on Modern East Asia, 1975). Publication Series Vol. 1, No. 1.

45. Kiang Wen-han, *The Chinese Student Movement* (New York: n.p., 1948), p. 97, as cited in ibid., p. 12; See Ch'ien Tuan-sheng, *The Government and Politics of China, 1921–1949* (Stanford: Stanford University Press, 1970), pp. 145–46 for similar admiration among some QuoMinDang (KMT) planners for Soviet central planning and the establishment but ineffectiveness of the Chinese Central Planning Board (1940–48).

46. Gewurtz, *Between America and Russia*, p. 13.

47. Ibid., p. 54.

48. Mark G. Field, *Soviet Socialized Medicine* (New York: Free Press, 1967); U.S. Department of Health, Education, and Welfare/Public Health Service, *Medical Care in the USSR: Report of U.S. Delegation on Health Care Services and Planning: May 16-June 3, 1970* (Washington, D.C.: DHEW Publication No. NIH 72-60, 1971), esp. pp. 10 and 15.

49. Compare, for example, "European Conference on Rural Hygiene: Report of Preparatory Committee on Principles Governing Organization of Medical Assistance, Public Health Services and Sanitation in Rural Districts," Warsaw, June 29-July 7, 1931 (Geneva: League of Nations Health Section *Document No. C.H. 1045*, June 1, 1931) with Bryant, *Health*, and Sidel and Sidel, *Serve the People*.

GLOSSARY

This glossary is designed to supplement the text. In the text, English language translations of important Chinese terms and phrases are accompanied by their *pinyin* romanizations given in parentheses. Readers may locate the Chinese character and Wade-Giles equivalents for textual terms and phrases by referring to the center column of the glossary where *pinyin* romanizations are ordered alphabetically. The character equivalents are presented in the left-hand column in standard form. Wade-Giles equivalents are presented in the right-hand column.

Chinese Characters	*Pinyin* Romanizations	Wade-Giles Romanizations
白話	baihua	pai-hua
八字	bazi	pa-tzu
北京大學學報	*Beijing daxue xuebao*	*Pei-ching ta-hsüeh hsüeh-pao*
北史	Beishi	Pei-shih
變化氣質	bianhua qizhi	pien-hau ch'i-chih
筆記	biji	pi-chi
才	cai	ts'ai
詞	ce	tz'u
紫薇斗數	Cewei doushu	Tz'u-wei tou-shu
陳風	Chen Feng	Ch'en Feng
陳獨秀	Chen Duxiu	Ch'en Tu-hsiu
秦	Chin	Ch'in

Chinese Characters	*Pinyin* Romanizations	Wade-Giles Romanizations
秦始皇	Chin Shihuang	Ch'in Shih-huang
瞿同祖	Chu Tongzu	Ch'u T'ung-tsu
戴東原 (震)	Dai Dongyuan (Zhen)	Tai Tung-yuan (Chen)
當權	dangchuan	tang-ch'üan
大我	dawo	ta-wo
大學	Daxue	Ta-hsüeh
大字報	dazibao	ta-tzu-pao
德先生	De xiansheng	Te hsien-sheng
得救	dejiu	te-chiu
鄧拓	Deng Tou	Teng T'o
鄧小平	Deng Xiaoping	Teng Hsiao-p'ing
地富反懷右	di, fu, fan, huai, you	ti, fu, fan, huai, yu

Chinese Characters	*Pinyin* Romanizations	Wade-Giles Romanizations
董仲舒	Dong Zhongshu	Tung Chung-shu
動機	dongji	tung-chi
東林	donglin	Tung-lin
遁甲	Dunjia	Tun-chia
多權	duochuan	tuo-ch'üan
范縝	Fan Zhen	Fan Chen
馮友蘭	Feng Yulan	Fung Yu-lan
風水	fengshui	feng-shui
傅玄	Fu Xuan	Fu Hsuan
負責任	fu zeren	fu tze-jen
鬼眉	guimei	kuei-mei
幹部	ganbu	kan-pu

Chinese Characters	*Pinyin* Romanizations	Wade-Giles Romanizations
高贊非	Gao Zanfei	Kao Tsan-fei
公	gong	kung
公益精神	gongyi jingshen	kung-i ching-shen
顧憲成	Gu Xiancheng	Ku Hsien-ch'eng
古文	guwen	ku-wen
關鋒	Guan Feng	Kuan Feng
關係	guanxi	kuan-hsi
光明日報	Guangming ribao	Kung-ming jih-pao
郭沫若	Guo Morou	Kuo Mo-jo
國家安全	guojia anchuan	kuo-chia an-ch'uan
海瑞	Hai Rui	Hai Jui
韓	Han	Han

Chinese Characters	*Pinyin* Romanizations	Wade-Giles Romanizations
韓非	Han Fei	Han Fei
杭州	Hangzhou	Hang-chou
合作	hezuo	ho-tso
合二為一	heer weiyi	ho-erh wei-i
紅旗雜誌	*Hongqi zazhi*	*Hung-ch'i tsa-chih*
洪世添	Hong Shidi	Hung Shih-ti
胡適	Hu Shi	Hu Shih
黃心川	Huang Xinchuan	Hung Hsin-ch'uan
黃炎培	Hung Yanpei	Huang Yen-p'ei
火	huo	huo
火形	huoxing	huo-hsing
賈島	Jia Dao	Chia Tao

Chinese Characters	*Pinyin* Romanizations	Wade-Giles Romanizations
江青	Jiang Qing	Chiang Ch'ing
假如	jiaru	chia-ju
家庭安全	jiating anchuan	chia-t'ing an-ch'uan
價值	jiazhi	chia-chih
接班人	jieban ren	chieh-pan jen
階級鬥爭	jieji douzheng	chieh-chi tou-cheng
金	jin	chin
繼續革命	jixu geming	chi-hsü ko-ming
景氣	jingchi	ching-ch'ih
競賽	jingsai	ching-sai
就	jiu	chiu
舊唐書	Jiu Tangshu	Chiu T'ang-shu

Chinese Characters	*Pinyin* Romanizations	Wade-Giles Romanizations
看手	kanshou	k'an-shou
看相	kanxiang	k'an-hsiang
弘嘉家店	Kongjia dian	Kong-chia tien
康生	Kang Sheng	K'ang Sheng
考古	*Kaogu*	*K'ao-ku*
寬恕	kuanshu	k'uan-shu
來生幸福	laisheng xingfu	lai-sheng hsing-fu
老子	Lao Ze	Lao Tzu
老成	laocheng	lao-ch'eng
禮	li	li
李三才	Li Sancai	Li San-ts'ai
李斯	Li Si	Li Ssu

Chinese Characters	*Pinyin* Romanizations	Wade-Giles Romanizations
李贄	Li Zhi	Li Chih
亮	liang	liang
梁啟超	Liang Qichao	Liang Ch'i-ch'ao
廉潔	lianjie	lien-chieh
廖沫沙	Liao Mosha	Liao Mo-sha
列子	Lie Ze	Lieh Tzu
林彪	Lin Biao	Lin Piao
林聿時	Lin Yushi	Lin Yü-shih
劉節	Liu Jie	Liu Chieh
六壬	Liu ren	Liu jen
劉少奇	Liu Shaoqi	Liu Shao-ch'i
劉師培	Liu Shipei	Liu Shih-p'ei

Chinese Characters	*Pinyin* Romanizations	Wade-Giles Romanizations
柳下	Liuxia	Liu-hsia
劉元彥	Liu Yuanyan	Liu Yüan-yen
柳宗元	Liu Zongyuan	Liu Tsung-yuan
六十四干支	liushisi ganzhi	liu-shih-ssu kan-chih
禮運	*Liyun*	*Li-yün*
陸定一	Lu Dingyi	Lu Ting-i
陸平	Lu Ping	Lu P'ing
魯迅	Lu Xun	Lu Hsün
呂振羽	Lu Zhenyu	Lu Chen-yü
龍井	lungzhing	lung-ching
馬南邨	Ma Nancun	Ma Nan-ts'un
卯	Mao	Mao

Chinese Characters	*Pinyin* Romanizations	Wade-Giles Romanizations
毛遠清	Mao Yuanqing	Mao Yuan-ch'ing
眉毛散亂	meimao sangluan	mei-mao sang-luan
明	Ming	Ming
木形	muxing	mu-hsing
南史	*Nanshi*	*Nan-shih*
內	nei	nei
劉懷懷	Peng Dehuai	P'eng Te-huai
劉真	Peng Zhen	P'eng Chen
平等	pingdeng	p'ing-teng
卜天壽	Pu Tianshou	P'u T'ien-shou
乾隆	Qianlong	Ch'ien-lung
煎驗	*Qianxian*	*Ch'ien-hsien*

Chinese Characters	*Pinyin* Romanizations	Wade-Giles Romanizations
錢偉長	Qian Weichang	Ch'ien Wei-ch'ang
親切	qinqie	ch'in-ch'ieh
群眾路線	Qunzhong luxian	ch'ün-chung lu-hsien
去私	qusi	ch'ü-ssu
仁	ren	jen
任繼愈	Ren Jiyu	Jen Chi-yü
人生的目標	rensheng di mubiao	jen-sheng ti mu-piao
人相	renxiang	jen-hsiang
仁學	renxue	jen-hsüeh
如果	ruguo	ju-kuo
賽先生	Sai xiansheng	Sai hsien-sheng
三綱	sangang	san-kang

Chinese Characters	*Pinyin* Romanizations	Wade-Giles Romanizations
三國演義	*Sanguo yanyi*	*San-kuo yen-i*
三家村札記	*Sanjia cun zhaji*	*San-chia ts'un cha-chi*
三庭	santing	san-t'ing
沙明	Shaming	Sha-ming
桑弘羊	Shang Hongyang	Shang Hung-yang
上庭	shangting	shang-t'ing
少正	Shaozheng	Shao-cheng
社會聖王	shehui shengwang	shih-hui sheng-wang
社會實踐	*shehui shijian*	*she-hui shih-chien*
生活舒適	shenghuo shushi	sheng-huo shu-shih
十干	shigan	shih-kan
十二支	shier zhi	shih-erh chih

Chinese Characters	*Pinyin* Romanizations	Wade-Giles Romanizations
世界和平	shijie heping	shih-chieh ho-p'ing
事事關心	"shishi guanxin"	"shih-shih kuan-hsin"
受人尊敬	shouren zunjing	shou-jen tsun-ching
四清	*siqing*	*ssu-ch'ing*
思想開通	sixiang kaitong	ssu-hsiang k'ai-t'ung
算卦	suangua	suan-kua
算命	suanming	suan-ming
孫傳芳	Sun Chuanfang	Sun Ch'uan-fang
孫子	Sun Zi	Sun Tzu
宋	Sung	Sung
態度	taidu	t'ai-tu
擇棋	*tanqi*	*t'an-ch'i*

Chinese Characters	*Pinyin* Romanizations	Wade-Giles Romanizations
譚嗣同	Tan Sitong	T'an Ssu-t'ung
唐	Tang	T'ang
湯用彤	Tang Yongtong	T'ang Yung-t'ung
天主實義	*Tianzhu shiyi*	*T'ien-chu shih-i*
體用	*tiyong*	*t'i-yung*
團體合作	tuanti hezuo	t'uan-t'i ho-tso
外	wai	wai
王安石	Wang Anshi	Wang An-shih
王充	Wang Chong	Wang Ch'ung
王船山	Wang Chuanshan	Wang Ch'uan-shan
王夫之	Wang Fuzhi	Wang Fu-chih
王海容	Wang Hairong	Wang Hai-jung

Chinese Characters	*Pinyin* Romanizations	Wade-Giles Romanizations
王陽明	Wang Yangming	Wang Yang-ming
魏源	Wei Yuan	Wei Yuan
文匯報	Wenhui bao	*Wen-hui pao*
文人	wenren	wen-jen
五.八.十.邵	wu, ba, shi, gong	wu, pa, shih, kung
五.八.十.匣	wu, ba, shi, guan	wu, pa, shih, kuang
五.八.十.室	wu, ba, shi, tang	wu, pa, shih, t'ang
吳哈	Wu Han	Wu Han
吳漢	Wu Han	Wu Han
吳南星	Wu Nanxing	Wu Nan-hsing
五術	wu shu	wu shu
吳虞	Wu Yu	Wu Yü

Chinese Characters	*Pinyin* Romanizations	Wade-Giles Romanizations
吳稚輝	Wu Zhihui	Wu Chih-hui
五常	wuchang	wu-ch'ang
無名星	wuming xing	wu-ming hsing
五行	wuxing	wu-hsing
武學	wuxue	wu-hsüeh
系統	xitong	hsi-t'ung
鄉約	xiangyue	hsiang-yüeh
孝	xiao	hsiao
小品文	xiaopin wen	hsiao-p'in wen
下庭	xiating	hsia-t'ing
新青年	*Xin Qingnian*	*Hsin ch'ing-nien*
新世紀	*Xin shihji*	*Hsin shih-chi*

Chinese Characters	*Pinyin* Romanizations	Wade-Giles Romanizations
新唐書	*Xin Tangshu*	*Hsin T'ang-shu*
心無定向	xin wu ding xiang	hsin wu ting hsiang
心安理得	xinan lide	hsin-an li-te
性善	xingshan	hsing-shan
性惡	xingwu	hsing-o
信任	xinren	hsin-jen
徐光啟	Xu Guangqi	Hsü Kuang-ch'i
學術討論會	xueshu taolun hui	hsüeh-shu t'ao-lun hui
學術研究	*Xueshu yanjui*	*Hsueh-shu yen-chiu*
顏回	Yan Hui	Yen Hui
楊榮國	Yang Rongguo	Yang Jung-kuo
陽宅	yang shou	yang shou

Chinese Characters	*Pinyin* Romanizations	Wade-Giles Romanizations
楊獻珍	Yang Xianzhen	Yang Hsien-chen
燕山夜話	*Yanshan yehua*	*Yen-shan yeh-hua*
要點	yaodian	yao-tien
姚文元	Yao Wenyuan	Yao Wen-yuan
一貫道	Yiguan dao	I-kuan tao
醫學	yixue	i-hsüeh
勇敢	yonggan	Yung-kan
有意義的生活	you yiyi de shenghuo	yu i-i ti sheng-huo
有禮	youli	yu-li
幽靈	youling	yu-ling
有名星	youming xing	yu-ming hsing
袁世凱	Yuan Shikai	Yuan Shih-k'ai

Chinese Characters	Pinyin Romanizations	Wade-Giles Romanizations
選反有理	zaofan youli	tsao-fan yu-li
資治通鑑	Zezhih tongjian	*Tzu-chih t'ung-chien*
章炳麟	Zhang Binglin	Chang Ping-lin
張載	Zhang Zai	Chang Tsai
張東孫	Zhang Dongsun	Chang Tung-sun
張飛	Zhang Fei	Chang Fei
章士釗	Zhang Shizhao	Chang Shih-chao
張之洞	Zhang Zhidong	Chang Shih-tung
張宗昌	Zhang Zongchang	Chang Tsung-ch'ang
趙紀彬	Zhao Jibin	Chao Chi-pin
哲學研究	Zhexue yanjiu	*Che-hsüeh yen-chiu*
真正的友誼	zhenzheng de youyi	cheng-cheng ti yu-i

Chinese Characters	*Pinyin* Romanizations	Wade-Giles Romanizations
正直	zhengzhi	cheng-chih
路	zhi	chih
智慧	zhihui	chih-hui
知識	zhishi	chih-shih
知識分子	zhishi fenze	chih-shih fen-tzu
知識活動	zhishi huodong	chih-shih huo-tung
金岳霖	Zhin Yuelin	Chin Yüeh-lin
忠	zhong	chung
仲尼	zhongni	chung-ni
中庭	zhongting	chung-t'ing
周恩來	Zhou Enlai	Chou En-lai
度誠	Zhucheng	chu-ch'eng

Chinese Characters	*Pinyin* Romanizations	Wade-Giles Romanizations
諸葛亮	Zhu Geliang	Chu-ko Liang
朱光潛	Zhu Guangqian	Chu Kuang-ch'ien
莊子	Zhuang Ze	Chuang Tzu
主流	zhuliu	chu-liu
君子	zhunzi	chün-tzu
宗教	zongjiao	tsung-chiao
總理	zongli	tsung-li
左傳	Zouzhuan	*Tso-chuan*
子平	zu ping	tze p'ing
祖國月刊	*Zuguo yuekan*	*Tsu-kuo yüeh-k'an*
自律	zulu	Tzu-lü

Chinese Characters	*Pinyin* Romanizations	Wade-Giles Romanizations
自由	zuyou	tzu-yu
尊敬别人	zunjing bieren	tsun-ching pieh-jen
做人的道理	zuoren de daoli	tso-jen ti tao-li

GLOSSARY (extended phrases)

Chinese Characters	*Pinyin* Romanizations	Wade-Giles Romanizations
不錯. 你怎麼知道？	"Bucuo, ni zenma zhidao?"	"Pu-ts'o, ni tsen-ma chih-tao?"
不對. 我從來沒有跟婦人吵架！	"Budui, wo conglai meiyou gen furen chaojia!"	"Pu-tui, wo ts'ung-lai mei-yu ken fu-jen ch'ao-chia!"
不要聽他的話；他總是這麼樣講.	"Buyao ting tade hua; t'a zong shi zhemayang jiang."	"Pu-yao t'ing t'a ti hua; t'a tsung-shih je-ma-yang chiang."
多謝. 你真幫我忙.	"Duoxieh, Ni zhen bang womang."	"Tou-hsieh, Ni chen pang wo mang."
對於孔子的批判和對於我國的尊孔思想的自我批判.	"Duiyu Kongzi de pipan ho duiyu wo guoqu de zunKong sixiang de zewo pipan."	"Tui-yü K'ung Tzu ti p'i-p'an ho tui-yü wo kuo-ch'ü ti tsun K'ung ssu-hsiang ti tzu-wo p'i-p'an."

Chinese Characters	*Pinyin Romanizations*	Wade-Giles Romanizations
反動階級的"聖人"孔子	*Fandong jieji de "shengren" Kong Ze*	*Fan-tung chieh-chi ti "sheng-jen" K'ung Tsu*
復古與復古兩條路線的鬥爭	*"Fugu yu fanfugu shi liangtiao luxian de douzheng."*	*"Fu-ku yü fan-fu-ku shih liang-t'iao lu-hsien ti tou-cheng."*
關於標題音樂無標題音樂問題的討論	*Guanyu biaoti yin yue, wubiaoti yinyue wenti de taolun.*	*Kuan-yü piao-t'i yin-yüeh, wu-piao-t'i yin-yüeh wen-t'i ti t'ao-lun.*
關於孔子誅少正卯問題	*Guanyu Kongze zhu Shaozheng Mao wenti*	*Kuan-yü K'ung Tzu chu Shao-cheng Mao wen-t'i*
漢唐佛教思想論集	*Han Tang Foujiao sixiang lunji*	*Han-T'ang Fo-chiao ssu-hsiang lun-chi*

Chinese Characters	*Pinyin* Romanizations	*Wade-Giles* Romanizations
"胡說，真沒有什麼出息！"	"Hushuo! Zhen meiyou shenma chuxi!"	"Hu-shuo! Chen mei-yu shen-ma ch'u-hsi!"
孔家店及其幽靈	Kongjiadian jiqi youling	K'ung-chia-tien chi-ch'i yu-ling
林彪是地地道道的孔老二的信徒	Lin Biao shih didi daodao de Kong Laoer de xintu	Lin Piao shih ti-ti tao-tao te K'ung lao-erh ti hsin-t'u
論中國佛教無"十宗"	"Lun Zhungguo Foujiao wu 'Shizong'"	"Lun Chung-kuo Fo-chiao su 'Shih-Tsung'"
論中國共產黨員的修養	Lun Gongchandangyuan de xiuyang	Lun Kung-ch'an-tang-yüan ti hsiu-yang
論尊儒反法	Lun zunRu fanFa	Lun tsun-Ju fan-Fa

Chinese Characters	*Pinyin* Romanizations	Wade-Giles Romanizations
" 明年三月五號你會開刀；不要緊。"	"Mingnian sanyue wuhao ni hui kaidao; buyaojin."	"Ming-nien san-yüeh wu-hao ni hui k'ai-tao; pu-yao-chin."
" 你將來會賺錢。"	"Ni daodeshang shi...."	"Ni tao-te-shang shih...."
" 你看，我對於你的問題什麼都知道。"	"Ni jianglai hui zhuanqian"	"Ni chiang-lai hui chuan-ch'ien"
" 你是什麼樣的人...."	"Ni kan, wo duiyu nide wenti shenma dou zhidao."	"Ni k'an, wo tui-yü ni ti wen-t'i shen-ma dou chih-tao."
" 你是一個...."	"Ni shi shenmayang de ren...."	"Ni shih shen-ma-yang ti jen...."
" 你認你從來沒有跟婦人以來，可是我看你的眉毛蓬亂心不會講錯。"	"Ni shi yige...."	"Ni shih i-ke...."
	"Ni shuo ni conglai meiyou gen furen chaojia, keshi wo kan nide meimao sangluan; bu hui jiangcuo."	"Ni shuo ni ts'ung-lai mei-yu ken fu-jen ch'ao-chia, k'o-shih wo k'an ni ti mei-mao sang-luan; pu hui chiang-ts'o."

Chinese Characters	*Pinyin* Romanizations	Wade-Giles Romanizations
"你說你你生意，你應該作官"	"Ni shuo ni zuo shengyi; ni yinggai zuo guan"	"Ni shuo ni tso sheng-yi; ni ying-kai tso kuan"
"你說我有個'母'字，有什麼意思？"	"Ni shuo wo you sange 'mu' zi, you shenma yisi?"	"Ni Shuo wo yu san-ke 'mu' tze, yu shen-ma i-sse?"
"你應該做一個⋯⋯"	"Ni yinggai zuo yige⋯⋯"	"Ni ying-kao tso i-ke⋯⋯"
"你以前作一個⋯⋯"	"Ni yiqian zuo yige⋯⋯"	"Ni i-ch'ien tso i-ke⋯⋯"
"你最近有沒有跟婦人吵架？"	"Ni zuijin youmeiyou gen furen chaojia?"	"Ni tsui-chin yu-mei-yu ken fu-jen ch'ao-chia?"
她"克己復禮"文章選輯	Pi "kezhi fuli" wenzhang xuanji	P'i "k'o-chi fu-li" wen-chang hsüan-chi

Chinese Characters	*Pinyin* Romanizations	Wade-Giles Romanizations
"評劉節先生 的"唯仁論"和 "天人合一"說	"Ping Liu Jie xiansheng de 'Weiren lun' he 'Tianren heyi' shuo"	"P'ing Liu Chieh hsien-sheng ti 'Wei-jen lun' ho 'T'ien-jen ho-i' shuo"
批判安東尼奧尼拍攝 的反華影片 中國"	Pipan Andongniaoni paishe de fanHua yingpian "Zhongguo"	P'i-p'an An-tung-ni-ao-ni p'ai-she ti fanHua ying-p'ien "Chung-kuo"
"卜天壽'論語 抄本後的 詩詞雜錄'"	"Pu Tianshou 'Lunyu chaoben huo de shicu zalu'"	"P'u T'ien-shou 'Lun-yü ch'ao-pen huo ti shih-ts'u tsa-lu'"
"我又是什麼什麼 人"	"Wo shi shenma shenma ren."	"Wo shih shen-ma shen-ma jen."
"我四十多年算卦; 遁甲的算法是 最可靠的"	"Wo sishi duo nian suangua; Dun Zhia de suanfa shi zui kekao de"	"Wo ssu-shih tou nian suan-kua; Tun Chia suan-fa shih tsui k'o-k'ao ti"

Chinese Characters	*Pinyin* Romanizations	Wade-Giles Romanizations
"我下個月想去 美國旅行 不曉得應該 不應該去."	"Wo xiage yue xiang qu Meiguo luxing; buxiaode yinggai buyinggai qu."	"Wo hsia-ke yüeh hsiang ch'ü Mei-kuo lu-hsing; bu-hsiao-te ying-kai bu-ying-kai ch'ü."
"五長之人, 骨貌粗, 只愛筋脈 去皮膚, 又嫌枯槁 無滋潤, 衣食看來不以知."	"Wuchang zhi ren, gu mao cu, Zhi you jing mai qu p'i-fu, You qian gu gao wu cu run, Yi shi kan lai bu shi qu."	"Wu-ch'ang chih jen, ku mao ts'u, Chih yu ching mai ch'ü p'i-fu, Yu ch'ien ku kao wu ts'e jun, i shih k'an lai bu shih ch'u."
"一分為二的 論戰與 楊獻珍的 是非真象"	"Yifen weier de lunzhan yu Yang Xianzhen de shifei zhenxiang"	"I-fen wei-erh ti lun-chan yü Yang Hsien-chen ti shih-fei chen-hsiang"

Chinese Characters	*Pinyin* Romanizations	Wade-Giles Romanizations
"因為你是什麼樣的人，所以你將來會⋯⋯"	"Yinwei ni shi shenmayang deren, soyi ni jianglai hui. . . ."	"Yin-wei ni shih shen-ma-yang ti jen, so-i ni chiang-lai hui. . . ."
"因為你少年的時候受苦，所以你跟同事的關係不大好。"	"Yinwei ni xiaonian de shihou shouhai, soyi ni gen tongshi de guanxi bu da hao."	"Yin-wei ni hsiao-nien ti shih-hou shou-hai, so-i ni ken t'ung-shih ti kuan-hsi bu ta hao."
"因為你有這麼一個問題，所以你將來會⋯⋯"	"Yinwei ni you zhema yige wenti, soyi ni jianglai hui. . . ."	"Yin-wei ni yu jen-ma yi-ke wen-t'i, so-i ni chiang-lai hui. . . ."
"再批也已復不禮"	*Zaipi "keji fuli"*	*Tsai p'i "k'o-chi fu-li"*
"真是莫名其妙；你一好像對我什麼都知道"	"Zhen shi moming qimiao; ni haoxiang dui wo shenma dou zhidao"	"Chen shih mo-ming ch'i-miao; ni hao-hsiang tui wo shen-ma dou chih-tao"

Chinese Characters	*Pinyin* Romanizations	*Wade-Giles* Romanizations
中國法律與 中國社會	Zhongguo falu yu Zhongguo shehui	Chung-kuo fa-lü yü Chung-kuo she-hui
中國古代史 的分期問題	"Zhongguo gudaishi de fenqi wenti"	"Chung-kuo ku-tai-shih ti fen-ch'i wen-t'i"
中國歷代 反孔和尊孔 的鬥爭	Zhongguo lidai fanKong he zunKong de douzheng	Chung-kuo li-tai fan-K'ung ho tsun-K'ung ti tou-cheng
中國哲學遺產 的繼承問題	"Zhongguo zhexue yichan de jicheng wenti"	"Chung-kuo che-hsüeh i-ch'an ti chi-ch'eng wen-t'i"

INDEX

ABOUT THE EDITORS
AND CONTRIBUTORS

EMILY M. AHERN is Professor of Anthropology at The Johns Hopkins University. Until 1974 she was Assistant Professor of Anthropology at Yale University. She is the author of *The Cult of the Dead in a Chinese Village* (Stanford University Press, 1973) and several articles on Chinese ritual and social organization. Dr. Ahern holds a B.A. from the University of Michigan and a Ph.D. from Cornell University.

SHELDON APPLETON is Professor of Political Science at Oakland University in Michigan. He has written books on U.S. foreign policy and on U.S. China policy, and articles, often concerning Taiwan, for *Asian Survey*, the *Public Opinion Quarterly*, the *China Quarterly*, *Pacific Affairs*, the *Journal of Asian Studies* and other journals. Professor Appleton received his B.A. and M.A. degrees from New York University, and his Ph.D. from the University of Minnesota. A former Foreign Service officer, he is currently serving as a member of the editorial board of the *American Journal of Political Science*, and of the Gabriel Almond Award Committee.

CAROLYN LEE BAUM is a psychiatric social worker at Harbor General Hospital, Los Angeles. She is a student of cross-cultural socialization practices. Her interest in Chinese child-rearing techniques was stimulated by a two-year residence in Taiwan and Hong Kong, 1966-68. She holds a B.A. from Pacific Oaks College, Pasadena, and an M.S.W. from U.C.L.A. She is a practicing consultant on early childhood education.

RICHARD BAUM is Professor of Political Science at U.C.L.A. He is a past member of The China Council of The Asia Society. His published books include *China in Ferment: Perspectives on the Cultural Revolution* (1971) and *Prelude to Revolution: Mao, the Party, and the Peasant Question, 1962-66* (1975). He holds a B.A. from U.C.L.A. and an M.A. and Ph.D. from the University of California, Berkeley. He has visited the People's Republic of China twice, in 1975 and 1978.

GORDON BENNETT is Associate Professor of Government at the University of Texas at Austin. He is co-author (with Ronald Montaperto) of *Red Guard: The Political Biography of Dai Siao-ai* (1971; re-issued in 1977 by Peter Smith Publishers); and author of *Yundong: Mass Campaigns in Chinese Communist*

Leadership (1976), *China's Finance and Trade: A Policy Reader* (1978), and *Huadong: The Story of a Chinese People's Commune* (1978).

Dr. Bennett is a member of the Asia Society's China Council, of the Board of Directors of the National Committee on U.S.-China Relations, and of the editorial board of *Contemporary China*. He is Program Director of the Texas Program for Educational Resources on Asia (TEXPERA). He holds a Ph.D. from the University of Wisconsin at Madison.

ALFRED H. BLOOM is Assistant Professor of Psychology and Linguistics and Director of the Linguistics Program at Swarthmore College, Swarthmore, Pennsylvania. He received his Ph.D. in Social Psychology from Harvard University in 1974. His research interests focus on the impact of language and culture on cognition and cognitive development. He has written articles for, among others, the *Journal of Social Psychology*, *The Handbook of Political Psychology*, and the *Journal of Peace Science*, and is presently working on a book examining the relationship of language to thought.

BETTY B. BURCH, formerly Professor of Political Science at Tufts University, Medford, Massachusetts, is presently Research Associate at the Fairbank Center for East Asian Research, Harvard University. Dr. Burch has published various books, including *Asian Political Systems*, as well as articles and reviews. She received her B.A. from Mt. Holyoke College, her M.A. from Bryn Mawr, and her Ph.D. from Harvard University.

SIDNEY L. GREENBLATT, Chairperson of the Department of Sociology at Drew University, Madison, New Jersey, is editor of *Chinese Sociology and Anthropology*, a quarterly journal of translation published by International Arts and Sciences Press, White Plains, New York. He is also editor of *The People of Taihang: An Anthology of Family Histories* (1976); co-editor of *Deviance and Social Control in Chinese Society* (1977); and author of "Organizational Elites: Peking University, 1949-1964" in Robert Scalapino, ed., *Elites in the People's Republic of China* (1972), reviews in *Political Science Quarterly*, and papers delivered at various conferences in the social sciences and the China field. Professor Greenblatt holds a B.A. from Harper College of the State University of New York and an M.A. and East Asian Institute Certificate from Columbia University.

ANELISSA LUCAS is Assistant Professor of Political Science at Livingston College-Rutgers University, New Brunswick, New Jersey. She is currently completing a book on Chinese medical modernization policies since the 1920s. Professor Lucas received her A.B. from the University of California at Berkeley and her M.A. and Ph.D. from Harvard University.

NANCY J. OLSEN has conducted field work in Taiwan on two occasions, and has published articles on Taiwanese family life in the *American Journal of Sociology*, the *Journal of Asian Studies*, and the *Journal of Marriage and the*

Family. She has taught at the University of Santa Clara and Oregon State University, and is currently Co-Director of Community Research Services in Palo Alto, California. Her Ph.D. is from Cornell University.

TU WEI-MING is Professor of History at the University of California, Berkeley. He has taught as Assistant Professor of East Asian Studies at Princeton University and as Visiting Lecturer at Tunghai University in Taiwan. Dr. Tu has published widely in the areas of Confucian thought, Chinese intellectual history and religious philosophy of East Asia. He is the author of *Neo-Confucian Thought in Action: Wang Yang-ming's Youth* (University of California Press, 1976) and *Centrality and Commonality: An Essay on Chung-yung* (The University Press of Hawaii, 1976). His articles and reviews have appeared in *Philosophy East and West,* the *Journal of Asian Studies, American Historical Review, Eastern Buddhist, Daedalus,* and the *Monist.* Born in Kunming, China, Dr. Tu holds a B.A. from Tunghai University and an M.A. and Ph.D. from Harvard University.

LYNN T. WHITE, III is Assistant Professor in the Woodrow Wilson School and the Departments of Politics and East Asian Studies, and an Associate of the Center of International Studies, all at Princeton University. His book on *Careers in Shanghai* was published in 1978 and articles have appeared in the *American Political Science Review,* the *Journal of Asian Studies, China Quarterly,* and other journals.

AMY AUERBACHER WILSON is Lecturer in Sociology at Douglass College, Rutgers University. In addition to editing *Deviance and Social Control in Chinese Society* (1977), she has also published articles and reviews on such features of modern Chinese society as women's liberation and student movements. Ms. Wilson received her B.A. from Douglass College and her M.A. from Princeton University. For her Ph.D. in sociology at Princeton University she is completing research on mass organizations in the People's Republic of China.

RICHARD W. WILSON is Professor of Political Science and Director of International Programs at Rutgers University. He has published widely in the area of political socialization. In addition to writing numerous articles, Professor Wilson is author of *Learning to be Chinese* (1970) and *The Moral State* (1974), and is co-editor of *Deviance and Social Control in Chinese Society* (1977). He received his A.B., M.A., and Ph.D. from Princeton University.